Data Security and Communication Networks

Data Security and Communication Networks

Edited by
Malcolm Becker

www.willfordpress.com

Published by Willford Press,
118-35 Queens Blvd., Suite 400,
Forest Hills, NY 11375, USA

ISBN: 978-1-68285-651-2

Cataloging-in-Publication Data

Data security and communication networks / edited by Malcolm Becker.
    p. cm.
Includes bibliographical references and index.
ISBN 978-1-68285-651-2
1. Data transmission systems. 2. Computer networks. 3. Communications software.
I. Becker, Malcolm.
TK5105 .D38 2019
004.6--dc23

For information on all Willford Press publications
visit our website at www.willfordpress.com

Contents

Preface

A computer network is a digital telecommunications network that allows the exchange of resources across nodes. These can be personal computers, servers, phones or networking hardware. The connections between these nodes are established over wireless media, optic cables or wires. The protection of digital data from unauthorized access and actions is called data security. Cyberattacks and data breaches can cause unwanted changes to data. Disk encryption, backups, data erasure, data masking, etc. are some of the technologies generally employed to ensure data security. Network security is an important consideration in data security. It is used on both private and public computer networks. This book explores all the important aspects of data security and communication networks in the present day scenario. It outlines the processes and applications of these fields in detail. This book, with its detailed analyses and data, will prove immensely beneficial to professionals and students involved in this area at various levels.

This book is a comprehensive compilation of works of different researchers from varied parts of the world. It includes valuable experiences of the researchers with the sole objective of providing the readers (learners) with a proper knowledge of the concerned field. This book will be beneficial in evoking inspiration and enhancing the knowledge of the interested readers.

In the end, I would like to extend my heartiest thanks to the authors who worked with great determination on their chapters. I also appreciate the publisher's support in the course of the book. I would also like to deeply acknowledge my family who stood by me as a source of inspiration during the project.

Editor

A Consensus Framework for Reliability and Mitigation of Zero-Day Attacks in IoT

Vishal Sharma, Kyungroul Lee, Soonhyun Kwon, Jiyoon Kim, Hyungjoon Park, Kangbin Yim, and Sun-Young Lee

Department of Information Security Engineering, Soonchunhyang University, Asan-si 31538, Republic of Korea

Correspondence should be addressed to Sun-Young Lee; sunlee@sch.ac.kr

Academic Editor: Antonio Skarmeta

"Internet of Things" (IoT) bridges the communication barrier between the computing entities by forming a network between them. With a common solution for control and management of IoT devices, these networks are prone to all types of computing threats. Such networks may experience threats which are launched by exploitation of vulnerabilities that are left unhandled during the testing phases. These are often termed as "zero-day" vulnerabilities, and their conversion into a network attack is named as "zero-day" attack. These attacks can affect the IoT devices by exploiting the defense perimeter of the network. The existing solutions are capable of detecting such attacks but do not facilitate communication, which affects the performance of the network. In this paper, a consensus framework is proposed for mitigation of zero-day attacks in IoT networks. The proposed approach uses context behavior of IoT devices as a detection mechanism followed by alert message protocol and critical data sharing protocol for reliable communication during attack mitigation. The numerical analysis suggests that the proposed approach can serve the purpose of detection and elimination of zero-day attacks in IoT network without compromising its performance.

1. Introduction

The communication networks are expected to go beyond 40% of the total devices in 2020, which were active in 2012 [1]. All these entities are grouped and studied as "Internet of Things" (IoT). IoT is now a common name and soon it will be a part of daily networking. IoT aims at reducing the gap between the isolated devices and service providers by forming a local network between them.

IoT includes computing components that are grouped together as a single subnetwork on the basis of similar functionalities. These subnetworks have recurrent operations and depend on a common firmware for their activities. A common firmware helps to integrate a vast range of communication devices irrespective of the technology being used by them. Such type of deployment allows easy integration as well as maintenance of IoT devices. A common platform allows easier updates as well as control on the behavior of IoT devices. In general, IoT devices operate in a secure environment and rely much on the security of firmware. However, in certain scenarios, their firmware is subject to various kinds of computing threats, which can infiltrate the operational defense of these devices [2].

The level of threats and possibility of perimeter breaking depend on the types of applications as well as the types of security mechanisms opted by an IoT network. The applications which are dependent on privileged access to a user for its operations are more prone to computing threats. These threats can be known or unknown attacks and depend entirely on IoT activities, such as diagnosis of IoT devices, fault management, firmware updates, mobility management, and information dissemination. Such activities are performed with access to crucial layers of IoT networks, which may provide unauthorized access to notorious groups leading to exploitation of their regular operations [3–5].

All the attacks which are known so far are applicable to IoT networks. The current enterprises are looking forward to nonhuman intervention in network setups. However, with everything being controlled by a computing entity, that too connected via a common network, the risk of falling prey to known or unknown attacks increases [6–9]. Such conditions demand efficient security solutions for protected operations of these networks.

Most of the business houses and technology developers focus on a common platform that can serve the purpose for "connectivity to all." However, the common platform comes with a workload of management and security issues. Since these operations are only applicable via software-defined solutions, such approaches make the system vulnerable to all kinds of software threats [67]. One of these threats is "zero-day vulnerabilities." These are extremely dangerous vulnerabilities in the network, which if left unidentified may lead to a zero-day attack, that may fail the entire network [52, 68].

Zero-day vulnerabilities exploit the network on the basis of their identification. If the security patches are released after the identification of such vulnerabilities by the notorious groups, there can be serious consequences. On the contrary, identification by in-house administrators can help in mitigation of these threats before making any public announcements. Thus, mode of identification and time of identification are the key role players in the case of zero-day attacks in IoT networks. A software bug can be identified during its testing phase; however, in some cases, it may get unnoticed and gets exploited after a long time of use. Such scenarios are dangerous and convert a zero-day vulnerability into a possible zero-day attack. The name is coined by considering the negligible time offered to the developers or the service providers for counterfeiting these vulnerabilities after their first identification.

IoT networks are highly sensitive as these may possess crucial currency exchange as well as health information of an individual. Thus, zero-day threats are one of the biggest issues for these networks. It is of utmost importance to analyze the operations of these networks and provide an efficient solution for their mitigation. In recent years, most of the researchers have focused on identification of zero-day attacks in IoT networks by analyzing the difference in operations of devices from their normal routine.

The existing approaches, such as detecting advanced persistent threats [64], self-protecting systems [65], and behavior information-based detection [66], are effective, but their scope is limited to detection. These approaches are unable to support communication during threat identification. Also, there are no evident mechanisms for alerting other nodes of the network about the attack formation. Further, these approaches do not account for reliable connectivity, which can continue its operations irrespective of the attack and number of nodes in the network.

In this paper, a study on zero-day attacks is presented followed by a solution, for the issues illustrated in the previous paragraph, which is governed by a consensus framework. The proposed consensus framework relies on behavior context of IoT devices for identification of attacks. The proposed approach not only identifies the zero-day threats in the network but also supports communication and alert messages once an attack is identified. The proposed approach uses two different protocols, one for alert messages and the other for critical data sharing during attacking conditions. The proposed approach is highly scalable and reliable even if the entire network is under the threat of zero-day vulnerabilities. Reliability and consensus cost are the two driving factors of the proposed approach. The results presented for network formulations and latency show that the proposed approach can successfully mitigate the zero-day attacks in IoT network without compromising its performance.

1.1. Background to Zero-Day Attacks. The term "zero-day" is coined considering the negligible time stipulated for overcoming the effects of identified vulnerabilities in a particular software. The number of days for which an anomaly remains unknown affects the countermeasures as well as its effects. This is directly affected by the steps taken to eliminate a known vulnerability. Users with less experience and those who delay the application of patches are the ones who suffer the most. The announcement of vulnerability should be immediately followed by patching of security updates for the identified software. Failing in doing so may lead to harsh consequences of zero-day attacks [69].

The mode of detection has a direct influence on the threat implications of zero-day attacks. Once identified by good guys (white hat hackers), these vulnerabilities can be overpowered with the timely release of security patches; however, identification by bad guys (black hat hackers) makes these systems prey to a different kind of known as well as unknown attacks. Apart from these concerns, the users of a computing entity play a crucial role and can reduce the threat level by following the guidelines for security updates.

Zero-day attacks have a direct influence on the working of an organization and nation. During last decade, a large number of zero-day vulnerabilities were identified in the government of many nations. Most of them were also released on the public domains, which allowed hackers to exploit their parent software by using some known attacks. The announcements of vulnerabilities on the public domains worsen the conditions as all the bugs are easily highlighted which attracts notorious groups of society leading to devastating effects. Such situations also affect the strategies of nations and their mutual agreements.

Every zero-day vulnerability does not lead to zero-day attacks. The ones whose security measures fall short of all possible attacks lose the game and get exploited. These shortcomings of an organization and an individual for implementing security mechanisms give hackers an exploitation window which may lead to zero-day attacks.

The vulnerability cycle for zero-day attacks varies for different situations. In some cases, these attacks are launched covertly once a bug is identified, while, in other cases, hackers may lead to an overt operation by publicizing over different domains [70, 71]. Thus, it is evident that not only do hackers lead to zero-day attacks, but also the delays in updating of security mechanisms also cause possibilities of zero-day attacks. The life cycle of zero-day attacks is studied with "Window of Vulnerability" (WoV). It is evaluated as a software timeline considering the discovery phase, security patching, intermediate exploitation phase, and patch applicability phase, as shown in Figure 1 [52, 70, 72].

The four phases of WoV are split into three sections (operations) as shown with different colors in Figure 1. The

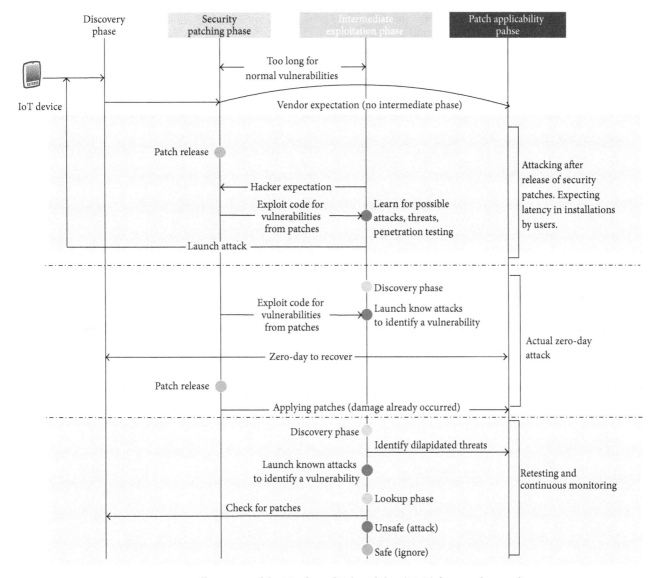

FIGURE 1: An illustration of the Window of Vulnerability (WoV) for zero-day attacks.

expectation of the vendors is a direct mapping between the security patching phase and its applicability once a vulnerability is discovered. However, such is possible only in the ideal case, which is not applicable for most of the scenarios. The figure shows that, in the first partitioning, after the release of a patch, the hackers expect to identify a bug in the patch by covert or overt operations. This is followed by the launch of known or unknown attacks expecting that users have not updated these patches and there might exist a possibility for zero-day attacks. The second partitioning is when the zero-day vulnerabilities are identified by the hackers themselves and the damage occurs prior to the launch of security patches. The third partitioning is the iterative procedure believing that there might be some vulnerabilities which are left unhandled. These are followed by a decision on safe and unsafe nature of the released patches.

No system is capable of providing a fool-proof security. Exploitation of zero-day vulnerabilities is a matter of time and range of access. There might exist a bug which is left

unnoticed for many years, while there might be others that are identified without many interventions. It is of utmost importance for the security analysts, network administrators, penetration testers, and network evaluators to covertly identify such issues and securely share the patches against the identified vulnerabilities.

1.2. Threat Implications and Detection of Zero-Day Attacks. Ever since the computing entities are capable of supporting connectivity between them, the level of threats has arisen to many folds. These threats leave a huge impact on the IoT systems which vary from a simple capturing to destruction and disruption of services [7]. However, these are the worse scenarios; there are other implications associated with the threats in IoT that can act as a silent killer in the form of zero-day attacks. These include the following:

(i) *Ethical Distortion.* Once a zero-day attack is launched, it destroys the usability ethics associated with any software. Exploitation of a zero-day vulnerability may affect the credibility of an organization leading to huge impact on the economic growth. Apart from destroying and capturing, zero-day attacks raise various ethical issues concerning the usability of a particular IoT device. Zero-day attacks are also used by organizations to destroy the reputation of other organizations leading to a strong ethical conflict and effects on customers and services.

(ii) *Trust Violations and Initiation of Other Attacks.* Zero-day attacks violate the trust and usability rules of any IoT device. Trust violations can cause immediate shutdown of secure services between the implanted IoT devices. These attacks can also release the personal information of an individual or organization on the public domain that makes it vulnerable to different other attacks leading to a major threat of full cyberwar. The network between the IoT devices is assumed to be validated on the basis of a trust as maintained by a particular entity or the service providers. An attack on the firmware or application software can directly affect the security perimeter of an organization. Further, such scenarios can easily influence the remote procedures which are considered to be the backbone of IoT networks.

(iii) *Sovereignty.* IoT devices have seen a tremendous growth in civilian as well as military activities. With a large number of devices involved in surveillance and security services, access to vulnerability can affect the sovereignty of a country leading to serious threats to the public as well as classified domains. During the last few years, the vulnerability in the management software of security services has led to stealing of classified information and its release over the public domain. Such cases are some of the serious implications of zero-day attacks in IoT.

(iv) *End Solutions' Credibility.* Nowadays, most of the enterprises focus on providing a single updatable version of software solutions without requiring reinstallation of firmware. In the case of IoT, such approach can easily be affected if a zero-day vulnerability is identified in endpoint software. The effects can vary and will depend on the actions regarding the updating of firmware. A zero-day attack or exploitation can certainly be harmful to any organization and can destroy its whole chain of software solutions. This is also related to the earlier point on trust violations.

(v) *Defenselessness.* In some cases of zero-day attacks, cascade vulnerabilities are identified leading to multiple zero-day threats. Such conditions in IoT networks can make the entire perimeter defenseless despite the strengths of firewall and other detection solutions. Such scenarios require large-scale alterations in the entire network and may require network replanning leading to huge cost overheads on the organizations.

(vi) *Conceptual Disfigurement.* The success of IoT networks lies in the depth of concept and planning. With zero-day vulnerabilities, the concept of security gets destroyed leading to the disfigurement of the entire idea. Such conditions also expose the strategic context as well as instances involved in decision-making leading to deformity at personal as well as team levels. Further, such attacks vandalize the IoT device in their deployment network without any use.

As discussed earlier, zero-day attacks do not give enough time to security analyzers and developers for overcoming the threats. It is difficult to identify and trace such threats even after years of development. However, covert analyses on the periodic basis can prevent the exploitation of zero-day vulnerabilities. Further, reverse engineering has also increased the chances of occurrence of such attacks. Detection of zero-day attacks in IoT should be fast and it should provide less time to hackers for developing exploit codes.

Identification of unknown attacks and behavior variations of each IoT device make it difficult to provide any countermeasures against such threats. Embedded IoT devices need to be secured by the means of secure embedded coding solutions [5]. Signature analysis and code validation should be performed periodically to analyze the frequency of a zero-day vulnerability in IoT systems. Evaluation of RFID security protocol and packet analyses should also be carried out for detecting any vulnerability. The remote procedures associated with the IoT updating process should be protected using channel security. However, this cannot prevent the zero-day attacks entirely but can ensure a latency to attackers in gathering information from the remote procedures [72]. Further, various techniques available for detecting zero-day possibilities in a network are listed in Table 1. The table discusses different types of detection approaches with their motivation, description, and applicability issues. The existing approaches can be classified into pattern-based detection, heuristic-based detection, reputation-based detection, behavior-based detection, virtualization-based detection, and irregular symptom-based detection. Most of these approaches rely on finding vulnerabilities in the exploited system but are not well-matched for real-time detection. Further, the communication between the devices after the identification of an attack is not discussed much in these solutions.

1.3. Motivation and Our Contribution. The devices in IoT networks are highly sensitive and depend on a common platform for the majority of their operations. With a common firmware from their business operators, these devices are operable on software technologies, which may fall prey to some bugs. These bugs may be noticed after a long period of time, or, as in some cases, these are ignored during testing phases. Such scenarios lead to vulnerabilities that can be exploited by the black hats for harming the operations of IoT networks. Thus, prevention of network against the known or unknown attacks which can be launched at any time in the near future is the motivation behind the development of the proposed framework. There are a lot of approaches for identifying zero-day attacks with a high accuracy, but (to the best of our knowledge) most of these are not able to withstand the communication burden and may halt the network during

TABLE 1: Zero-day detection techniques applicable in IoT.

Detection techniques	Motivation or background	Description	Issues
Pattern-based [10–17]	To detect and analyze malicious codes incoming promptly from outside	After defining the specific pattern of existing malicious codes as their characteristics, malicious codes are detected and blocked by matching defined pattern with a pattern of incoming codes	(i) This technique can support fast detection by just comparing defined signatures (ii) However, new and variant malicious codes are not defined in pattern and are not detected
Heuristic-based [18–24]	To detect and analyze new and variant malicious codes	This technique determines specific behavior of malicious codes, so this can check new and variant codes by analyzing abnormal behavior not signatures	(i) It is hard to define criteria for comparison of similarities of abnormal behavior (ii) This causes false positive by detecting normal program as malicious code
Reputation-based [25–28]	To detect and analyze new and variant malicious codes	(i) This technique is similar to pattern-based technique (ii) In particular, if new malicious codes are emerged, reliability is determined based on feedback for opinions of a large number of users (iii) Reputation information is defined on the basis of number of users, manufacturer of codes, etc. (iv) Accuracy and reliability depend on possession and analysis of a large amount of reputation information	(i) Accuracy and reliability are only dependent on user's opinions (ii) If reputation information is not enough, accuracy and reliability are decreased
Behavior-based [29–42]	(i) Signature, pattern, and reputation information are hard to analyze by malicious code analyst preferentially (ii) There is a limitation to collect or analyze malicious codes when the number of codes increases exponentially (iii) It is a difficult approach for analyzing malicious codes realistically because of reasons that the rate of malicious code generation is much faster than the speed of analysis	(i) This technique detects faulty behavior when malicious codes are executed (ii) This is an improved version of heuristic-based technique (iii) Malicious behavior is revealed not only in executable files, but also in document files, such as PDF, DOC, and HWP (iv) This technique determines characteristics of malicious behavior based on file, registry, network, process, etc.	The system can be infected because behavior is analyzed during execution process in the actual system
Virtualization-based [43–48]	An environment to analyze malicious behavior in a separated space from actual system is required	(i) This approach is closely related to dynamic heuristic-based technique (ii) Malicious codes are analyzed in virtual system	This does not detect attacks efficiently and takes a lot of time to penetrate the system, even after collecting various pieces of information and utilizing unknown attacks
Abnormal/irregular symptom-based [49–51]	To detect and analyze unknown and zero-day attacks	(i) To detect abnormal behavior, this technique collects and integrates logs, which are generated in the system, and analyzes the correlated information (ii) In particular, this is required for detecting infected systems, with unknown new malicious code, and it helps to determine whether transmitted traffic is normal or abnormal	(i) In case of security system, if the system does not process information in real time, the system gets exposed to security threats (ii) It is technically difficult to collect and analyze correlation for high-capacity and high-speed traffic from network

attack scenarios. This also motivated the need for a common solution which can handle both the identification of zero-day attacks as well as reliable communication during such possibilities.

The proposed approach forms a consensus framework which uses behavior context of IoT devices for identifying zero-day vulnerabilities in the network. Next, the proposed approach uses alert message protocol for notifying network components about the infected nodes as well as subnetworks. Finally, the proposed approach uses a critical data sharing protocol for disseminating information despite the presence of zero-day vulnerabilities. The proposed approach uses reliability and consensus cost to form their solution and it also suggests mechanisms for security patching and reestablishment of trust.

The rest of the paper is structured as follows: Section 2 presents related works. Section 3 gives insight into the network model, proposed approach, and protocols. Section 4 presents the performance analysis. Section 5 concludes the paper with a future scope.

2. Related Works

Zero-day attacks have been studied by a lot of researchers in different forms and environments. The existing works have focused on the elimination of these attacks on the basis of fixed parameters, such as false positive ratio, false negative ratio, accuracy, and the area under curves. These approaches operate towards the elimination of possible zero-day threats in a connected environment. However, very few of them have highlighted the consequences and solutions for zero-day in IoT networks. Intelligent solutions are required for countering these threats and preserve communication despite the level of damage. Machine learning can be used as one possible ground for intelligent mechanisms that can help to understand threat implications and provide a suitable remedy accordingly [73].

Recently, Singh et al. [66] proposed a solution for detecting zero-day attacks by using device signatures and behavior. The approach uses a hybrid technique for detecting threats. This solution can be useful in analyzing streaming data against zero-day threats but is unable to provide a reliable communication mechanism for rest of the network. Duessel et al. [74] focused on application-layer based zero-day attack detection. The authors relied on investigating anomalies by using contextual information. The authors used text-based solutions and binary application-layer protocols for detecting zero-day anomalies. Similar to other existing techniques, this approach is limited to detection over a node and does not account for network attacks and management when encountered with zero-day vulnerabilities.

Chamotra et al. [75] suggested that honeypot baselining can be an efficient solution for analysis in an attacker environment. The authors particularly emphasized the use of honeypot baselining in detecting zero-day attacks. Their approach is based on the XML mapping, but this can be manipulated if the structure of files is known to the attackers. How the rest of the network will operate is still an open issue with this solution. Sun et al. [76] proposed a probabilistic

solution for zero-day attacks. Their approach is based on high infection probabilities for detecting zero-day paths. With a proper network-based extension, this can be a useful solution in mitigating extreme threat implications of zero-day attacks. However, with an erroneous measurement of probability, this approach can lead to excessive computations, which is not desirable.

Self-protecting computing systems, as suggested by Chen et al. [65], are desirable for detecting zero-day threats in an IoT environment. The authors gave a prototype by using virtual machines for building self-protecting systems. Their solution is efficient and can be considered for extending to IoT networks. However, the present state of this approach requires a much contextual evaluation of devices before considering it for zero-day analysis of IoT networks. Host-based intrusion detection system can be used for detecting zero-day attacks [77]. Such solutions use a window-based dataset to form a system capable of detecting zero-day threats by analyzing normal as well as abnormal data. This kind of solutions has limited scope and can be manipulated by multiple attacks. Also, such solutions need a considerable extension for real-time analysis of zero-day attacks in IoT networks.

Apart from the related works presented above, some key aspects of general zero-day attacks and zero-day attacks in IoT are presented in Tables 2 and 3, respectively. Most of the existing solutions, discussed in these tables, focus on identifying programming errors by using strong debugging, executable operations through attachments, data forging through authentication failures, and so on. Further, the subsisting solutions are vulnerably susceptible to threats as the analysis phase itself can lead the system to zero-day attacks. Apart from these, the dependence on data accumulating and lateral analysis does not ensure a real-time solution for zero-day susceptibility detection in IoT networks.

From the study presented in this paper, it is evident that existing solutions are capable of identifying zero-day attacks by using various mechanisms, but (to the best of our knowledge) most of them are unable to provide a strategy for reliable communication during these attacks. Also, these approaches lack aftermath of zero-day exploitation.

3. Proposed Work

The proposed approach aims at mitigating aftereffects of zero-day attacks and providing a strategy for analyzing the communication across the entire network. With the efficient identification of falsifying groups, the proposed approach uses a consensus framework for reliable communication even during zero-day attacks.

3.1. System Model. The network comprises a set $\mathcal{M}$ of IoT devices out of which some are independent while others are Corresponding Nodes (CNs). The CNs operate as a single network under a control of common Home Gateway (HGW) and a network can have multiple HGWs represented by a set $\mathcal{H}$. The devices under each HGW are represented by $M_1, M_2, \ldots, M_{|\mathcal{M}|}$, such that $\mathcal{M} = \bigcup_{i=1}^{|H|} M_i$. Further, the

TABLE 2: Zero-day attacks.

Attack techniques	Mechanism	Focus	Methodology
Network attack vector [52, 53]	Launch the attack's malicious payload and propagate itself	Programming errors	Protocols and network-aware processes
Application attack vector [52, 53]	Launch executable files	Open e-mail attachment	Executable files
Control system attack vector [54]	Destroy control system such as SCADA and PLC	Server Service (MS08-067), Windows Shell (MS10-046), Print Spooler Service (MS10-061), and Windows Kernel-Mode Drivers (MS10-073)	Third parties, LAN, and removable flash drives
Worm propagation [54]	Propagate worms or bots inside the network	Infection of Web server	IIS
Targeted attack (APT) [54]	Penetrate targeted system	Misplaced diversity	Weakest path
Moving target [54, 55]	Evade antivirus detection	Limit the exposure of attackers and opportunities and mitigate system resiliency	Continually shift and change over time to increase complexity and cost

TABLE 3: Zero-day attacks in IoT.

Attack techniques	Mechanism	Focus	Methodology
Asynchronous attack [56]	Lead to instability of a real-time energy market	Erroneous control	Desynchronizing of smart meters
Simple packet delay attack [56]	Desynchronizing the slave nodes	Manipulate of a slaves' clock	Delay of the transmissions of the NTP or PTP packets
DDoS [57, 58]	Denial of services, service unavailable	Unknown or new attack, exploiting vulnerabilities, overload resources	UDP flood, ICMP/PING flood, SYN flood, Ping of Death, etc.
Advanced persistent threats (APT) [58]	Unauthorized person attempts to gain access to the system	Stealing data	Bypassing authentication
Man-in-the-Middle (MITM) attack [58–60]	Gain illegitimate access to the system or the network	A program or person masquerades as another program or person	Spoofing and sniffing attack
Replay attack [58, 61, 62]	Disguise valid entities or messages	Bypassing integrity	Valid message containing some valid data is repeated again and again

network uses a set $\mathscr{B}$ for Base Stations (BSs) and a set $\mathscr{A}$ for Access Points (APs) for communicating with IoT device directly or indirectly via HGW. The network includes a set $\mathscr{N}$ of Mobile Nodes (MNs) which aim at sharing context as well as information with IoT devices. The network also has inter-IoT device communication between all the elements of set $\mathscr{M}$. An illustration of the initial and proposed network architectures is shown in Figure 2 with hierarchical view in Figure 3.

The problem in this paper is presented as cost-reliability formulation [78]. The cost involves the "cost of consensus," whereas the reliability is the belief a node exhibits on every other entity in the network including itself. Both of these parameters are used to derive the level of connectivity, which helps to analyze whether a connection exists between any two nodes as well as helping in predicting the possibilities of connectivity on the basis of given behavior of a node. The

proposed system is affected by the number of diagnosis systems that monitor a single node. In the network, considering that every infrastructure possesses a diagnosis system, the total number of subnetworks γ will be equal to $|\mathscr{H}| + |\mathscr{A}'|$, where $\mathscr{A}'$ is the set of APs that do not interact with any HGW. With α being the initial connectivity constant between any two entities, $\mathscr{I}$ being the set of diagnosis system in charge for a given set of nodes, s being the alternative routes for each device, and τ being the trustworthy components, the reliability $\mathscr{R}$ of the network can be calculated as [78]

$$\mathscr{R} = \prod_{i=1}^{\gamma}\left(1 - \sum_{j=1}^{|\mathscr{I}|}\sum_{\tau}\prod_{k=1}^{s_i}\left(\binom{\mathscr{E}_{i,k}}{\tau'}\alpha_{ik}^{\tau'}\left(1 - \alpha_{ik}^{\mathscr{E}_{ik}-\tau'}\right)\right)\right). \quad (1)$$

Here, τ' is the difference between the actual connections and the active connections available for a graph $\mathscr{G} = (\mathscr{V}, \mathscr{E})$ formed between the network entities, such that $\mathscr{V}$ is the

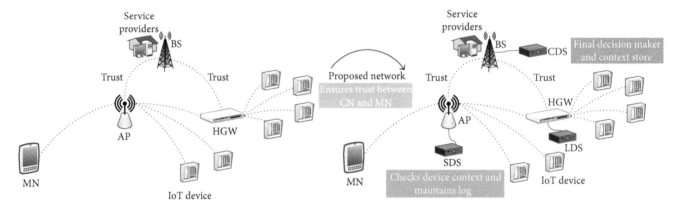

FIGURE 2: An illustration of the initial and proposed network architectures.

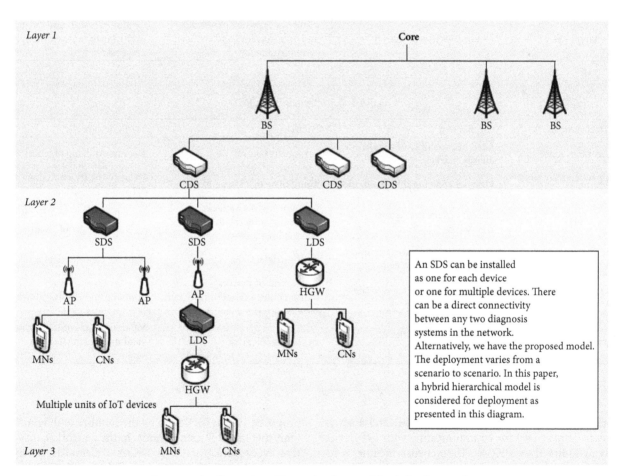

FIGURE 3: An illustration of hierarchical view of the defined network.

union of all the network entities and $\mathscr{E}$ refers to the set of connections per node. Let $\mathscr{W}$ be the weight associated with every link which is active in the network, such that, for a single instance, $\max(\mathscr{W}) = |\mathscr{E}|((|\mathscr{E}| - 1)/2)$. In the proposed approach, the consensus cost means the minimum cost of connectivity that enables maximum reliability for maintaining communication in the network. The consensus cost is derived as a mutual cooperation between $\mathscr{E}$, γ, halt time $\mathscr{T}$, and τ'. In the proposed approach, the mitigation of zero-day attacks is followed by realization of reliable communication

between the nodes. Thus, for optimal solution, the proposed approach relies on following conditions:

$$\mathscr{R} = \max, \quad C_o = \min,$$
$$\mathscr{R} = \mathscr{R}_{\mathrm{TH}}, \quad C_o = \min, \tag{2}$$

where $\mathscr{R}_{\mathrm{TH}}$ are the threshold limits for the reliability of the network during attacks and C_o is the consensus cost defined over multiple parameters, such that, for given instances η,

$$C_o = \mathscr{W}\mathscr{T} \times \left(1 - \frac{\tau'}{\max(\mathscr{E})}\right)^{\eta}, \qquad (3)$$

provided that all the variables are at minimum even after a vulnerability is exploited.

3.2. IoT Diagnosis System. The proposed approach forms a consensus framework for mitigating the effects of zero-day attacks and provides reliable communication once an attack is identified. In the proposed approach, MNs are secured via trust, which is maintained by the service providers who are also in charge of the BSs. The diagnosis system forms the backbone of the proposed consensus framework and helps in diagnosing the issues at different operational layers of the network. The diagnosis systems are just like the monitoring devices which manage the context of IoT devices and help in maintaining reliability between the network entities. The diagnosis system can be installed centrally or distributively. The details of diagnosis systems are provided below:

(i) *Centralized Diagnosis System (CDS).* CDS is the main diagnosis system which is installed on the central BS that manages multiple APs as well as HGWs. CDS is the key entity in managing the trust as well as generating updates for the entire network. The updates are shared via security mechanisms and communication protocol provided in the later part of this paper. In general cases, the behavioral aspects of IoT devices are available with the CDS and it shares them with the other diagnosis system whenever required or demanded. CDS is highly active in reliable communication between IoT as well as in alarming devices once a particular attack is registered in its database.

(ii) *Local Diagnosis System (LDS).* LDS is the near-user diagnosis system which is installed on the HGW. LDS manages the operability of IoT devices which indirectly interact with the BSs via HGW. LDS is critical for some of the applications, such as smart home management system and smart monitoring. LDS also obtains the context of its devices and stores them locally. However, an issue with the LDS may expose the entire network to different kind of attacks. Thus, the information of devices in HGW needs to be encrypted. Also, the details can be stored distributively, by storing ID at HGW and the corresponding information at the CDS. It is assumed that LDS are secured prior to communication and the service providers have sufficient information regarding the operations of LDS.

(iii) *Semi-Diagnosis System (SDS).* SDS is installed on the AP for supporting the IoT devices which do not act as a CN. SDS interacts directly with the CDS, and, in some cases, it is capable of retrieving information from the LDS. SDS helps in sustaining communication when LDS is irresponsive or it violates the rules of communication. In highly dense networks, SDS is not believed to handle context of devices, and the data collected from them is shared directly with the CDS. Further, the context and data sharing protocols help in checking the authenticity of each device once a vulnerability is exploited in the network.

The proposed approach deals with both scenarios of storing context at the centralized and distributed diagnosis systems. The evaluation part of this paper uses both of these strategies for analyzing the performance of the proposed approach. Also, the level of abstraction and distribution of information depend on the context and amount of data to be shared and transmitted between the IoT devices as well as the network infrastructure.

3.3. IoT Context and Behavior Formulation. The context is a driving force behind the formation of a reliable network which can operate effectively even in the presence of zero-day attack without exposing the entire network. The context helps in forming a strategy which can be employed for generating trust rules between the IoT devices. The context may vary for different IoT devices. In this paper, general IoT context is considered in the formation of behavior rules. These rules can be further exaggerated depending on the requirements as well as the application scenario.

The context is decided by the CDS after registering all the devices during initialization of the network. These contexts are stored in every diagnosis system and shared mutually between the demanding diagnosis systems. The values are stored periodically and appended in a single file for every device. The size of storage depends on the level of feedback expected from the network operators as well as on the memory of diagnosis systems. Note that CDS does not possess a constraint to memory, but HGWs and APs have limited memory; thus, logs should be shared with the CDS on a timely basis. In the proposed approach, it is assumed that the CDS, SDS, and LDS are connected via a secure path; thus, security of logs is not a concern in the proposed approach. At present, the general information available for each IoT device is selected as a context. This can be altered depending on the types of devices and network configurations. The details of the context used in the proposed approach are provided below:

(i) *Device Signatures* $(\mathscr{D}_s)$. This is the unique ID of a device allocated once it registers itself with the CDS. Note that $\mathscr{D}_s$ are allocated in lieu of physical address of every requesting device. These signatures are embedded in the device and also shared with the corresponding SDS or LDS.

(ii) *Pseudo Signatures* $(\mathscr{S}_s)$. This is the pseudo ID generated from the local entity for communication with the fellow devices. It is to be noted that every CN in the network recognizes another device by its $\mathscr{S}_s$. In the adverse cases, the local entity can shuffle these IDs, but with updates to every CN; otherwise, it may lead to sharing of wrong information to a wrong device.

(iii) *Update Counter* ($\mathcal{U}_c$). This is the firmware update counter which tells the number of times the firmware of a device is accessed and updated. The value of $\mathcal{U}_c$ may be different for each subgroup. It is fixed by the CDS by selecting a random value for every requesting subgroup. These counters do not interfere with the performance of the network and help in determining the level as well as the depth of updates performed in the IoT network. The update counters are stored at the central level and local level as well as at the device.

(iv) *Traffic Type* ($\mathcal{F}_t$). This is one of the crucial parameters which helps in deciding the content shared between the IoT devices. $\mathcal{F}_t$ governs the rules of traffic, which is expected from a particular IoT device and focuses on the exact outcomes as intended in the network. Usually, one set of IoT devices operating in the same domain has similar values for $\mathcal{F}_t$. However, depending on the level of interactions, the log for some devices may have multiple entries for $\mathcal{F}_t$.

(v) *Header Length* ($\mathcal{H}_l$). This includes the metadata of the IoT device and its controlling diagnosis system. Header fields are also subjected to some random integers generated by their corresponding diagnosis system. These random integers are selected by the diagnosis systems during the initialization of the network and are periodically updated. For the complex security of network parameter, corresponding diagnosis systems of each device may induce alterations in these random values to make IoT device unaware of the exact settings.

(vi) *Memory Range* ($\mathcal{Y}_r$). This controls the size of packets which are shared between the network entities. $\mathcal{Y}_r$ includes overall size of the packets including the code and binaries. In the case of exploitation of binaries, this metric can help in determining its correctness.

(vii) *Route* ($\mathcal{O}_r$). This field helps to check the route followed by the traffic coming from a particular IoT device. The diagnosis system matches the route with the path defined by it. This does not help in determining vulnerabilities but rather helps in checking the path which is followed by a device identified as a potential threat of zero-day attack.

The above context helps in defining the behavior formulations as well as the rules for analyzing the operations of any IoT device subjected to the possibilities of zero-day vulnerabilities. The context above can have fixed or variable lengths and has a lot to do with the content of applicability of a device in practical conditions. The behavior formulation for each device is performed by forming a network of context described above and storing the general values into a tabular log for easier assessment. Various rules that are to be followed for ensuring consensus and trust between the network entities, as well as the diagnosis systems, are as follows:

(i) CDS is the one in charge and has the capacity of altering the context requirements in the network.

(ii) CDS can ensure trusted parties and such entities can be ignored from context matching. However, in the case of critical situations, all the entities fall under the proposed threat elimination categories and must ensure their trust before proceeding with the data exchanges.

(iii) Each diagnosis system has the capacity of deriving its dominance chart for the given set of context and can alter it periodically. This creates an ambiguous situation for the in-house attacker as it is always unaware of the checking rules.

(iv) One-to-one or single context mapping can be done depending on the situations and also on the transmission rates. Since mapping and matching of entire context consume time, unnecessary evaluations may lead to network overheads. However, the proposed approach takes care of such situations and the context strategy is a lightweight that does not cause many overheads.

(v) SDS and LDS can operate in dual mode seeking context from the CDS as well as the MN and the CN. They can form a local context decision system on the basis of their diagnosis results for every connection. This provides an extra layer of security but at the cost of excessive computations.

(vi) Any entity whose application access is altered as per its initial configurations needs to register its new format with the CDS as well as the corresponding LDS and SDS.

(vii) LDS and SDS have the capabilities of limiting the access to any device in the network, connected to their subgroups, in the case of alert messages.

The dominance of each context may vary with time and is fixed by the CDS. The dominance helps in retaining control over the evaluations in the network. This allows management of network without burdening the diagnosis systems. An illustration of exemplary curves for context, interaction module, and the context storing table is shown in Figure 4. The curves can follow any trend and the interaction module remains the same. The log and context storing table changes in accordance with the values set by CDS. The contexts from different entities are matched to analyze the behavior of IoT device allowing a platform for the formation of context graphs and strategic decision system.

3.4. Context Graphs and Strategic Decision System. The context graphs and strategic decision system are an integral part of the proposed approach. Both of these account for correct working as well as mitigation of zero-day attacks in IoT network by following the previously defined context rules. Let $\mathcal{G}' = (V', E')$ be the context graph formed for each node, where V' is the number of computational stages including input and output states. The context graphs are derived for every IoT device and the results are stored only for the first (input) as well as the final (output) stages. This helps in saving memory as well as knowing the exact state of every device

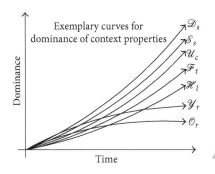
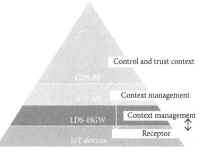

Properties	CDS	SDS*	LDS	IoT	Match
$\mathscr{D}_s$	—	—	—	—	Yes/no
$\mathscr{S}_s$	—	—	—	—	Yes/no
$\mathscr{U}_c$	—	—	—	—	Yes/no
$\mathscr{F}_t$	—	—	—	—	Yes/no
$\mathscr{H}_l$	—	—	—	—	Yes/no
$\mathscr{Y}_r$	—	—	—	—	Yes/no
$\mathscr{O}_r$	—	—	—	—	Yes/no

*NA: if not applicable as per the hierarchy model.

FIGURE 4: An illustration of exemplary curves for context, interaction module, and the context storing table.

in the network. In some cases, the intermediate stages can be saved. Such mechanisms allow in-depth evaluations by analyzing the working of every IoT device. However, these are subject to memory constraints and may cause many overheads. The context is derived individually depending on the dominance of context properties. In the context graphs, E' refers to the connectivity between the IoT referring to cohesion and coupling between the stages. Low values for context edges mean string-like one-to-one mapping, which is easier to follow and analyze. The size of $\mathscr{G}'$ may vary depending on the complex behavior of an IoT device.

The proposed strategic context graph-based solutions are applicable in the network during the deployment phase, rather than the development phase. However, these must be provided as an inbuilt facility in all the IoT devices. Thus, the proposed strategy comes handy only when a vulnerability is identified in the lateral stages of operations by either the development team or the security analysts. It can also be considered while releasing security patches and updates for a possible zero-day attack in the network. Operating on the behavior of every device, the proposed approach helps to track their stage-wise operations.

The management of IoT devices against the zero-day attacks is much affected by the strategic decisions. For this, CDS follows a rule of updating $\mathscr{U}_c$ with a random value anytime during transmissions. Once the values are decided, these can be used to identify the number of times a firmware of a device has been updated in real time and its actual value has been stored in the device. This helps in understanding if the firmware of a device is manipulated or not. The success of this depends on the exact matching of the context between the device and the diagnosis systems. An illustration of the operational view with an exemplary scenario for context graphs is shown in Figure 5. Once the context is shared between the diagnosis system, a simple rule of mutual exclusion is followed for analyzing values of selected or all contexts. The input and output stages are crucial as these include the entry and exit of intruders in the IoT firmware as well as the subnetwork. More intermediate states for every device allows much time for analyzing the context and behavior of a device. However, if the intermediate states are less or fast, delays can be added in the proposed strategy. The procedures in the proposed approach are described as four stages, as follows:

(i) *Stage 1.* The IoT device interacts with network entities for its registration and permissions for context sharing. The interaction procedures are secured via trust rules and security mechanisms for communications. This is the input stage and is followed by self-processing of IoT devices.

(ii) *Stages 2 and 3.* These are the intermediate stages and are referred to as a self-processing mechanism for the IoT devices. A procedure can have n number of stages depending on the type of context and configuration of the network. Stages 2 and 3 are operated as processing stages between the input and the output stages. These stages are accompanied by information gathering and processing by respective diagnosis systems. A high number of intermediate stages ensures more time for information processing. However, an excessively larger value for n may induce excessive overheads.

(iii) *Stage 4.* This is the final step for taking a decision on any IoT device and invoking a consensus data sharing protocol if intended because of the irregular behavior of IoT device or identification of misleading context. Any misleading device is identified after completion of stage 4 in the proposed approach.

The steps for strategic decisions on the basis of retrieved context through these stages are presented in Algorithm 1. The algorithm monitors the network continuously and its operational complexity is dependent on the amount of context as well as the connected components. Once a possibility of an attack is identified, the proposed approach uses consensus data sharing protocols which operate for alerting the network entities as well as reliable data sharing without being exploited by the zero-day vulnerabilities. The network operating with standard context matches the exactness with constant time, but, in the general case (proposed scenario), the complexity of Algorithm 1 will be given on the count of number of IoT devices and is equal to the complexity of forming a graph $\mathscr{G}'$.

3.5. Consensus Data Sharing Protocols. The consensus protocols are used once a zero-day vulnerability is identified in the network. These protocols can be used in case any node violates the reliability rules of the network. In the proposed approach, two different mechanisms are used for

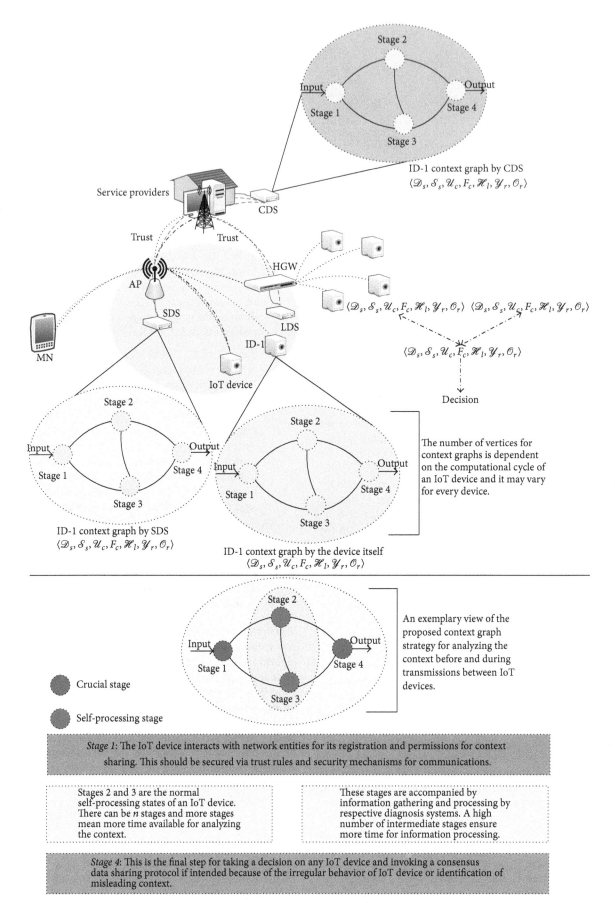

FIGURE 5: An illustration of exemplary scenario for context graph formation and evaluation of communicating IoT devices.

```
(1) Input: 𝒢 = (𝒱), 𝓔, 𝒟ₛ, 𝒮ₛ, 𝒰_c, 𝓕_t, 𝓗_l, 𝒴_r, 𝒪_r
(2) Output: context decision
(3) Register IoT devices with CDS, SDS, LDS
(4) set 𝒰_c
(5) while transmission! = NULL do
(6)     set a periodic counter for evaluation
(7)     Retrieve context from IoT device
(8)     Form 𝒢' = (V', E')
(9)     Mark input and outputs
(10)    Initialize context table
(11)    if |𝒱| = min && 𝓡 < 𝓡_TH && C_o = max then
(12)        Mark the device
(13)        Check 𝒰_c with CDS, SDS, LDS
(14)        Analyze 𝒟ₛ, 𝒮ₛ, 𝒰_c, 𝓕_t, 𝓗_l, 𝒴_r, 𝒪_r
(15)        Update context table
(16)        Generate alert messages (context table)
(17)        Follow consensus data sharing protocol
(18)    else
(19)        Continue
(20)    end if
(21)    Operate till trust is not ensured
(22) end while
(23) exit
```

ALGORITHM 1: Strategic decision on retrieved context.

protecting the network against unaware circumstances as well as intrusions. The details of both the protocols are provided in the following subsections.

(1) Alert Protocol. The alert protocol is invoked as a part of Algorithm 1. This protocol helps disseminate the alert messages across the network, allowing the formation of a secure workgroup. An illustration of the alert messages protocol is shown in Figure 6. The protocol initiates with reports and moves on taking a decision on the behavior of an IoT device. The steps followed by this protocol are explained below:

(i) The first step is the reporting by an MN about the unresponsive behavior of an IoT device to the CDS. The CDS begins investigation procedures which aim at retrieval of information from the required nodes.

(ii) The investigations are followed by the request messages for different context to the SDS and the LDS. The context messages are distinguished on the basis of the difference in the total information required as well as the IDs used for reporting.

(iii) The LDS operates towards fetching of results and logs from every connected device, which responds by sharing their reports.

(iv) Following this, $\mathcal{U}_c$ is checked at the CDS which is received from the LDS and the SDS.

(v) Next, all the diagnosis systems analyze the routes and maintain a report, which is followed by identification of false nodes.

(vi) Finally, a decision is taken and, in the case of unsafe nodes, alert messages are sent to the corresponding diagnosis systems. Using this, LDS selects the problematic device and alerts all other devices about its state.

(2) Critical Data Sharing Protocol. The alert message protocol is followed by a critical data sharing protocol (Figure 7). This protocol helps to disseminate information and maintains data flow even during unfavorable conditions. This protocol operates on an assumption that a secure path exists between all the diagnosis systems. The detailed procedures for this protocol are explained below:

(i) The first step begins with gathering alarming information, which is done by the previous alert protocol. LDS continuously fetches and maintains the log for every connected device.

(ii) All the connected components, namely, SDS, LDS, and MN, send their alarming updates and reports to CDS. This is done to acquire information of the subnetwork as a single CDS may be managing one or more subnetworks.

(iii) Next, the CDS fetches route logs and context from LDS as well as for the intended IoT device from the MN. Once the initial steps are performed, the CDS changes the pseudo IDs of every IoT device and reallocates them to the appropriate device via SDS and LDS.

(iv) The LDS maintains a policy of nondisclosure of new IDs to unsafe nodes. It is to be noted that the unsafe nodes always possess the same ID throughout the transmission that was allocated to them during initialization of the network.

(v) Once done with these steps, the LDS sends failed nodes information across the network and receives log reports and acknowledgments from every connected device.

(vi) Finally, the CDS shares the available information to all the intended entities and allows communication to begin in normal flow.

The combination of both consensus protocols helps to maintain a reliable communication and mitigate the zero-day attacks in IoT networks.

3.6. Context Management, Security Patching, and Reestablishment of Trust. The proposed approach relies on efficient decision-making over the context shared between the diagnosis systems. By analyzing the context, the proposed approach decides on rules for mitigating the threats of zero-day attacks. Further, it employs two protocols for alarming and data sharing between the correct devices across the network. However, with the proposed strategy, there are three major issues which should be handled for fault-free operations of the network in case a vulnerability is exploited. These include context management, security patching, and reestablishment of trust.

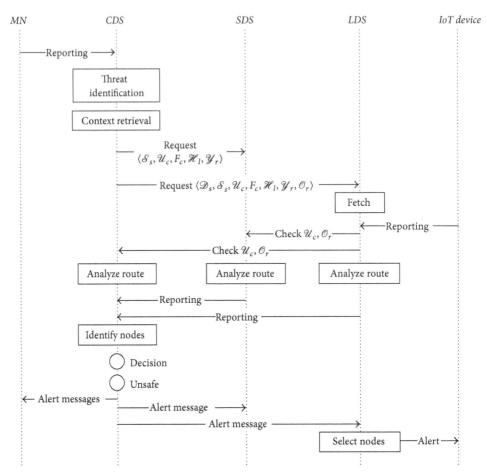

FIGURE 6: Consensus: alert protocol for zero-day attacks.

Context management is the responsibility of diagnosis systems and they use a secure channel for transmitting it across the network. Currently, the proposed approach is illustrated with a limited amount of context and decision solutions. This can be extended by an in-depth evaluation of IoT devices and generation of more contextual information which can help in identifying any device during regular operations. The context is updatable and can be modified with permissions of CDS as well as the trust establishing authorities. The context is stored as log files which are periodically updated and follows append mode which is dependent on a particular backup time for the replacement. SDS and LDS can also have a local storing point; however, this can overcome the issues of overheads involved in transmitting context across the network but raises issues related to local authentication as well as memory consumption. In the proposed approach, limited context is managed by the SDS and LDS and a majority of it is invoked directly from the device or CDS.

Once a vulnerability is exploited by a notorious group or a zero-day attack is launched, it is the responsibility of the proposed approach to counterfeit its effects and provide consensus rules for communication. After applicability of the proposed approach, it is the responsibility of the developers or network administrators to update the IoT firmware with new security patches using on-site or off-site mechanisms. On-site mechanisms are the traditional way of supporting an affected system, whereas, for off-site patching, the proposed approach can depend on the LDS or the SDS for reestablishing the trust and updating the firmware. However, the choice between the two is dependent on the fact whether a vulnerability is found or exploited. In the former case, off-site patching is successful, whereas, in the latter case, on-site patching is recommended. However, in any of the scenarios, the proposed approach can continue its mechanisms and support communication between the corrected devices without falling prey to the faulty nodes.

The final phase of mitigating a zero-day attack in IoT networks is the reestablishment of trust between the devices. Once security patching is done, the proposed approach operates as a counterpart and asks for context from the updated device. Since this is the first time after patching that the device is active, the default metrics are obtained from the security patches or the developers. By using default communications, the context is checked and a new pseudo ID is given to the recovered devices. Further, if the behavior of the device is found to be normal and aligned with the previous logs, the device is secured and its trust is reestablished. Since the proposed approach is iterative and continuously monitors the IoT devices as well as the connections between the MNs

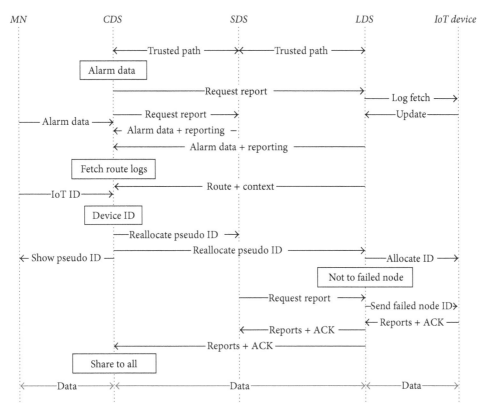

FIGURE 7: Consensus: critical data sharing protocol for zero-day attacks.

and the CNs, most possibilities of zero-day exploitations are counterfeited in a single attempt.

4. Performance Evaluations

The proposed approach is evaluated by using numerical simulations. The proposed approach is analyzed in two parts. The first part presents the network analysis by considering the zero-day attacks, and the second part presents the latency analysis for the two protocols proposed in this paper for mitigation of zero-day threats in IoT networks.

4.1. Network Analysis. These evaluations are performed in a numerically analyzed network by using *Matlab™*. A network with a single BS is considered which supports connectivity between MNs and CNs via APs. As described in the system model, the network is operated with three diagnosis systems with two protocols and an algorithm defined in the proposed approach. The network operates with 90% trustworthy components, the rest of which are under zero-day threat and may or may not lead to a full zero-day attack. This part of analysis presents the trends for reliability and consensus cost by varying the network size. Considering the parameter configurations given in Table 4, a randomized graph is formed between the network entities aiming at transmitting data between the MNs and the CNs.

First of all, the analysis is recorded for $\mathcal{R}$ against the variation in network size. The network size is the sum of all the nodes active in the network and possessing a connection

TABLE 4: Parameter configurations.

Parameter	Value	Description
$\lvert\mathcal{M}\rvert$	80	IoT devices
$\lvert\mathcal{H}\rvert$	2	HGWs
$\lvert\mathcal{B}\rvert$	1	BS
$\lvert\mathcal{N}\rvert$	10	MNs
$\lvert\mathcal{A}\rvert$	5	APs
$\lvert\mathcal{A}'\rvert$	2	Independent APs
$\mathcal{G} = (\mathcal{V}, \mathcal{E})$	100	Network graph
τ	90%	Trustworthy components
s	$\left((\tau)^4 \times \left(1 - \tau^{\tau-2}\right)\right) / (1 - \tau)$	Alternative routes [63]
α	0-1	Connectivity constant for $\mathcal{V}$
$\mathcal{T}$	5 ms	Halt time
$\mathcal{W}$	α	Link weight
η	2 per node	Instances per connection

with at least one of the MNs or the CNs. Figure 8 shows the reliability curve for the initial network and a network with and without infected nodes. The initial network curve serves as the baseline, and it can be analyzed that once the nodes with zero-day possibilities are removed from the communication by using the proposed approach, the value of $\mathcal{R}$ gradually increases and reaches a maximum where every possibility of zero-day threat is mitigated.

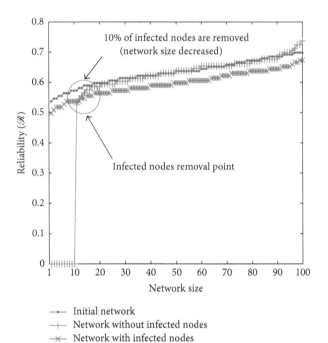

FIGURE 8: Reliability $\mathcal{R}$ versus network size.

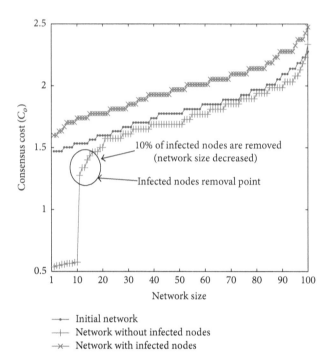

FIGURE 9: Consensus cost C_o versus network size.

The network can be operated with $\mathcal{R}_{\text{TH}}$ as discussed in the system model. Considering this figure, 0.5 can be treated as the threshold value for $\mathcal{R}_{\text{TH}}$. Below this value, a network cannot be considered reliable for communications and any value above it makes network safe despite the presence of infected nodes. It can be noticed that the network with infected nodes despite their identification has lesser reliability than the network with complete removal of such nodes. Thus, it is necessary to eliminate such nodes from the network as some traffic may still be passed to such nodes without expecting any forwarding mechanisms. This may cause excessive overheads and can further decrease the reliability of the network.

Contrary to $\mathcal{R}$, the consensus cost operates in a minimum way and the network with the removal of infected nodes has a better cost which is lower than the baseline as well as the network with infected nodes. Further, a network, which possesses infected nodes even after the identification, has higher values for C_o because infected nodes are also included while deriving actual cost for the network. These trends are presented in Figure 9. It is clear from the figure that, similar to $\mathcal{R}$ curves, it is important to operate a network with much knowledge allowing nontransmission of packets towards the infected nodes. Such behavior can be attained by the application of the proposed approach.

Figures 10 and 11 show values of $\mathcal{R}$ for baseline compared with attacker environment having 10% infected nodes and a network with the removal of the infected nodes, respectively. The red color in the former presents the lower values for reliability illustrating that the network which suffers from zero-day threats should be identified and moved towards their elimination as shown in the latter figure. Once the infected nodes are removed, as shown by a point of removal

in Figure 11, the reliability of network can be managed and made comparable with the baseline.

Further, the network analysis is presented by statistical variations of the numerical results following $\mathcal{R}$ and C_o, as shown in Figures 12 and 13. Figure 12 shows the variation of network density versus $\mathcal{R}$. The curve fitting with a normal distribution of values shows the comparison for reliability values in baseline mode and in the network with and without infected nodes. Similar observations are seen for C_o in Figure 13. It can be seen that a network without infected nodes possesses lower values for consensus cost and higher values for reliability. However, reliability curves are dominated by the baseline, whereas the network with infected nodes dominates the consensus cost negatively. The behavior of these curves is aligned with (1)–(3).

The results presented in this section are able to justify that the proposed approach can maintain reliable communication despite the presence of infected nodes in the network. However, the success of the proposed approach depends on the number of alternative routes available for communication in a highly infected network. A network with extremely large effects of zero-day threats may possess a low value for $\mathcal{R}$, and such scenarios can lead to complete failure of the network. However, the alarming mechanisms of the proposed approach take care of such scenarios and prevent complete failure or shutdown of the network in extreme zero-day possibilities.

4.2. Latency Analysis. In the proposed approach, two different protocols are used for alert messaging as well as for data sharing during critical instances in the network. This section presents latency analysis for both the protocols and helps to understand the communication overheads caused due to

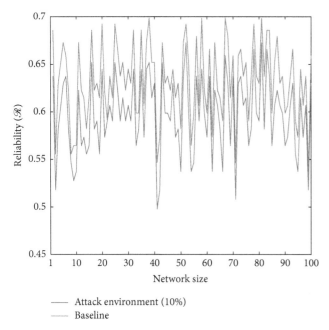

Attack environment (10%)

Baseline

FIGURE 10: Reliability $\mathcal{R}$ attacker environment versus network size.

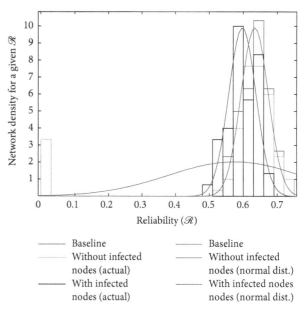

Baseline

Without infected nodes (actual)

With infected nodes (actual)

Baseline

Without infected nodes (normal dist.)

With infected nodes (normal dist.)

FIGURE 12: Statistical evaluation: network density for all values of $\mathcal{R}$ versus reliability $\mathcal{R}$.

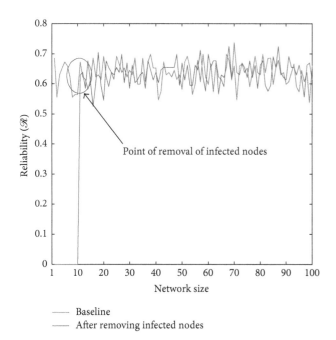

Baseline

After removing infected nodes

FIGURE 11: Reliability $\mathcal{R}$ without infected nodes versus network size.

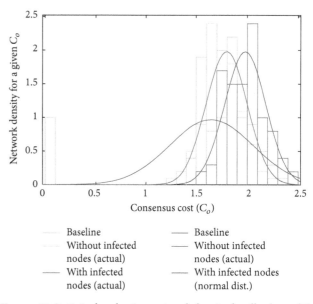

Baseline

Without infected nodes (actual)

With infected nodes (actual)

Baseline

Without infected nodes (actual)

With infected nodes (normal dist.)

FIGURE 13: Statistical evaluation: network density for all values of C_o versus consensus cost C_o.

messaging between the network entities. Various metrics, their notations, and descriptions used in this section are given in Table 5. The results are observed by varying the network nodes in normal and infected scenarios. Similar to network analysis, the network size includes all the nodes involved in communication between the MNs and the CNs. The values for numerical analysis are used by observing the number of iterations required for generating a particular message. However, subjected to a particular environment,

these values can be changed according to the configuration of the communication protocol used between the nodes.

The critical instances in both the protocols are marked by the identification of network nodes under a possible zero-day attack. For alert message protocol, the alert message generating latency $\mathcal{L}^A$ is calculated as

$$\mathcal{L}^A = 2\mathcal{T}_{\text{mn-cds}} + 3\mathcal{T}_{\text{cds-sds}} + 4\mathcal{T}_{\text{cds-lds}} + \mathcal{T}_{\text{sds-lds}} \\ + 2\mathcal{T}_{\text{lds-iot}}, \tag{4}$$

and final alert message generating latency after decisions is calculated as

$$\mathscr{L}_f^A = \mathscr{L}^A + 4\mathcal{Q}_{cds} + \mathcal{Q}_{sds} + 3\mathcal{Q}_{lds}. \tag{5}$$

However, in networks with equal decision-making delay, (4) can be rewritten as

$$\mathscr{L}_f^A = \mathscr{L}^A + 8\mathcal{Q}_{tds}. \tag{6}$$

Now, for a wired link between the CDS, SDS, and LDS, one-way packet transport delay is calculated as [79, 80]

$$\mathscr{D}_e(\mathscr{P}, \mathscr{X}) = \frac{\mathscr{P} \times \mathscr{X}}{\beta} + \mathscr{D}_{wired}, \tag{7}$$

and, for wireless links, one-way packet transport delay is calculated as [79, 80]

$$\mathscr{D}_{el}(\mathscr{P}) = \mathscr{F}_s + (\mathscr{X} - 1)t. \tag{8}$$

Now, by using the above equations, the communication overheads for alert messaging can be calculated as

$$\mathscr{C}_{overheads} = 2\mathscr{D}_{el}(\mathscr{P}_{mn}) + 2\mathscr{D}_{el}(\mathscr{P}_{iot})$$
$$+ 3\mathscr{D}_e(\mathscr{P}, \mathscr{X}_{cds-sds}) + \mathscr{D}_e(\mathscr{P}, \mathscr{X}_{sds-lds}) \tag{9}$$
$$+ 4\mathscr{D}_e(\mathscr{P}, \mathscr{X}_{cds-lds}) + \mathscr{L}_f^A.$$

In the second part, the analysis is performed for critical data sharing protocol. For this, the message generation latency is calculated as

$$\mathscr{L}^C = 3\mathscr{T}_{mn-cds} + 3\mathscr{T}_{cds-sds} + 2\mathscr{T}_{sds-lds} + 4\mathscr{T}_{cds-lds}$$
$$+ 5\mathscr{T}_{lds-iot}, \tag{10}$$

and final critical message generating latency after decisions is calculated as

$$\mathscr{L}_f^C = \mathscr{L}^C + 4\mathcal{Q}_{cds} + \mathcal{Q}_{lds}. \tag{11}$$

Now, similar to alert message protocol, with equal decision time, (11) can be rewritten as

$$\mathscr{L}_f^C = \mathscr{L}^C + 5\mathcal{Q}_{tds}. \tag{12}$$

Finally, the communication overheads for critical data sharing protocol can be calculated as

$$\mathscr{C}_{overheads}^{\mathscr{D}} = 3\mathscr{D}_{el}(\mathscr{P}_{mn}) + 5\mathscr{D}_{el}(\mathscr{P}_{iot})$$
$$+ 3\mathscr{D}_e(\mathscr{P}, \mathscr{X}_{cds-sds})$$
$$+ 2\mathscr{D}_e(\mathscr{P}, \mathscr{X}_{sds-lds}) \tag{13}$$
$$+ 5\mathscr{D}_e(\mathscr{P}, \mathscr{X}_{cds-lds}) + \mathscr{L}_f^C.$$

Now, by using the above-defined analysis model and the values from Table 5, results are observed for message latency as well as communication overheads. The numerical and

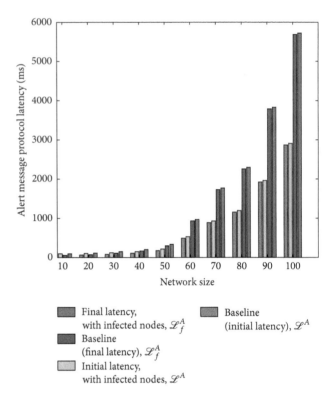

FIGURE 14: Alert message protocol latency versus network size.

timing analyses suggest that the proposed approach is capable of handling zero-day attack scenarios efficiently as a minimal difference is observed for alert message latency, as shown in Figure 14. It is evident from this graph that the proposed approach can handle network under zero-day attack with sufficient efficiency as the variation between the baseline and the actual observed values during attacks for alert message protocol is negligible. This graph shows results for $\mathscr{L}^A$ and $\mathscr{L}_f^A$ in the baseline as well as infected mode.

Similarly, these results are recorded for analyzing the message latency for critical data sharing protocols by following the formulations in (10) and (12). The less difference between the message latency in the baseline and that in the infected scenario suggests the efficient operations of the proposed approach. These trends can be visualized in Figure 15. Despite the fact that message latency increases with an increase in the network size, the overall difference between the actual scenario and the observed scenario is less; thus, the proposed approach can be used for performance-based reliable communication during mitigation of zero-day attacks in IoT networks.

Finally, the overall performance of the proposed approach in different modes with details on communication overheads can be observed in Figure 16. This graph presents results for $\mathscr{C}_{overheads}$ and $\mathscr{C}_{overheads}^{\mathscr{D}}$. The graph considers variation in one-way transport delay which is affected by the frame error rate. The values for F_s are observed by varying frame error rate between 0 and 0.9 on a stepping scale of 0.1.

The results shown in this figure suggest that the overheads increase with an increase in one-way transport delay, and

TABLE 5: Latency analysis (notations).

Notations	Values	Description
$\mathscr{L}^A$	TBC	Alert message latency
$\mathscr{L}_f^A$	TBC	Final/total alert message latency
$\mathscr{T}_{mn-cds}$	$\delta \times |\mathscr{N}| \times |\mathscr{M}| \times |\mathscr{B}| \times |\mathscr{A}| \times |\mathscr{H}|$	Evaluation time between MN and CDS
δ	Exponential: 1–30 packets	Traffic arrival time
$\mathscr{T}_{cds-sds}$	5 ms	Evaluation time between CDS and SDS
$\mathscr{T}_{cds-lds}$	5 ms	Evaluation time between CDS and LDS
$\mathscr{T}_{sds-lds}$	10 ms	Evaluation time between SDS and LDS
$\mathscr{T}_{lds-iot}$	10 ms	Evaluation time between LDS and IoT
$\mathscr{Q}_{tds}$	5 ms	Average decision time per component
$\mathscr{Q}_{cds}$	5 ms	Decision time for CDS
$\mathscr{Q}_{sds}$	5 ms	Decision time for SDS
$\mathscr{Q}_{lds}$	5 ms	Decision time for LDS
$\mathscr{P}$	256 bytes	Message size
$\mathscr{F}_s$	$\mathscr{D}_o * (1 - \omega)$	One-way frame transport delay
ω	0–0.9, step 0.1	Frame error
$\mathscr{F}$	10–100	Number of hops
β	10 MHz	Bandwidth
$\mathscr{D}_{wired}, \mathscr{D}_o$	20 ms	Delay
$\mathscr{X}$	0.5	Ratio packet size to frame size
t	20 ms	Interframe time
$\mathscr{F}_{cds-sds}$	10	Hop distance between CDS and SDS
$\mathscr{F}_{cds-lds}$	10	Hop distance between CDS and LDS
$\mathscr{F}_{sds-lds}$	10	Hop distance between SDS and LDS
$\mathscr{L}^C$	TBC	Critical message latency
$\mathscr{L}_f^C$	TBC	Final/total critical message latency

*TBC: to be calculated with formula in Section 4.2.

this increase can also be observed for the baseline scenarios. More overheads are observed in the proposed approach when a network is under extreme zero-day attack. However, considering the level of reliability provided by the proposed approach during the presence of attackers, these results can be considered efficient for IoT networks. The excessive overheads are caused by security patching procedures, regeneration of alert messages, and reestablishment of trust. Out of these, regeneration of alert messages can be ignored, which will definitely affect the performance of the proposed approach on the better side. However, a network with a lower rate than a network with complete failure is much desirable in highly critical scenarios. Thus, considering the results and performance evaluations, it can be concluded that the proposed approach can mitigate the zero-day attacks without much effect on the performance of uninfected nodes.

To the best of our knowledge, there are no competitive approaches for IoT networks which can handle zero-day attacks simultaneously with reliable communication. However, on the basis of relativity, some of the recently proposed state-of-the-art solutions are used for comparison with the proposed solution as shown in Table 6. The existing solutions are efficient in detecting vulnerabilities and possibilities leading to zero-day attacks in IoT networks. However, these solutions do not emphasize much on alerting the connected nodes for the identified attack in the network. Further, these solutions do not show any sufficient mechanism for handling communication once an attack is identified. Thus, with these analyses, it is evident that the proposed approach can serve as a benchmark solution for real-time mitigation of zero-day attacks along with reliable communication in IoT networks.

5. Conclusions

"Zero-day" vulnerabilities and attacks are highly critical for IoT networks. These attacks can affect IoT devices by exploiting the defense perimeter of their network. In this paper, a detailed study was presented on zero-day attacks in IoT networks. Next, a consensus framework was proposed for mitigation of zero-day attacks in IoT networks. The proposed approach used context-behavior of IoT devices as a detection mechanism followed by alert message protocol and critical data sharing protocol for reliable communication during attack mitigation. The proposed protocol was evaluated numerically and the results suggested that the

TABLE 6: Comparative analysis with state-of-the-art solutions.

Approach	Authors	Network type	Zero-day detection	Scalability	Overheads	Latency	Response time	Reliable communication	Alert messages	Usability
DFA-AD	Sharma et al. [64]	IoT	Yes	—	—	Medium	—	No	No	Distributed
Self-protecting computing systems	Chen et al. [65]	IoT	Yes	—	Low	Low	—	No	No	Centralized
Hybrid layered architecture	Singh et al. [66]	General	Yes	—	—	Medium	—	No	No	Centralized
Proposed	Sharma et al.	IoT	Yes	High	Low	Low	Low	Yes/high	Yes	Distributed

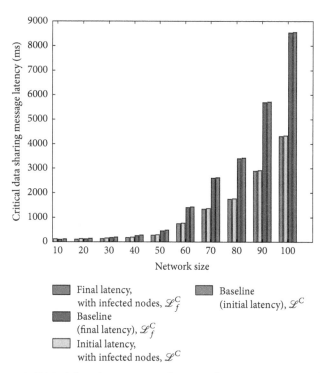

FIGURE 15: Critical data sharing protocol message latency versus network size.

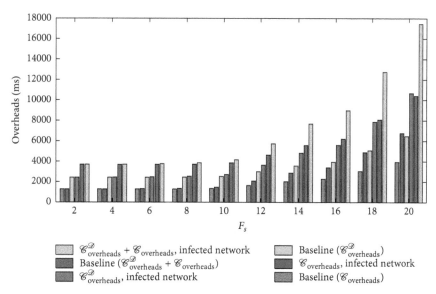

FIGURE 16: Communication overheads for alert message protocol and critical data sharing protocol versus one-way frame transport delay F_s.

proposed approach can serve the purpose of detection and elimination of zero-day attacks in IoT network without compromising its performance. A state-of-the-art comparison was also presented that justified the performance as well as the benchmark standard fixed by the proposed approach. The results for latency and overheads suggest high-performance network formation even in the presence of zero-day attacks.

In the future, the focus will be given on securing the passes of alert message protocol and critical data sharing protocol by investigating them with different security mechanisms. Further, the proposed approach will be analyzed by considering the actual behavior and message size for different IoT devices.

Disclosure

A part of this paper was presented at a Conference on Information Security and Cryptography (CISC-S 17), June 22-23, 2017, Asan, South Korea.

Acknowledgments

This research was supported by the Basic Science Research Program through the National Research Foundation of Korea (NRF) that is funded by the Ministry of Education (NRF-2015R1D1A1A01057300) and in part by the Soonchunhyang University Research Fund.

References

[1] K. Zhang, X. Liang, R. Lu, and X. Shen, "Sybil attacks and their defenses in the internet of things," *IEEE Internet of Things Journal*, vol. 1, no. 5, pp. 372–383, 2014.

[2] V. Sharma, J. D. Lim, J. N. Kim, and I. You, "SACA: Self-Aware Communication Architecture for IoT Using Mobile Fog Servers," *Mobile Information Systems*, vol. 2017, pp. 1–17, 2017.

[3] A.-R. Sadeghi, C. Wachsmann, and M. Waidner, "Security and privacy challenges in industrial internet of things," in *Proceedings of the 52nd ACM/EDAC/IEEE Design Automation Conference (DAC '15)*, pp. 1–6, IEEE, San Francisco, Calif, USA, June 2015.

[4] V. Desnitsky, D. Levshun, A. Chechulin, and I. Kotenko, "Design technique for secure embedded devices: Application for creation of integrated cyber-physical security system," *Journal of Wireless Mobile Networks, Ubiquitous Computing, and Dependable Applications*, vol. 7, no. 2, pp. 60–80, 2016.

[5] I. You and K. Yim, "Malware obfuscation techniques: a brief survey," in *Proceedings of the 5th International Conference on Broadband Wireless Computing, Communication and Applications (BWCCA '10)*, pp. 297–300, November 2010.

[6] I. Kotenko and A. Chechulin, "Attack modeling and security evaluation in siem systems," *International Transactions on Systems Science and Applications*, vol. 8, pp. 129–147, 2012.

[7] M. J. Covington and R. Carskadden, "Threat implications of the Internet of Things," in *Proceedings of the Cyber Conflict (CyCon), 2013 5th International Conference*, pp. 1–12, 2013.

[8] I. Agrafiotis, A. Erola, M. Goldsmith, and S. Creese, "Formalising policies for insider-threat detection: A tripwire grammar," *Journal of Wireless Mobile Networks, Ubiquitous Computing, and Dependable Applications*, vol. 8, no. 1, pp. 26–43, 2017.

[9] F. Kammüller, M. Kerber, and C. W. Probst, "Insider threats and auctions: Formalization, mechanized proof, and code generation," *Journal of Wireless Mobile Networks, Ubiquitous Computing, and Dependable Applications*, vol. 8, no. 1, pp. 44–78, 2017.

[10] P. Firstbrook and N. MacDonald, *A buyers guide to endpoint protection platforms*, https://www.gartner.com/doc/2973617/buyers-guide-endpoint-protection-platforms.

[11] R. Tian, L. Batten, R. Islam, and S. Versteeg, "An automated classification system based on the strings of trojan and virus families," in *Proceedings of the 2009 4th International Conference on Malicious and Unwanted Software, MALWARE 2009*, pp. 23–30, can, October 2009.

[12] D. Bilar, "Opcodes as predictor for malware," *International Journal of Electronic Security and Digital Forensics*, vol. 1, pp. 156–168, 2007.

[13] G. Bonfante, M. Kaczmarek, and J.-Y. Marion, "Morphological detection of malware," in *Proceedings of the 3rd International Conference on Malicious and Unwanted Software, MALWARE 2008*, pp. 1–8, usa, October 2008.

[14] A. Pektas, M. Eris, and T. Acarman, "Proposal of n-gram based algorithm for malware classification," in *in Proceedings of the Fifth International Conference on Emerging Security Information, Systems and Technologies*, pp. 21–27, French Riviera, France, 2011.

[15] I. Santos, F. Brezo, J. Nieves et al., "Idea: Opcode-sequence-based malware detection," *Lecture Notes in Computer Science (including subseries Lecture Notes in Artificial Intelligence and Lecture Notes in Bioinformatics): Preface*, vol. 5965, pp. 35–43, 2010.

[16] M. Egele, E. Kirda, and C. Kruegel, "Mitigating drive-by download attacks: Challenges and open problems," *IFIP Advances in Information and Communication Technology*, vol. 309, pp. 52–62, 2009.

[17] A. Niki, "Drive-by download attacks: Effects and detection methods," in *Proceedings of the in 3rd IT Security Conference for the Next Generation*, 2009.

[18] Z. Ruili, P. Jianfeng, T. Xiaobin, and X. Hongsheng, "Application of CLIPS expert system to malware detection system," in *Proceedings of the 2008 International Conference on Computational Intelligence and Security, CIS 2008*, pp. 309–314, chn, December 2008.

[19] E. Al Daoud, I. H. Jebril, and B. Zaqaibeh, "Computer virus strategies and detection methods," *International Journal of Open Problems in Computer Science and Mathematics*, vol. 1, no. 2, pp. 12–20, 2008.

[20] T. Dube, R. Raines, G. Peterson, K. Bauer, M. Grimaila, and S. Rogers, "Malware target recognition via static heuristics," *Computers & Security*, vol. 31, no. 1, pp. 137–147, 2012.

[21] N. Nissim, R. Moskovitch, L. Rokach, and Y. Elovici, "Novel active learning methods for enhanced PC malware detection in windows OS," *Expert Systems with Applications*, vol. 41, no. 13, pp. 5843–5857, 2014.

[22] H. Lu, X. Wang, B. Zhao, F. Wang, and J. Su, "ENDMal: An anti-obfuscation and collaborative malware detection system using syscall sequences," *Mathematical and Computer Modelling*, vol. 58, no. 5-6, pp. 1140–1154, 2013.

[23] C. Williams, "Applications of genetic algorithms to malware detection and creation," 2009.

[24] I. Santos, F. Brezo, X. Ugarte-Pedrero, and P. G. Bringas, "Opcode sequences as representation of executables for data-mining-based unknown malware detection," *Information Sciences*, vol. 231, pp. 64–82, 2013.

[25] F. Bao, I. Chen, and J. Guo, "Scalable, adaptive and survivable trust management for community of interest based Internet of Things systems," in *Proceedings of the 2013 IEEE Eleventh International Symposium on Autonomous Decentralized Systems (ISADS)*, pp. 1–7, Mexico City, Mexico, March 2013.

[26] D. Chen, G. Chang, and D. Sun, "TRM-IoT: a trust management model based on fuzzy reputation for internet of things," *Computer Science and Information Systems*, vol. 8, no. 4, pp. 1207–1228, 2011.

[27] R. Neisse, G. Steri, I. N. Fovino, and G. Baldini, "SecKit: a model-based security toolkit for the internet of things," *Computers & Security*, vol. 54, pp. 60–76, 2015.

[28] A. M. Ortiz, D. Hussein, S. Park, S. N. Han, and N. Crespi, "The cluster between internet of things and social networks: Review and research challenges," *IEEE Internet of Things Journal*, vol. 1, no. 3, pp. 206–215, 2014.

[29] C. Modi, D. Patel, B. Borisaniya, H. Patel, A. Patel, and M. Rajarajan, "A survey of intrusion detection techniques in cloud,"

Journal of Network and Computer Applications, vol. 36, no. 1, pp. 42–57, 2013.

[30] O. L. Barakat, A. R. Ramli, F. Hashim, K. Samsudin, I. A. Al-baltah, and M. M. Al-Habshi, "Scarecrow: Scalable malware reporting, detection and analysis," *Journal of Convergence Information Technology*, vol. 8, no. 14, p. 1, 2013.

[31] Y. Qiao, Y. Yang, L. Ji, and J. He, "Analyzing malware by abstracting the frequent itemsets in API call sequences," in *Proceedings of the 12th IEEE International Conference on Trust, Security and Privacy in Computing and Communications (TrustCom '13)*, pp. 265–270, July 2013.

[32] Y. Park, D. S. Reeves, and M. Stamp, "Deriving common malware behavior through graph clustering," *Computers & Security*, vol. 39, pp. 419–430, 2013.

[33] R. Islam, R. Tian, L. M. Batten, and S. Versteeg, "Classification of malware based on integrated static and dynamic features," *Journal of Network and Computer Applications*, vol. 36, no. 2, pp. 646–656, 2013.

[34] Z. Chen, M. Roussopoulos, Z. Liang, Y. Zhang, Z. Chen, and A. Delis, "Malware characteristics and threats on the internet ecosystem," *The Journal of Systems and Software*, vol. 85, no. 7, pp. 1650–1672, 2012.

[35] L. Feng, X. Liao, Q. Han, and H. Li, "Dynamical analysis and control strategies on malware propagation model," *Applied Mathematical Modelling*, vol. 37, no. 16-17, pp. 8225–8236, 2013.

[36] D. Debarr, V. Ramanathan, and H. Wechsler, "Phishing detection using traffic behavior, spectral clustering, and random forests," in *Proceedings of the 11th IEEE International Conference on Intelligence and Security Informatics, IEEE ISI 2013*, pp. 67–72, usa, June 2013.

[37] M. Scheutz and V. Andronache, "Architectural mechanisms for dynamic changes of behavior selection strategies in behavior-based systems," *IEEE Transactions on Systems, Man, and Cybernetics, Part B: Cybernetics*, vol. 34, no. 6, pp. 2377–2395, 2004.

[38] A. P. Lauf, R. A. Peters, and W. H. Robinson, "Embedded intelligent intrusion detection: A behavior-based approach," in *Proceedings of the 21st International Conference on Advanced Information Networking and Applications Workshops/Symposia, AINAW'07*, pp. 816–821, can, May 2007.

[39] J. Hu, "Host-based anomaly intrusion detection," *Handbook of Information and Communication Security*, pp. 235–255, 2010.

[40] A. S. Ashoor and S. Gore, "Intrusion detection system: case study," in *in Proceedings of the International Conference on Advanced Materials Engineering*, vol. 15, pp. 6–9, 2011.

[41] S. S. Murtaza, W. Khreich, A. Hamou-Lhadj, and M. Couture, "A host-based anomaly detection approach by representing system calls as states of kernel modules," in *Proceedings of the 2013 IEEE 24th International Symposium on Software Reliability Engineering, ISSRE 2013*, pp. 431–440, usa, November 2013.

[42] H. Kaur and N. Gill, "Host based Anomaly Detection using Fuzzy Genetic Approach (FGA)," *International Journal of Computer Applications*, vol. 74, no. 20, pp. 5–9, 2013.

[43] S. Cesare and Y. Xiang, "A fast flowgraph based classification system for packed and polymorphic malware on the endhost," in *Proceedings of the 24th IEEE International Conference on Advanced Information Networking and Applications (AINA '10)*, pp. 721–728, Perth, Australia, April 2010.

[44] D. Song, D. Brumley, and H. Yin, "BitBlaze: a new approach to computer security via binary analysis," in *The Journal of Information System Security*, vol. 5352 of *Lecture Notes in Computer Science*, pp. 1–25, Springer, Berlin, Germany, 2008.

[45] K. Yoshioka, Y. Hosobuchi, T. Orii, and T. Matsumoto, "Vulnerability in public malware sandbox analysis systems," in *Proceedings of the 2010 10th Annual International Symposium on Applications and the Internet, SAINT 2010*, pp. 265–268, kor, July 2010.

[46] G. Willems, T. Holz, and F. Freiling, "Toward automated dynamic malware analysis using CWSandbox," *IEEE Security & Privacy*, vol. 5, no. 2, pp. 32–39, 2007.

[47] D. Inoue, K. Yoshioka, M. Eto, Y. Hoshizawa, and K. Nakao, "Automated malware analysis system and its sandbox for revealing malware's internal and external activities," *IEICE Transaction on Information and Systems*, vol. E92-D, no. 5, pp. 945–954, 2009.

[48] S. Miwa, T. Miyachi, M. Eto, M. Yoshizumi, and Y. Shinoda, "Design and implementation of an isolated sandbox with mimetic internet used to analyze malwares," in *DETER*, 2007.

[49] W. Jiang, R. Wang, Z. Xu, Y. Huang, S. Chang, and Z. Qin, "PRUB: A Privacy Protection Friend Recommendation System Based on User Behavior," *Mathematical Problems in Engineering*, vol. 2016, Article ID 8575187, 2016.

[50] X. M. Choo, K. L. Chiew, D. H. A. Ibrahim, N. Musa, S. N. Sze, and W. K. Tiong, "Feature-based phishing detection technique," *Journal of Theoretical and Applied Information Technology*, vol. 91, no. 1, pp. 101–106, 2016.

[51] V. Sharma, I. You, and R. Kumar, "ISMA: Intelligent Sensing Model for Anomalies Detection in Cross Platform OSNs With a Case Study on IoT," *IEEE Access*, vol. 5, pp. 3284–3301, 2017.

[52] R. Kaur and M. Singh, "A survey on zero-day polymorphic worm detection techniques," *IEEE Communications Surveys & Tutorials*, vol. 16, no. 3, pp. 1520–1549, 2014.

[53] R. Kaur and M. G. Singh, *Efficient Zero-day Attacks Detection Techniques [Ph.D. thesis]*, 2016.

[54] M. Zhang, L. Wang, S. Jajodia, A. Singhal, and M. Albanese, "Network Diversity: A Security Metric for Evaluating the Resilience of Networks Against Zero-Day Attacks," *IEEE Transactions on Information Forensics and Security*, vol. 11, no. 5, pp. 1071–1086, 2016.

[55] W. House, "Trustworthy cyberspace: Strategic plan for the federal cybersecurity research and development program," *Report of the National Science and Technology Council, Executive Office of the President*, 2011.

[56] S. Viswanathan, R. Tan, and D. K. Y. Yau, "Exploiting Power Grid for Accurate and Secure Clock Synchronization in Industrial IoT," in *Proceedings of the 2016 IEEE Real-Time Systems Symposium, RTSS 2016*, pp. 146–156, prt, December 2016.

[57] K. Sonar and H. Upadhyay, "A survey: Ddos attack on internet of things," *International Journal of Engineering Research and Development*, vol. 10, no. 11, pp. 58–63, 2014.

[58] A. Sajid, H. Abbas, and K. Saleem, "Cloud-Assisted IoT-Based SCADA Systems Security: A Review of the State of the Art and Future Challenges," *IEEE Access*, vol. 4, pp. 1375–1384, 2016.

[59] M. Conti, N. Dragoni, and V. Lesyk, "A survey of man in the middle attacks," *IEEE Communications Surveys & Tutorials*, vol. 18, no. 3, pp. 2027–2051, 2016.

[60] T.-H. Cho and G.-M. Jeon, "A method for detecting man-in-the-middle attacks using time synchronization one time password in interlock protocol based internet of things," *Journal of Applied and Physical Sciences*, vol. 2, no. 2, pp. 37–41, 2016.

[61] J. Liu, Y. Xiao, and C. P. Chen, "Authentication and access control in the Internet of things," in *Proceedings of the 32nd IEEE International Conference on Distributed Computing Systems*

Workshops (ICDCSW '12), pp. 588–592, IEEE, Macau, China, June 2012.

[62] S. Na, D. Hwang, W. Shin, and K.-H. Kim, "Scenario and countermeasure for replay attack using join request messages in lorawan," in *Proceedings of the Information Networking (ICOIN, 2017 International Conference*, pp. 718–720, 2017.

[63] J. L. Martin, "Complete graphs," https://www.math.ku.edu/jmartin/courses/math105-F11/Lectures/chapter6-part2.pdf.

[64] P. K. Sharma, S. Y. Moon, D. Moon, and J. H. Park, "DFA-AD: a distributed framework architecture for the detection of advanced persistent threats," *Cluster Computing*, vol. 20, no. 1, pp. 597–609, 2017.

[65] Q. Chen, S. Abdelwahed, and A. Erradi, "A model-based validated autonomic approach to self-protect computing systems," *IEEE Internet of Things Journal*, vol. 1, no. 5, pp. 446–460, 2014.

[66] S. Singh, P. K. Sharma, S. Y. Moon, and J. H. Park, "WITH-DRAWN: A hybrid layered architecture for detection and analysis of network based Zero-day attack," *Computer Communications*, vol. 106, pp. 100–106, 2017.

[67] D. Kim, Y. Kim, J. Moon, S.-J. Cho, J. Woo, and I. You, "Identifying windows installer package files for detection of pirated software," in *Proceedings of the 8th International Conference on Innovative Mobile and Internet Services in Ubiquitous Computing, IMIS 2014*, pp. 287–290, gbr, July 2014.

[68] J. Gubbi, R. Buyya, S. Marusic, and M. Palaniswami, "Internet of Things (IoT): a vision, architectural elements, and future directions," *Future Generation Computer Systems*, vol. 29, no. 7, pp. 1645–1660, 2013.

[69] G. Portokalidis, A. Slowinska, and H. Bos, "Argos: An emulator for fingerprinting zero-day attacks for advertised honeypots with automatic signature generation," in *Proceedings of the 2006 EuroSys Conference*, pp. 15–27, bel, April 2006.

[70] K. Palani, E. Holt, and S. Smith, "Invisible and forgotten: Zero-day blooms in the IoT," in *Proceedings of the 13th IEEE International Conference on Pervasive Computing and Communication Workshops, PerCom Workshops 2016*, aus, March 2016.

[71] B. Wanswett and H. K. Kalita, "The Threat of Obfuscated Zero Day Polymorphic Malwares: An Analysis," in *Proceedings of the 7th International Conference on Computational Intelligence and Communication Networks, CICN 2015*, pp. 1188–1193, ind, December 2015.

[72] L. Bilge and T. Dumitras, "Before we knew it: An empirical study of zero-day attacks in the real world," in *Proceedings of the 2012 ACM Conference on Computer and Communications Security, CCS 2012*, pp. 833–844, usa, October 2012.

[73] J. B. Fraley and J. Cannady, "The promise of machine learning in cybersecurity," in *Proceedings of the SoutheastCon 2017*, pp. 1–6, Concord, NC, USA, March 2017.

[74] P. Duessel, C. Gehl, U. Flegel, S. Dietrich, and M. Meier, "Detecting zero-day attacks using context-aware anomaly detection at the application-layer," *International Journal of Information Security*, pp. 1–16, 2016.

[75] S. Chamotra, R. K. Sehgal, and R. S. Misra, "Honeypot Baselining for Zero Day Attack Detection," *International Journal of Information Security and Privacy*, vol. 11, no. 3, pp. 63–74, 2017.

[76] X. Sun, J. Dai, P. Liu, A. Singhal, and J. Yen, "Towards probabilistic identification of zero-day attack paths," in *Proceedings of the 2016 IEEE Conference on Communications and Network Security, CNS 2016*, pp. 64–72, usa, October 2016.

[77] W. Haider, G. Creech, Y. Xie, and J. Hu, "Windows based data sets for evaluation of robustness of Host based Intrusion Detection Systems (IDS) to zero-day and stealth attacks," *Future Internet*, vol. 8, no. 3, article no. 29, 2016.

[78] D. W. Coit and A. E. Smith, "Reliability optimization of series-parallel systems using a genetic algorithm," *IEEE Transactions on Reliability*, vol. 45, no. 2, pp. 254–263, 1996.

[79] I. You and J. Lee, "SPFP: Ticket-based secure handover for fast proxy mobile IPv6 in 5G networks," *Computer Networks*, 2017.

[80] J.-H. Lee, J.-M. Bonnin, I. You, and T.-M. Chung, "Comparative handover performance analysis of IPv6 mobility management protocols," *IEEE Transactions on Industrial Electronics*, vol. 60, no. 3, pp. 1077–1088, 2013.

BAS: The Biphase Authentication Scheme for Wireless Sensor Networks

Rabia Riaz,[1] **Tae-Sun Chung,**[2] **Sanam Shahla Rizvi,**[3] **and Nazish Yaqub**[1]

[1]*Department of CS & IT, University of Azad Jammu and Kashmir, Muzaffarabad 13100, Pakistan*
[2]*Department of Software, Ajou University, San 5, Woncheon-dong, Yeongtong-gu, Suwon 443-749, Republic of Korea*
[3]*Department of Computer Sciences, Preston University, 15 Shahrah-e-Faisal, Banglore Town, Karachi 75350, Pakistan*

Correspondence should be addressed to Sanam Shahla Rizvi; sanam_shahla@hotmail.com

Academic Editor: Huaizhi Li

The development of wireless sensor networks can be considered as the beginning of a new generation of applications. Authenticity of communicating entities is essential for the success of wireless sensor networks. Authentication in wireless sensor networks is always a challenging task due to broadcast nature of the transmission medium. Sensor nodes are usually resource constrained with respect to energy, memory, and computation and communication capabilities. It is not possible for each node to authenticate all incoming request messages, whether these request messages are from authorized or unauthorized nodes. Any malicious node can flood the network by sending messages repeatedly for creating denial of service attack, which will eventually bring down the whole network. In this paper, a lightweight authentication scheme named as Biphase Authentication Scheme (BAS) is presented for wireless sensor networks. This scheme provides initial small scale authentication for the request messages entering wireless sensor networks and resistance against denial of service attacks.

1. Introduction

A wireless sensor network (WSN) consists of a number of tiny devices called sensor nodes and a base station. These tiny devices may be few or thousands in number; it depends on the size of network. Sensor nodes can be easily deployed and the distance is normally less than few meters between two sensor nodes. Sensors can cooperate with each other to observe physical or environmental situations such as temperature, motion, and pressure. Nodes are used to detect, collect, and process environmental data. Due to small size, sensor nodes are resource constrained with respect to energy, memory, and computational and communicational capabilities [1, 2]. Nodes life period depends on their battery power. The base station is authoritative data processing and storage center and it is also called sink [3]. It usually serves as entryway to another network, is more dominant, and is resource enriched than sensor nodes. Any new node which wants to join the existing network, whether it is authentic user or not, is checked through base station [4].

There are two types of devices defined in IEEE 802.15.4 for WSN [5]. These devices are full-function devices (FFDs) and reduced-function devices (RFDs). RFDs have minimal resources and less memory capacity than FFDs. FFDs act as a personal area network (PAN) coordinator [6] but RFDs only work as worker node. FFDs can communicate with RFDs and all other FFDs in network, but RFDs can only communicate with near neighboring RFDs and FFDs.

WSNs are used in healthcare applications, military applications, environment and habitat monitoring, home automation, and traffic control. Due to their extensive usage in various domains, authenticity of communicating entities is vital for proper functionality of WSN. The purpose of authentication is to enable a sensor node to make sure of the identities of entities communicating with it. Authentication in WSNs is always a stimulating task due to the wireless nature of transmission media. The following two characteristics of WSNs make it challenging to provide an authentication mechanism for secure communication in WSNs.

(1) Resource Constraints. Sensor nodes have limited communicational and computational capabilities. Nodes have limited memory and energy availability. As sensor nodes are resource constrained [7–9], it is not possible for each node to authenticate all incoming request messages, whether these request messages are from authorized or unauthorized nodes. Any malicious node can easily send request message to join the network. All these resource constraints require that the authentication process should be efficient and lightweight for effective working of WSNs.

(2) Network Constraints. WSNs use wireless open channel. An invader can easily get access to the network and insert bogus messages in network. The network may transmit these fake request packets inserted by an invader many hops before they are identified by base station. Any malicious node can flood the network by sending fake request messages repeatedly to bring down the network by creating denial of service (DoS) attack. This results in consumption of network bandwidth and nodes energy, obstruction of communication among nodes, and disruption of the service to a specific system. As a result, it makes the system or service unavailable for the legitimate users. All these problems inversely affect the network lifetime and gradually reduce the functionality as well as the overall performance of the entire network. So there is requirement of some authentication mechanism, which can prevent the transmission of messages in the network, injected by an adversary, and provide partial authentication if not complete at initial message exchange time.

This research aims to exploit the problems of authentication in WSNs. In this study, an authentication scheme named as "Biphase Authentication Scheme" is proposed to make authentication process efficient and to overcome the authentication vulnerability in WSNs. The purpose of this scheme is to

(i) defend sensor network against DoS attack,

(ii) reduce network traffic,

(iii) save nodes battery powers,

(iv) increase the lifetime of WSN.

The functionality as well as the performance of the entire network improves by using the proposed scheme.

This paper is divided into following sections. Section 2 presents security requirements for WSNs, and some existing protocols, used for authentication process in WSNs, are reviewed with their advantages and limitations indicated. Section 3 provides an overview of the authentication process in WSNs. The main objective of this section is to introduce an authentication scheme named as Biphase Authentication Scheme (BAS) for WSNs. Section 4 highlights the network model used for performance evaluation. Section 5 provides the results obtained from the analysis of BAS by comparing it with previously proposed methods. Conclusion and recommendations for future work are presented in Sections 6 and 7, respectively.

2. Related Work

There are numerous schemes that provide authentication in WSNs [5, 10–17]; the most relevant of them are discussed in detail here.

2.1. Sensor Protocol for Information via Negotiation (SPIN). SPIN is a security scheme that provides authentication for WSN. It provides security but with great consumption of energy. SPIN has two main components, secure network encryption protocol (SNEP) and micro timed efficient stream loss-tolerant authentication (μTESLA) [10].

SPIN provides confidentiality, two-party data authentication, data integrity, and data freshness [11]. This protocol uses the trusted third party, which is central key distribution center (KDC), and overall communication between nodes takes place through it. In this scheme all key creation activities are performed through the base station. Its responsibility is to authenticate and create the session keys between nodes and send shared keys to communicating nodes. The KDC can communicate with nodes either directly or indirectly. In SPIN every node and the server share a unique key. Each node has an individual shared master key and this key is used for validation purpose of node by base station. All further keys are evaluated from the shared key.

This protocol depends on KDC for communication. Session keys are created and distributed through KDC. There is a lot of burden on base station in this scheme. Two nodes cannot directly establish a secret key with each other. If they wish to create secure communication session keys, they must first talk with the base station. In enormous scale network, the base station is many hops away. This feature is a drawback of this protocol; all the information passes through the base station. The traffic flow on sensor nodes nearby the base station is increased which results in consumption of energy [12].

In SPIN protocol, no proper solution is provided for information leakage or if a node is captured. The scalability of SPIN protocol is limited and it cannot easily applied to large scale sensor networks. It also suffers from denial of service (DoS) attack [13]. An adversary can easily send a request to the target node, and the target node forwards its request to KDC for authentication purpose. The adversary node can send network joining messages repeatedly to bring down the network by creating DoS attack, due to which the receiver node may lose its energy.

2.2. Broadcast Session Key Protocol (BROSK). BROSK is a broadcasting negotiation protocol which is used for secure communication in WSNs. In this protocol, no trusted party or server is used just like SPIN and it consumes less energy as compared to SPIN. Each node directly constructs a session key with its neighboring node by sending a key negotiation message [14]. This protocol uses a single master key in each sensor node for the entire WSN, and a message authentication code (MAC) is used to provide authentication. A sensor node will attempt to negotiate a shared session key by transmitting the key negotiation message. When node receives the message transmitted by its neighbor, it can establish the mutual-session keys by creating the MAC and use these shared keys for secure message exchange.

The scalability of BROSK protocol is significant and it can easily apply to large scale sensor networks. In this protocol master key is not managed in a proper way and there is no proper information about master key, that is, what is done with the master key once the broadcasting process has completed. In BROSK protocol the same master key is shared by each node. This key is used by nodes to verify other nodes: whether node is authorized or unauthorized user. In this scheme no proper solution is provided for the problem if master key is compromised. An intruder can effortlessly compromise the whole network communication and create all further keys [15].

2.3. Localized Encryption and Authentication Protocol (LEAP).
LEAP is used to provide security in sensor network [5]. In LEAP four types of keys are used which are individual keys, pairwise keys, cluster keys, and group keys. By using an individual key, a node can inform the base station about the anomalous behavior of its surrounding nodes. The base station uses this key to give instruction to a specific node. A master key is used to produce the individual keys and these keys are stored in nodes before their deployment.

Pairwise keys are shared by a node and its neighbors. These keys are used for secure communication. A node can establish pairwise keys by sending a message to the neighboring node. Cluster keys are shared by a node and its multiple neighbors. The node uses the pairwise key to encrypt the cluster key so that only the legitimate neighbors are able to decrypt the message to get access to the cluster key. A group key which is also called global key is shared by all nodes in the entire network. This key is used by the base station to encrypt data, and encrypted data is transferred to all the nodes in the group. This key removes the need for a base station to encrypt and send the same message to individual nodes with individual keys.

This protocol is effective in terms of communication and energy. It provides mechanisms for authentication broadcasting of a base station, data packets, and key revocation. The drawback of this protocol is security weakness during the process of key formation and the high cost of capacity needed to save the four keys for each node. In neighbor discovery phase of the pairwise key creation an invader can force a node to compute pairwise keys with many or all nodes. In this way any invader can easily compromise the node and get access to the pairwise keys without any information about the initial key.

2.4. A Dynamic User Authentication Scheme for Wireless Sensor Networks.
A user authentication scheme for WSN prevents unauthorized users from querying the sensor data from any sensor node in network [16]. The computational overhead of this scheme is low. For authentication purpose, this scheme uses user's password and uses cryptographic hash functions. This scheme comprises three phases: registration, login, and authentication phase. This scheme permits only authentic users to query sensor data.

During registration phase, a user sends ID and a password for registration purpose to a gateway node. The gateway node stores the user ID and password in its database and tells the user about successful registration. When the user wants to query sensor data, it has to log in to a sensor login-node. The user sends its ID and password to the login-node. When the login-node receives the login request from the user, it checks the dataset list to find the user ID. If the ID is not found, then a rejection message is sent to the user. If the ID is found, then the login-node sends a message for authentication purpose to the gateway node. When the gateway node receives the message from the login-node, it checks its database to find the user ID. If the ID is not found, a rejection message is sent to the login-node. If the ID is found, then the gateway node sends an acceptance message to the login-node. The login-node then sends an acceptance message to the user.

This scheme has some flaws. It cannot provide resistance against replay and forged attacks. It also suffers from stolen-verifier attack; both gate way and login-node have the look-up table which contains secret information about registered users. Passwords may be exposed by any of the sensor nodes and the user is unable to alter the password.

2.5. An Improved Dynamic User Authentication Scheme for Wireless Sensor Networks.
It is a user authentication scheme [17] to overcome the flaws of user authentication scheme by [16] as it provides resistance against reply attack and forged attack, and it is a modified version of the user authentication scheme by [16]. In this scheme user can easily change password and can log in to the network from any sensor node and this scheme does not require additional computation.

This scheme comprises four phases which are registration, login, authentication, and password-changing phase. The registration, login, and authentication phases work in a similar way to the phases in the user authentication scheme by [16]. When a sensor node receives the login request from a user, it forwards this request to the gateway node. The gateway node confirms the legitimacy of the user. User registration is also performed at the gateway node. In password-changing phase, when a user wants to alter its password, it sends its ID, original hashed password, and new hashed password to the gateway node. When the gateway node receives the request for password change from the user, it checks the user ID and whether the hashed password sent by user is correct or not. If the ID is not found in its database or the hashed password is incorrect, then the gateway node sends a rejection message to the user. Otherwise, it changes the user password and sends the user a password change message. This scheme overcomes the flaws of the user authentication scheme by [16] but it also suffers from security flaws and is unable to provide resistance against node compromise attack.

3. Proposed Biphase Authentication Scheme (BAS)

Sensor nodes are usually resource constrained with respect to energy, memory, and computational and communication capabilities. It is not possible for each node to authenticate

Legend:
  /: Modulo 2 division operation
  $\mathfrak{T}$: Truncates the input stream to 128 bits if r > 128
  KM: Master key of 1024 bits
  S: Generator polynomial of 64 bits
  R: Remainder after division between master key and seed
  r: Number of bits in remainder
  KE: 128 bits Encryption key
Begin Proc
        $R = KM/S$
        If $r\{R\} > 128$
            $KE = \mathfrak{T}(R)$
        Else
            $KE = R$
End Proc

ALGORITHM 1: Key generation algorithm.

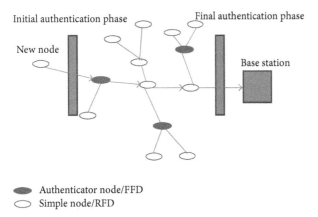

FIGURE 1: Authentication process using Biphase Authentication Scheme.

all the incoming messages. This scheme provides initial small scale authentication of the messages entering to WSNs.

There are two types of devices defined in IEEE 802.15.4 for WSN: full-function devices (FFDs) and reduced-function devices (RFDs). In this proposed scheme, FFDs will act as authenticator nodes. These authenticator nodes will forward the outside request messages to the base station as shown in Figure 1. In case of unauthorized node request message, these nodes will block the request message and will not forward it to the base station.

BAS comprises two phases: initial authentication phase and final authentication phase.

3.1. Initial Authentication Phase. The initial authentication phase is performed with the help of authenticator nodes. This phase acts as a filter, and authenticator nodes act as gateway nodes. Any new node that wants to join the network sends its request to the authenticator node. This phase blocks the request messages sent by an adversary in the network. Only authorized nodes request messages are sent to the base station for final authentication.

3.2. Final Authentication Phase. The final authentication phase is performed with the help of the base station. The base station matches the (ID, Key) pair sent by the authenticator node in its database. If they are matched, then the new node is successfully approved, and complete access to network will be permitted. An acceptance message will be sent to the new node through the authenticator node. If the (ID, Key) pair is not found, then the new node is not successfully approved, no access to network will be permitted, and a rejection message is sent to the authenticator node.

In BAS, each node is preloaded with *node ID, master key* K_M, *key generation algorithm,* and *pairwise shared key with base station* K_{NB} before their deployment. This scheme has been designed to be very lightweight and uses symmetric keys. Symmetric key system requires less storage than asymmetric key system, so this system is better than asymmetric key system for sensor networks [15]. Each node has its *unique ID, master key* K_M *of 1024 bits,* and *pairwise key* K_{NB} *of 128 bits* [18]. A base station has *[ID, K_{NB}]* pair for every node in its database and uses it to authenticate every sensor node at the time of node joining the network. K_{NB} is a unique pairwise key of each node with the base station. Base station can use this key to directly communicate with nodes.

In BAS, we use a modified form of key generation algorithm [19]. This algorithm is used to create the encryption key K_E from any random seed S of 64 bits. This random seed S is used for security purpose; when any authenticator node receives network joining request from any new node, it calculates the encryption key K_E from any random seed S by using key generation algorithm and sends the same random seed to new node. New node calculates its own encryption key K_E from random seed sent by authenticator node, then sends its calculated encryption key K_E to authenticator node, and authenticator node checks that encryption key calculated by new node is correct or not by comparing it with its own calculated K_E. This algorithm is depicted in Algorithm 1.

In BAS mechanism, initial authentication is performed between new node (A) and authenticator node (AN) and consists of the following steps if the node A is new node and it wants to join the network.

(1) The node A sends its ID to authenticator node.

$$M_1 = A \longrightarrow AN : [ID_A] \qquad (1)$$

(2) Authenticator node receives message M_1 from A and performs the following functions.

    (a) It calculates encryption key (K_E) using any random seed S and key generation algorithm; see Algorithm 1.

    (b) It sends the same random seed to new node A.

$$M_2 = AN \longrightarrow A : [S] \qquad (2)$$

(3) If node A is authorized user and it has master key K_M, it can easily obtain its own K_E by using the random seed S sent by the authenticator node and the key generation algorithm; see Algorithm 1.

(4) The node A sends K_E to authenticator node.

$$M_3 = A \longrightarrow AN : [K_E] \qquad (3)$$

(5) Authenticator node receives M_3 from A and performs the following functions.

    (a) It checks the K_E; if it is correct, it agrees to become its agent and an [In-Progress] message is sent to node A which means that node A is working on the authentication process.

$$M_4 = AN \longrightarrow A : [\text{In-Progress}] \qquad (4)$$

    (b) If K_E is incorrect, it refuses to become its agent and does not send new node request to base station.

(6) When node A receives message M_4 from authenticator node, it forwards its pairwise key K_{NB} to authenticator node.

$$M_5 = A \longrightarrow AN : [K_{NB}] \qquad (5)$$

(7) Authenticator node forwards node A request to base station (BS).

$$M_6 = AN \longrightarrow BS : [ID_A, K_{NB}] \qquad (6)$$

Final authentication is performed with the help of base station and consists of the following steps.

(8) BS receives message from authenticator node; it decrypts message, checks K_{NB} and ID_A sent by authenticator node by comparing them with values presented in its database, and performs the following functions.

    (a) If they are matched, then new node is successfully approved and access to network is granted and [Accept] message is sent to authenticator node.

$$M_7 = BS \longrightarrow AN : [\text{Accept}] \qquad (7)$$

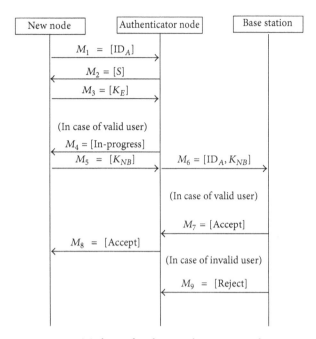

FIGURE 2: Working of Biphase Authentication Scheme.

    (b) If they are not matched, then new node is not approved and no access to network is granted and [Reject] message is sent to authenticator node.

$$M_8 = BS \longrightarrow AN : [\text{Reject}] \qquad (8)$$

(9) Authenticator node only sends [Accept] message to node A.

$$M_9 = AN \longrightarrow A : [\text{Accept}] \qquad (9)$$

(10) On receiving [Reject] message authenticator node will not forward it to node A.

Complete authentication process of proposed scheme is summarized in Figure 2.

4. Network Model

We consider a WSN of 100 Mica2 sensor nodes and a base station. The network is arranged using the cluster-based topology [20]. Sensor nodes are arranged in cluster form, and every cluster has a node that acts as the cluster head (CH). In BAS network model, FFDs will act as CHs and all new nodes that want to join the network will forward their request messages to the CH. Each CH will send request to another nearby CH. Finally the request reached base station through multihop wireless communication via CHs.

The base station is also a Mica2 node with greater energy and computation capabilities. In cluster-based topology each node in cluster is one hop away from its CH. Each CH is one hope away from its neighboring CHs and many hops away from other CHs. Each CH forwards data to its closest CH. In our network model the farthest CH is at a distance

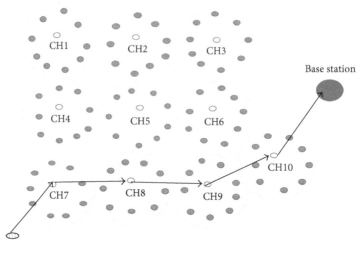

FIGURE 3: Cluster-based topology in SPIN.

of D hops from base station. For our scheme, we assume that $D = 4$. In BAS, CHs will also work as authenticator nodes. Mica2 nodes send and receive messages consuming $16.25\,\mu J$/byte and $12.25\,\mu J$/byte energy, respectively [21]. This energy consumption is for one hop distance and transmission energy consumption varies with respect to number of hops. Authenticator nodes/CHs consume $0.73\,\mu J$ energy [19] to obtain encryption key K_E by using key generation algorithm.

The following equations are used to calculate energy consumption of nodes in proposed network model.

(i) T_x is transmitting energy, R_x is receiving energy, and K_x is energy consumption to obtain encryption key.

(ii) E_{T_x} is total transmitted energy consumption of messages, which will be calculated as

$$E_{T_x} = (T_x * n) * H \qquad (10)$$

Here n is the number of sent bytes by each CH and H is the number of hops used to send message to BS.

(iii) E_{R_x} is total received energy consumption of messages, which will be calculated as

$$E_{R_x} = (R_x * n) \qquad (11)$$

Here n is the total number of received bytes in network.

(iv) E_{K_x} is the total energy consumption to obtain encryption key K_E, which is calculated as

$$E_{K_x} = (K_x * X) \qquad (12)$$

Here X is the number of times encryption keys are generated by authenticator nodes in BAS.

(v) E_{Tot} is the total energy consumption, which will be calculated as

$$E_{\mathrm{Tot}} = E_{T_x} + E_{R_x} + E_{K_x} \qquad (13)$$

(vi) M_{Tot} is the total number of sent and received messages in the network, which will be calculated as

$$M_{\mathrm{Tot}} = M_{S_x} + M_{R_x} \qquad (14)$$

Here M_{S_x} is the number of sent messages and M_{R_x} is the number of received messages in the network.

5. Performance Evaluation

The performance of the proposed scheme BAS is evaluated for different metrics like energy consumption, packets ratio, and DoS attack. BAS was compared with one of the existing schemes, SPIN, by applying both schemes to the network model explained in Section 4.

5.1. Energy Consumption. When a new node wants to join the network, it has to send request to the base station and receive the reply message from it. The authentication of a node is checked at base station. This will result in consumption of nodes energy and an increase in network traffic. The basic purpose of BAS is to prevent the transmission of packets in the network injected by an adversary to enhance the life period of sensor network.

In SPIN protocol a new node which is an adversary sends request to CH, that is, CH_7 as shown in Figure 3. Then CH_7 forwards its request to nearby CH_8. Finally the request reached the base station after multihop wireless communication.

The total transmitted energy consumption is calculated by (10); see Section 4. In this case, four CHs are involved in

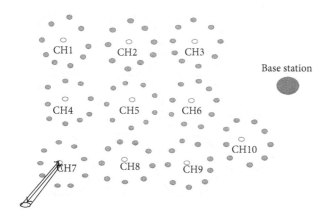

Simple node
Cluster head node
Adversary node

FIGURE 4: Cluster-based topology in BAS.

routing process (CH_7, CH_8, CH_9, and CH_{10}). The number of hops D is 4 as the farthest CH is four hops away from the base station. In SPIN protocol the length of message which consists of ID, symmetric key, and nonce bits is 36 bytes [22].

$$E_{T_x} = (16.25 * 36) * 4$$
$$E_{T_x} = 2{,}340 \, \mu J \tag{15}$$

The total received energy consumption is calculated by (11). In the case shown in Figure 3, 36 bytes are received by each CH in network, so the total number of received bytes in network including the received bytes of base station is $n = 36 * 5 = 180$ bytes.

$$E_{R_x} = (12.25 * 180)$$
$$E_{R_x} = 2{,}205 \, \mu J \tag{16}$$

The energy consumption to obtain encryption key in SPIN is zero as it is only used in BAS. The total energy consumption for SPIN is calculated by (13).

$$E_{Tot} = 2{,}340 \, \mu J + 2{,}205 \, \mu J = 4{,}545 \, \mu J \tag{17}$$

In BAS new node A sends its ID to authenticator node. Authenticator node sends seed [S] to node A. The size of ID, seed, and encryption key K_E is 2, 8, and 16 bytes, respectively. Node A will send its own key K_E to authenticator node. Authenticator node checks new node's key; if it is incorrect, then it does not forward its request to base station. In this case, as shown in Figure 4, two messages are received by authenticator node and only one message is transmitted by it.

The total transmitted energy consumption in this case is calculated by (10).

$$E_{T_x} = (16.25 * 8) * 1 = 130 \, \mu J \tag{18}$$

TABLE 1: Energy consumption comparison between SPIN and BAS.

Energy consumption $E_{Tot} = E_{T_x} + E_{R_x} + E_{K_x}$	SPIN	BAS
E_{T_x}	$2{,}340 \, \mu J$	$130 \, \mu J$
E_{R_x}	$2{,}205 \, \mu J$	$220.5 \, \mu J$
E_{K_x}	0	$0.73 \, \mu J$
E_{Tot}	$4{,}545 \, \mu J$	$351.23 \, \mu J$

Here $H = 1$ as new node (adversary) is one hop away from the CH and the number of sent bytes of seed is $n = 8$ bytes.

The total received energy consumption is calculated by (11).

$$E_{R_x} = (12.25 * 18) = 220.5 \, \mu J \tag{19}$$

Here the number of the received bytes is $n = 18$ bytes, including 2-byte ID and 16-byte encryption key.

The energy consumption in generating key K_E by authenticator node is calculated by (12).

$$E_{K_x} = 0.73 \, \mu J * 1 = 0.73 \, \mu J \tag{20}$$

Here $X = 1$, as only one key is generated by authenticator node.

The total energy consumption is calculated by (13).

$$E_{Tot} = 130 \, \mu J + 220.5 \, \mu J + 0.73 \, \mu J = 351.23 \, \mu J \tag{21}$$

An adversary can send request to some specific number of CHs to involve all CHs in the network. The total energy consumption will vary with respect to the number of CHs involved in routing process and with the total number of sent and received messages in the network. However, the energy consumption will be less in BAS compared to SPIN. Table 1 shows the energy consumption comparison between both schemes.

Simulation is used to evaluate the performance of proposed scheme. The results of this simulation are performed by using MATLAB. Figure 5 presents the energy consumption graph of BAS and SPIN scheme with respect to the number of adversary nodes. When the number of adversary nodes increases, the level of energy consumption also increases. This is because a higher number of CHs get involved in the routing process.

The results prove that energy consumption in proposed scheme BAS is much less as compared to SPIN scheme. So our scheme is helpful to improve the network performance and its lifetime by saving nodes battery power.

5.2. Packets Overhead. In SPIN protocol when an adversary sends a request to any node in the network, each node forwards the request to the base station. As a result, the traffic in the network near the base station increases, which reduces the performance of the whole network. In SPIN protocol when an adversary sends a request to CH_7 in the network, as shown in Figure 3, 4 packets will be sent and 5 packets will be received in the network.

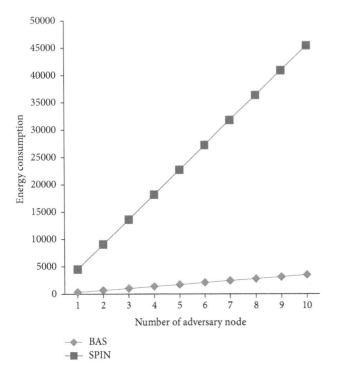

FIGURE 5: Variation of energy consumption with respect to number of adversary nodes.

TABLE 2: Packets overhead comparison between SPIN and BAS.

Total packets overhead $M_{\text{Tot}} = M_{S_x} + M_{R_x}$	SPIN	BAS
In case when an adversary sends request to CH_7	9	3

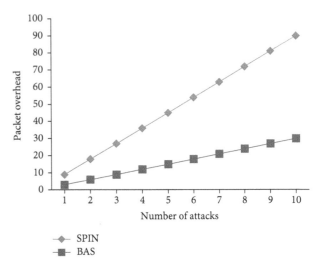

FIGURE 6: Variation of packets overhead with respect to the number of adversary nodes.

The total number of sent and received messages M_{Tot} is calculated by (14).

$$M_{\text{Tot}} = M_{S_x} + M_{R_x}$$
$$M_{\text{Tot}} = 4 + 5 \qquad (22)$$
$$M_{\text{Tot}} = 9$$

In BAS only one packet will be transmitted by authenticator node and 2 packets will be received by it as shown in Figure 4.

The total number of sent and received messages M_{Tot} is calculated by (14).

$$M_{\text{Tot}} = M_{S_x} + M_{R_x}$$
$$M_{\text{Tot}} = 1 + 2 \qquad (23)$$
$$M_{\text{Tot}} = 3$$

An adversary can send request to some specific number of CHs to involve all CHs in the network. The number of data packets will vary with respect to the number of CHs involved in routing process and the total number of sent and received packets in the network. However, the number of data packets will be less in BAS compared to SPIN scheme. Table 2 shows the data packets overhead comparison between both schemes.

We use simulation to evaluate the performance of the proposed scheme. Figure 6 presents the data packets overhead of BAS and SPIN scheme with respect to the number of adversary nodes. When the number of adversary nodes

increases, the packets overhead in the network also increases. This is because a higher number of CHs get involved in the routing process, so the ratio of sent and received packets in the network is also high. However, the data packets overhead will vary with respect to the number of adversary nodes and the number of cluster heads involved in the routing process.

Results show that the total number of sent and received packets in the network will be less in BAS compared to SPIN scheme. So our scheme is helpful to improve the network performance and its lifetime by reducing network traffic.

5.3. Repeated Attacks (DoS Attack). DoS attack, also known as jamming attack, is main physical layer attack in WSN [23]. In this attack, an adversary repetitively send malicious requests in the network. Its purpose is to block availability of service to legitimate users, by creating DoS attack, by sending a number of messages continuously in the network.

In SPIN protocol when an adversary sends request to any CH or a number of CHs in the network, the whole authentication process will be performed to check authenticity of adversary node. Any malicious node or a number of malicious nodes can send the request messages repeatedly after short intervals of time, due to which all the CHs will be involved in the routing process and will gradually lose their battery powers. DoS attack will occur in the network, which will make the system or service unavailable for the authorized users.

In BAS when an adversary sends request to any CH in the network, only one packet will be transmitted by CH and 2 packets will be received by it. Similarly even if the same adversary node sends request to some specific number of CHs or to all CHs in the network, only one packet will be transmitted and 2 packets will be received by every CH. There is no risk of DoS attack in the network and no disruption to the availability of the service to authorized users.

So the proposed BAS scheme is helpful to defend WSN against DoS attacks and improve the functionality and performance of the entire network.

6. Conclusion

The proposed Biphase Authentication Scheme (BAS) improves the performance and increases the lifetime of network. The main objective is to provide outside authentication for the user that wants to join the existing WSN. By using the proposed scheme, request messages of nodes can be filtered and messages of only partially authorized users are sent to the base station for final authentication. Initial authentication phase reduces the network traffic, and through final authentication phase only authorized nodes are able to become a part of the network. This scheme is helpful to overcome the flaws in existing schemes, that is, SPIN and BROSK.

It provides the solution for issues in SPIN scheme. SPIN protocol suffers from DoS attack, energy consumption, and network traffic problem. BAS overcomes these issues as shown in Section 5, so this scheme is better than SPIN scheme and improves the performance of the network.

In BROSK protocol the same master key is shared by each node. All other keys for communication are created from the master key. If the master key is compromised, then an invader can easily compromise the whole network and create all further keys.

BAS provides a solution for this problem. If the master key is compromised, an adversary cannot compromise the entire network and cannot produce further keys for communication. So this scheme provides more secure environment for network functionality than BROSK protocol and removes security vulnerabilities.

7. Future Work

WSNs are exposed to security attacks due to wireless nature of the media. Current authentication schemes used for WSNs cannot provide satisfactory solution for authentication vulnerabilities in network. There are other problems such as data integrity and confidentiality in WSNs. Further authentication schemes should be developed to provide outside as well as inside network security in WSN. Several extensions of this research work can be further developed. For future work our plan is to extend the proposed Biphase Authentication Scheme to provide inside network security such as data integrity, data freshness, and data confidentiality. This will overcome inside network authentication vulnerabilities in WSN like authentication vulnerabilities in network, will provide more secure environment for proper functionality of WSNs, and would be very effective to increase network performance. The effect of various nondeterministic factors, such as distance between nodes, remaining energy level of CH, and so forth, on BAS will also be carried out.

Acknowledgments

This research was supported by the Ministry of Science and ICT (MSIP) under ICT R&D program (2017-0-01672) supervised by the Institute for Information & Communications Technology Promotion (IITP).

References

[1] S. S. Rizvi and T.-S. Chung, "PIYAS-Proceeding to intelligent service oriented memory allocation for flash based data centric sensor devices in wireless sensor networks," *Sensors*, vol. 10, no. 1, pp. 292–312, 2010.

[2] I. F. Akyildiz, W. Su, Y. Sankarasubramaniam, and E. Cayirci, "Wireless sensor networks: a survey," *Computer Networks*, vol. 38, no. 4, pp. 393–422, 2002.

[3] S. S. Rizvi and T. S. Chung, "Performance evaluation of indices-based query optimization from flash-based data centric sensor devices in wireless sensor networks," *International Journal of Distributed Sensor Networks*, vol. 2012, Article ID 258080, 10 pages, 2012.

[4] R. Riaz, S. S. Rizvi, E. Mushtaq et al., "OSAP: online smart-phone's user authentication protocol," *International Journal of Computer Science and Network Security*, vol. 17, no. 3, pp. 7–12, 2017.

[5] J. Zheng and M. J. Lee, "Will IEEE 802.15.4 make ubiquitous networking a reality?: a discussion on a potential low power, low bit rate standard," *IEEE Communications Magazine*, vol. 42, no. 6, pp. 140–146, 2004.

[6] A. Koubaa, M. Alves, and E. Tovar, "IEEE 802.15.4 for wireless sensor networks: a technical overview," in *Proceedings of the 11th IEEE International Conference*, pp. 400–406, 2005.

[7] M. Hoberl, I. Haider, and B. Rinner, "Towards a Secure Key Generation and Storage Framework on Resource-Constrained Sensor Nodes," in *Proceedings of the International Conference on Embedded Wireless Systems and Networks*, pp. 313–318, 2016.

[8] S. Prasad, S. Jaiswal, N. S. V. Shet, and P. Sarwesh, "Energy aware routing protocol for resource constrained wireless sensor networks," in *Proceedings of the 1st International Conference on Informatics and Analytics, ICIA 2016*, August 2016.

[9] D. Granlund, P. Holmlund, and C. Åhlund, "Opportunistic mobility support for resource constrained sensor devices in smart cities," *Sensors*, vol. 15, no. 3, pp. 5112–5135, 2015.

[10] C. Karlof and D. Wagner, "Secure routing in wireless sensor networks: attacks and countermeasures," in *Proceedings of the 1st IEEE International Workshop on Sensor Network Protocols and Applications*, pp. 113–127, May 2003.

[11] B. Lai, S. Kim, and I. Verbauwhede, "Scalable session key construction protocol for wireless sensor network," in *Proceedings of IEEE Workshop on Large Scale Real Time and Embedded Systems (LARTES)*, pp. 1–6, 2006.

[12] S. S. Rizvi and T.-S. Chung, "Investigation of in-network data mining approach for energy efficient data centric wireless sensor networks," *International Review on Computers and Software*, vol. 8, no. 2, pp. 443–447, 2013.

[13] J. Gul, S. Mushtaq, and R. Riaz, "Optimal guard node placement using SGLD and energy factor," *Journal of Computing*, vol. 4, no. 6, pp. 87–92, 2012.

[14] B.-C. C. Lai, S. P. Kim, I. Verbauwhede, and D. D. Hwang, "Reducing Radio Energy Consumption of Key Management

Protocols for Wireless Sensor Networks," in *Proceedings of the 2004 International Symposium on Low Power Electronics and Design, ISLPED 2004*, pp. 351–356, August 2004.

[15] K. Kifayat, M. Merabti, Q. Shi, and L. J. David, "Security in wireless sensor networks," in *Handbook of Information and Communication Security, 2010, Part E*, pp. 513–552, 2010.

[16] K. H. M. Wong, Y. Zheng, J. Cao, and Wang, "A dynamic user authentication scheme for wireless sensor networks," in *Proceedings of the IEEE International Conference on Sensor Networks, Ubiquitous, and Trustworthy Computing*, pp. 318–327, 2006.

[17] H. R. Tseng, R. H. Jan, and W. Yang, "An improved dynamic user authentication scheme for wireless sensor networks," in *Proceedings of the 50th Annual IEEE Global Telecommunications Conference (GLOBECOM '07)*, pp. 986–990, November 2007.

[18] R. Riaz, *A Unified Security Framework for IP Based Wireless Sensor Networks [Ph.D. thesis]*, 2008.

[19] R. Riaz, A. Naureen, A. Akram, A. H. Akbar, K. H. Kim, and H. Farooq Ahmed, "A unified security framework with three key management schemes for wireless sensor networks," *Computer Communications*, vol. 31, no. 18, pp. 4269–4280, 2008.

[20] Q. Mamun, "A qualitative comparison of different logical topologies for wireless sensor networks," *Sensors*, vol. 12, no. 11, pp. 14887–14913, 2012.

[21] J. Hill, R. Szewczyk, A. Woo, S. Hollar, D. Culler, and K. Pister, "System architecture directions for networked sensors," in *In Proceedings of the ACM ASPLOS IX*, pp. 93–104, 2000.

[22] Y. Wang, G. Attebury, and B. Ramamurthy, "A survey of security issues in wireless sensor networks," *IEEE Communications Surveys & Tutorials*, vol. 8, no. 2, pp. 2–22, 2006.

[23] Y. Zou, J. Zhu, X. Wang, and L. Hanzo, "A survey on wireless security: technical challenges, recent advances, and future trends," *Proceedings of the IEEE*, vol. 104, no. 9, pp. 1727–1765, 2016.

3

An Improved Privacy-Preserving Framework for Location-Based Services Based on Double Cloaking Regions with Supplementary Information Constraints

Li Kuang,[1] Yin Wang,[1] Pengju Ma,[1] Long Yu,[1] Chuanbin Li,[1] Lan Huang,[1] and Mengyao Zhu[2]

[1]*School of Software, Central South University, Changsha 410075, China*
[2]*School of Communication and Information Engineering, Shanghai University, Shanghai 200444, China*

Correspondence should be addressed to Mengyao Zhu; zhumengyao@shu.edu.cn

Academic Editor: Lianyong Qi

With the rapid development of location-based services in the field of mobile network applications, users enjoy the convenience of location-based services on one side, while being exposed to the risk of disclosure of privacy on the other side. Attacker will make a fierce attack based on the probability of inquiry, map data, point of interest (POI), and other supplementary information. The existing location privacy protection techniques seldom consider the supplementary information held by attackers and usually only generate single cloaking region according to the protected location point, and the query efficiency is relatively low. In this paper, we improve the existing LBSs system framework, in which we generate double cloaking regions by constraining the supplementary information, and then k-anonymous task is achieved by the cooperation of the double cloaking regions; specifically speaking, k dummy points of fixed dummy positions in the double cloaking regions are generated and the LBSs query is then performed. Finally, the effectiveness of the proposed method is verified by the experiments on real datasets.

1. Introduction

In recent years, with the rapid development of cellular network and GPS (Global Positioning System) positioning technology, the use of LBSs (location-based services) devices (such as phone, PAD) became more and more popular, while driving the rapid growth of LBSs applications. The typical LBSs applications include retrieval of POI (such as MeiTuan), map (such as Google Maps), GPS navigation (such as Amap), and location-aware social networks (such as Wechat). It can be said that LBSs have penetrated into many aspects of life, and the invocation of LBSs undoubtedly brings great convenience to people's life.

At the same time, LBSs privacy risks also attract the attention of the society, because when the user requests LBSs, specific location information is needed to submit, and the locations which are involved in a large number of user's query data [1, 2] may reveal user's privacy, such as home address, living habits, and social relations. In the era of big

data security, the emphasis is put on the problem of security of data being sent, data at rest, and data being processed and deleted from the system [3]. If such information is leaked to malicious attackers, the user will be exposed to a serious threat. In practice, there is no server that is absolutely secure; LBSP (location-based services providers) itself may also be an attacker, and even anonymizer on third parties cannot be trusted absolutely. In addition, the client receives a large number of results returned by anonymizer, which will increase the cost of computation, and they may wait for the service due to too many dummy positions; therefore the user may be not satisfied by the application usage experience.

The existing LBSs framework is shown as Figure 1. The client sends user's request Q_U to the anonymizer. The Q_U includes the UID (User ID), the specific location l_u, the privacy protection requirement k, and the query content con, The anonymizer then sends the processed request Q_A to the LBSPs. Q_A includes randomly generated query requests for k dummies locations. Location information is different

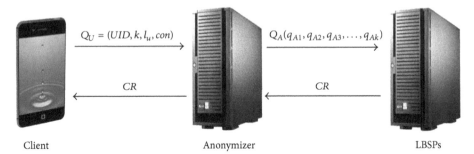

FIGURE 1: A centralized framework of LBSs.

from user's location in each q_{Ai}, while the remaining request information is the same. LBSP then returns the candidate results CR of the request Q_A to the anonymizer, and the anonymizer passes CR to the client, and finally the client filters the best result from the returned CR as the final result of the request.

The traditional LBSs privacy protection algorithms seldom consider that the anonymizer is not credible, so that the user's specific location information is sent directly to the anonymizer. If the data in anonymizer is leaked and used by the attackers, the user's location data will be disclosed directly. In addition, the attacker may make a fierce attack based on the probability of inquiry, map data, POI, and other supplementary information. For example, if a region is covered by a very low query number of locations such as lakes and mountains, the attacker can exclude the region with a large probability, so that the risk of user's exposure in the remaining region will be increased.

In this paper, we propose improving the existing LBSs framework and design several related algorithms within the framework. First, user's actual location which is contained in the query request is generalized into grid id, and the user's grid region is matched to another region by a dynamic matching algorithm, so that double cloaking regions are formed by considering that the attacker has a background of the number of historical queries; second, k fixed dummy positions are generated in double cloaking regions to achieve k-anonymous requirements by the proposed dummies generation algorithm; and, finally, the queries in dummy positions of double cloaking regions are sent to LBSPs and the candidate results are filtered and sent back to the user. Our proposed framework as well as the algorithms can solve the contradiction between service quality, privacy and resource overhead effectively.

The remainder of the paper is organized as follows. Related work is discussed in Section 2. The preliminaries of this paper are given in Section 3. The proposed approach is illustrated in Section 4. The experimental results are presented in Section 5. And finally, the conclusions and future work are given in Section 6.

2. Related Work

At present, researchers have put forward a lot of privacy protection methods for LBSs, and k-anonymous [4–16] is

the core idea of many methods. Gruteser and Grunwald [4] propose the concept of location k-anonymity. K-anonymity requires that when a user sends a location request data to a LBSPs, the cloaking region in which a query user is located must contain at least the other $k - 1$ users, so that the probability that the location query user is identified does not exceed $1/k$. Yiu et al. [5] propose a Space Twist solution which introduces a trusted third party; after the user sends their real location information to the trusted third party, it will send a dummy coordinate to LBS service rather than user's real coordinate. Mokbel et al. [6] propose a k-anonymity protection method, which introduces a third party anonymous server; when the user sends a request to the LBSPs, the location information is sent to the anonymous server first. The anonymous server generalizes the user's location into a region of k-anonymity nature, and then the anonymous server sends the request to the LBSPs and returns the candidate result set to the user; finally, the user selects the best one.

Spatial cloaking [17–25] is a fairly popular mechanism. Chow et al. [17] propose Casper cloak algorithm, which uses a quad-tree data structure and allows users to determine the size of k and the minimum anonymous area, but the privacy can be guaranteed only when users' positions are distributed evenly. Jin and Papadimitratos [18] allow P2P responses to be validated with very low fraction of queries affected even if a significant fraction of nodes are compromised. Chen and Pang [21] propose that the cloaking region is randomly chosen from the ones with top-k largest position entropy.

Dummy position [26–30] generation is also a common method for location privacy protection. Kido et al. [26, 27] first propose a dummy position generation mechanism. Guo et al. [28] combine the dynamic pseudonym transformation mechanism with the user's personalized features to protect user's location privacy. Palanisamy and Liu [29] propose a Mix-zone approach for protecting user's privacy.

Encryption-based methods [12, 31–37] make user's location completely invisible to the server by encrypting LBSS query. Although encryption-based methods have high privacy and high quality of service, the calculation and communication costs are large, the deployment is complex, and the optimization algorithm is needed. Khoshgozaran et al. [12, 34] propose an encryption method based on the Hilbert curve to transfer user's position as well as his POI from two-dimensional coordinates to one-dimensional encryption space; the one-dimensional encryption space transformed by two different parameters of Hilbert curve still maintains the proximity in two-dimensional space, so that k-nearest neighbor query and range query can also be performed in one-dimensional encrypted space. PIR (Private Information Retrieval) [35] method is used to protect user's query privacy, and it has the advantages of high privacy protection and good service quality. Lu et al. [36] propose the PLAM privacy protection framework, which uses homomorphic encryption to protect user privacy, but with much time overhead. Fu et al. [37] use the powerful computing power of the server to propose a retrieval encryption scheme to meet the privacy requirements of different threat models.

In summary, the existing location privacy protection mechanisms and methods still have the following problems: (1) the existing methods often do not consider the supplementary information when generating cloaking region; if the attacker has supplementary information, the success rate of the attack will be increased and the privacy security of the user will be challenged. (2) In the existing framework, the candidate results that anonymizer returns to the user often include a large number of useless dummy positions, which not only increase the computational overhead, but also reduce users' experience. (3) Dummy position coordinates are often generated randomly without considering whether it will affect the quality of final service.

The differences of this paper include the following: (1) we propose generating double cloaking regions while assuming that the attacker has a background of supplementary information, so the privacy protection can be greatly improved; (2) the proposed anonymizer in the LBSs framework will not return all candidate results but merely returns a half to the client, so that the computation overhead is reduced and user's waiting time is reduced; (3) we propose generating fixed dummy positions according to the value of k and uniform distribution rule, which can solve the contradiction between service quality, privacy, and resource overhead effectively.

3. Preliminaries

3.1. Strong Attack and Its Illustrating Examples.
In this paper, we assume that the attacker is a strong attacker. LBSPs can be seen as strong attackers, since LBSPs not only have supplementary information, such as the number of historical queries, but also know the privacy protection mechanism. A strong attacker usually infers the region where the user is located and then combines the supplementary information to filter the user's region and even makes reverse attack based on the privacy protection mechanism, so that the attacker can uniquely identify the user's region, then infer the user's real location from the region, and finally access the user's privacy.

For example, as shown in Figure 3(a), if the user's region randomly matches a cloaking region with history query number of 1, obviously, it is a region with very low number of historical queries, while if the user's real location is in the region with history query number of 20, there will be a great possibility of determining the user's real region.

The strong attacker may not only have the supplementary information, but also know the privacy protection mechanism. Suppose that we simply use the region which is the closest to the user's history query as the generation mechanism of double cloaking region, and the attacker knows the mechanism. As shown in Figure 3(b), the query time in user's region is 20, and the region with query times 22 will form the double cloaking regions. If the attacker is the LBSP itself, it will analyze the two regions; if the user's real region is that with query times 22, the closest one is the region with 23. To form a double cloaking region, the region with query times 22 will select that with 23 instead of 20, so it can be determined that the user's real region is that with 20. Therefore, if attackers have supplementary information and know the privacy protection mechanisms, it will increase the risk of users to disclose the specific location.

3.2. Problem Definition and Related Concepts

Definition 1 (space division based on quad-tree). As shown in Figure 4, this paper uses the quad-tree data structure [8]. The space is divided layer by layer from top to bottom, and each layer is divided into 4^h grids; especially speaking, the 0th layer of the entire space is divided into 1 grid, the 1st layer contains 4 grids, the 2nd layer contains 16 grids, and so on, until the side length of each grid reaches the threshold L, and the space will be divided into H layers. The total number of the history query times on each layer is the same, but the entire spatial area is subdivided so that the length L of each grid is gradually reduced. The smaller the L, the lower the level of privacy protection and the higher the quality of service; on the contrary, the bigger the L, the higher the level of privacy protection and the lower the quality of service. The information in each grid is contained in the hash table, where the *GID* is the number of the grid and *NoU* is the user's history query times in each grid.

Definition 2 (query request from user Q_U (*UID*, k, h, *GID*, *con*)). As shown in Figure 2, the query request submitted by the user to the anonymizer is denoted as Q_U (*UID*, k, h, *GID*, *con*), where *UID* is the user's identification information; k is user's requirement on k-*anonymous* protection mechanism, which determines the number of dummies to generate; h is user's requirements on the generalization level of space, which is required to be larger than 2, since the query would be too poor if h is less than or equal to 2. Both the user and the anonymizer use the quad-tree data structure to store the spatial information. The *GID* is the grid ID which is generated according to the user's specific location; *con* is the query content, which is not the focus of this study.

Definition 3 (query request from anonymizer Q_A (q_{A1}, q_{A2}, q_{A3},...,q_{Ak})). The query request passed by the anonymizer to LBSPs is denoted as $Q_A(q_{A1}, q_{A2}, q_{A3},...,q_{Ak})$, where $q_{Ai}(DID, l_{di}, con)$ is a request for each dummy and *DID* (Dummies ID) is the identification information of the k dummies generated by the anonymizer; l_{di} is the location information of k dummies; *con* is the query content.

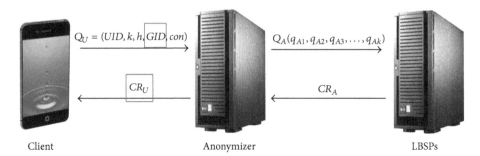

FIGURE 2: Improved framework of LBSs system.

1	2	25	26
18	24	33	45
28	20	22	30
51	43	23	13

1	2	25	26
18	24	33	45
28	20	22	30
51	43	23	13

(a) Cloaking region is formed by randomly matching the number of queries

(b) Cloaking region is formed according to the closest number of query

FIGURE 3: Two mechanisms of generating cloaking region.

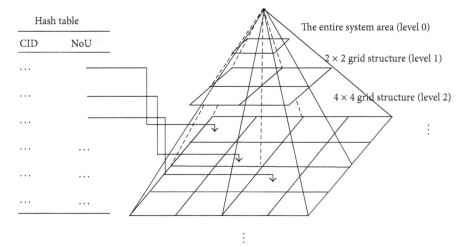

FIGURE 4: Data storage structure.

Definition 4 (candidate results to anonymizer CR_A). The LBSPs return the candidate results to the anonymizer as CR_A, which is the results of the request for k dummies in the double cloaking region. Each request result corresponds to the *DID* of the query request.

Definition 5 (candidate results to user CR_U). The anonymizer returns candidate results to the user as CR_U, which only includes the query results of the dummies in the *RCR*.

Definition 6 (quality of service). The quality of service obtained by the user is measured by the Euclidean distance between the dummy and the user. If the user is closer to the dummy position, the location of request and the result are more similar; therefore the service quality would be higher. Assume that the user's specific position is l_u, its latitude and longitude coordinate is (lon_u, lat_u), and l_{di} ($i = 1, 2, 3, \ldots, k$) is the ith dummy position; its latitude and longitude coordinate is (lon_{di}, lat_{di}). r is the radius of the earth, generally taken as 6371 km. The distance between user and dummy is calculated as formula (1):

$$\text{dis}_i\left(l_u, l_{di}\right) = 2r * \arcsin\left(\sqrt{\sin\left(\frac{d_{lati}}{2}\right)^2 + \cos\left(lat_{di}\right) * \cos\left(lat_u\right) * \sin\left(\frac{d_{loni}}{2}\right)^2}\right), \tag{1}$$

where

$$d_{loni} = \frac{\pi\left|lon_{di} - lon_u\right|}{180},$$

$$d_{lati} = \frac{\pi\left|lat_{di} - lat_u\right|}{180}. \tag{2}$$

The smaller the value of $\text{dis}_i(l_u, l_{di})$, the better the quality of service of ith dummy, and we can take the query result of the ith dummy as the final query result.

Problem Definition. We know that the user, the anonymous server, and LBSPs share the *space division based on quad-tree*. And we also know that the user submits Q_U to anonymizer, and the anonymizer passes Q_A to LBSPs, the LBSPs return CR_A to anonymizer, and the anonymizer returns CR_U to client. In this process, it is assumed that the anonymizer and LBSPs are not fully credible, so the strong attacker is most likely to guess the specific location of the user according to the background knowledge which includes the number of historical queries and privacy protection mechanism, thus causing the user's privacy to be disclosed. The problem that we want to solve is improving the *quality of service* experienced by the user and reducing the computing overhead of the user, when he accesses the LBSs, while ensuring his location security.

3.3. Symbolic Correspondence. For simplicity, we list the notations used in this paper as Notation section shows.

4. Privacy-Preserving Framework and Algorithms for LBSs

4.1. Approach Overview. In order to protect the user's real location which is contained in the query request, we employ the double cloaking region mechanism. The double cloaking region includes real cloaking region (*RCR*) and fake cloaking region (*FCR*). The *RCR* is the user's grid, and the anonymizer generates *FCR* by dynamic clustering method. *FRC* has three main functions: (1) *FCR* and *RCR* together generate k dummy positions to reach k-anonymous requirements; (2) *FCR* and *RCR* form a double cloaking region against strong-attacks; (3) when the anonymizer returns the candidate results to the client, the candidate results of the request for the dummies in the *FCR* are filtered directly. The dummies in the double cloaking region are sent to the LBSPs to request the service.

The whole process of our proposed solution is shown as Figure 5 (the system execution order is demonstrated by the numbers): (1) a *RCR* is generated according to the user's

specific location; (2) the query request Q_U is submitted to the anonymizer; (3) Dynamic Matching Algorithm (*DMA*) is employed by the anonymizer to generate a *FCR* according to the *GID* in Q_U, so that a double cloaking region with similar query times is formed; (4) $k/2$ dummy positions are generated in the two regions, respectively, by using the dummies generation algorithm (*DGA*), and the two dummy sets are denoted *DSs1* and *DSs2*; (5) the query request Q_A from the dummy positions in *DSs1* and *DSs2* is submitted to LBSPs together; (6) LBSP answers CR_A according to Q_A; (7) CR_A are replied to the anonymizer; (8) the anonymizer forms CR_U according to the *DIDs* (Dummy IDs) in CR_A to filter out the query results in *DSs1*; (9) CR_U is returned to the client, and the client selects the query result q_{Ai} of the dummy whose $\text{dis}_i(l_u, l_{di})$ is minimum as the query result according to formula (1).

In our improved framework, there are two important algorithms, which are dynamic matching algorithm (*DMA*) and dummies generation algorithm (*DGA*), and we will illustrate the two algorithms in the following subsections.

4.2. Dynamic Matching Algorithm. The main idea of dynamic matching algorithm (DMA for short) is to separate the regions with relatively large, relatively small, and zero number of queries, so that the two regions with obviously different number of queries will not be matched together to form a double cloaking region. As shown in Figure 6(a), the points represent the positions where users make historical requests. The position coordinates are projected into a 2D map, and the whole region is divided into 4^h grids according to the generalization level of space h. *RCR* where the user located is represented by the region with black solid line. The region is divided into 9×9 grids in Figure 6(a) as an example.

As shown in Figure 6(b), first, a 4×4 grid region which contains *RCR* is allocated randomly, and *FCR* will be matched in this region as well; second, the number of historical queries in each grid is counted and stored in a matrix represented by $G_{4 \times 4}$. An example of $G_{4 \times 4}$ is shown in Figure 7, where the number of queries in *RCR* is 25, and the number of historical queries in each grid of the 4×4 region with black line in Figure 6(b) is also shown.

And then the numbers of queries in the 4×4 region are divided into three categories, relatively large, relatively small, and zero, which are realized by the classical dynamic clustering algorithm [38]. To form a double cloaking region, we remove the region with zero number of queries firstly, and then *FCR* is only selected randomly from the regions with the number in the same category as *RCR*.

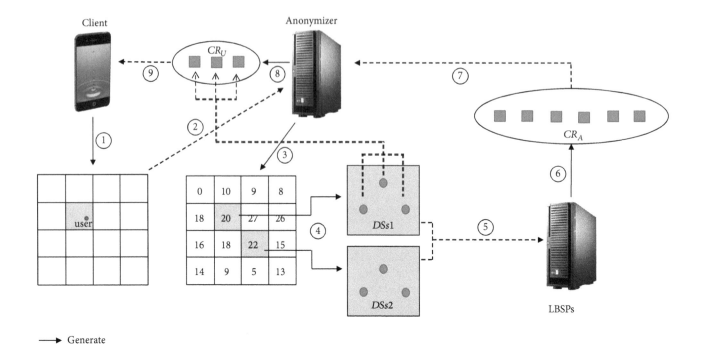

FIGURE 5: The improved framework.

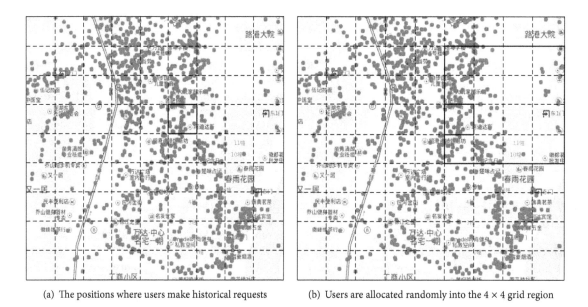

(a) The positions where users make historical requests   (b) Users are allocated randomly into the 4 × 4 grid region

FIGURE 6: Historical requests on the map.

Take the data in Figure 7 as an example, *DMA* first divides the number of queries into three categories, {14, 16, 22, 25, 25, 27}, {1, 1, 1, 6, 6, 8, 9}, and {0, 0, 0}, respectively. Assume that the query number of the user's region is 25; the *FCR* may be the grid with the query number 22, and the two regions will form a double cloaking region.

The pseudocode of *DMA* is shown as Algorithm 1.

4.3. Dummies Generation Algorithm. The core idea of dummies generation algorithm *(DGA)* is to generate k fixed dummy positions to approximate the user's real position, and it tries to distribute the fixed dummy positions over the region as evenly as possible, and then the answer to the query request by the user will be approximated by that from the best dummy location. It is common to generate

27	14	0	8
25	6	0	6
25	9	1	1
16	22	1	0

FIGURE 7: Number of historical queries in 4×4 region.

Input: Privacy protection level h, User's grid ID *GID*
Output: Double Cloaking Region (*RCR* and *FCR*)
(1) **Anonymizer selects the spatial hierarchy according to the privacy protection level** h
(2) **Randomly match the user's grid into a grid region** $G_{4\times4}$
(3) **for query count in** $G_{4\times4}$
(4)   **if query count** $\neq 0$ **then**
(5)   **add query count to Sets**
(6)   **end if**
(7) **end for**
(8) **The Sets are randomly divided into** set_1 **and** set_2 equally
(9) **Do**
(10) avg_1 = average(set_1); avg_2 = average(set_2);
(11)   **for** s **in** Sets
(12)   **if** $(s - avg_1)^2 < (s - avg_2)^2$ **then**
(13)   s **belong to** c_1
(14)   **else**
(15)   s **belong to** c_2
(16)   **end if**
(17)   **end for**
(18) **while** there are changes on the elements **in** c_1 **and** c_2
(19) **if the number of** *GID* **belongs to** c_1 **then**
(20)   *FCR* **is** selected randomly from the regions with the number in c_1 except *RCR*
(21) **else** *FCR* **is selected randomly from the regions with the number in** c_2 **except** *RCR*
(22) **end if**
(23) **return** *FCR* **and** *RCR*

ALGORITHM 1: DMA (dynamic matching algorithm).

---

dummy positions randomly in the double cloaking regions; however, we propose defining two rules to generate fixed dummy positions according to k. In Figure 8, the red solid circle represents the user's real position and the solid circles represent the fixed dummy positions according to our rules, while the dotted circles represent the dummy positions generated randomly. As shown in Figure 8(a), when $d_1 > d_2$, that is, the shortest distance between the user and the fixed dummy is shorter than that between the user and the random dummy, we say that the quality of service of the fixed dummy positions is higher than that of the random dummy positions according to Definition 6. On the contrary, as shown in Figure 8(b), when $d_1 < d_2$, we say that the quality of service of the fixed dummy positions is lower than that of the random

dummy positions. We verify that the service quality of *DGA* is higher than that of random way in Section 5.2.

The coordinate system of the two-dimensional coordinate origin is established at the lower left vertex of the grid. In the anonymizer, there is data of each grid length L in each spatial hierarchy. k_1 and k_2 both equal to $k/2$, and they represent the number of dummy positions to be generated in *RCR* and *FCR*, respectively. There are two core rules in *DGA*.

Base Rule R_1. When k_1 (or k_2) ≤ 5, the fixed dummy positions when k_1 (or k_2) = 1, 2, 3, 4, 5 are shown as Figures 9(a)–9(e), respectively.

(1) When k_1 (or k_2) = 1, the dummy position is set at $(L/2, L/2)$, as shown in Figure 9(a);

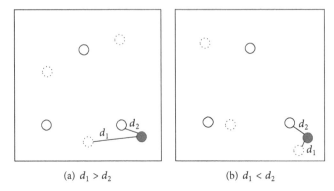

FIGURE 8: The shortest distance between the user and the random dummy d_1 compared to that between the user and the fixed dummy d_2.

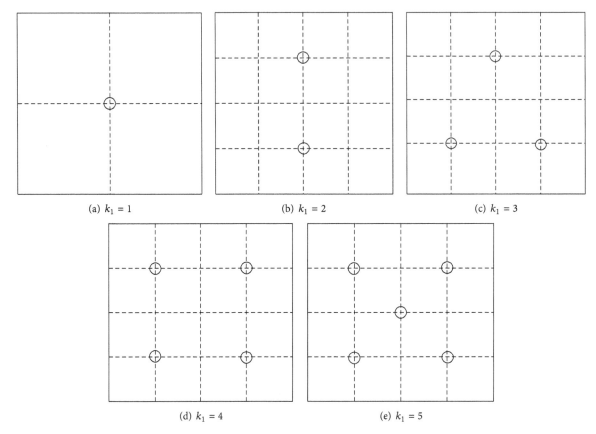

(a) $k_1 = 1$ (b) $k_1 = 2$ (c) $k_1 = 3$

(d) $k_1 = 4$ (e) $k_1 = 5$

FIGURE 9: Base rule R_1.

(2) When k_1 (or k_2) = 2, the dummy positions are $(L/2, L/4)$, $(L/2, 3L/4)$, as shown in Figure 9(b);

(3) When k_1 (or k_2) = 3, the dummy positions are $(L/4, L/4)$, $(L/2, 3L/4)$, $(3L/4, L/4)$, as shown in Figure 9(c);

(4) When k_1 (or k_2) = 4, the dummy positions are $(L/4, L/4)$, $(3L/4, L/4)$, $(L/4, 3L/4)$, $(3L/4, 3L/4)$, as shown in Figure 9(d);

(5) When k_1 (or k_2) = 5, the dummy positions are $(L/4, L/4)$, $(3L/4, L/4)$, $(L/4, 3L/4)$, $(3L/4, 3L/4)$, $(L/2, L/2)$, as shown in Figure 9(e).

Generalization Rule R_2. When k_1 (or k_2) = n and $n > 5$, we have the following:

First, divide the whole region into 4 grids, and each value in the 4 grids is as follows:

(1) If $n\% \ 4 \ = \ 0$, $n/4$ dummy positions are assigned in each of the 4 grids;

(2) If $n\% \ 4 = 1$, $(n/4) + 1, n/4, n/4, n/4$ dummy positions are assigned in the 4 grids, respectively, starting from the left upper corner, continuing in the clockwise direction;

(3) If $n\% \ 4 \ = \ 2$, $(n/4) + 1, (n/4) + 1, n/4, n/4$ dummy positions are assigned in the 4 grids, respectively;

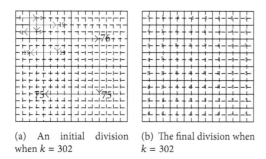

(a) An initial division when $k = 302$

(b) The final division when $k = 302$

FIGURE 10: An illustrating example of *DGA*.

Input: The value of k in the k-anonymity, *RCR, FCR*
Output: k_1 *dummies* in *RCR* and k_2 *dummies* in *FCR*, ID at each Dummy *DID*
(1) **Generate** $4^{\lceil \log_4 \lceil k_1/5 \rceil \rceil}$, $4^{\lceil \log_4 \lceil k_2/5 \rceil \rceil}$ small grids in *RCR* and *FCR*
(2) **Generate** fixed dummies in *RCR* and *FCR* based on R_1, R_2
(3) **Add ID** for each dummy
(4) **return** k_1, k_2 dummies, ID at each Dummy *DID*

ALGORITHM 2: DGA (dummies generation algorithm).

(4) If $n\% \ 4 = 3$, $(n/4)+1$, $(n/4)+1$, $(n/4)+1$, $n/4$ dummy positions are assigned in the 4 grids, respectively.

Second, if $(n/4)+1$ or $n/4$ is still larger than 5, repeat the first step; otherwise, follow the base rule R_1 to distribute the dummy positions.

In total, $4^{\lceil \log_4 \lceil n/5 \rceil \rceil}$ small grids will be generated in the region.

Take $k_1 = 302$ as an example, as shown in Figure 10, (1) in the first level of division; the region will be divided into 4 grids, and dummy positions in each grid are 76, 76, 75, and 75, respectively; (2) since 76 or 75 is larger than 5, in the second level of division, the 4 grids will be divided into 4 grids further; for example, the left upper grid with 76 will be divided into 4 grids with 19, 19, 19, and 19 dummy positions, respectively; and the other three grids follow the same way; (3) since 19 is larger than 5, in the third level of division, the grid with 19 will be divided into 4 grids with 5, 5, 5, and 4 dummy positions, respectively; and the other three grids follow the same way; (4) since 5 or 4 is not larger than 5, the division stops and in total $4^{\lceil \log_4 \lceil k_1/5 \rceil \rceil} = 64$ grids are generated, and the generation of fixed positions in the 64 small grids follows rule R_1.

According to *DGA*, anonymizer can store *DD* (Dummies data) that satisfies various k values in the database, so that the query requests for services can be responded to quickly. The pseudocode of *DGA* is shown as Algorithm 2.

5. Experiment and Analysis

5.1. Experiment Setting. In this paper, we use the historical GPS sampling point data within the range of 5.5 km × 3.5 km in Hefei city as historical inquiry points, which includes more than 60,000 sampling points produced by more than 30,000 people. The data consists of ID, latitude, and longitude, in which "ID" is the user's unique identifier; "longitude" and "latitude" together tell the location where the user submits a query. For convenience, the experiment selects an area of 3.2 km × 3.2 km and sets the threshold of edge length L to 50 m. The space is divided into 64 × 64 grids, and the spatial region is divided into 7 layers, from 0th to 6th layer.

We will compare the dummy algorithm (DA) and naive algorithm (NA) with our proposed *Double Cloaking Algorithm* (*DCA* for short, which consists of *DMA* and *DGA*). As shown in Figure 11, the *DA* is similar to the *DCA* process, except the red box in Figure 11. Specially speaking, *DCA* generates fixed dummy positions according to *DGA*, while *DA* generates random dummy positions in the double cloaking regions. We aim to compare the quality of service for *DA* and *DCA*.

As shown in Figure 12, *NA* is similar to the *DCA* process, except the red boxes in Figure 12. *NA* does not generate double cloaking regions; the anonymizer generates k dummy positions directly in the user's region and sends the queries in dummies to LBSPs, then receives the candidate results from LBSPs, and passes to the user without filtration. We aim to compare the time cost of *NA*, *DA*, and *DCA*.

The coding language is Python and the experiment runs with the 64 bit Windows 10 operating system configured as Intel (R), Core (TM), i5-4590, CPU, and 8 GB.

5.2. Experimental Result and Analysis

5.2.1. The Time Cost of Generating Dummies. As shown in Figure 13, when k changes within (2, 50), the time cost of *DCA* for generating dummy positions is steady, always 0.17 ms. Because *DCA* can be divided into two steps, *DMA* and then *DGA*, the time cost of *DMA* is not affected by k; moreover, the k-anonymous fixed dummy positions have already been set and stored, so it only needs to choose the fixed positions

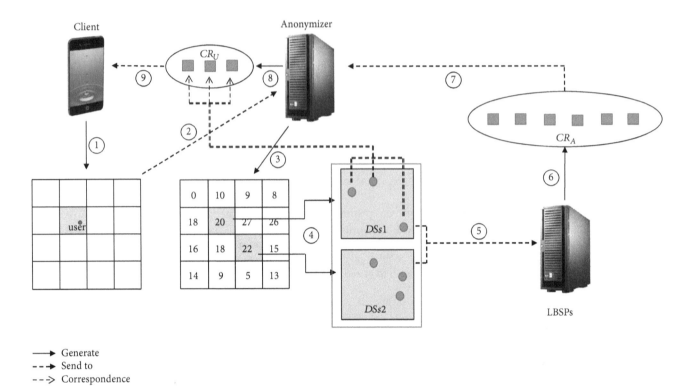

FIGURE 11: Dummy algorithm.

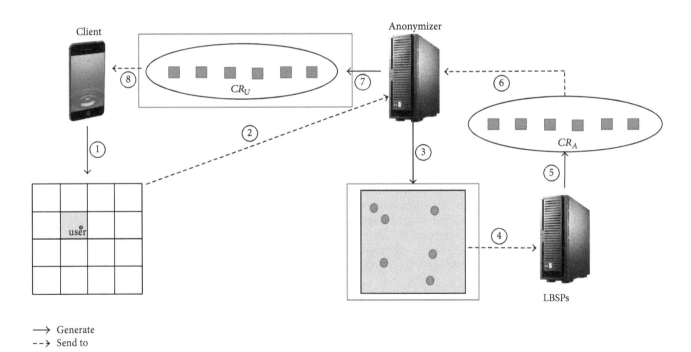

FIGURE 12: Naive algorithm.

according to k; therefore, the time cost of DCA is relatively fixed and remains a constant value.

DA can also be divided into two steps; the first step is the same as DCA, and the second step is to generate random dummy positions, which should be computed in real time,

so it will take more time than DCA to generate each dummy position, and the bigger the value of k, the more time it takes.

While NA only takes time to generate the k dummy positions randomly, when k is less than 28, NA takes less time than DCA; when k is equal to 28, DCA and NA spend the

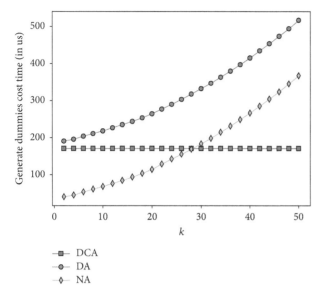

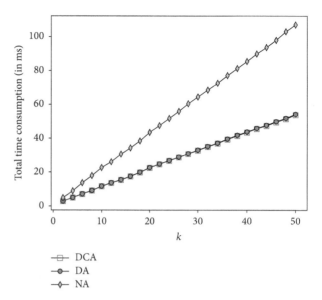

FIGURE 13: Comparison on time cost of generating dummies.

FIGURE 15: Comparison on total time consumption.

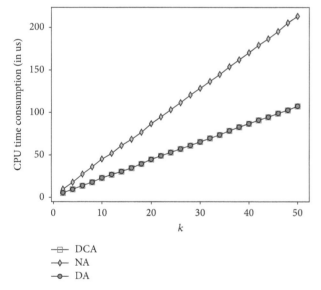

FIGURE 14: Comparison on time cost of result processing on client side.

same time; with the continuous increase of k, NA begins to take more time than DCA.

5.2.2. The Time Cost of Result Processing. As shown in Figure 14, the time cost of NA for result processing on the client side is almost twice as that in DCA and DA. Because when the anonymizer sends CR_U to the client, DCA and DA generate the double cloaking regions, the k dummy positions are equally distributed into two regions, and only the candidate results in RCR are returned to the client by the anonymizer; NA generates k dummy positions in one cloaking region; the anonymizer returns a set of candidate results for k dummy positions to the client. The number of

candidate results in NA is twice of that in DCA and DA; in order to select the optimal dummy position, the client needs to calculate the $\mathrm{dis}_i(l_u, l_{di})$ between all dummy positions in the candidate results and the user's specific position. So there is an obvious difference among NA and DCA/DA on the time cost of result processing on the client.

Please note the experiment is simulated on computer, and the unit of the experimental result is microsecond (us), but in actual environment, when the results are processed by client on smart phones, the unit of time cost will fall into millisecond (ms) level.

5.2.3. Total Time Consumption. In this section, we will compare the total time cost of the three algorithms, taking into account the device performance of the anonymizer and the client. In general, the computing power of our PC is much better than that of phones used by the client. Theoretically the floating-point computing power of 1.3 GHz frequency quad-core ARM processor is about 10 MFLOPs/s, and that of 2.5 GHz frequency Intel quad-core Q8300 is 25GFLOPs/s; the two differ 2500 times. Due to the different computing power of different devices, we deem conservatively that the computing power of PC is 500 times as much as the client device, while the computing power of anonymizer is the same as PC; therefore the total time consumption is

$$\text{Total Time} = \text{Time of Generating Dummies} + 500 \times \text{Time of Result Processing.} \tag{3}$$

According to formula (3), it can be known that the time cost on the client side is much larger than that on the anonymizer, and the result processing accounts for the majority percentage of the total time consumption. As shown in Figure 15, the total time consumed by NA is about twice as much as DCA and DA when k is given. In terms of time

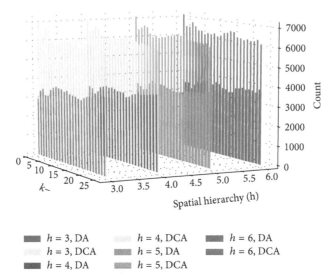

FIGURE 16: Comparison on the probability of getting better quality of service.

efficiency, *DCA* and *DA* are better than *NA*. Since *NA* does not generate double cloaking regions, its privacy protection capability is weaker than DCA and DA, and in the next experiment we only compare *DCA* and *DA*.

5.2.4. Comparison on Quality of Service between DCA and DA. In order to compare *DCA* and *DA* on the quality of service, we first conduct 10,000 times of experiments on different values of h and k and count the times when $d_1 > d_2$ and $d_1 < d_2$, as shown in Figures 8(a) and 8(b). As shown in Figure 16, given k and h, for the 10000 experiment, if $d_1 > d_2$, the count of *DCA* adds 1, if $d_1 < d_2$, the count of *DA* adds 1.

When h is specific while k varies between (1, 25), the count of *DGA* ranges between 6000 and 7200, and the count of *DA* ranges between 2,800 and 4000; when h varies, the count range of *DGA* and *DA* does not change much, because although h becomes larger and L becomes smaller in the cloaking region, the ratio of the fixed dummy positions to L stays the same, and the position of the random dummy positions is also independent of L.

In summary, *DCA* has a greater probability of getting better quality of service than *DA*.

We further compare the average quality of service of *DCA* and *DA*. We conduct 10,000 times of experiments on different values of h and k and compute the average quality of service. In the experiment, k ranges from 1 to 25 and h ranges from 3 to 6. According to Definition 6, we can see that the smaller the distance from the user, the better the quality of service. In Figures 17(a)–17(d), with the decrease of h, the average quality of service of *DCA* and *DA* is decreasing, but the average quality of service of *DCA* is always better than *DA*. With the increase of k, the average quality of service of *DCA* and *DA* is increasing, and when k is larger than 15, the trend of increasing becomes slow. In summary, *DCA* has a better average quality of service than *DA*.

6. Conclusion

In this paper, we propose an improved privacy-preserving framework for location-based services based on double cloaking regions with supplementary information constraints. Compared to previous work, our method is effective in solving the strong attack with supplementary information, and, comparing to generating random dummy positions, generating fixed ones improves the service quality but reduces the computational overhead for the client. However, when the distribution of the information data is extremely nonuniform, the dynamic matching algorithm is difficult to match the region of similar information and forms double cloaking regions with the user's region. In the future, we plan to improve the dynamic matching algorithm; in addition, we will consider the continuous query requests of the mobile user.

Notations

LBSPs: Location-Based Services Providers
GID: Grid ID
DIDs: Dummies IDs
UID: User ID
Q_U: A set of query requests submitted by the user to the Anonymizer
Q_A: A set of query requests passed by the Anonymizer to LBSPs
CR_A: The set of candidate results sent by LBSPs to Anonymizer
CR_U: The set of candidate results sent by Anonymizer to Client
$G_{4\times4}$: RCR randomly matches into the grid of 4×4
h: Spatial hierarchy
LS: Level saturated

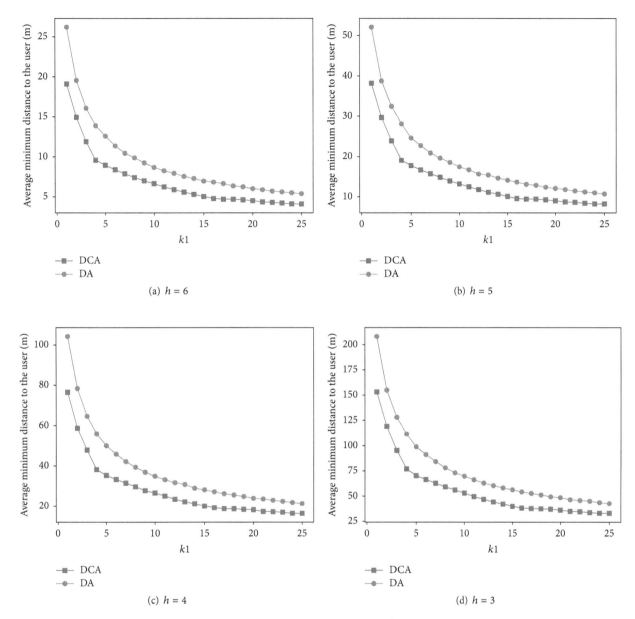

FIGURE 17: Comparison on the average quality of service.

$dis_i(l_u, l_{di})$: Euclidean distance between user and
dummy
DD: Dummies Data.

Acknowledgments

The research is supported by "National Natural Science Foundation of China" (no. 61772560), "Natural Science Foundation of Hunan Province" (no. 2016JJ3154), "Key Support Projects of Shanghai Science and Technology Committee" (no. 16010500100), "Scientific Research Project for Professors in Central South University, China" (no. 904010001), and "Innovation Project for Graduate Students in Central South University" (no. 1053320170313).

References

[1] D. Vatsalan, Z. Sehili, P. Christen et al., *Privacy-Preserving Record Linkage for Big Data: Current Approaches and Research Challenges*, Handbook of Big Data Technologies, Springer International Publishing, 2017, 851–895.

[2] H. Ye, X. Cheng, M. Yuan, L. Xu, J. Gao, and C. Cheng, "A survey of security and privacy in big data," in *Proceedings of the 16th International Symposium on Communications and Information Technologies, ISCIT 2016*, pp. 268–272, Qingdao, China, September 2016.

[3] A. Jakóbik, *Big Data Security*, Resource Management for Big Data Platforms, Springer International Publishing, 2016, 241–261.

[4] M. Gruteser and D. Grunwald, "Anonymous usage of location-based services through spatial and temporal cloaking," in *Proceedings of the 1st International Conference on Mobile Systems, Applications and Services*, pp. 31–42, ACM, San Francisco, Calif, USA, May 2003.

[5] M. L. Yiu, C. S. Jensen, X. Huang, and H. Lu, "SpaceTwist: managing the trade-offs among location privacy, query performance, and query accuracy in mobile services," in *Proceedings of the IEEE 24th International Conference on Data Engineering (ICDE '08)*, pp. 366–375, IEEE Press, Cancun, Mexico, April 2008.

[6] M. Mokbel F, C. Chow Y, and G. Aref W, "The new casper: Query processing for location services without compromising privacy," in *Proceedings of the 32nd international conference on Very large data bases*, pp. 763–774, VLDB Endowment, 2006.

[7] X. Pan, J. L. Xu, and X. F. Meng, "Protecting location privacy against location-dependent attacks in mobile services," *IEEE Transactions on Knowledge and Data Engineering*, vol. 24, no. 8, pp. 1506–1519, 2012.

[8] X. Zhu, H. Chi, B. Niu, W. Zhang, Z. Li, and H. Li, "MobiCache: When k-anonymity meets cache," in *Proceedings of the 2013 IEEE Global Communications Conference, GLOBECOM 2013*, pp. 820–825, IEEE, Atlanta, GA, USA, December 2013.

[9] Y. Wang, D. Xu, X. He, C. Zhang, F. Li, and B. Xu, "L2P2: location-aware location privacy protection for location-based services," in *Proceedings of the IEEE Conference on Computer Communications (INFOCOM '12)*, pp. 1996–2004, IEEE, Orlando, Fla, USA, March 2012.

[10] T. Hashem, L. Kulik, and R. Zhang, "Countering overlapping rectangle privacy attack for moving kNN queries," *Information Systems*, vol. 38, no. 3, pp. 430–453, 2013.

[11] B. Yao, F. Li, and X. Xiao, "Secure nearest neighbor revisited," in *Proceedings of the IEEE 29th International Conference on Data Engineering (ICDE '13)*, pp. 733–744, IEEE, Brisbane, Australia, April 2013.

[12] A. Khoshgozaran, C. Shahabi, and H. Shirani-Mehr, "Location privacy: Going beyond K-anonymity, cloaking and anonymizers," *Knowledge and Information Systems*, vol. 26, no. 3, pp. 435–465, 2011.

[13] R. Shokri, G. Theodorakopoulos, P. Papadimitratos, E. Kazemi, and J.-P. Hubaux, "Hiding in the mobile crowd: Location privacy through collaboration," *IEEE Transactions on Dependable and Secure Computing*, vol. 11, no. 3, pp. 266–279, 2014.

[14] Y. Elmehdwi, B. K. Samanthula, and W. Jiang, "Secure k-nearest neighbor query over encrypted data in outsourced environments," in *Proceedings of the 30th IEEE International Conference on Data Engineering (ICDE '14)*, pp. 664–675, Chicago, IL, USA, April 2014.

[15] H. Hu and J. Xu, "Non-exposure location anonymity," in *Proceedings of the 25th IEEE International Conference on Data Engineering, ICDE 2009*, pp. 1120–1131, Shanghai, China, April 2009.

[16] B. Gedik and L. Liu, *A Customizable k-Anonymity Model for Protecting Location Privacy*, Georgia Institute of Technology, 2004.

[17] C.-Y. Chow, M. F. Mokbel, and W. G. Aref, "Casper*: query processing for location services without compromising privacy," *ACM Transactions on Database Systems (TODS)*, vol. 34, no. 4, article 24, 2009.

[18] H. Jin and P. Papadimitratos, "Resilient privacy protection for location-based services through decentralization," in *Proceedings of the the 10th ACM Conference*, pp. 253–258, Boston, Mass, USA, July 2017.

[19] H. Jadallah and Z. Al Aghbari, "Aman: Spatial cloaking for privacy-aware location-based queries in the cloud," in *Proceedings of the International Conference on Internet of Things and Cloud Computing, ICC 2016*, New York, NY, USA, March 2016.

[20] F.-Y. Tai, J.-K. Song, Y.-C. Tsai, and H.-P. Tsai, "Cloaking sensitive patterns Td preserve location privacy for LBS applications," in *Proceedings of the 3rd IEEE International Conference on Consumer Electronics-Taiwan, ICCE-TW 2016*, Nantou, Taiwan, May 2016.

[21] X. Chen and J. Pang, "Measuring query privacy in location-based services," in *Proceedings of the the second ACM conference*, pp. 49–60, San Antonio, Tex, USA, Feburary 2012.

[22] M. Li, Z. Qin, and C. Wang, "Sensitive semantics-aware personality cloaking on road-network environment," *International Journal of Security and Its Applications*, vol. 8, no. 1, pp. 133–146, 2014.

[23] Y. Huang, Z. Huo, and X.-F. Meng, "Coprivacy: a collaborative location privacy-preserving method without cloaking region," *Chinese Journal of Computers*, vol. 34, no. 10, pp. 1976–1985, 2011.

[24] Y. Cai and G. Xu, *Cloaking with Footprints to Provide Location Privacy Protection in Location-Based Services*, U.S. Patent, 2017.

[25] C. Li and B. Palanisamy, "De-anonymizable location cloaking for privacy-controlled mobile systems," in *Proceedings of the International Conference on Network and System Security*, pp. 449–458, Springer, Cham, Switzerland.

[26] H. Kido, Y. Yanagisawa, and T. Satoh, "An anonymous communication technique using dummies for location-based services," in *Proceedings of the 2nd International Conference on Pervasive Services (ICPS '05)*, pp. 88–97, IEEE Press, Santorini, Greece, July 2005.

[27] H. Kido, Y. Yanagisawa, and T. Satoh, "Protection of location privacy using dummies for location-based services," in *Proceedings of the 21st International Conference on Data Engineering Workshops (ICDEW '05)*, p. 1248, Tokyo, Japan, April 2005.

[28] M. Guo, N. Pissinou, and S. S. Iyengar, "Pseudonym-based anonymity zone generation for mobile service with strong adversary model," in *Proceedings of the 2015 12th Annual IEEE Consumer Communications and Networking Conference, CCNC 2015*, pp. 335–340, Las Vegas, NV, USA, January 2015.

[29] B. Palanisamy and L. Liu, "Attack-resilient mix-zones over road networks: Architecture and algorithms," *IEEE Transactions on Mobile Computing*, vol. 14, no. 3, pp. 495–508, 2015.

[30] B. Niu, Z. Zhang, X. Li, and H. Li, "Privacy-area aware dummy generation algorithms for location-based services," in *Proceedings of the1st IEEE International Conference on Communications, ICC ('14)*, pp. 957–962, Sydney, Australia, June 2014.

[31] S. Papadopoulos, S. Bakiras, and D. Papadias, "Nearest neighbor search with strong location privacy," in *Proceedings of the VLDB Endowment*, pp. 619–629.

[32] K. Mouratidis and M. L. Yiu, "Shortest path computation with no information leakage," in *Proceedings of the VLDB Endowment*, pp. 692–703.

[33] Z. Liao, L. Kong, X. Wang et al., "A visual analytics approach for detecting and understanding anomalous resident behaviors in smart healthcare," *Applied Sciences (Switzerland)*, vol. 7, no. 3, article no. 254, 2017.

[34] A. Khoshgozaran and C. Shahabi, "Blind evaluation of nearest neighbor queries using space transformation to preserve location privacy," *Advances in Spatial and Temporal Databases*, pp. 239–257, 2007.

[35] R. Paulet, M. G. Kaosar, X. Yi, and E. Bertino, "Privacy-preserving and content-protecting location based queries," *IEEE Transactions on Knowledge and Data Engineering*, vol. 26, no. 5, pp. 1200–1210, 2014.

[36] R. Lu, X. Lin, Z. Shi, and J. Shao, "PLAM: A privacy-preserving framework for local-area mobile social networks," in *Proceedings of the 33rd IEEE Conference on Computer Communications, IEEE INFOCOM 2014*, pp. 763–771, Canada, May 2014.

[37] Z. Fu, X. Sun, Q. Liu, L. Zhou, and J. Shu, "Achieving efficient cloud search services: multi-keyword ranked search over encrypted cloud data supporting parallel computing," *IEICE Transactions on Communications*, vol. 98, no. 1, pp. 190–200, 2015.

[38] R. Verde, F. A. T. Carvalho, and Y. Lechevallier, *A Dynamical Clustering Algorithm for Multi-Nominal Data*, Data Analysis, Classification, and Related Methods, Springer, Berlin, Germany, 2000.

4

Constructing APT Attack Scenarios based on Intrusion Kill Chain and Fuzzy Clustering

Ru Zhang, Yanyu Huo, Jianyi Liu, and Fangyu Weng

Information Secure Center, Beijing University of Posts and Telecommunications, 10 West Tucheng Road, Haidian District, Beijing, China

Correspondence should be addressed to Ru Zhang; zhangru@bupt.edu.cn

Academic Editor: Zhenxing Qian

The APT attack on the Internet is becoming more serious, and most of intrusion detection systems can only generate alarms to some steps of APT attack and cannot identify the pattern of the APT attack. To detect APT attack, many researchers established attack models and then correlated IDS logs with the attack models. However, the accuracy of detection deeply relied on the integrity of models. In this paper, we propose a new method to construct APT attack scenarios by mining IDS security logs. These APT attack scenarios can be further used for the APT detection. First, we classify all the attack events by purpose of phase of the intrusion kill chain. Then we add the attack event dimension to fuzzy clustering, correlate IDS alarm logs with fuzzy clustering, and generate the attack sequence set. Next, we delete the bug attack sequences to clean the set. Finally, we use the nonaftereffect property of probability transfer matrix to construct attack scenarios by mining the attack sequence set. Experiments show that the proposed method can construct the APT attack scenarios by mining IDS alarm logs, and the constructed scenarios match the actual situation so that they can be used for APT attack detection.

1. Introduction

Nowadays, attacks on the network are becoming more and more complex, and, among them, APT attacks are increasingly frequent [1]. Unlike traditional attacks, APT attacks are not launched to interrupt services, but to steal intellectual property rights and sensitive data [2]. An APT attack has the stage and longevity characteristics and uncertain attack channel. Therefore, the Intrusion Detection System (hereinafter referred to as IDS) cannot detect an APT attack and can only generate alarms to certain steps in the attack. In 2012, Kabbah and Comodo companies' source codes were stolen [3]; in 2015, the OceanLotus Organization launched APT attacks on a number of essential institutions, including the Chinese government, certain research institutes, and maritime organizations in China [4]. Since then, APT attack has become a hot research topic. This paper focuses on how to correlate a large number of IDS security logs to dig out an APT attack scenario, and ultimately identifies an APT attack. Attack scenarios reflect the actual state of the network and can help defenders to take corresponding precautionary measures.

Correlating alarm logs is an important step to dig out attack scenarios. At present, researchers working on APT attack correlation built a full-scale attack model based on the phases of an APT attack and then correlated security logs with the attack model to generate the attack context. However, the establishment of APT attack model requires expert knowledge, and if the attack model is incomplete, some alarmed events will be unmatched and discarded, resulting in an incomplete attack route. In this paper, we propose a new method to solve this problem. We adopt fuzzy clustering correlation method to form clusters using multidimensional properties of alarm logs, so the correlated alarms are clustered to an APT attack route. Although each case is different, all APT attacks are phased, which conform to the feature of the intrusion kill chain model. According to this feature, we improve the fuzzy clustering algorithm by adding attack event property. We divide an APT attack process into several phases according to the intrusion kill chain model and categorize the attack events into different phases according to the characteristic of each phase, the behavior of each attack event, and the degree of harm. Then we compare the attack events of two alarms in the process of clustering, and if the attack event of latter alarm is in the subsequent attack phase relative to the attack event of previous one, then the correlation of the two alarms is stronger. The merits of taking the attack event as a cluster dimension are that it improved the correlation of alarms in an attack sequence, and there is no need to establish the attack model beforehand, and the alarm will not be lost because its event cannot match. Finally, we analyze the clustering results, combine the repeated attacks, delete the incomplete attack fragments, and then establish the probability transfer matrix to mining the attack scenario.

2. Literature Review

An APT attack is targeted, camouflaged, and phased, and it cannot be identified effectively with traditional detection technologies [5]. Friedberg et al. used the whitelist method to detect APT attacks. This method studied normal system behaviors and reported those operations different from system normal model, to find out Zero-day Threats [2]. Choi et al. used the extraction of normal behavior and anomaly patterns to detect the anomalies of APT attacks and proposed a method to detect anomalies by mining unknown anomaly patterns [6]. The APT attack model is often used in security log-based APT attack detection [7]; Tankard [8] established an APT attack model to monitor the network to discover the rules of actual attacking process. And Zhang et al. [3] constructed the attack tree model based on the intrusion kill chain and analyzed the attack logs to form the attack route to predict an APT attack. Three security researchers from Lock Martin first proposed the intrusion kill chain model on the ICIW Conference in March 2011 [9]. From the perspective of intrusion detection, this model decomposes the attacking process into 7 steps of reconnaissance, weaponization, delivery, exploitation, installation, command and control, and actions on objectives, and this model meets the phase characteristic of APT attack. APT attack detecting methods based on attacking model rely on expert knowledge predefining model. If the attack model is incomplete, attack scenario will be disrupted. If an attacker does not attack by well-defined rules and bypasses a phase in other ways, then a complete attack scenario cannot be constructed. Therefore, in this paper, fuzzy clustering is used in correlation to resolve these problems.

In the context of using fuzzy clustering to correlate alarms, the alarms are correlated to form an attack sequence by calculating the similarity between the alarms [10]. In terms of alarms correlation, most papers studied in general multistep attacks and made no adjustment according to different complex attacks. Feng et al. [11] used the correlation of the IP address in clustering, but the causation of two alarms is not just reflected in IP addresses. In this paper, we divide the attack events using the intrusion kill chain model and use multidimensional properties including the IP address, the attack event, and the time stamp in fuzzy clustering. This method resolves problems such as inability in constructing the complete attack scenario using expert knowledge, and loose coupling of clustering using single property. Finally, the attack sequences are fused by the transfer matrix, which

avoids small-frequency attack sequences being omitted when using frequently occurring item sets.

3. Mining an APT Attack Scenario

IDS alarm log is a kind of log generated when attack operations occur. It shows security situation of the entire network.

Definition 1 (alarm logs). We represent IDS alarm log as alarms = $\{a_1, a_2, a_3, \ldots, a_n\}$, where a_i indicates the ith alarm and is a six-tuple:

$$a_i = (\text{timestamp}, \text{sIP}, \text{dIP}, \text{sPort}, \text{dPort}, \text{alarm\_event}). \quad (1)$$

The meaning of each attribute is shown in Table 1.

Definition 2 (attack sequence). An attack sequence is a sequence of IDS alarms that is produced by an attacking process. We represent the attack sequence as AS = $\{a_1, a_2, a_3, \ldots, a_n\}$, where all the alarms are listed in temporal order.

Definition 3 (attack scenario). The attack scenario shows the intrusion process of many different attack actions according to a certain time and logical sequence, which can be described in the form of graphs. Therefore, it can be said that the attack scenario consists of many single attack steps, which are the attack alarm information detected by the safety device.

3.1. The Entire Process. As is shown in Figure 1, there are four steps in the entire process:

(1) Data preprocessing: the IDS alarm log is normalized to the six-tuple format as in Definition 1 after a simple elimination of false positives in the data.

(2) Attack event classification: the APT attack is divided into several phases based on the intrusion kill chain model, and the attack events are classified according to the purpose of each phase and the behaviors of each attack event.

(3) Fuzzy clustering: the similarity function of each property used in fuzzy clustering is defined so that fuzzy clustering can be conducted. The attack sequence set ASS = $\{AS_1, AS_2, \ldots, AS_q\}$ is formed after fuzzy clustering, where each attack sequence $AS_i = \langle a_1, a_2, a_3, \ldots, a_n \rangle$ represents a possible APT attacking process, where a_i is an alarm.

(4) Attack scenario mining: we analyze all attack sequences generated after fuzzy clustering and delete isolated attack sequences without subsequent data transmission. A probability transfer matrix is established using multiple attack sequences where each row and each column represents an attack event. And finally, the probability transfer matrix is converted into a probabilistic attack scenario graph that can be used to identify APT attacks in the network.

TABLE 1: The meaning of each attribute.

The attribute of an alarm	Meaning
timestamp	The time when the attack occurred
sIP	The source IP address
dIP	The destination IP address
sPort	The source port
dPort	The destination port
alarm_event	The IDS alarm event

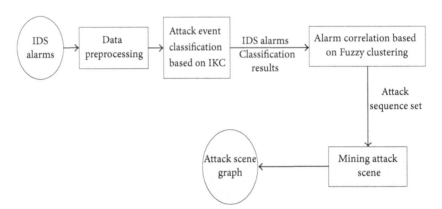

FIGURE 1: The entire process.

3.2. Attack Events Classification Based on IKC. In some papers, the intrusion kill chain (IKC) model is widely used in constructing APT attack model. The attack event is an important property of an APT attack; therefore, the attack event dimension is included in fuzzy clustering, and all the attack events in the alarm log are classified by the purpose of each phase and the behavior of the attack event in the model, to calculate the correlation between two alarms in the fuzzy clustering. The two adjacent alarmed attack events are compared in clustering. If the latter alarmed attack event is in subsequent attack phase relative to the former alarmed attack event, the correction of the two alarms is higher.

We divide an APT attack into four phases based on the IKC model. Each phase has different purpose and different behavior.

(1) Information collection phase: it is the first step of an attack, including reconnaissance and information collecting, using some technical means such as scanning, probing, and social engineering.

(2) Intrusion phase: the attacker induces the target user to click on the phishing website or to download the malicious email attachment or install a backdoor through Trojan upload or loophole exploitation, to upgrade access permission to the target host.

(3) Latent expansion phase: the attacker maintains connection to the controlled host to obtain more valuable data and get ready for expansion. The **attacker** continues penetrating in the interior by using the host with permission as a stepping stone.

(4) Information theft phase: this is the confidential information transmission phase. The data will be transferred to the attacker's server after the attack has reached the host. The transport process often uses SSL or TLS secure transport protocol to encrypt data for camouflage. In addition to obtaining information, APT attackers can disrupt the facilities in the target network and interfere with the normal operation of the system.

We analyze the behavior and hazard of each attack event and classify all attack events into a certain phase. The classification process is shown in Figure 2.

3.3. Alarm Correlation Based on Fuzzy Clustering. Fuzzy clustering analysis generally constructs fuzzy matrix according to the property of the object and determines the clustering relationship according to the degree of membership. The properties of the alarm log are nonnumericand are typically measured in the following manner.

$x_i, x_j \in A$ where A is the alarm set, and the membership function of x_i and x_j in fuzzy clustering is defined as $S(x_i, x_j) = (\sum_{k=1}^{m} \alpha_k \cdot \delta(x_{ik}, x_{jk}))/m$, where m is the number of properties for an alarm, α_k is the weight of each property, and $\delta(x_{ik}, x_{jk})$ is the similarity function for each property, generated by the nature of property.

3.3.1. The Similarity Function. We define the similarity function of properties in fuzzy clustering according to different meanings of different properties. We define the similarity function of three properties including IP address, timestamp, and attack event as follows.

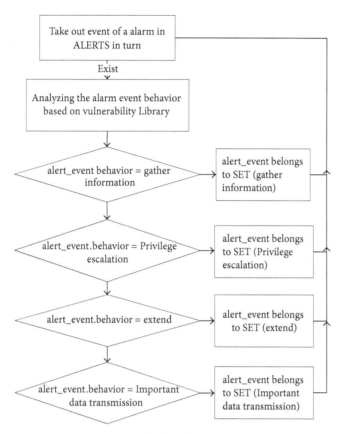

FIGURE 2: The classification process.

a_i is an original alarm, and a_j is a classified alarm using fuzzy clustering. We use similarity of a_i and a_j to measure a_i's membership of the class containing a_j, that is, $F(a_i, a_j) = \delta_k F_k(a_i, a_j)$, where δ_k is the weight of each property, and k refers to alarm event, IP address, and timestamp three properties.

(1) The Attack Event Similarity Function. In terms of the attack event dimension, the similarity function of a_i and a_j to an attack sequence is as follows:

$$F_{\text{alarm\_event}}\left(a_i, a_j\right) = \begin{cases} 1, & \Delta\alpha = 0 \text{ or } 1 \\ e^{-(\Delta\alpha-1)}, & \Delta\alpha > 1 \\ 0, & \text{else,} \end{cases} \quad (2)$$

$$\Delta\alpha = \alpha\left(a_i.\text{alarm\_event}\right) - \alpha\left(a_j.\text{alarm\_event}\right).$$

$\alpha\left(a_i.\text{alarm\_event}\right)$ indicates the phase of a_i's attack event, and $\Delta\alpha$ is the difference between the phases of the two alarms. From the attacker's point of view, the attack of subsequent phase is more complex and purposeful and has higher access permission, so if $\Delta\alpha$ equals to 0 or 1, the degree of correlation between these two attack events is higher.

(2) The IP Similarity Function

$$F_{\text{IP}}\left(a_i, a_j\right) = \frac{N}{32}, \quad (3)$$

where $N = \max\{H(a_i.\text{sIP}, a_j.\text{dIP}), H(a_i.\text{sIP}, a_j.\text{sIP}), H(a_i.\text{dIP}, a_j.\text{sIP})\}$, sIP means the source IP, dIP means the destination IP, and $H(\text{IP1}, \text{IP2})$ is maximum same digits of the two IP from the high to low in binary. If two alarms have the same source IP or the same destination IP, or IPs of two alarms are in the same network domain, the two alarms may belong to an attack. Such as, if two alarms have different sIP, but the same dIP, then the attack is launched against the same host, for example, the alarm to an attack with a fake source IP address, such as Syn_flood.

(3) The Timestamp Similarity Function. APT attackers do not tend to profit in a short time, instead, they use the "controlled host" as a stepping stone for persistent searching until a thorough grasp of the target is achieved. In an attacking process, the time interval is relatively short when two attacks are in the same phase, and the time interval may be longer when two attacks occur in different phases, and when there is a long latency following the previous access. For this reason, we do not set time window for alarm logs. The similarity function of the timestamp property is as follows:

$$F_{\text{time}}\left(a_i, a_j\right) = e^{-\Delta t}, \quad (4)$$

$$\Delta t = a_i.\text{time} - a_j.\text{time}, \text{ the unit of } \Delta t \text{ is day.}$$

The complete similarity is calculated using the following function:

$$F\left(a_i, a_j\right) = \delta_{\text{alarm}_{\text{event}}} F_{\text{alarm}_{\text{event}}}\left(a_i, a_j\right) + \delta_{\text{IP}} F_{\text{IP}}\left(a_i, a_j\right) \quad (5)$$
$$+ \delta_{\text{time}} F_{\text{time}}\left(a_i, a_j\right).$$

IDS alarm logs are in ascending order by the timestamp, and the similarity of two alarms is calculated using the complete similarity function with multidimensional properties. When the similarity is greater than the threshold value, two alarms are considered triggered by the same attack.

3.3.2. Clustering Algorithm Process

Input: alarm log ALARMS = $\{a_1, a_2, a_3, \ldots, a_n\}$, and attack sequence set ASS = Ø.

Output: attack sequence set ASS = $\{AS_1, AS_2, \ldots, AS_q\}$, where each attack sequence $AS_i = \langle a_1, a_2, a_3, \ldots, a_n \rangle$ is a set of alarms and reflects a probable APT attack.

① For each original alarm a_i, calculate its membership to each attack sequence AS_i. If the attack sequence set ASS = $\{AS_1, AS_2, \ldots, AS_q\}$ is empty, then make $AS_1 = \{a_i\}$, and repeat step ①. If ASS is not empty, then use AS_1 in the ASS set in step ②.

② Scan attack sequence $AS_i = \langle a_1, a_2, a_3, \ldots, a_k \rangle$. First determine whether the phase of the alarm event a_i is equal to or later than the phase of AS_i (the phase in which the latest timestamp in AS_i occurs). If the answer is yes, go to step ③, and if the answer is no, then go to step ④.

③ Calculate the similarity between a_i and each element in AS_i separately using the similarity function and use the maximum value of the results as a membership degree of a_i to AS_i. If the membership degree is greater than or equal to the preset threshold value λ, then add a_i to attack sequence $AS_i = \{a_1, a_2, a_3, \ldots, a_k, a_i\}$ and go to step ④.

④ Take the next AS_i in ASS, if it exists, repeat step ②; if not, it means that all the attack sequences in the ASS have been scanned. If the membership degree of a_i to every attack sequence is less than λ, then create a new element $AS_r = \{a_i\}$ and add AS_r to ASS = $\{AS_1, AS_2, \ldots, AS_q, AS_r\}$, before going to step ⑤.

⑤ Repeat step ① to step ④ above until all ALARMS are analyzed.

3.4. Mining Out the Attack Scenario. We filter attack sequence set combining purpose and phase characteristic of APT attack and delete the incomplete attack sequence of all IP addresses not involving key assets. In the process of converting an attack sequence into a directed graph, alarms with timestamps approximate to the same attack event are merged into one attack event node. This is because the attacker would use different automation tools during the attack to make continuous malicious requests, generating alarms temporally approximate to the same attack event. Finally, the multiple directed graphs are converted to an attack scenario graph

through the probability transfer matrix. The key steps of mining algorithm are shown in Figure 3.

Input: attack sequence set ASS = $\{AS_1, AS_2, \ldots, AS_n\}$ and the IP set IIP of key assets

Output: attack scenario graph

① Get a new $AS_i = \langle a_1, a_2, a_3, \ldots, a_n \rangle$ from ASS, $a_1, a_2, a_3, \ldots, a_n$ is sorted by timestamp. Determine whether the phase of the last alarm in AS_i is ahead of phase 3, and whether the length of AS_i equals 1. If one of the two conditions is met, and none of the IPs of AS_i is in IIP (key asset IP), then discard this attack sequence and repeat step ①; otherwise go to step ②.

② Convert the first alarm in AS_i to an event node that contains the alarmed attack event and scan from the second alarm, before going to step ③.

③ Take unspecified alarms in turn as a_i, and determine if its corresponding attack event is the same as the attack event of the previous alarm a_j. If the answer is yes then do not create a new node and repeat step ③, or, if the answer is no, convert a_i to a node that contains an attack event, and add a side from a_j node to a_i node. Repeat ③ until the last alarm in AS_i is processed. Then use the matrix to save the directed graph.

④ Go to step ①, if all attack sequences have been analyzed go to step ⑤.

⑤ Initialize a transfer matrix of an empty attack event, where each row and each column represents an attack event in the directed graph. Scan each directed graph, and if there is a directed side between the two attack event nodes A and B, add 1 to the value of location (A, B) in the matrix, and if a new attack event cannot be found in the matrix, add a row and a column in the transfer matrix to represent this attack event. Then each numeric in a row is converted to its proportion to the sum of all the numerical values in that row. The final matrix is expressed in the form of a directed graph.

4. Experiment Analysis

In order to prove the effectiveness of our method for mining out APT attacking scenario, we have used the IDS monitoring environment of a certain company and have simulated 10 advanced persistent attacking processes to steal data. Firstly, we use advanced transverse scan to probe an attack and exploit the vulnerabilities of the key hosts so as to increase access permission. In the process, attack tools such as Nmap, Sqlmap, and chopper are used in sending emails with malicious attachments and exploiting vulnerabilities. For example, Namp is used to scan multiple machines, and some of the vulnerable hosts are targeted with further attacks to extract permission. The entire process lasted one month, during which time IDS alarm logs were collected, and there are 1000 or so valid alarms after false positives were eliminated, some of which have similar timestamps.

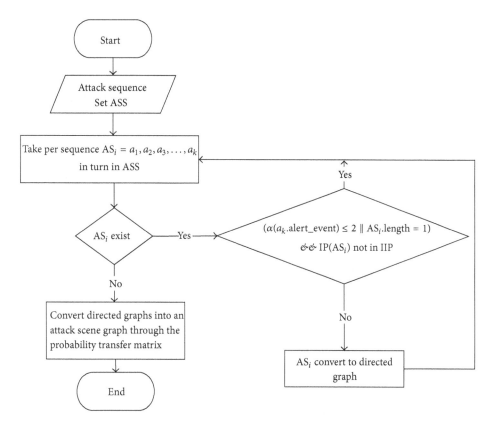

FIGURE 3: The process of mining out the attack scenario.

Different alarms to the same attack event are generated by the automated tools.

We then classify all the attack events in the experimental data into four phases of an APT attack before carrying out fuzzy clustering.

4.1. Clustering Algorithm Implementation.
Alarms are sorted by timestamp in temporal order. Each alarm is normalized to the six-tuple format as in Definition 1.

The similarity function with multidimensional properties defined in Section 3.3.1 and the clustering algorithm defined in Section 3.3.2 are then used to cluster the IDS alarms ($\lambda =$ 0.65, $\delta_{alarm\_event} = 0.4$, $\delta_{IP} = 0.4$, $\delta_{time} = 0.2$).

After clustering, 25 attack sequences are formed, some of which only have scanning and probing behaviors.

4.2. Attack Scenario Mining.
We analyze the set of attack sequences generated above and discard any attack sequence where the last alarm is generated in the first or second phase of an attack event. There were 14 relatively complete attacks. Since attackers used different network hosts to launch attacks during the APT attack, attack alarms generated in one attack-planning process were distributed into different attack sequences, resulting in incomplete attack sequences. Eight attack sequences that conformed to the planning process were found after analyses were made. The eight attack sequences were then converted to directed graphs according to the

algorithm in Section 3.4. Some directed graphs are shown in Figure 4.

The probability transfer matrix corresponding to all attack sequences is shown in Figure 5.

The probability transfer matrix is then converted into an attack scenario as shown in Figure 6.

Figure 6 shows that we can construct attack scenario by our proposed method. For an attack sequence, the attack means gradually changing from elementary to advanced, obtained permissions are getting more and more powerful, and suspicious files transmission or Trojan back door connection should happen in the end, which meet the phased characteristic of an APT attack. In order to verify the validity of the mined attack scenario, we analyze the attack scenario of an APT attack case named "Sea Lotus" detected by a certain organization. The attack event was unfolding when an intranet host user clicked the malicious mail attachment disguised as a normal file, resulting in the server's terminal virus infection and being controlled by an illegal APT organization, who then implanted the Trojan file qq.exe.bak in the folder c:\users\user\appdata\roaming\tencent, where communication was made with a hacker IP address and a small-amount data transmission was done. By analysis of the whole APT process, we find a series of events including alarms against a large number of malicious mail attachments, DNS requests from malicious domains, suspicious file transfers, and malicious domain connections. These events

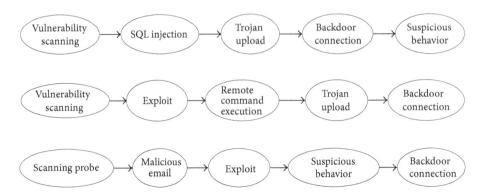

FIGURE 4: Part of the directed graph of an attack sequence.

	Scanning probe	CGI attack	Trojan upload	Exploit	Backdoor connection	Suspicious behavior	Remote command execution	Malicious email	Suspicious file directory access
Scanning probe		0.25		0.5				0.25	
CGI attack			0.33			0.67			
Trojan upload					0.5		0.2		0.3
Exploit						0.33	0.33		0.33
Backdoor connection						1			
Suspicious behavior					1				
Remote command execution			0.33						0.67
Malicious email				0.6		0.4			
Suspicious file directory access					1				

FIGURE 5: The probability transfer matrix.

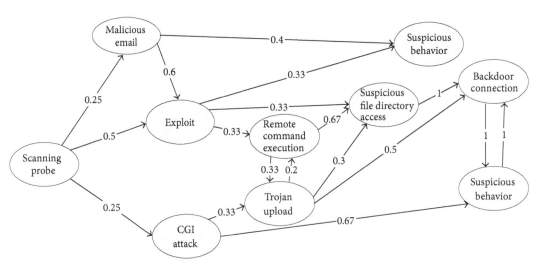

FIGURE 6: An attack scenario.

conform to the mined APT attack scenario, meaning that the attack scenario we mined reflects the true APT attack chain and is useful for the detection and defense of an APT attack.

Additionally, we use accuracy rate $R_r = N_c/N_n$ to evaluate the APT attack scenario mining method, where N_c is the effectively mined attack sequence by our mining method and N_n is the APT attack sequence that should be mined out. All the mined attack sequences include some attack sequences that do not match our attack strategy, and we delete such attack sequences, $R_r = 80\%$.

Feng et al.'s paper [11] used alert clustering based on the correlation of IP addresses to produce alarm cluster sets. We

TABLE 2: Results of clustering algorithms with different dimensions.

Clustering algorithm	Dimensions of clustering algorithm	Result
Fuzzy Clustering which includes the attack-event dimension	alarm_event, IP address, timestamp	Escalating attack mechanism, and there is higher correlation in an attack sequence
Fuzzy Clustering which exclude the attack-event dimension	IP address, timestamp	Attack events intersect, and there is small correlation in an attack sequence

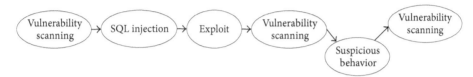

FIGURE 7: Attack sequence fragment.

use the clustering algorithm excluding the attack event dimension to process the same experimental data and do not classify attack events. We cluster with IP address and timestamp and analyze attack sequence set without considering attack events. We can get an attack sequence as shown in Figure 7.

In Figure 7, detection scanning occurs after either vulnerability exploitation or suspicious behaviors and attack events of different phases intersect. The clustering method that uses only two dimensions of the IP and the timestamp tends to correlate the attacking processes on the same asset by multiple attackers and/or certain misoperations to one attack sequence, resulting in decreased correlation between different alarms in an attack sequence. The results of clustering algorithms with different dimensions are shown in the Table 2.

By adding an extra dimension of the attack event, our proposed method can reduce the occurrence of decreased correlation. Thus, our method increases the degree of correlation between different alarms in an attack sequence, and it does not rely on any attack model built with expert knowledge.

5. Conclusion

In this paper, the attack events in an IDS log are classified based on the IKC model, the method of fuzzy clustering is used to correlate the alarm logs to produce the attack sequence set, and the nonaftereffect property of the probability transfer matrix is used to excavate the attack scenario from the attack sequence set. Based on the phased characteristic of an APT attack, in this paper, the purpose of an APT attack in each phase is analyzed and attack events are classified. In addition to the IP address and the timestamp, the use of the attack event as another key dimension in fuzzy clustering also improves the correlation degree of alarms in the same attack sequence. The effectiveness of this method has been proved by experiments. The method proposed in this paper can automatically construct attack scenario based on IDS logs and the attack scenario provides guidance for the detection and defense of APT attacks.

Acknowledgments

This work was supported by the National key Research and Development Program of China (2016YFB0800903) and the NSF of China (U1636212, U1636112).

References

[1] P. Chen, L. Desmet, and C. Huygens, "A study on advanced persistent threats," in *Communications and Multimedia Security: 15th IFIP TC 6/TC 11 International Conference, CMS 2014, Aveiro, Portugal, September 25-26, 2014. Proceedings*, vol. 8735 of *Lecture Notes in Computer Science*, pp. 63–72, Springer, Berlin, Germany, 2014.

[2] I. Friedberg, F. Skopik, G. Settanni, and R. Fiedler, "Combating advanced persistent threats: from network event correlation to incident detection," *Computers & Security*, vol. 48, no. 7, pp. 35–57, 2015.

[3] X.-S. Zhang, W.-N. Niu, G.-W. Yang et al., "Method for APT prediction based on tree structure," *Journal of University of Electronic Science and Technology of China*, vol. 45, no. 4, pp. 582–588, 2016.

[4] SkyEye: OceanLotus APT Report [2015-05-29], https://ti.360.net/static/upload/report/file/OceanLotusReport.pdf.

[5] K. Munro, "Deconstructing flame: The limitations of traditional defences," *Computer Fraud and Security*, vol. 2012, no. 10, pp. 8–11, 2012.

[6] C. Choi, J. Choi, and P. Kim, "Abnormal behavior pattern mining for unknown threat detection," *Computer Systems Science & Engineering*, vol. 32, no. 2, pp. 171–177, 2017.

[7] Y. Fu, H. LI, X.-p. Wu, and J. Wang, "Detecting APT attacks: a survey from the perspective of big data analysis," *Journal on Communications*, vol. 36, no. 11, pp. 1–14, 2015.

[8] C. Tankard, "Advanced Persistent threats and how to monitor and deter them," *Network Security*, vol. 2011, no. 8, pp. 16–19, 2011.

[9] E. M. Hutchins, M. J. Cloppert, and R. M. Amin, "Intelligence-driven computer network defense informed by analysis of adversary campaigns and intrusion kill chains," in *Proceedings of the 6th International Conference on Information Warfare and Security (ICIW '11)*, pp. 113–125, Curran Associates Inc, Washington, Wash, USA, March 2011.

[10] H.-B. Mei, J. Gong, and M.-H. Zhang, "Research on discovering multi-step attack patterns based on clustering IDS alert sequences," *Journal on Communications*, vol. 32, no. 5, pp. 63–69, 2011.

[11] X. Feng, D. Wang, M. Huang, and J. Li, "A mining approach for causal knowledge in alert correlating based on the markov property," *Jisuanji Yanjiu yu Fazhan/Computer Research and Development*, vol. 51, no. 11, pp. 2493–2504, 2014.

5

Quantum-to-the-Home: Achieving Gbits/s Secure Key Rates via Commercial Off-the-Shelf Telecommunication Equipment

Rameez Asif[1,2] and William J. Buchanan[1,2]

[1]Centre for Distributed Computing, Networks, and Security, School of Computing, Edinburgh Napier University, Edinburgh EH10 5DT, UK
[2]The Cyber Academy, Edinburgh Napier University, Edinburgh EH10 5DT, UK

Correspondence should be addressed to Rameez Asif; r.asif@napier.ac.uk

Academic Editor: Vincente Martin

There is current significant interest in Fiber-to-the-Home (FTTH) networks, that is, end-to-end optical connectivity. Currently, it may be limited due to the presence of last-mile copper wire connections. However, in near future, it is envisaged that FTTH connections will exist, and a key offering would be the possibility of optical encryption that can best be implemented using Quantum Key Distribution (QKD). However, it is very important that the QKD infrastructure is compatible with the already existing networks for a smooth transition and integration with the classical data traffic. In this paper, we report the feasibility of using off-the-shelf telecommunication components to enable high performance Continuous Variable-Quantum Key Distribution (CV-QKD) systems that can yield secure key rates in the range of 100 Mbits/s under practical operating conditions. Multilevel phase modulated signals (m-PSK) are evaluated in terms of secure key rates and transmission distances. The traditional receiver is discussed, aided by the phase noise cancellation based digital signal processing module for detecting the complex quantum signals. Furthermore, we have discussed the compatibility of multiplexers and demultiplexers for wavelength division multiplexed Quantum-to-the-Home (QTTH) network and the impact of splitting ratio is analyzed. The results are thoroughly compared with the commercially available high-cost encryption modules.

1. Introduction

The optical broadband world is taking shape and as it does so, researchers are carefully designing the networks and proposing the applications it will carry [1, 2]. Next-generation (NG) services such as cloud computing, 3D high definition television (HDTV), machine-to-machine (M2M) communication, and Internet of things (IoT) require unprecedented optical channel bandwidths. High-speed global traffic is increasing at a rate of 30–40% every year [3]. For this very reason, the M2M/IoT applications will not only benefit from fiber-optic broadband but also require it. Both M2M/IoT are using the Internet to transpose the physical world onto the networked one. Bandwidth-hungry applications are driving adoption of fiber-based last-mile connections and raising the challenge of moving access network capacity to the next level, 1–10 Gbits/s data traffic to the home, that is, Fiber-to-the-Home (FTTH)

[4]. The researchers believe that FTTH is the key to develop a sustainable future, as it is now widely acknowledged that it is the only future-proof technology, when it comes to bandwidth capacity, speed, reliability, security, and scalability.

With more and more people using IoT devices and applications, data security is the area of endeavor, concerned with safeguarding the connected devices and networks in the IoT. Encryption is the key element of data security in NG networks. It provides physical layer of protection that shields confidential information from exposure to the external attacks. The most secure and widely used methods to protect the confidentiality and integrity of data transmission are based on symmetric cryptography. Much enhanced security is delivered with a mathematically unbreakable form of encryption called a one-time pad [5], whereby data is encrypted using a truly random key/sequence of the same length as the data being encrypted. In both cases, the main

TABLE 1: Overview of recent CV-QKD demonstrations.

Sr #	Reference	Protocol	Receiver bandwidth	Repetition rate	Transmission distance	Secure key rates
(1)	J. Lodewyck et al. (2005)	Gaussian	10 MHz	1 MHz	55 km	Raw key rate up to 1 Mbits/s
(2)	Qi et al. (2007)	Gaussian	1 MHz	100 kHz	5 km	30 kbits/s
(3)	Y. Shen et al. (2010)	Four-state	100 MHz	10 MHz	50 km	46.8 kbits/s
(4)	W. Xu-Yang et al. (2013)	Four-state	N/A	500 kHz	32 km	1 kbits/s
(5)	Jouguet et al. (2013)	Gaussian	N/A	1 MHz	80.5 km	0.7 kbits/s
(6)	S. Kleis et al. (2015)	Four-state	350 MHz	40 MHz	110 km	40 kbits/s
(7)	R. Kumar et al. (2015)	Gaussian + classical	10 MHz	1 MHz	75 km	0.49 kbits/s
(8)	Huang et al. (2016)	Gaussian	5 MHz	2 MHz	100 km	500 bits/s
(9)	S. Kleis et al. (2016)	Four-state	350 MHz	50 MHz	100 km	40 kbits/s
(10)	Qu et al. (2016)	Four-state	23 GHz	20 GHz	Back-to-back	$\geq$12 Mbits/s

practical challenge is how to securely share the keys between the concerned parties, that is, Alice and Bob. Quantum Key Distribution (QKD) addresses these challenges by using quantum properties to exchange secret information, that is, cryptographic key, which can then be used to encrypt messages that are being communicated over an insecure channel.

QKD is a method used to disseminate encryption keys between two distant nodes, that is, Alice and Bob. The unconditional security of QKD is based on the intrinsic laws of quantum mechanics [6, 7]. Practically, any eavesdropper (i.e., commonly known as Eve) attempting to acquire information between Alice and Bob will disturb the quantum state of the encrypted data and thus can be detected by the bona fide users according to the noncloning theorem [8] by monitoring the disturbance in terms of quantum bit-error ratio (QBER) or excess noise. The quest for long distance and high bit-rate quantum encrypted transmission using optical fibers [9] has led researchers to investigate a range of methods [10, 11]. Two standard techniques have been implemented for encrypted transmission over standard single mode fiber (SSMF), that is, DV-QKD [12, 13] and CV-QKD [14–16]. DV-QKD protocols, such as BB84 or coherent one-way (COW) [17], involve the generation and detection of very weak optical signals, ideally at single photon level. A range of successful technologies has been implemented via DV-QKD protocol but typically these are quite different from the technologies used in classical communications [18]. CV-QKD protocols have therefore been of interest as these protocols can make use of conventional telecommunication technologies. Moreover, the secure key is randomly encoded on the quadrature of the coherent state of a light pulse [19]. Such an approach has potential advantages because of its capability of attaining high secure key rate with modest technological resources.

During the last few years, there has been growing interest in exploring CV-QKD, as listed in Table 1. The key feature of this method is the use of a classical coherent receiver that can be used for dedicated photon-counting [20]. After transmission, the quadratures of the received signals are measured using a shot-noise limited balanced coherent receiver using either the homodyne or heterodyne method. The lack of an advanced reconciliation technique at low SNR values limits

the transmission distance of CV-QKD systems to 60 km, which is lower than that for DV-QKD systems [21]. The secure key rate of CV-QKD is limited by the bandwidth of the balanced homodyne detector (BHD) and the performance of reconciliation schemes, which is degraded by the excess noise observed at high data rates [22].

In this article, we present the initial results, based on numerical analysis, to characterize and evaluate the distribution of secure data to the subscribers by implementing the Quantum-to-the-Home (QTTH) concept. We have systematically evaluated the performance of using (a) phase encoded data, that is, m-PSK (where $m = 2, 4, 8, 16, \ldots$), to generate quantum keys and (b) limits of using a high-speed BHD, in terms of electronic and shot noise for commercially available coherent receiver to detect the CV-QKD signals. Furthermore, the transceivers, noise equivalent power (NEP) contributions from analogue-to-digital converter (ADC), and transimpedance amplifier (TIA) are modeled according to the commercial off-the-shelf (COTS) equipment. Both single-channel and especially wavelength division multiplexed (WDM) transmissions are investigated. We have also implemented (a) local local oscillator (LLO) concept to avoid possible eavesdropping on the reference signal and (b) a phase noise cancellation (PNC) module for offline digital signal processing of the received signals. Moreover, we have depicted the trade-off between the secure key rates achieved and the split ratio of the access network considering the hybrid classical-quantum traffic. These detailed results will help the people from academics and industry to implement the QTTH concept in real-time networks. Furthermore, the designed system is energy efficient and cost effective.

2. Characterization of Alice and Bob for Coherent Transmission

The schematic of the proposed simplified QTTH network with m-PSK based quantum transmitter (Alice) and LLO based coherent receiver (Bob) is depicted in Figure 1. At Alice, a narrow line-width laser is used at the wavelength of 1550 nm having a line width of $\leq$5 kHz allowing it to maintain low phase noise characteristics. A pseudo-random binary sequence (PRBS) of length $2^{31} - 1$ is encoded for

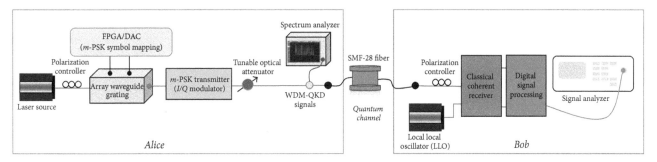

FIGURE 1: Schematic of the m-PSK based quantum transmitter (Alice) and quantum receiver (Bob) for QTTH applications.

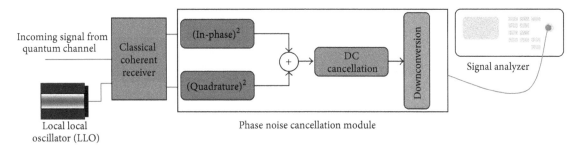

FIGURE 2: Schematic of the digital signal processing (phase noise cancellation) module for quantum receiver (Bob).

single-channel transmission and delay decorrelated copies are generated for the WDM transmission. Furthermore, we perform pulse shaping at the transmitter according to the Nyquist criterion to generate intersymbol interference (ISI) free signals. Resultant 1 Gbaud 4-PSK (four-state phase-shift keying) signal is generated after the radio-frequency (RF) signals are modulated via an electrooptical I/Q modulator, where RF frequency is kept at 2 GHz. The complete mathematical model of CV-QKD protocol is explained in "Appendix A." The modulation variance is modeled with the help of a variable optical attenuator (VOA) just before the quantum channel. We used the standard single mode fiber (SMF-28) parameters to emulate the quantum channel and losses, that is, attenuation (α) = 0.2 dB/km, dispersion (β) = 16.5 ps/nm·km, and nonlinear coefficient (γ) = $1.2 \text{ km}^{-1} \cdot \text{W}^{-1}$. As the QKD transmission occurs at a very low power level, the impact of optical Kerr effects is considered negligible. The polarization mode dispersion (PMD) is considered as $\leq 0.2 \text{ ps}/\sqrt{\text{km}}$ that enables more realistic simulations, that is, comparative to the real-world installed fiber networks.

For implementing the coherent receiver, COTS equipment has been modeled. The receiver module (Bob) consists of a 90° optical hybrid and a high optical power handling balanced photodiodes with 20 GHz bandwidth. The responsivity, gain of TIA, and noise equivalent power (NEP) of the receiver at 1550 nm are 0.8 A/W, 4 K·V/W, and 22 pW/$\sqrt{\text{Hz}}$, respectively. For our analysis, we have kept the high power, narrow line-width local oscillator at the receiver, that is, integral part of Bob in order to avoid any eavesdropping on the reference signal. That is why it is termed as local local oscillator (LLO). The LLO photon level is considered as 1×10^8

photons per pulse. A classical phase noise cancellation (PNC) based digital signal processing (DSP) is implemented to minimize the excess noise as shown in Figure 2. The PNC stage has two square operators for in-phase and quadrature operators, one addition operator, and a digital DC cancellation block assisted by a downconverter. The detailed implementation of the PNC module is explained in "Appendix B" [23]. The coherent receiver requires a specific signal-to-noise ratio (SNR) to detect the m-PSK signal.

As first step, we quantified the coherent receiver to detect the m-PSK signals as we know that specific modulation formats require a particular optical signal-to-noise ratio (OSNR) in order to be detected at bit-error rate (BER) threshold. After modulating the 4-PSK and 8-PSK signals, back-to-back signals are detected at the coherent receiver and normalized signal-to-noise ratio (E_b/N_0, the energy per bit to noise power spectral density ratio) is plotted against BER. The results are plotted in Figure 3(a). The BER threshold is set to be 3.8×10^{-3} (Q-factor of ≈ 8.6 dB), corresponding to a 7% overhead, that is, hard-decision forward error correction (HD-FEC), while soft-decision FEC (SD-FEC) level of BER 2.1×10^{-2} (Q-factor of ≈ 6.6 dB) can also be used corresponding to 20% overheard. From the results, we can depict that minimum of 10 dB and 6 dB E_b/N_0 values is required for the 8-PSK and 4-PSK signals at HD-FEC, while this limit can further be reduced to smaller values but at the cost of 20% overheard in data rates, that is, SD-FEC. We also investigated the ADC requirements to detect the m-PSK signals. The results are plotted in Figure 3(b). The ADC resolution (bits) is investigated with respect to the SNR penalty for 1 and 4 Gbaud m-PSK signals. From the results, it is clear that 6–8-bit ADC can be used to detect the m-PSK signals at different baud rates while keeping the SNR penalty ≤ 1 dB. It is worth

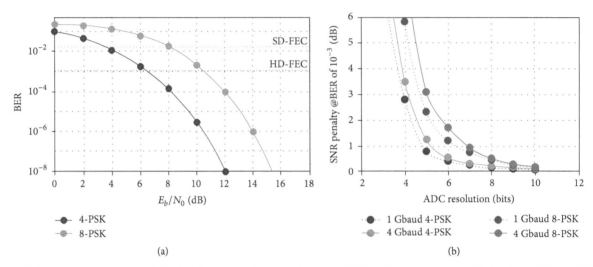

FIGURE 3: Performance comparison of classical data transmissions: (a) averaged SNR with respect to m-PSK signals at different FEC levels and (b) SNR penalty with respect to ADC resolution for different baud rates for m-PSK signals.

TABLE 2: Summary of the ADC minimum requirements to process the m-PSK signals.

Sr #	Modulation	ADC bandwidth	ADC sampling rate ($T_s/2$)
(1)	4-PSK (4 Gbaud)	4 GHz	8 GS/s
(2)	8-PSK (4 Gbaud)	4 GHz	8 GS/s
(3)	8-PSK (2.66 Gbaud)	2.66 GHz	5.33 GS/s

mentioning here that high resolution ADCs can give you better performance but on the other hand they have high electronic noise that is not beneficial for high secure key rates in terms of QTTH. We have also summarized the ADC requirements [24] in terms of ADC bandwidth and ADC sampling rate ($T_s/2$), as listed in Table 2.

3. Results and Discussions

3.1. Point-to-Point QKD Network. Since the noise equivalent power (NEP) determines electronic noise of the detection system, it is essential to select a TIA and ADC with lower NEP in order to achieve a low electronic noise to shot noise ratio (ESR). In addition, as the NEP of the TIA is amplified by the TIA itself, it dominates the total electronic noise. However, the ESR negligibly changes as the bandwidth of the detector is increased. This is because both electronic and shot-noise variances linearly increase with bandwidth, so it is beneficial to use the receivers having 1–20 GHz bandwidth. Since 20 GHz receivers are easily commercially available, we have modeled them for our analysis. Furthermore, the quantum link comprises the standard SMF and VOA to model the channel loss. Meanwhile, the variance of the excess noise is mainly due to the bias fluctuation of the I/Q modulator and timing jitter of the Bob, that is, receiver modules. It is estimated that the excess noise can be limited to be as small as 0.01 [25] below the zero key rate threshold. After optimizing the transmission model, (a) the corresponding

power is $\approx$−70 dBm [26], (b) the detector efficiency is 60%, and (c) reconciliation efficiency is 95%.

Based on the above-mentioned values, we extended our studies to calculate the secure key rates (SKR) at different transmission distances, that is, transmittance values. We have kept the input power constant for every iteration. Furthermore, SKR for both the 4-PSK and 8-PSK modulation formats under collective attack [22] are depicted in Figure 4(a). The maximum of 100 Mbits/s SKR can be achieved with this configuration by employing COTS modules for transmittance $(T) = 1$ for 4-PSK modulation, while SKR are $\approx$25 Mbits/s and 1 Mbit/s at $T = 0.8$ and 0.6, respectively. From the graph it can also be concluded that the maximum transmission range for CV-QKD based network is 60 km. Hence it is recommended that this QKD protocol can efficiently be used for access network, that is, QTTH. We have also investigated the performance of 8-PSK modulation and the results are plotted in Figure 4(a). We have seen degradation in the transmission performance as compared to 4-PSK modulation and this is due to the PNC algorithm that is implemented to process the received quantum signal. This concept of generating seamless quantum keys can further be enhanced for wavelength division multiplexed (WDM) networks that will help to generate high aggregate SKR via multiplexing the neighboring quantum channels. In this paper, we have multiplexed 12 WDM quantum channels to generate the aggregate SKR with the channel spacing of 25 and 50 GHz. The WDM-QKD results, based on 4-PSK modulation, are shown in Figure 4(b).

The results depict that the classical multiplexing techniques can efficiently be used to multiplex quantum signals without any degradation in the SKR. We have multiplexed the signals by using 25 and 50 GHz channel spacing, while aggregate secure key rate can reach up to 1.2 Gbits/s for a 12-channel WDM quantum system at $T = 1$. The importance of these results is due to the fact that next-generation PON services are already aiming at Gbits/s data rates, so QKD can match the data rates. The 50 GHz channel spaced

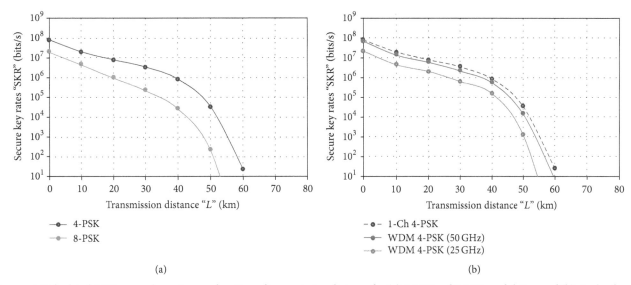

(a)   (b)

FIGURE 4: Calculated QKD secure key rates as a function of transmission distance for (a) 4-PSK and 8-PSK modulation and (b) single-channel (1-Ch) 4-PSK modulation and 12-channel WDM 4-PSK modulation with 25 and 50 GHz channel spacing. Simulations are performed by assuming 60% detector efficiency and 95% reconciliation efficiency.

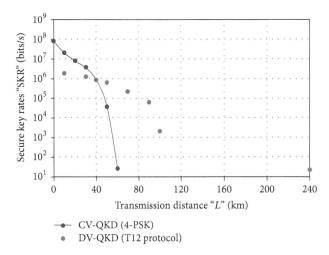

FIGURE 5: Performance comparison of CV-QKD versus DV-QKD for access and metro networks.

system shows negligible performance degradation as compared to single-channel transmission case, whereas the 25 GHz channel spaced system depicts loss in SKR due to the fact of intersymbol interference between the neighboring channels. This degradation can be easily compensated with the help of efficient raised-cosine filters for pulse shaping at the transmitter. From the results we can also infer that the quantum signals are compatible with traditional passive optical add-drop multiplexers (OADMs) but the insertion loss from add/drop modules can impact the SKR.

A comparison of distance dependent secure key generation rates between CV-QKD using 20 GHz BHD and state-of-the-art DV-QKD systems based on T12 protocol [27, 28] is shown in Figure 5. The transmission distance of CV-QKD systems, limited by the lack of advanced reconciliation techniques at lower SNR, is far lower than that

for DV-QKD demonstrations. However, comparison of DV-QKD and CV-QKD shows that CV-QKD has the potential to offer higher speed secure key transmission within an access network area (100 m to 50 km). Especially within 0–20 km range, that is, typical FTTH network, the SKR generated by using the traditional telecommunication components are 10 s of magnitude higher than those of DV systems.

3.2. QTTH Network. Most of the efforts on the QKD system design and experimental demonstrations are limited to lab environments and point-to-point transmissions, while actual FTTH networks have in-line optical devices including but not limited to routers, switches, passive splitters, add-drop multiplexers, and erbium doped fiber amplifiers (EDFA), as envisioned in Figure 6(a). This restricts the deployment of QKD networks along with the classical data channels. However, in this paper we have investigated the compatibility of optical network components and their impact on the secure key rates. We have emulated the scenario of a typical quantum access network as shown in Figure 6(b).

The optical line terminal (OLT) consists of a QKD transmitter; that is, in this paper a *m*-PSK modulated transmitter is modeled. The optical distribution comprises (a) standard single mode fiber of 5 km length and (b) passive optical splitter with different split ratios. The commercially available splitters have insertion loss that is listed in Table 3. The variable splitting ratio is vital for the secure key rates as it will contribute to the attenuation and excess noise of the system. To test the simulation model under realistic conditions we have also added 0.15 dB splicing loss for every connection with the passive optical splitter. The results are depicted in Figure 7 where we have plotted the SKR with respect to the splitting ratio of the system. It can be deduced from the graph that for a 1 × 2 splitting ratio the SKR drops down to ≈10 Mbits/s per user, while the SKR of 1 Mbits/s can be achieved with the splitting ratio of 1 × 4. Moreover,

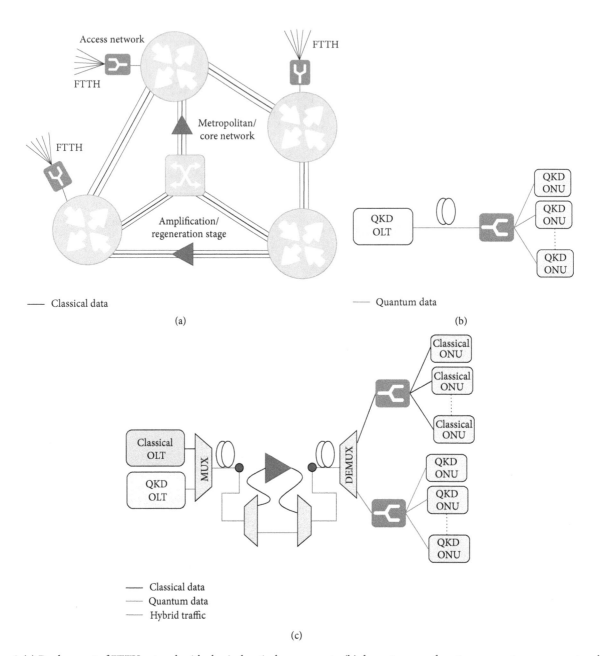

FIGURE 6: (a) Deployment of FTTH network with classical optical components, (b) downstream and upstream quantum access network, and (c) hybrid classical-quantum traffic in access networks.

the classical telecommunication components can be used to design a seamless QTTH network and for short range transmission as well as for data center applications it can perform better as compared to the much expensive DV-QKD systems [10].

3.3. Hybrid Classical-Quantum Traffic in Access Networks. For the commercial compatibility of quantum signals with the existing optical networks, the wavelength and optimum power assignment to the signals are very much important. Different wavelength assignment [29–31] techniques have been investigated to avoid possible intersymbol interference

TABLE 3: Summary of the average attenuation (dB) associated with the standard passive optical splitters.

Sr #	Split ratio	Average loss (dB)
(1)	1×2	3 dB
(2)	1×4	7.5 dB
(3)	1×8	11 dB
(4)	1×16	14.2 dB
(5)	1×32	17.8 dB
(6)	1×64	21.1 dB
(7)	1×128	23.8 dB

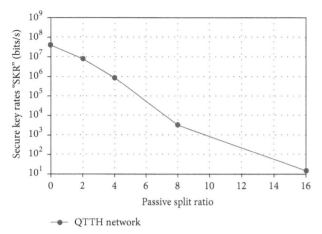

FIGURE 7: Performance comparison of QTTH network with diverse passive split ratios as a function of achieved secure key rates.

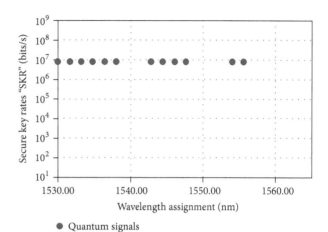

FIGURE 8: Optimum system performance and wavelength assignment for hybrid classical-quantum traffic in an access network.

between the classical and quantum signals. The best possible solution is to place the classical channels at 200 GHz channel spacing [31] in order to avoid any interference with the weakly powered quantum signals. Most importantly, we have implemented the concept of LLO; hence local oscillator signal is not generated from transmitter by using 90 : 10 coupler [18]. So, apparently with LLO and 200 GHz channel spacing, there is no cross-talk among the hybrid classical-quantum signals in the quantum channel. This is very much ideal for commercially available telecommunication components in the C-band (1530 to 1565 nm). Furthermore, with 200 GHz channel spacing the classical channels can be encoded up to 400 Gbit/s line rate with advanced modulation formats, that is, dual-polarization m-QAM ($m = 16, 32, 64, \ldots$). But most importantly, high data rate classical channels need sophisticated high bandwidth receivers that inherently have high electronics noise. Due to this reason, they are not suitable for quantum multiplexed signals as shown in Figure 6(c). As we are investigating a 20 GHz coherent receiver, we have kept the data rate at 2.5 Gbit/s/polarization of quadrature phase-shift keying (QPSK) signals for classical data. The power of the classical data channels is optimized below −15 dBm. The quantum channel loss in this analysis corresponds to the 20 km of the optical fiber. The results for quantum signals at diverse wavelengths are depicted in Figure 8. The wavelength windows that are not occupied with the quantum channels are used for classical data transmission of QPSK signals. These signals are efficiently detected below the HD-FEC level, while the SKR of the quantum signals are ≈10 Mbits/s. We can conclude from the results the compatibility of quantum signals with the classical telecommunication components. Furthermore, L-band (1565–1625 nm, extended DWDM band) can also be used to generate the hybrid classical-quantum signals as broadband lasers are readily available commercially.

4. Conclusion

To summarize, we have theoretically established a QTTH transmission model to estimate the potential of using the commercially available modules to generate the quantum keys. From the results, we can depict that CV-QKD protocol is beneficial for short range transmission distances and it is concluded that 100 Mbits/s SKR can be achieved for $T = 1$, while, for FTTH networks, 25 Mbits/s SKR can be achieved for $T = 0.8$, that is, equivalent 10 km of the optical fiber transmission. These key rates are much higher than the commercially available encrypters based on DV protocol. The CV-QKD protocol is compatible with network components like multiplexers and demultiplexers. Due to this benefit, we can multiplex several quantum signals together to transfer aggregate high SKR in the range of 1 Gbits/s. Moreover, the splitting ratio associated with the commercially available optical passive splitters influences the SKR and dramatically decreases beyond 1 × 8 splitting ratio. These results provide a solid base to enhance the existing telecommunication infrastructure and modules to deliver end-to-end optical data encryption to the subscribers.

Appendix

A. Mathematical Model for CV-QKD Signals

Alice generates random m-PSK symbols that can be optimized from pseudo-random binary sequence (PRBS) at the transmitter; that is, $I(t), Q(t) \in \{-1, +1\}$. These random symbols are upconverted to radio-frequency (RF) domain with corresponding in-phase and quadrature signals [25] that are denoted by $S_I(t)$ and $S_Q(t)$. Mathematically these two components can be expressed as in

$$S_I(t) = I(t) \cos(\omega_1 t) - Q(t) \sin(\omega_1 t),$$
$$S_Q(t) = I(t) \sin(\omega_1 t) + Q(t) \cos(\omega_1 t),$$
(A.1)

where ω_1 is the RF angular frequency. The output is then used as the input of I/Q modulator, Mach-Zehnder modulator

(MZM). The resultant optical field can be expressed as in (A.2) and further simplified as in (A.3)

$$E(t) = \left\{ \cos \left[AS_I(t) + \frac{\pi}{2} \right] + j \cos \left[AS_Q(t) + \frac{\pi}{2} \right] \right\}$$
$$\cdot \sqrt{P_s} e^{j[\omega t + \varphi_1(t)]},$$
(A.2)

$$E(t) \simeq \sqrt{2P_s} e^{j[\omega t + j\pi/4]} - A \cdot [I(t) + jQ(t)]$$
$$\cdot \sqrt{2P_s} e^{j[(\omega + \omega_1)t + \varphi_1(t)]},$$
(A.3)

where A refers to the modulation index and P_s, ω, and $\varphi_1(t)$ represent the power, angular frequency of the carrier, and phase noise. For evaluating the modulation variance V_A of the optical signal, expressed as shot-noise units (SNUs), the parameter A and variable optical attenuator (VOA) are modeled. To further simply the mathematical model, the quantum channel loss is expressed as the attenuation of the optical fiber. Moreover, channel introduced noise variance is expressed as in

$$\chi_{\text{line}} = \frac{1}{T} + \epsilon - 1,$$
(A.4)

where T is the transmittance (relation between transmission length and attenuation, i.e., $T = 1$ for back-to-back and $T = 0.2$ for 80 km fiber transmission) and ϵ is the excess noise. Practically, possible excess noise contributions, expressed as SNUs [18, 32], may come from the imperfect modulation, laser phase noise, laser line width, local oscillator fluctuations, and coherent detector imbalance [33].

In this paper, we have used the concept of a local local oscillator (LLO). It is a very vital configuration to keep the laser at the receiver, that is, Bob's side, in order to prevent any eavesdropping attempt on the quantum channel to get the reference information of the incoming signal. The electric field of the LLO can be expressed as in

$$E_{\text{LLO}}(t) = \sqrt{P_{\text{LLO}}} e^{j[\omega_{\text{LLO}} t + \varphi_2(t)]},$$
(A.5)

where P_{LLO}, ω_{LLO}, and $\varphi_2(t)$ represent the power, angular frequency, and phase noise of the LLO, respectively. The structure of the Bob comprises a 90° optical hybrid and two balanced photodetectors. The coherent receiver has an overall efficiency of η and electrical noise of V_{el}. Practically, V_{el} comprises electrical noise from transimpedance amplifiers (TIA) as well as contribution from the analogue-to-digital converters (ADCs). The receiver added noise variance can be expressed as in

$$\chi_{\text{det}} = \frac{(2 + 2V_{\text{el}} - \eta)}{\eta}.$$
(A.6)

Furthermore, the total noise variance of the system, including Alice and Bob, can be expressed as in

$$\chi_{\text{system}} = \frac{\chi_{\text{line}} + \chi_{\text{det}}}{T}.$$
(A.7)

B. Digital Signal Processing (DSP) Module

Conventionally, in order to detect the weakly powered incoming quantum signals, a high power local oscillator is required. It is very important to select the local oscillator with narrow line width, so that the laser fluctuations cannot contribute to the system excess noise. Furthermore, it will help the coherent receiver to have a low complex digital signal processing (DSP) module, that is, phase noise cancellation (PNC) algorithm. As a prerequisite for PNC module, the photocurrents of the in-phase and quadrature signals, after the balanced photodetectors, have to be measured accurately. Mathematically, they can be expressed as in

$$i_I(t)$$
$$\propto \sqrt{2} \cos \left[(\omega - \omega_{\text{LO}})t + \varphi_1(t) - \varphi_2(t) + \frac{\pi}{4} \right]$$
$$- AI(t) \cos \left[(\omega + \omega_1 - \omega_{\text{LO}})t + \varphi_1(t) - \varphi_2(t) \right]$$
$$+ AI(Q) \cos \left[(\omega + \omega_1 - \omega_{\text{LO}})t + \varphi_1(t) - \varphi_2(t) \right]$$
$$+ n_I,$$
(B.1)

$$i_Q(t)$$
$$\propto \sqrt{2} \sin \left[(\omega - \omega_{\text{LO}})t + \varphi_1(t) - \varphi_2(t) + \frac{\pi}{4} \right]$$
$$- AI(t) \cos \left[(\omega + \omega_1 - \omega_{\text{LO}})t + \varphi_1(t) - \varphi_2(t) \right]$$
$$+ AI(Q) \cos \left[(\omega + \omega_1 - \omega_{\text{LO}})t + \varphi_1(t) - \varphi_2(t) \right]$$
$$+ n_Q,$$

where n_I and n_Q define the in-phase and quadrature components of the additive phase noise that needs to be compensated. We have implemented the phase noise cancellation (PNC) algorithm [25]. By combining the squares of the in-phase and quadrature component of photocurrents, as in (B.1), that is, $i_I^2(t) + i_Q^2(t)$, and cancelling the DC component, the final result can be expressed as in

$$i_S(t) \propto 2\sqrt{2} AI(t) \cos \left(\omega_1 t - \frac{\pi}{4} \right) + 2\sqrt{2} AQ(t)$$
$$\cdot \cos \left(\omega_1 t - \frac{\pi}{4} \right) + 2\sqrt{2} \left\{ n_I \right.$$
$$\cdot \cos \left[(\omega - \omega_{\text{LO}})t + \varphi_1(t) - \varphi_2(t) + \frac{\pi}{4} \right] n_Q$$
$$\cdot \sin \left[(\omega - \omega_{\text{LO}})t + \varphi_1(t) - \varphi_2(t) + \frac{\pi}{4} \right] \right\}.$$
(B.2)

The final step in the DSP module is to downconvert the RF signal. The resultant in-phase and quadrature components can be expressed as in

$$r_I = \text{LPF} \left[i_S(t) \cos \left(\omega_1 t - \frac{\pi}{4} \right) \right] = -\sqrt{2} AI + n_I',$$
$$r_Q = \text{LPF} \left[i_S(t) \sin \left(\omega_1 t - \frac{\pi}{4} \right) \right] = -\sqrt{2} AQ + n_Q',$$
(B.3)

where n'_I and n'_Q are the equivalent additive noise that is added during the transmission and detection processes prior to DSP module. By considering (B.3), it is concluded that the original m-PSK signals can be detected without any frequency and phase distortions.

Acknowledgments

The authors would like to acknowledge the project research support from Edinburgh Napier University, UK, for Project STRENGTH (Scalable, Tuneable, Resilient and Encrypted Next Generation Transmission Hub).

References

[1] R. Asif, "Advanced and flexible multi-carrier receiver architecture for high-count multi-core fiber based space division multiplexed applications," *Scientific Reports*, vol. 6, Article ID 27465, 2016.

[2] Y. Ding, V. Kamchevska, K. Dalgaard et al., "Reconfigurable SDM switching using novel silicon photonic integrated circuit," *Scientific Reports*, vol. 6, Article ID 39058, 2016.

[3] C. Lam, H. Liu, B. Koley, X. Zhao, V. Kamalov, and V. Gill, "Fiber optic communication technologies: what's needed for datacenter network operations," *IEEE Communications Magazine*, vol. 48, no. 7, pp. 32–39, 2010.

[4] C. F. Lam, "Fiber to the home: getting beyond 10 Gb/s," *Optics and Photonics News*, vol. 27, no. 3, pp. 22–29, 2016.

[5] R. Horstmeyer, B. Judkewitz, I. M. Vellekoop, S. Assawaworrarit, and C. Yang, "Physical key-protected one-time pad," *Scientific Reports*, vol. 3, Article ID 03543, 2013.

[6] N. Gisin, G. Ribordy, W. Tittel, and H. Zbinden, "Quantum cryptography," *Reviews of Modern Physics*, vol. 74, no. 1, pp. 145–195, 2002.

[7] H.-K. Lo, M. Curty, and K. Tamaki, "Secure quantum key distribution," *Nature Photonics*, vol. 8, no. 8, pp. 595–604, 2014.

[8] W. K. Wootters and W. H. Zurek, "A single quantum cannot be cloned," *Nature*, vol. 299, no. 5886, pp. 802-803, 1982.

[9] B. Fröhlich, M. Lucamarini, J. F. Dynes et al., "Long-distance quantum key distribution secure against coherent attacks," *Optica*, vol. 4, no. 1, p. 163, 2017.

[10] B. Fröhlich, J. F. Dynes, M. Lucamarini et al., "Quantum secured gigabit optical access networks," *Scientific Reports*, vol. 5, Article ID 18121, 2015.

[11] L. C. Comandar, M. Lucamarini, B. Fröhlich et al., "Quantum key distribution without detector vulnerabilities using optically seeded lasers," *Nature Photonics*, vol. 10, no. 5, pp. 312–315, 2016.

[12] X. Ma, B. Qi, Y. Zhao, and H.-K. Lo, "Practical decoy state for quantum key distribution," *Physical Review A - Atomic, Molecular, and Optical Physics*, vol. 72, no. 1, Article ID 012326, 2005.

[13] Y. Zhao, B. Qi, X. Ma, H.-K. Lo, and L. Qian, "Experimental quantum key distribution with decoy states," *Physical Review Letters*, vol. 96, no. 7, Article ID 070502, 2006.

[14] D. B. S. Soh, C. Brif, P. J. Coles et al., "Self-referenced continuous-variable quantum key distribution protocol," *Physical Review X*, vol. 5, no. 4, Article ID 041010, 2015.

[15] P. Jouguet, S. Kunz-Jacques, A. Leverrier, P. Grangier, and E. Diamanti, "Experimental demonstration of long-distance continuous-variable quantum key distribution," *Nature Photonics*, vol. 7, no. 5, pp. 378–381, 2013.

[16] D. Huang, P. Huang, H. Li, T. Wang, Y. Zhou, and G. Zeng, "Field demonstration of a continuous-variable quantum key distribution network," *Optics Letters*, vol. 41, no. 15, pp. 3511–3514, 2016.

[17] D. Stucki, C. Barreiro, S. Fasel et al., "Continuous high speed coherent one-way quantum key distribution," *Optics Express*, vol. 17, no. 16, pp. 13326–13334, 2009.

[18] B. Qi, L.-L. Huang, L. Qian, and H.-K. Lo, "Experimental study on the Gaussian-modulated coherent-state quantum key distribution over standard telecommunication fibers," *Physical Review A - Atomic, Molecular, and Optical Physics*, vol. 76, no. 5, Article ID 052323, 2007.

[19] I. Derkach, V. C. Usenko, and R. Filip, "Preventing side-channel effects in continuous-variable quantum key distribution," *Physical Review A - Atomic, Molecular, and Optical Physics*, vol. 93, no. 3, Article ID 032309, 2016.

[20] Y. Painchaud, M. Poulin, M. Morin, and M. Têtu, "Performance of balanced detection in a coherent receiver," *Optics Express*, vol. 17, no. 5, pp. 3659–3672, 2009.

[21] A. Leverrier, R. Alléaume, J. Boutros, G. Zémor, and P. Grangier, "Multidimensional reconciliation for a continuous-variable quantum key distribution," *Physical Review A - Atomic, Molecular, and Optical Physics*, vol. 77, no. 4, Article ID 042325, 2008.

[22] Y.-M. Chi, B. Qi, W. Zhu et al., "A balanced homodyne detector for high-rate Gaussian-modulated coherent-state quantum key distribution," *New Journal of Physics*, vol. 13, no. 1, Article ID 013003, 2011.

[23] R. Asif and W. J. Buchanan, "Seamless cryptographic key generation via off-the-shelf telecommunication components for end-to-end data encryption," in *Proceeding of the 10th IEEE International Conference on Internet of Things (iThings) '17*, Paper ID SITN–2, June 2017.

[24] C.-Y. Lin, R. Asif, M. Holtmannspoetter, and B. Schmauss, "Nonlinear mitigation using carrier phase estimation and digital backward propagation in coherent QAM transmission," *Optics Express*, vol. 20, no. 26, pp. B405–B412, 2012.

[25] Z. Qu, I. B. Djordjevic, and M. A. Neifeld, "RF-subcarrier-assisted four-state continuous-variable QKD based on coherent detection," *Optics Letters*, vol. 41, no. 23, pp. 5507–5510, 2016.

[26] A. Karlsson, M. Bourennane, G. Ribordy et al., "Single-photon counter for long-haul telecom," *IEEE Circuits and Devices Magazine*, vol. 15, no. 6, pp. 34–40, 1999.

[27] L. C. Comandar, B. Fröhlich, M. Lucamarini et al., "Room temperature single-photon detectors for high bit rate quantum key distribution," *Applied Physics Letters*, vol. 104, no. 2, Article ID 021101, 2014.

[28] B. Korzh, C. C. W. Lim, R. Houlmann et al., "Provably secure and practical quantum key distribution over 307km of optical fibre," *Nature Photonics*, vol. 9, no. 3, pp. 163–168, 2015.

[29] R. Asif, F. Ye, and T. Morioka, "λ-selection strategy in C+L band 1-Pbit/s (448 WDM/19-core/128 Gbit/s/channel) flex-grid space division multiplexed transmission," in *Proceedings of the European Conference on Networks and Communications, EuCNC 2015*, pp. 321–324, fra, July 2015.

[30] M. Razavi, "Multiple-access quantum key distribution networks," *IEEE Transactions on Communications*, vol. 60, no. 10, pp. 3071–3079, 2012.

[31] S. Bahrani, M. Razavi, and J. A. Salehi, "Optimal wavelength allocation in hybrid quantum-classical networks," in *Proceedings of the 24th European Signal Processing Conference, EUSIPCO 2016*, pp. 483–487, hun, September 2016.

[32] S. Fossier, E. Diamanti, T. Debuisschert, A. Villing, R. Tualle-Brouri, and P. Grangier, "Field test of a continuous-variable quantum key distribution prototype," *New Journal of Physics*, vol. 11, no. 4, Article ID 045023, 2009.

[33] D. Huang, D. Lin, C. Wang et al., "Continuous-variable quantum key distribution with 1 Mbps secure key rate," *Optics Express*, vol. 23, no. 13, Article ID 017511, pp. 17511–17519, 2015.

6

Predictive Abuse Detection for a PLC Smart Lighting Network based on Automatically Created Models of Exponential Smoothing

Tomasz Andrysiak, Łukasz Saganowski, and Piotr Kiedrowski

Institute of Telecommunications and Computer Science, Faculty of Telecommunications, Computer Science and Electrical Engineering, University of Technology and Life Sciences in Bydgoszcz (UTP), Ul. Kaliskiego 7, 85-789 Bydgoszcz, Poland

Correspondence should be addressed to Tomasz Andrysiak; andrys@utp.edu.pl

Academic Editor: Steffen Wendzel

One of the basic elements of a Smart City is the urban infrastructure management system, in particular, systems of intelligent street lighting control. However, for their reliable operation, they require special care for the safety of their critical communication infrastructure. This article presents solutions for the detection of different kinds of abuses in network traffic of Smart Lighting infrastructure, realized by Power Line Communication technology. Both the structure of the examined Smart Lighting network and its elements are described. The article discusses the key security problems which have a direct impact on the correct performance of the Smart Lighting critical infrastructure. In order to detect an anomaly/attack, we proposed the usage of a statistical model to obtain forecasting intervals. Then, we calculated the value of the differences between the forecast in the estimated traffic model and its real variability so as to detect abnormal behavior (which may be symptomatic of an abuse attempt). Due to the possibility of appearance of significant fluctuations in the real network traffic, we proposed a procedure of statistical models update which is based on the criterion of interquartile spacing. The results obtained during the experiments confirmed the effectiveness of the presented misuse detection method.

1. Introduction

In the last decade, digital technologies started to cover cities, creating a skeleton of immense intelligent infrastructure based on information and communication technologies (ITC). The aim of building such a ubiquitous system is to create Smart Cities (SC), which have the ability to manage their resources in a better way to enhance the quality of life and safety of their citizens.

One of the key elements of a Smart City is a system of management, monitoring, and smart steering of street lights. This system allows for optimal use of the lighting infrastructure and facilitates reduction of lighting operating costs. It mostly involves prolonged operation of light sources and, as a result, a less often need to exchange them, which is costly. A decrease in the consumption of electric energy also causes limitation of CO_2 emission. Data presented in

[1, 2] show that, in the recent decade, approximately 20 per cent of the received electricity is consumed by lighting, where the biggest share concerns roads and streets. Reduction of energy consumption thanks to the use of energy-saving light sources and introduction of Smart Lighting (SL) is performed in numerous ways, of which the most important are (i) reduction of the intensity of light in a given time and space, (ii) switching on and off the lamps precisely in time, and (iii) taking into account the variable capacity of light sources in long-term operation. Utilization of such type of activities ensures optimization of light management costs and limits the electricity consumption costs even up to 40 per cent.

Usually, the Smart Lighting system is an extension of already existing traditional lighting systems. Its implementation is based on installing controllers/drivers in every lamp. The controllers communicate with the steering server via an existing energetic network with the use of LonWorks protocol

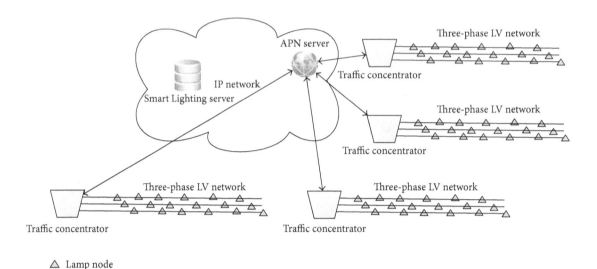

△ Lamp node

FIGURE 1: Smart Lighting critical infrastructure.

and Power Line Communication (PLC) technology. The steering server safely communicates through a data transmission network with a central management and control system. The central management system facilitates full control over all of the supervised lamps. This allows for configuration of parameters such as scenarios of switching on/off the lamps and time for initiation of the energy-saving function. It also supplies us with information concerning the current performance of the infrastructure, and it reports failures and provides data about lamps which work defectively [3].

In Figure 1, we can see the general block scheme of a Smart Lighting Communication Network (SLCN). The network consists of lamp nodes (yellow triangles) connected by three-phase low-voltage (LV) power mains by means of PLC modems. Traffic from the lamp nodes is received by a traffic concentrator (TC). The traffic concentrator also plays a role of a gateway between the PLC network and the Internet Protocol (IP) network. The Access Point Name Server (APN) allows us to make a connection by means of packet communication (e.g., Long-Term Evolution (LTE)) to the PLC lighting network.

Smart Lighting systems can be classified in two ways. The first way treats them as a subset of Smart City systems, which are further understood as a subset called the Internet of Things. Such classification does not include the whole area of SL application (e.g., it does not contain Road Lighting systems, which in fact are identical to the street lighting systems in terms of communication solutions). Therefore, the authors believe that a better way of classification is to define the Smart Lighting as a part of the Smart Grid (SG) system. This is a result of the fact that the Smart Lighting communication systems, next to Smart Metering (SM), are the biggest communication systems in Smart Grid when it comes to the number of nodes and the size of the geographic area where they operate. The second key similarity is the technologies used in the fields of the last-mile area of those communication systems. In SL, four technologies are applied, namely, PLC, Radio Frequency (RF), General Packet Radio

Service (GPRS), and Meter-Bus (M-BUS), while in Smart Metering there are only two: PLC and RF. As far as RF technologies are concerned, in Smart Lighting and Smart Metering, the used solutions are identical. However, in case of PLC, the differences are significant, of which the most important are the following: (i) in terms of SM, the standard PLC interfaces are applied [4], while in case of SL they are not (the existing Digital Addressable Lighting Interface (DALI) [5] has only local use, e.g., steering a few lamps located on the same pole, not to control hundreds of lamps in a lighting course/string); (ii) the SM devices must communicate in Band A according to CENELEC [6], and SL devices must communicate in Band A if the system's operator is an energy supplier, or in Band B, C, or D if it is the receiver of energy; (iii) there is a requirement to encrypt the transmitted information in case of SM, while for SL there is no such obligation.

Even though, on the market, there are PLC chips equipped with encryption modules (mostly AES-128), this function is seldom used. There are numerous reasons for this fact, for instance, (i) bothersome distribution of encryption keys, (ii) extending the transmission frames and thus improving the unreliability and transmission time, and (iii) finally the cost of implementation.

Actions connected with violating the safety rules in Smart Lighting Communication Networks (especially in the last-mile area) may be deliberate or unaware. Unaware interference usually happens when the LV network powers both streets and households, in which there are connected loads that do not meet the standards of electromagnetic compatibility. On the other hand, the deliberate interference in a communication system consists in intentional switching into not only loads not being able to fulfil the norms, but also elements such as capacitors, interfering generators, or terminals emulating a hub. Switching such devices even into the LV networks dedicated only to lighting is not difficult; therefore, an intruder may use them imperceptibly for a longer period of time.

There are different reasons why the smart lights operator needs anomaly and intrusion detection for the PLC smart lights network. In case of attacks, the smart light operator is responsible for proper operation of the PLC smart lights network. The smart lights network operator is also responsible to the customer in case of improper network operation and may be exposed to penalties. Intentional and unintentional damage cause additional costs to the operator when the attacker changes smart lights to ones instantly on with maximum luminosity. Reaction on anomalies in the smart lights network is also important for public transport safety (especially in intersections) when the attacker might switch off entire segments of the PLC smart lights network. Switching lights off may also be responsible for decreasing public safety in areas where smart lights are off by an attacker. Due to similar reasons, energy suppliers use anomaly and intrusion detection systems in Smart Grid networks especially for detecting energy thefts. Energy operators detect abuses in, for example, WSN (Wireless Sensor Network) smart meter infrastructures [7].

In our system, we propose a solution concerning detection of different types of abuses in the network traffic for the SL infrastructure, which is based on automatically created models of exponential smoothing. To detect abnormal behavior that may be a symptom of possible malpractice, we counted the values of variance between the forecast in the estimated model of traffic and its real variability. In the abovementioned process, we used a two-step method of abuse detection. In the first step of the proposed solution, we identified and then eliminated outliers using the criterion based on Mahalanobis's distance. In the second step, however, we estimated proper statistical models smoothed exponentially for the analyzed network traffic parameters. As a result, the respective operations presented differences in the tested SLCN parameters, which point at possible occurrence of malpractice.

The article is organized as follows. After the Introduction, Section 2 describes the communication protocol used in the last-mile testbed network. Next, Section 3 presents related work on existing abuse detection solutions for Smart Lighting Communications Networks. Section 4 focuses on the main security risks related to the PLC network. Section 5 presents the structure and operation of the proposed solution. In Section 6, a real-life experimental setup and experimental results are presented and discussed. Finally, Section 7 concludes our work.

2. Communication Protocol Used in the Considered Solution

A communication protocol in last-mile Smart Lighting networks was proposed in 2010 and published in 2011 in [8] as EGQF protocol (Energy Greedy Quasi-Flooding) by one of the coauthors. In the same year, this protocol was implemented in Smart Metering networks, which used a low-power RF technology for communication. The EGQF protocol is independent of communication media types and may be applied in networks using RF, PLC, or even RF/PLC hybrid technologies. This protocol is dedicated to tiny communication nodes based on short distance devices connected to shared communication mediums. It uses the multihop technique for transmission range extension and also uses the multipath technique to improve reliability of data transfer. The multipath scheme is useful for delivering data in unreliable environments, such as PLC. The retransmission mechanism is used only by the destination node, without any extra RAM memory occupation, because the RESPONSE packet is already kept in the transmission buffer of a transceiver. The decision to launch the retransmission is as follows: after sending the RESPONSE, the destination node starts a retransmission timer. After the timer expires, the destination node sends RESPONSE again and stops the timer. This timer can also be stopped if a copy of RESPONSE or ACK/Cancel is received during the period of the timer's operation. The number of retransmissions is reduced by a protocol parameter, RC (Retransmission Counter). In our experiments, RC was set to 1. The architecture of the presented network is very simple because it can operate with only two types of nodes, that is, a traffic concentrator and a terminal (a lamp). All the traffic is forced and coordinated by the traffic concentrator. Due to the lack of memory, terminals do not know the network topology and even do not know the addresses of neighboring nodes.

The EGQF protocol uses a small set of packet types, that is, command packets, response packets, and ACK/Cancel packets. Command packets, in most cases, are used by the traffic concentrator for controlling or querying the lamp or the pole. The answer or acknowledgement from the lamp is transported over the response packet. The ACK/Cancel packet is a packet which acts as the low layer ACK for the destination node and as the relaying process canceler for the other nodes. The ACK/Cancel packet is sent only by the traffic concentrator to confirm the reception of the response and to cancel the flooding process of response, or even command copies. The relaying process in nodes, which are neither destination nor source nodes, depends on transmitting the copy of the packet after the sum of constant short time (60 ms) and random time in the condition of an undetected carrier. The difference between the typical flooding protocol and the EGQF protocol is that while using a typical flooding protocol, the nodes always send a copy of the packet once, whereas while using the EGQF protocol, copies are sent as often as needed, for instance, once, twice, or never. The decision of whether a copy of the packet should be sent is made when the transfer discriminator value of the packet is greater than the previously stored one. The initial (or set at the end of the process) transfer discriminator value is zero. The transfer discriminator consists of two fields organized in the following order: the packet type code and the time-to-live (TTL) counter. The TTL occupied three least significant bits of the control field of the packet, while the packet type code occupied two more significant bits in the same field. Commands are coded as 00, responses as 01, and ACK/Cancel as 11, so that the transfer process of the command packet is always canceled after receiving a response packet. This is the same as response packet propagation after receiving ACK/Cancel. The above cases show us a situation where the relaying process was canceled, which is a difference with regard to the typical flooding protocol. The solution adopted in EGQF reduces the risk of collision. Using the same schema, it is possible to send a copy of the same packet type more than once. Such situation occurs when, after sending the copy of the packet, the same packet is received again with a greater value of TTL than the already copied packet. This situation occurs very seldom (e.g., when a packet with a greater number of hops comes earlier than a packet with a smaller number of hops), and it increases reliability [9].

3. Related Work

Every administrator of a Smart Lightning network or a safety specialist would like to be timely informed about any nontypical behaviors in the infrastructure that he is in control of (whether they are connected to attacks, abuses, or improper performance of devices or applications) [10]. The most important issue is to aim for the detection of new threats and such hazards that would break through the traditional defense mechanisms. One of the possible solutions is the use of systems based on Network Behavior Anomaly Detection (NBAD) [11]. These solutions do not utilize knowledge about the attacks'/abuses' signatures [12] but they are based on behavioral analysis [13]. Such an approach allows for the detection of numerous threats, which "manifest" their presence with nontypical behaviors in the network [14].

Generally, NBAD systems use statistical profiles or behavioral models to detect potential threats/anomalies. Most often, the model approaches are autoregressive ones, for example, AutoRegressive Moving Average (ARMA) or AutoRegressive Fractional Integrated Moving Average (AFIMA) [15], or mixed models composed of autoregressive and exponential smoothing ones [16] (combined to improve the forecasting process). There can also be found solutions applied to anomaly detection in the network traffic, which are based only on traditional, exponential smoothing models [17]. However, all those approaches do not use the processes of optimization to find defined exponential smoothing models, best matching the input data. In the subject literature, there can also be found other works (theoretical ones in particular), that is, Gardner [39, 40], Ord and Lowe [20], or Archibald [41], describing procedures of automatic prediction of future time series' values, based though on defined exponential smoothing models. In the solution proposed by us, we use a mathematical methodology presented by Hyndman [38, 43] which depends on seeking an optimal model (in the process of nonlinear optimization) and automatic procedure of prediction to find the future values of the analyzed time series. Then, detection of anomalies consists in comparing the variability of the real, time series' values with the estimated model of that traffic. Such a solution has not been yet used for anomaly/abuse detection in the Smart Lightning network traffic.

However, exhaustive description of methods and techniques of detection of anomalies and/or outlier observations can be found in review articles [14, 24]. They describe diverse approaches to anomaly detection, starting with machine learning methods, through data mining and information theory, and finishing on spectral solutions. Nevertheless, analysis of those solutions should be conveyed in close connection with their application.

Extensive research has been conducted on security in Smart Grids; most of them are done for anomaly detection in backbone networks and/or all areas of networks based on TCP/IP or UDP/IP protocol stack [25]. Not only does anomaly detection in LV network concern Smart mMtering systems, but also data transmitted over the LV network must be encrypted. In Smart Lighting systems, there are no security requirements for the transmitted data. Most works focus on data transfer reliability [26] in Smart Lighting last-mile communication networks, which is realized by using two independent technologies, for instance, PLC and wireless. In this work, the authors proposed a decentralized method of anomaly detection, similar to the one in [27], but the difference is that our method is proposed for Smart Lighting systems, not for Smart Metering.

In spite of that, we did not find anomaly/attack detection publications for Smart Lighting PLC based networks; there are different methods of anomaly detection used in Wireless Sensor Networks (WSN) or Smart Metering networks. In general, the anomaly detection methods used so far for sensor networks (especially for WSN) were divided into [18, 19] statistical methods (e.g., statistical chi-square test, kernel density estimator), signal processing methods (e.g., based on frequency analysis like Discrete Wavelet Transformation (DWT)), data mining (e.g., clustering methods like K-means, Support Vector Machines (SVM)), computational intelligence (e.g., Self-Organizing Maps (SOM)), rule-based methods, graph based methods (e.g., tree construction), and hybrid methods [18, 19, 21]. Part of the anomaly/attack detection methods work in lower protocol layers (e.g., data link layer or network layer) while others are focused on the application layer (especially for the Advanced Metering Infrastructure (AMI) used by energy operators).

4. Security Risks in PLC Smart Lighting Communication Networks

In Smart Cities, security of critical infrastructures is essential for providing confidentiality, accessibility, integrity, and stability of the transmitted data. The use of advanced digital technologies (ITC), which connect more and more complicated urban infrastructures, is risky because there may appear different types of abuses which may hamper or completely disenable proper functioning of a Smart City. Undoubtedly, one of the biggest frailties of a Smart City is the Smart Lighting system when taking into account the size of the area where it functions, potentially big number of the system's devices, and the generated operational costs. Therefore, providing a proper level of security and protection becomes a crucial element of the SLCN solutions [28].

The task of a Smart Lighting system is not only to light the streets. Depending on the kind of pavement, it must control the brightness of the lighting, its dimming, homogeneity, and reflectivity, providing drivers and pedestrians with maximum safe visibility. Therefore, lighting installations with luminaires, which are used as light sources, must be easily controllable. Such controlling may include whole groups or even individual lamps, which may be turned on or off according to a specified schedule or dimmed up to any degree at specified times, and the state of individual devices must be easy to control. In comparison to a traditional autonomic lighting system, Smart Lighting solutions are characterized by much bigger functionality and flexibility; however, due to their intelligent nature, they may be liable to different types of abuses (attacks). Such actions may be realized by both the sole receiver of the service and intruders wanting to enforce a specific state of infrastructure [29].

The receiver most often causes destructive actions to the SLCN, which interfere with the transmission of control signals (by active or passive influence) to achieve a change in period and/or intensity of the light. Increasing the intensity of lighting in front of the receiver's property allows for switching off the light on his land, which may result in significant economic benefits. However, a much bigger problem seems to be protection against intended attacks. There are numerous reasons for performing such attacks, the main one being to disturb the controlling system in order to set a different value of lighting than the one established by the operator. Switching off the light or reduction of its intensity in some area may facilitate criminal proceedings. Another reason is malicious activity consisting in hindering the lives of neighbors or local authorities by forcing a change in the schedule of lighting (e.g., switching off the light at night or turning it on during the day). However, a much more serious challenge seems to be protection against attacks realized for criminal purposes. Then, every potential Smart Lighting lamp may become a point by means of which an attack on SLCN may be performed [10].

Such actions, in particular in the area of the last mile, may have a conscious or unconscious nature. The unconscious interference most often happens when the LV network feeds both the streets and the users' households, where the included loads do not meet electromagnetic compatibility standards. The conscious form of interference in the communication system is related to deliberate activity that consists in switching into the SLCN infrastructure such elements as capacitors, interfering generators, or terminals emulating a hub. Loading such devices, even in LV networks dedicated only to lighting, is not difficult, and using them by an intruder may remain unnoticed for a longer time.

Smart Lighting network security and protection from such attacks seems to be a harder task to solve than the prevention of possible abuses (to achieve quantifiable but limited economic benefits) from the receivers' side.

Attacks on Smart Lighting Communication Networks can be divided into two basic categories: passive and active. Passive attacks are any activities aiming to gain unauthorized access to the data or SLCN infrastructure, for which the attacker does not use emission of signals that may disturb and/or disenable correct performance of the signal. Active attacks, on the other hand, are all the attempts of illegal access to the data or the SLCN system's infrastructure by means of any signals or realization of any actions which may be detected [30].

Realizing a passive attack on the SLCN, the intruder camouflages one's presence and attempts to gain access to the transmitted data by passively listening to such a network. It is most often realized by switching into the network additional node which has similar functionalities to the original one. In such situation, we can distinguish three cases: (i) pretending to be a hub, (ii) pretending to be a particular lamp, (iii) or participating only in transferring frames in the transmission process.

To provide protection from such events, appropriate cryptographic mechanisms are most often used. Another kind of passive attack on the SLCM is activities for analyzing the traffic inside the network. In this case, the intruder's intention is not to know the content of the transmitted packets of data, but to get topological knowledge enabling the learning of the structure of the attacked network.

Contrary to the above presented passive forms of attacks on the SLCN infrastructure, in case of realization of an active attack, the intruder influences indirectly or directly the contents of the sent information and/or functionality of the system. Attacks of this kind are much easier to detect in comparison to the passive ones, because they cause visible disturbances in the SLCN performance. An effect of conducting an active attack may be degradation of a specific service or, in extreme cases, complete loss of control over the whole or some part of the SLCN infrastructure.

Due to the form, purpose, and manner of realization, active attacks can be divided into three types: (i) physical attacks aiming at destroying and/or disturbing correctness of the SLCN's node operation by means of an electromagnetic pulse (EMP), (ii) attacks on integrity and confidentiality of the transmitted data, and (iii) and attacks oriented onto particular layers of the SLCN (especially for the provided services).

Physical attacks are all kinds of destructive activities whose aim is to completely destroy or damage the SLCN infrastructure. One of their forms may be activities performed by means of an electromagnetic pulse (EPM) or injecting high pulse distortion into the power supply network [31].

Attacks directed onto the integrity or confidentiality of data, however, are especially dangerous, because they enable the attacker to gain unauthorized access to the information transmitted via the SLCN. This type of attack was presented in [32].

Another kind of attack in the SLCN consists in overloading the attacked network infrastructure, which is visible in the lack of correct data transmission or disenabling access to specific services. Such actions are usually realized by introducing to the network bigger traffic than can be served. They can also have other forms; for instance, they can occur in the physical layer performing jamming activities, and in the layer of data link they can flood the network with packets, causing as a result a collision of data and a necessity to retransmit them. The simplest way to perform such an attack is to connect an additional capacitor to the power circuit. This will cause suppression of the PLC modem carrier signal. Another method is to load into the SLCN a generator broadcasting in the transmission band of the system, which causes reduction of the signal/noise gap more, rendering a higher level of interfering signal. Reduction of the gap causes then an increase in the number of transmission errors. Another solution is to add any PLC modem, transmitting in the same band that is used by the Smart Lighting system. This solution is a bit more advanced than the use of a generator and causes the modems remaining within the intruder's reach to stay in the "receive" state without the ability to switch to the "broadcast" mode in the period when it transmits, for instance, when it broadcasts without a break or with short breaks [9].

To ensure protection against the above presented threats, especially different kinds of active and passive attacks, it is necessary to provide a high level of security to the critical SLCN infrastructure by continuous monitoring and control of the network traffic. One of the possible solutions to the so-stated problem can be to implement a detection system of anomalies reflected in defined SLCN traffic parameters. In consequence, the detected nonstandard behaviors of specific parameters may indicate a possibility of a given abuse or any other form of attack. The present paper focuses on the above stated question.

5. The Proposed Solution: Predictive Abuse Detection System

For ensuring a high level of security to Smart Lighting Communication Network systems, it is required that they are properly protected by means of passive actions (network monitoring, storing incidents, and reporting) and active actions (constant supervision to enforce the adopted security policy). Realization of the so-stated tasks ensures connection between technologies: Intrusion Detection System (IDS) and Intrusion Prevention System (IPS). In the hierarchy of network infrastructure protection, these systems are located just after security elements, such as a firewall.

The aim of the IPS systems is to undertake actions to prevent an attack, minimize its results, or actively respond to violation of security rules. From the technical side, IPS, in big simplification, is an IDS connected with a firewall. As far as topology is concerned, IPS systems can be divided into network solutions based on (i) a passive probe connected to the monitoring port of the switch analyzing all packets in a given network segment (ii) or a probe placed between two network segments operating in a transparent bridge mode that transmits all packets in the network. The basic aim of such solution is to compare between the real network traffic and the remembered attack signatures [12].

However, IDS systems are used to increase the security of the protected network both from the inside and from the outside. Their advantage is that they can be used for network traffic analysis and use diverse threat identification techniques. One of them consists in the detection of known attacks with the use of specified features (signatures), which describe changes in the network traffic. The second, on the other hand, is based on monitoring normal network's performance in order to find deviations from the norms (anomalies), which may indicate a break-in to the protected network infrastructure.

Anomaly detection (abuses) consists in recognition of nonstandard patterns of behaviors reflected in the network traffic parameters. All incidents deviating from those patterns (which are profiles that describe normal behavior of the network traffic) are classified as potentially dangerous and might signify an attempt of an attack or abuse. High efficiency and effectiveness of methods based on anomaly detection are closely related to the ability of recognition of unknown attacks (abuses). These methods operate on the basis of knowledge of not how a given attack runs (what is its signature), but what exceeds the defined network traffic pattern. Therefore, systems based on anomaly detection work better than those using signatures while detecting new, unknown types of attacks (abuses) [14].

In the present article, we propose a predictive abuse detection system for PLC Smart Lighting Networks based on automatically created models of exponential smoothing. Assuming that the correctness of the created statistical model directly depends on the quality of data used for designing it, at the initial stage, we identified and eliminated outlying data by means of Mahalanobis's distance (see Section 5.1). For the so-prepared data, statistical models were created (which constituted patterns) for particular network traffic parameters. This process was realized by means of exponential smoothing methods which, in turn, assume that the future forecasted value depends not only on the last observed value, but also on the whole set of the past values. Simultaneously, the influence of past values (former ones) is weaker than the influence of the newer values, that is, earlier ones (this methodology is further developed in Section 5.2). It should be noticed that the presented assumption agrees with the generally accepted rules of prediction. Bearing in mind the possibility of occurrence of essential real network traffic fluctuations (triggered by natural factors), a procedure of the pattern models' update was proposed on the basis of the interquartile spread criterion (see Section 5.3).

In Figure 2, we presented a block scheme of the proposed anomaly/attack solution for smart lights Power Line Communication networks. The presented solution is spread out across two physical localizations. On the right part of Figure 2, we can see the analyzed smart light PLC network with smart light marked as a yellow triangle connected to different phases of low-voltage power mains. The PLC traffic from different localizations of smart light PLC networks (in our case, we used 3 localizations on different streets) is gathered by the traffic concentrator and repacked into IP packets in order to send PLC network traffic by means of standard IP WAN network to distant locations where we perform anomaly/attack detection steps. We used two routers equipped with different WAN (Wide Area Network) ports or LTE (Long-Term Evolution) modems in order to connect these two localizations by means of dedicated safe connection through VPN (Virtual Private Network).

On the left of Figure 2, we can see the second part of our anomaly/attack detection solution placed on a distant location (in our case, the university building). The proposed solution is divided into two branches. The first branch is responsible for calculation of reference models for PLC anomaly/attack detection purposes. The second branch

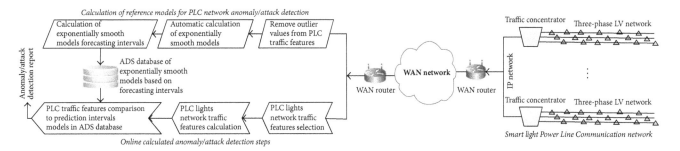

FIGURE 2: Block scheme of the proposed anomaly/attack solution for smart lights Power Line Communication network.

consists of steps performed online during anomaly/attack detection steps. In order to achieve reference models for PLC network traffic, we extracted traffic features from the PLC network traffic (more details are presented in Section 6.2). After removing outlier values for every traffic feature, we performed automatic calculation of exponential smoothing models and, in the end, forecasting intervals based on these models (details are presented in Section 5.2). Connection between the two branches of the proposed model is realized by means of ADS database where forecasting intervals based on exponential smoothing models are stored separately for every extracted PLC network traffic feature. Additionally, the reference models are updated when necessary to prevent the models from aging in case of changes in, for example, traffic characteristics or physical architecture (by providing additional segments of PLC smart light network). Recalculation of the model is controlled by a trigger condition presented in more detail in Section 5.3.

The second branch of the proposed model also consists of selection and calculation of the PLC network traffic features (see Section 6.2). PLC network traffic features are sampled and calculated with fixed time intervals, appropriate for smart light networks. In order to detect anomalies, we compare online calculated traffic features to prediction intervals read from the ADS database where the prediction intervals based on exponential smoothing models are stored. When the online calculated traffic features are outside the prediction intervals estimated by the model, we generate an anomaly detection report for a given traffic feature (more details are provided in Section 6).

5.1. Outliers Detection and Elimination Based on the Mahalanobis's Distance. The quality of a statistical model directly depends on the quality of data used to design it. The values of variables describing observations in actual datasets are often outlying (not typical). This is due to the specifics of the examined phenomenon or different kinds of errors. The outlier observations may have a very strong influence on the results of analysis and therefore they require special attention.

The notion of outliers is not directly defined in the literature. In the present work, a general definition, taken from Hawkins's work [33], is used. An outlier is such an observation that deviates from the remaining observations to such an extent that it generates an assumption that it was

created by another mechanism; for instance, it comes from a different distribution in the dataset. It is worth noticing that, according to the above definition, such emergence indicates not fulfilling one of the most basic assumptions concerning the analyzed dataset, namely, that it is an i.i.d. set (independent and identically distributed). In that case, occurrence of an outlier means that it comes from a different distribution and should not be analyzed with other elements of the examined set of data.

Analyzing particular elements and the operational environment of Smart Lighting Communication Networks, it becomes obvious that there may appear real possibilities of considerable fluctuations of the analyzed network traffic parameters (and, as a consequence, emergence of outliers). These fluctuations may have diverse sources, for instance, (i) environmental, connected with interruptions caused by high-energy electromagnetic pulse; (ii) technical, related to changes in the infrastructure; (iii) devices' damage; (iv) as a consequence of a network attack; or (v) intentional, unfair interference in the SLCN infrastructure. Thus, an important element of the preliminary analysis of data should be the evaluation of the impact that particular observations may have on the final result, and in case of detection of outliers they should be deleted from the set of data.

In our approach, identification of outliers in the analyzed SLCN traffic parameters is performed by means of a method utilizing Mahalanobis's distance. The essence of this method lies in the estimation of the distance between the analyzed observation vector x and the average value in the examined dataset based on the calculated matrix of variance and covariance [34]:

$$MD^2(x) = (x - \widehat{\mu})\,\widehat{\Sigma}\,(x - \widehat{\mu}), \tag{1}$$

$$\widehat{\Sigma} = \frac{1}{n-1}\sum_{i=1}^{n}(x_i - \widehat{\mu})(x_i - \widehat{\mu}), \tag{2}$$

where $\widehat{\mu}$ is the average value from the analyzed dataset and $\widehat{\Sigma}$ is the matrix of variance and covariance.

To underline the generality of our method, we left the original Mahalanobis's measure matrix record (the case of multiple regression); however, with time series, we have a one-dimensional case. Identification of outliers is performed by comparing Mahalanobis's square distance for each of the observations with critical values taken from χ^2 distribution. If there are significant differences (at an accepted level of importance), the given observation is treated as an outlier. This approach has one drawback though; namely, the value of the criterion (1) itself directly depends on statistics which are very sensitive to the occurrence of distant values. To eliminate this disadvantage, modifications were proposed for calculating the meter (1) by exchanging the average $\hat{\mu}$ with a resistant positional parameter. One of the proposals is the use of Minimum Volume Ellipsoid Estimator (MVE) [35]. In this case, $\hat{\mu}$ takes the value of the center of gravity of the ellipsoid with a minimum volume containing at least h observations of a given set, where $h = (n/2) + 1$, and n is the complete set of elements of the analyzed dataset. The second proposal is to designate a positional parameter $\hat{\mu}$ in formula (1) according to the following rule [35]: $\hat{\mu}$ is an average from these h observations of the given set, for which the determinant of covariance matrix is the smallest. Such a resistant positional estimator is called Minimum Covariance Determinant (MCD) estimator. The third approach suggested in the paper [36] uses the analysis of main components and identifies the distant observations just after transformation of all observations in space of main components by determining in this space Mahalanobis's square distance. The authors of this approach propose, at the stage of preparing analytical data, to standardize the variables by means of a median as a positional parameter and MAD, that is, median absolute deviation, as a dispersion parameter. After using such standardization, calculation of Euclidean distance in space of main components is equivalent to the calculation of the resistant variant of Mahalanobis's distance.

In summary, it is necessary to state that the MD measure modifications presented above are trying to eliminate the basic drawback of the described method, that is, not always reliable inference on the basis of classical statistics, which are very sensitive to the occurrence of nontypical observations. Therefore, to make an optimal choice, numerous experiments were performed on datasets containing the subject parameters of SLCN traffic, for both the original Mahalanobis's method and its presented modifications. As a result of the analysis of the obtained results, that is, the size, location, and number of outliers, for further consideration, we chose the approach proposed by Filzmoser et al. This method uses analysis of main components for identification of outliers and it is further developed in [36].

5.2. The SLCN Traffic Features' Forecasting Using Exponential Smoothing Models. Forecasting is still one of the main tasks of the time series analysis. Construction of those predictions is usually a multistage process, including matching the adequate model on the basis of historical data and evaluation of the quality of this matching (diagnostics). Correct conduct of such analysis requires appropriate knowledge and experience. It is usually also time-consuming, which may become an obstacle when it is necessary to collect forecasts for numerous time series simultaneously. Thus, in practice, there is a natural need to automate this forecasting.

In case of some stages connected to matching the optimal model for data, complete automatization is not possible.

Particularly, finding an appropriate compromise between the complexity of the model and the quality of its matching to the data often requires interpretation of the results by an analyst. Automation of the optimal model's choice usually requires adopting some assumptions simplifying the whole process (e.g., defining the statistical criterion, which will be used as a measure of matching quality of the model or the possible ranges of variation of model parameters) [37].

Algorithms allowing for automatic construction of forecasts should realize all the stages of the analysis, that is, (i) the choice of the optimal model for data, (ii) parameters' estimation, and (iii) the forecasts' construction (point and/or interval). While searching for an optimal model, it is important to use proper criteria which will protect from too good matching of the model to the learning data, which in turn may lead to bad quality of forecasts for the new periods. The algorithms should also be resistant in case of occurrence (in the analyzed time series) of outlier observations, or they should be equipped with mechanisms of their detection and elimination. Additionally, the algorithms should be easily used for a big number of diverse time series without the necessity of an analyst's interference, and they should be characterized by acceptable computational complexity [20].

One of the possible solutions to the so-stated problem of automatic forecasting is the ExponenTialSmoothing or ErrorTrendSeason (ETS) models, which constitute a family of adaptive models developed by Hyndman et al. [38], which uses generalized algorithms of exponential smoothing. Their crucial advantages are simplicity, relatively quick adaptive matching algorithm, and ease of understanding and interpretation of the results. The common denominator of these methods is assigning (exponentially) the weights, decreasing with distance in time, to the past observations during the process of designating a new forecast for a future observation. This is due to the fact that the classical assumptions of the quantitative prediction come down to the postulate of the relative invariability of the development mechanism of the studied phenomena and events. In methods based on ETS, exponential smoothing may be realized by means of different models, properly adjusted to the analyzed data.

When the time series' character and variability are analyzed, it is easy to notice that they are optionally composed of four elements: a trend, seasonal fluctuations, periodical fluctuations, and random disturbances. The seasonal fluctuations usually have an approximately constant period of time, whereas the time of the complete cycle of cyclical fluctuations is usually changeable. Optionally, the components of the analyzed time series may be connected in two ways: additively and multiplicatively [39]. In the exponential smoothing models, the trend is a combination of level c and increment g values. These two components may be connected in four different ways, including the attenuation parameter $\phi \in [0, 1]$. We then obtain diverse types of trends, such as the following [40]:

$$\text{No trend: } V_h = c, \tag{3a}$$

$$\text{Additive: } V_h = c + gh, \tag{3b}$$

Multiplicative: $V_h = cg^h$,   (3c)

Attenuated: $V_h = cg^{(\phi + \phi^2 + \cdots + \phi^h)}$,   (3d)

where V_h describes the character of the trend and h parameter describes the forecast's horizon.

If we take into consideration three possible combinations of the seasonal component with a trend, that is, lack of seasonality, the additive variant, and multiplicative variant, then we obtain twelve exponential smoothing models, which can be written as

$$l_t = \alpha P_t + (1 - \alpha) Q_t,$$ (4a)

$$b_t = \beta R_t + (\phi - \beta) b_{t-1},$$ (4b)

$$s_t = \gamma T_t + (1 - \gamma) s_{t-m},$$ (4c)

where l_t denotes the series level at time t, b_t denotes the slope at time t, s_t denotes the seasonal component of the series at time t, and m denotes the number of seasons in a given period; the values of P_t, Q_t, R_t, and T_t vary according to which of the cells the method belongs to, and $\alpha, \beta, \gamma, \phi \in [0, 1]$ are constants denoting model parameters [38].

The method with fixed level (constant over time) is obtained by setting $\alpha = 0$, the method with fixed trend (drift) is obtained by setting $\beta = 0$, and the method with fixed seasonal pattern is obtained by setting $\gamma = 0$. Note also that the additive trend methods are obtained by letting $\varphi = 1$ in the damped trend methods [41].

The works [42] discuss specific cases of state space models with a single source of error, which may be a basis for some methods of exponential smoothing. Including the possible character of these errors, we may present the state space models for all twelve types of exponential smoothing as follows:

$$Y_t = w(z_{t-1}) + r(z_{t-1}) \epsilon_t,$$ (5a)

$$z_t = f(z_{t-1}) + g(z_{t-1}) \epsilon_t,$$ (5b)

where $z_t = [l_t, b_t, s_t, s_{t-1}, \ldots, s_{t-m+1}]^T$ denotes the state vector, $w(x), r(x), f(x)$, and $g(x)$ are continuous functions with continuous derivatives, and $\{\epsilon_t\}$ is a Gaussian white noise process with mean zero and variance σ^2, and $\mu_t = w(z_{t-1})$ [42]. The error ϵ_t may be included in the model in an additive or multiplicative way. The model with additive errors has $r(z_{t-1}) = 1$, so that $Y_t = \mu_t + \epsilon_t$. The model with multiplicative errors has $r(z_{t-1}) = \mu_t$, so that $Y_t = \mu_t(1 + \epsilon_t)$. Thus, $\epsilon_t = (Y_t - \mu_t)/\mu_t$ is the relative error for the multiplicative model. The models are not unique. Apparently, any value of $r(z_{t-1})$ will lead to identical point forecasts for Y_t [38].

From the twelve exponential smoothing models described by dependency (4a), (4b), and (4c) after including the additive and multiplicative error ϵ_t, we obtain 24 adaptive models in the states' space. The choice of an adequate exponential smoothing model in a particular prognostic task requires the selection of the best form of the model as well as initialization of the z_0 vector's components and parameters estimation $\Theta = [\alpha, \beta, \gamma, \phi]^T$.

It is necessary to calculate the values of z_0 and Θ parameters; otherwise, the models will not be useful for the prognostic process. It is not difficult to compute the likelihood of the innovations state space model (LISSM*) (see (6)); achieving the maximum likelihood estimates (MLE) is similarly easy [38].

$$\text{LISSM}^*(\Theta; z_0) = n \log \left(\sum_{t=1}^{n} \frac{\epsilon_t^2}{z_{t-1}} \right) + 2 \sum_{t=1}^{n} \log |r(z_{t-1})|, \quad (6)$$

where n is the observations' number.

Calculating the above is not difficult when recursive equations are used [43]. Minimizing LISSM* is a procedure used to calculate the parameter Θ and the initial state z_0.

The present model was selected by means of the Akaike Information Criterion (AIC):

$$\text{AIC} = \text{LISSM}^*(\widehat{\Theta}; \widehat{z}_0) + 2k,$$ (7)

where k is the number of parameters in Θ plus the number of free states in z_0 and $\widehat{\Theta}$ and z_0 define the estimates of Θ and z_0. From all the models applicable to the data, we selected the one which minimizes the AIC [44].

The AIC is also a method which enables us to choose between the additive and multiplicative error models. However, there is no difference between the point forecasts of the two models, to make it impossible for the standard accuracy measures, like the mean squared error (MSE) or mean absolute percentage error (MAPE), to differentiate between the error types.

The presented methodology, connected to optimal searching for proper models of exponential smoothing, requires providing some initial values. Usually, the values of parameters α, β, and γ are included in the range $(0, 1)$. However, to avoid the problem with instability, we use a narrower range of parameters, that is, $0.1 \leq \alpha \leq 0.9$, $0.1 \leq \beta \leq 0.9, 0.1 \leq \gamma \leq 0.9$, and $\beta \leq \phi \leq 1$. We also limit the values of the initial states z_t of the vector's elements. This is done in such a way that the seasonality indexes were summed up do zero for the additive model and added to m for the multiplicative model. As the initial values in the nonlinear optimization, we use $\alpha = \beta = \gamma = 0.5$ and $\phi = 0.9$.

When we summarize the above ideas, we obtain an automatic forecasting algorithm. It operates in compliance with the following three-stage formula: (i) all proper models are applied to each of the series to optimize the parameters (smoothing the variable's initial stage), (ii) selection of the best matching model according to AIC, and (iii) creation of point forecasts on the grounds of the most effective model (with optimized parameters) for a necessary number of future stages [38].

All the above described kinds of exponential smoothing models are created in compliance with the prediction theory's assumptions, including the ongoing degradation processes (i.e., possible lack of stability in the variable correctness in time). Big flexibility of those models and their adaptive ability in case of irregular changes of the direction of speed of the trend, or deformations and shifts in seasonal fluctuations, make them a comfortable tool for short-term forecasting and prediction. Hyndman et al. [38, 43] provide a detailed description of the proposed algorithm.

5.3. The Condition of Statistical Model's Update. The process of statistical models' designation on the basis of experimental data is usually a complex task which depends on the knowledge about the object and attributes of the measuring results (observations). The quality of the designated statistical model directly depends on the quality of data used for its estimation.

In the present work, the experimental object is network traffic of an SLCN infrastructure and data characterizing the state of the Smart Lighting system. Both datasets are represented by defined time series. While analyzing the character of the examined dependencies, in particular the SLCN traffic parameters, it is necessary to notice the possibility of occurrence of significant fluctuation of data. The reasons of this phenomenon are to be sought in possible changes in the SLCN infrastructure, that is, aging of devices, replacement with new/other models, or modifications in the topology of the network. Obviously, when the nature of the analyzed data changes, there should be made a new estimation and creation of an updated statistical model on the basis of datasets composed of the subject fluctuations. As a result, this should cause adaptation of the proposed method of anomaly detection to the changing conditions (which are not an aftermath of any attack or abuse).

For the initial data selection, that is, checking if we are dealing with significant fluctuations in the analyzed time series, we use the one-dimensional quartile criterion [45]. For every analyzed set of data, we calculate the first (Q1) and third (Q3) quartiles and the interquartile range (IRQ) IRQ = Q3 − Q1. As influential observations, we accept those whose values exceed the range (Q1 − 1,5IRQ, Q3 + 1,5IRQ). As extremely influential observations, however, we understand those exceeding the range (Q1 − 3IRQ, Q3 + 3IRQ).

In the next step, for every detected influential observation, we check fulfilling the condition of whether it fits the range of forecasts of the appropriate reference model, that is, the following condition:

$$x_i \in \left(\mu_f - \sigma_f, \mu_f + \sigma_f \right) \quad i = 1, 2, \ldots, n, \quad (8)$$

where $\{x_1, x_2, \ldots, x_n\}$ is a time series limited by n-element analysis window, μ_f is the average forecast of the given reference model in the analysis window, and σ_f is the standard deviation of appropriate prognosis.

The estimation condition of the new standard model should be an ability to detect (in the analyzed time series) significant and possibly stable statistic changeability. Therefore, updating the statistical model will be realized when in the analyzed time series over 30 per cent of analysis windows in a weekly period contain observations not fitting the acceptable prognosis range of the appropriate reference model. The above condition is a consequence of the observed dependency that the value of the false positive (FP) parameter of the presented anomaly detection system increases exponentially when in over 30 per cent analysis windows in a weekly period we note significant changeability in data.

TABLE 1: PLC data link and network layer traffic features extracted from the traffic concentrators.

Network feature	PLC smart lights network traffic feature description
DLN$_1$	RSSI: received signal strength indication for PLC lamps [dBm]
DLN$_2$	SNR: signal-to-noise ratio [dBu]
DLN$_3$	PER: packet error rate per time interval [%]
DLN$_4$	PPTM: number of packets per time interval
DLN$_5$	TTL: packet time-to-live value

TABLE 2: PLC application layer traffic features extracted from the traffic concentrators.

Network feature	PLC smart lights network traffic feature description
APL$_1$	ENE: power consumption by PLC lamp [Wh]
APL$_2$	TEMP: lamp temperature [°C]
APL$_3$	LUL: lamp luminosity level in % (value: 0–100%)
APL$_4$	NR: number of lamp resets per time interval
APL$_5$	PS: power supply value [V]

6. Experimental Installation and the Anomaly/Attack Detection Method and Results

In Figure 2, we presented a block scheme which consists of the main steps in the proposed anomaly/attack detection method. In the first step, we extracted the PLC traffic features from two experimental PLC smart lights networks (additional explanation can be found in Section 6.1). There are two main branches in the proposed method: calculation of reference models for PLC network anomaly detection and the second branch consisting of online steps for extraction of traffic features, comparison of traffic features for reference model in ADS reference models database, and generation of an anomaly/attack detection report for a given traffic feature.

Values of the PLC traffic features can be captured in an arbitrary time interval but usually a 15-minute time interval is sufficient for the PLC smart light network. The extracted PLC network traffic features (see Tables 1 and 2) are represented as a one-dimensional time series. In case of a reference model generation, we have to remove suspicious values first by removing outlier values from network traffic features (see Section 5.1). After that step, we can start to calculate exponential smoothing models (see Section 5.2) and in the end exponential smoothing models forecasting intervals. We calculate a separate model for every PLC traffic feature and store them in a database of reference models. The reference models are calculated for a one-week period with a 15-minute resolution window. An example of the calculated forecasting intervals for traffic features can be seen in Figure 3. We can see two prediction intervals for signal-to-noise ratio (SNR) PLC traffic feature. When the online calculated network traffic feature is within boundaries set by two prediction intervals (see Figure 3), we assume that there is no anomaly/attack in

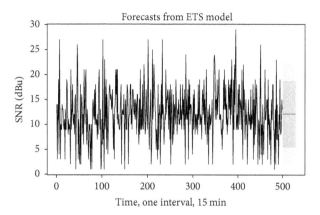

FIGURE 3: Two prediction forecast intervals (80% narrower, 95% wider) and 30-sample prediction interval calculated with the use of exponential smoothing model (PLC traffic feature, signal-to-noise ratio (SNR) [dBu]).

this case. We expect that 80 or 95% of the values for a given PLC traffic feature will lie inside these intervals (see Figure 3).

The second branch in our anomaly/attack detection method consists of steps calculated online during normal work of the PLC network anomaly/attack detection method. In the first two steps, we extract and calculate PLC lights network traffic features from Tables 1 and 2. Next, for every traffic feature, we check if the online calculated traffic feature values are within the intervals designated by reference models stored in ADS reference database models. When the online calculated traffic features are outside reference intervals, we generate a detection report about possible anomaly/attack triggered by the given PLC traffic feature.

The main issue of the so far proposed anomaly/attack detection conception is the problem of reference models' aging. This phenomenon comes from the fact that the PLC lights network has a dynamic structure. Connecting additional segments of PLC smart lights networks will result in changing of network traffic characteristics and, as a consequence, the necessity of changing reference models. Nonupdated reference models will cause as a result a constant increase of false positive values (FP [%]). To alleviate this drawback, we propose a trigger condition responsible for the recalculation process of the reference models (see Section 5.3 for more details). Reference models are calculated in a one-week period with the use of 15-minute windows. Based on empirical experiments, we recalculate all reference models when trigger conditions (see (8)) are not satisfied in 30% of the 15-minute analysis windows during the one-week period. We started to use new recalculated models at the beginning of the new week (the new model is valid for a minimum of one-week period).

6.1. Experimental Testbed.

The analyzed data were captured in two locations: Nieszawska Street in Toruń City (Poland) and University of Technology and Life Sciences (UTP) campus in Bydgoszcz City (Poland). We also used an additional separate Smart Lighting low-voltage LV PLC network testbed constructed during studies in GEKON project [46].

The first PLC network, located in Nieszawska Street, which was dedicated to a Smart Lighting low-voltage LV network, has a length of 3 km (see Figure 4), divided by a traffic concentrator located in the middle of the street. The PLC smart lights network contains 108 lamps (only one lamp is located on every electric pole). Old gas-discharge lamps were gradually replaced by smart LED lights. We used this network for testing traffic concentrators and experiments for detecting anomalies/attacks in PLC traffic.

The second network was placed at the University of Technology and Life Sciences (UTP) campus (see Figure 4). In this case, it was not a dedicated network with a separate power supply (offices, classrooms, and labs were powered by the same power supply network). The testbed in UTP campus consisted of 36 lamps.

Tests were performed in the laboratory (located in UTP campus) with different types and numbers of lamps (gas-discharge lamps and LED lamps). The PLC traffic from both locations was captured from the WAN (from Nieszawska Street) and local network placed in the university laboratory.

6.2. Experimental Setup and Results.

In this section, we present the methodology and results achieved for the proposed anomaly/attack detection with the use of exponential smoothing based models. We propose a set of different scenarios for evaluating the usability of the proposed method.

All experiments were carried out by means of two real-world PLC lights networks (see Section 6.1). A part of the testbed located in the university campus can be seen in Figure 5. The picture presents different types of smart lights used in the experiments. Connections between the 36 lamps for the testbed partially presented in Figure 5 are presented in Figure 7. We can see connection schemes between lamps assigned to three-phase power mains with signed possible high-quality and low-quality links. The entire traffic as mentioned earlier is accessible by the traffic concentrator (red rectangle in Figure 7).

Every lamp consists of a PLC modem used for communication, a lamp microprocessor controller, and a power supply. An opened LED lamp with signed internal elements is presented in Figure 6.

The first step in our method requires capturing the PLC traffic from smart lights networks presented in Section 6.1.

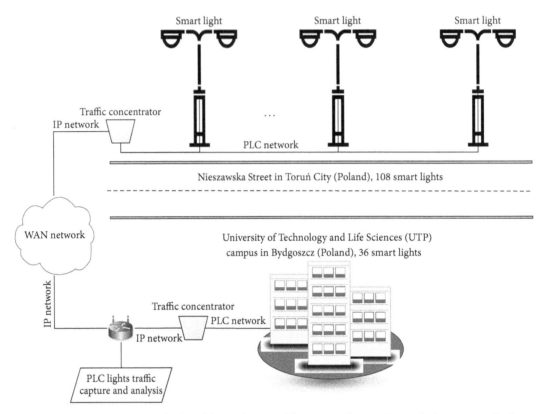

FIGURE 4: Experimental testbed used for evaluation of the proposed anomaly/attack detection method.

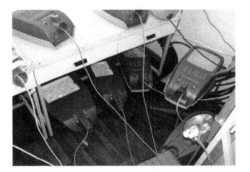

FIGURE 5: Part of the testbed used for achieving experimental results, located in the university campus.

FIGURE 6: Opened LED smart light used in experiments.

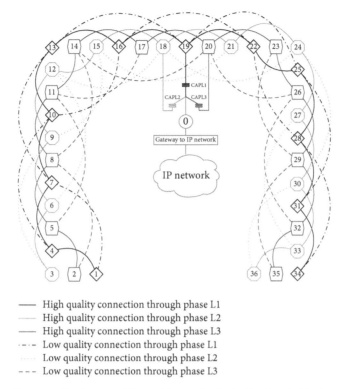

- High quality connection through phase L1
- High quality connection through phase L2
- High quality connection through phase L3
-·-· Low quality connection through phase L1
······ Low quality connection through phase L2
- - - Low quality connection through phase L3

FIGURE 7: Schematic connection between 36 smart lamps for the testbed located in the university campus.

We collect PLC traffic from traffic concentrators which are responsible for translating the PLC network packets into IP packets. In the next step, we extract the PLC traffic features in order to analyze these features for anomaly/attack detection.

In our experiments, we extracted features that belong to every layer of a PLC protocol stack. In Tables 1 and 2, we can see the extracted PLC traffic features together with explanations.

Traffic features from Table 1 are extracted based on data link and network layers of PLC communication stack. DLN_1 and DLN_2 features give us information about the quality of the received signals transmitted through the power mains. RSSI gives us information about the received signal strength where the signal power may come from any sources (e.g., different modulations, background radiation). RSSI does not give us information about the possibility of signal decoding. SNR [dBu] measure gives us information about the relation between the desired signal and the noise level. DLN_3 traffic feature stands for Packet Error Rate (PER) per time interval. In our case, we used a 15-minute time interval. PER is calculated as a quotient between the number of destroyed packets received by the traffic concentrator and the number of all packets received by the traffic concentrator for a given period of time. DLN_4 feature PPTM stands for the number of packets per time interval. The last feature from layer 2/layer 3 DLN_5 gives us TTL information connected to packets received by the PLC concentrator. In Table 2, there are traffic features extracted from the data payload (application layer) of the PLC packets. The application layer

traffic features are connected with parameters used by the energy supplier/operator management staff. APL_1 feature gives us information about power consumption for a given period of time separately for a given lamp. APL_2 carries information about the temperature read from smart lights. LUL (lamp luminosity level, in [%]) feature has values of luminosity sent by the lamp to the traffic concentrator. APL_4 carries the number of lamp resets per time interval (the value is stored in the Static Random Access Memory (SRAM) with backup power provided by a supercapacitor). The last value extracted from the data payload is PS (power supply) in volts [V] which is useful information for maintenance systems.

After PLC network features extraction, we can analyze subsequent traffic features in order to detect possible anomalies/attacks. We propose scenarios (as realistic as possible) in order to evaluate the efficiency of the proposed anomaly detection methodology.

There are different purposes of attacking smart lights PLC networks. First of all, the attacker would like to disturb the control system of a smart light operator in order to change the settings of the lamps parameters. Switching lamps off or lights' intensity reduction for a given area may cause an increase in crime or can be dangerous for car traffic (highest possibility of car accidents especially at intersections). Intentional damage or setting lamps instantly on near selected attacker possessions causes additional financial losses to the operator.

Detecting anomalies is also an important thing for the smart lights operator. The operator will be able to react faster

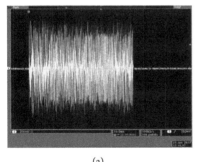 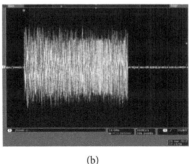 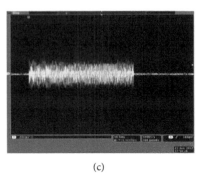

(a)   (b)   (c)

FIGURE 8: Impact (on signal received by the smart light) of 470 nF capacitance connected to the power line: (a) without capacitor, (b) capacitor connected close to the traffic concentrator, and (c) capacitor connected inside the lamp pole.

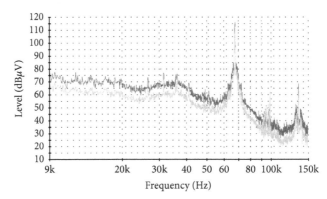

FIGURE 9: Characteristics of the interference signal generated by damaged notebook switching supply.

on damage, intentional damage, and network attacks, so it will be possible to limit the negative economic and social consequences.

We can divide the proposed scenarios into two main groups: (i) the first type of scenario requires physical access to the PLC network infrastructure in case of attacks on the physical infrastructure of a PLC smart lights network and (ii) the second type of attack requires knowledge about devices used in the PLC network and protocols used in the smart lights network.

Scenario 1. The first type of attack belongs to Group I of attacks. It is an attack on the physical layer and requires connection of a capacitor to the power line. The bigger the value of capacitor we connect, the higher the attenuation of PLC signal we achieve. In our case, we connected a 470 nF capacitor to the power line. In Figure 8, we can see oscillograms: Figure 8(a) without connected capacitor, Figure 8(b) with the same value capacitor connected near the traffic concentrator, and Figure 8(c) with capacitor 470 nF connected directly inside the lighting pole. In the presented oscillogram, we can see decreasing values of modulated PLC signals. When we connect a capacitor with higher values, for example, 4.7 uF, close to the PLC, the transmitter' modem would not be able to transmit any packet because of the too low current efficiency of power supply or line amplifier.

A different method of attack on the physical layer is connection of a signal generator to the power line. The connected generator has to transmit the signal with values that belong to the PLC frequency band used by the attacked network. The higher the level of the injected signal, the bigger the values of PER (DLN$_3$ feature) and the lower values of the SNR traffic feature. We performed such an attack by means of a damaged/prepared switching power supply which comes from a notebook computer. This is an easy and cheap way to perform such attack. We transmitted a narrow bandwidth signal with 90 dBuV power close to the disturbed device. In Figure 9, we can see the characteristics of the interference signal that comes from the damaged laptop power supply.

We also disturbed PLC power mains by a professional Electrical Fast Transient (EFT)/Burst generator [22] that is used during electromagnetic compatibility (EMC) tests and capacitive coupling clamp (in this case, there is no need for a galvanic connection to the power mains) according to the IEC 61000-4-4 [47] recommendation.

In our experiments, the capacitors and generator were connected constantly but the attacker can arbitrarily connect these elements by a microcontroller controlled device and take into consideration, for example, sunrise and sunset.

Attacks from Scenario 1 have an impact mainly on data link and the network layer from Table 1. In Table 3, we can see the results of the proposed anomaly/attack detection method.

TABLE 3: DR [%] and FP [%] for anomalies/attacks performed on the SLCN in Scenario 1.

Network feature	DR [%]	FP [%]	Description
DLN_1	90.80	4.80	—
DLN_2	98.00	3.60	The biggest impact on DLN_2 in Scenario 1
DLN_3	97.00	3.20	The biggest impact on DLN_3 in Scenario 1
DLN_4	81.40	5.20	—
DLN_5	75.40	7.40	—

TABLE 4: DR [%] and FP [%] for anomalies/attacks performed on the SLCN in Scenario 2.

Network feature	DR [%]	FP [%]	Description
DLN_1	91.40	4.30	—
DLN_2	98.80	3.80	The biggest impact on DLN_2 in Scenario 2
DLN_3	97.60	3.10	The biggest impact on DLN_3 in Scenario 2
DLN_4	82.60	6.40	—
DLN_5	78.60	7.80	—

TABLE 5: DR [%] and FP [%] for anomalies/attacks performed on the SLCN in Scenario 2.

Network feature	DR [%]	FP [%]	Description
APL_1	98.40	2.80	—
APL_2	91.20	5.20	—
APL_3	96.80	3.80	—
APL_4	—	—	Not important in this scenario
APL_5	—	—	Not important in this scenario

Scenario 2. In the second scenario, the attacker would like to generate random packets by means of a connected unauthorized smart lamp or a PLC modem. This is a more sophisticated attack than in case of using a generator (see Scenario 1). Constantly generated packets by the attacker's PLC modem cause modems which are within the impact of this transmission to be constantly in the receiving mode and to be unable to transmit or receive any packets. The attacker transmits packets with the use of carrier frequency/frequencies used in the attacked network one by one with the shortest delays as possible between consecutive packets. Packets transmitted by the attacker may be understandable or not from the smart lights network's point of view. Results of DR [%] and FP [%] for anomaly detection in case of Scenario 2 are presented in Tables 4 and 5.

Indirectly, this type of attack can also be seen in application layer parameters because part of the lamps will switch to maximum luminosity after three connection attempts to the traffic concentrator (we set 900 seconds between attempts). In this case, energy consumption will increase and other parameters that depend on energy consumption also will change (e.g., the lamp's temperature).

Scenario 3. The attack performed in Scenario 3 belongs to Group II of attacks. This type of attack requires knowledge about the PLC smart lights network topology, devices used in the smart lights network, communication protocols used for every layer of PLC communication stack, and so forth.

The attacker, in the presented scenario, connected an additional traffic concentrator (with the same MAC address

as the valid traffic concentrator). The attacker's traffic concentrator pretends to be a valid communication device and takes part in packet exchange between lamps. The attacker is placed near lamps and wants to change the lamps' settings. In this case, the attacker is far from the concentrator and the valid concentrator does not receive the command (or a command copy) sent by the fake concentrator. In order to prevent the command from reaching the valid concentrator, it is best to send a command with TTL = 0.

We also performed a similar attack when the attacker was close to the valid concentrator. In this case, anomaly is revealed by the registration command packet with TTL = TTLmax. The valid concentrator will never hear packets' copy with TTLmax. In a proper situation, the packet should have TTL < TTLmax. In this case, the attacker does not care that packets will not arrive to the valid concentrator. Results for the presented scenario are presented in Table 6.

Scenario 4. In the presented scenario, the attacker connected an additional device with a PLC modem and tried to change and retransmit packets with destroyed bits. This action causes an increasing number of corrupted packets with wrong Cyclic Redundancy Check (CRC) bytes. In this case, we can see an increasing value of Packet Error Rate (PER) (DLN_3) network feature. For example, if we send a command to lamps with new luminosity settings, some lamps may not get this information. When a lamp does not receive any command after three connection attempts to the concentrator (number of attempts' parameter NA and time between attempts are protocol parameters in our experiments set to NA = 3

TABLE 6: DR [%] and FP [%] for anomalies/attacks performed on the SLCN in Scenario 3.

Network feature	DR [%]	FP [%]	Description
DLN_1	—	—	Not important in this scenario
DLN_2	—	—	Not important in this scenario
DLN_3	—	—	Not important in this scenario
DLN_4	90.60	4.60	—
DLN_5	98.60	3.40	—

TABLE 7: DR [%] and FP [%] for anomalies/attacks performed on the SLCN in Scenario 4.

Network feature	DR [%]	FP [%]	Description
DLN_1	—	—	Not important in this scenario
DLN_2	—	—	Not important in this scenario
DLN_3	98.40	3.40	—
DLN_4	85.40	7.24	—
DLN_5	92.60	6.60	—

TABLE 8: DR [%] and FP [%] for anomalies/attacks performed on the SLCN in Scenario 4.

Network feature	DR [%]	FP [%]	Description
APL_1	98.80	2.40	—
APL_2	90.30	4.80	—
APL_3	96.50	3.60	—
APL_4	—	—	Not important in this scenario
APL_5	—	—	Not important in this scenario

and time 900 seconds), then they will switch to maximum luminosity. This situation causes additional costs to the installation's operator. This type of attack can be especially seen in application layer network features, such as APL_1 (ENE, power consumption by PLC lamp [Wh]), APL_3 (LUL, lamp luminosity level received from the lamp), and, indirectly, the lamp's temperature (APL_2). Detection rate DR [%] and false positive FP [%] results for Scenario 4 are presented in Tables 7 and 8.

Scenario 5. In the next scenario, the attacker would like to prevent receiving the broadcast command (e.g., a command that wants to set a group of lamps to certain luminosity) by lamps. When the attacker's PLC modem detects a broadcast command sent by a traffic concentrator, it transmits an arbitrary command (i.e., no operation command (NOP)) in the unicast mode. Transmission in the unicast mode has a higher priority and lower delay, which is why this transmission will reach first the lamp. The lamp will respond to this packet by switching to the acknowledge ACK/awaiting state. Broadcast command receiving is only possible for lamps in IDLE state. Results for this scenario are presented in Tables 9 and 10.

Additional explanation requires application network features APL_4 (number of lamp resets per time interval (NR)) and APL_5 (power supply (PS) value). These parameters are mainly important for the smart lights network operator and were not affected by the attack simulated in our experiments. Such parameters are important for smart lights network management and may indirectly have an impact on the transmission parameter, but we did not have the chance to observe the impact of these parameters during our experiments.

Taking into account all scenarios, the detection rate (DR) values change from 75.40 to 98.80%, while the false positive ranged from 7.80 to 2.40%. We can see that, depending on the attack scenario, only part of the network traffic features selected from the PLC traffic give us meaningful information from the anomaly/attack detection's point of view. For example, in Scenario 4, we can see a direct impact on data link and network layer features and indirect influence on application layer features extracted from the data payload.

Results achieved by the proposed anomaly/attack detection proved the usefulness of the proposed method. Anomaly detection systems are characterized by higher values of false positive in comparison to classic intrusion detection systems (IDS), which are based on the database of already known attacks.

We verified the achieved results by comparing the proposed solution to methods available in the literature. Although we did not find anomaly and intrusion detection for smart lights PLC network operating in data link, network layer, and application layer, there are anomaly and intrusion detection systems applied to WSN smart meter networks in Smart Grid AMI (Advanced Metering Infrastructure). Such solutions are mainly designed for energy theft detection and for failure and maintenance purposes and operate usually in network and application layers. Anomaly and intrusion detection systems for energy theft detection use, for example,

TABLE 9: DR [%] and FP [%] for anomalies/attacks performed on the SLCN in Scenario 5.

Network feature	DR [%]	FP [%]	Description
DLN_1	—	—	Not important in this scenario
DLN_2	—	—	Not important in this scenario
DLN_3	—	—	Not important in this scenario
DLN_4	92.40	7.74	—
DLN_5	90.20	7.70	—

TABLE 10: DR [%] and FP [%] for anomalies/attacks performed on the SLCN in Scenario 4.

Network feature	DR [%]	FP [%]	Description
APL_1	94.20	2.60	—
APL_2	88.40	4.40	—
APL_3	98.40	2.40	—
APL_4	—	—	Not important in this scenario
APL_5	—	—	Not important in this scenario

the HMM (Hidden Markov Models) [48], rule-based solutions [13], and statistical methods by means of, for example, Bollinger Bands [49]. Different kinds of methods are for estimation of metering errors in AMI infrastructure with the use of, for example, DTW (Dynamic Time Warping) [23]. In general, anomaly detection systems are very diverse and so a straightforward comparison is not easy, though it can be stated, bearing in mind the available literature [7, 11, 13, 15, 16, 23, 48–50], that false positive values for anomaly detection type systems are generally less than 10% [18, 19, 21]. This level of false positive parameter is acceptable for the proposed class of systems, especially for anomaly detection systems.

We also proposed a mechanism that prevents the aging of exponential smoothing models (see Section 5.3). Such an installation like smart lights networks or Wireless Sensor Networks (WSN) changes over time, so it is important to predict such a situation and update anomaly detection reference profiles in order to prevent the increase of false positive values.

7. Conclusions

The number of potential threats in dynamically created Smart Cities, and in particular in their critical communication infrastructures, is very big and is increasing every day. Thus, protection from constantly newer vectors of attacks is becoming more complicated and requires the use of highly specific solutions. Currently, the most often used mechanisms ensuring an adequate level of security in such infrastructures are the methods of detection and classification of abuses (attacks) unknown so far, often directed onto defined sources of critical communication infrastructures. The basic aims of such solutions are the early detection and reaction to the symptoms of nontypical behavior of network traffic which may indicate various abuses originating both outside and inside the protected infrastructure.

The article presents effective solutions concerning the detection of different types of abuses in network traffic for

the critical infrastructure of Smart Lighting. It proposes and describes the structure of the SLCN created for the purposes of the experiment. The structure was built with the use of Power Line Communication technology. The key security problems are also discussed, which have a direct impact on proper operation of the Smart Lighting critical infrastructure; that is, the authors described the possibilities of emergence of both external factors and active forms of attacks aiming at gaining influence on the informational contents of the transmitted data. The article proposes an efficient and effective method of abuse detection in the analyzed Smart Lighting network traffic. At the initial stage of the solution, there is identification and elimination of outliers, which is performed by means of Mahalanobis's distance. The objective of such an activity was correction of data for automatic creation of statistic models (standards) based on exponential smoothing methods. The choice of optimal values of the estimated statistical models was realized as minimization of their forecast error. The article also presents a procedure of recalculation (update) of the standard models in case there are permanent changes in the character of the SLCN traffic. The next step is the calculation of the difference value between the forecast in the estimated traffic model and its real variability in order to detect abnormal behavior, which may indicate an attempt of an abuse, for example, a network attack or unauthorized interference in the SLCN infrastructure.

The proposed anomaly/attack detection system based on predictive analysis with the use of exponential smoothing method was evaluated by five attack scenarios. The proposed scenarios have an impact on every layer of PLC communication stack. In order to detect an anomaly/attack, we extracted 10 network features from the PLC traffic network. For all scenarios, we achieved detection rate (DR) values changes from 75.40 to 98.80%, while the false positive ranged from 7.80 to 2.40%. In order to prevent ADS reference models' aging, we added a trigger condition used for reference profiles recalculation. The achieved results are promising and proved that statistical analysis of traffic features with the use of exponential smoothing models can be useful for anomaly/attack detection and maintenance purposes for smart lights operators.

Acknowledgments

This research was supported by the National Centre for Research and Development and also by the National Fund for Environmental Protection and Water Management under the realized GEKON program (Project no. 214093), and it also was supported by the Polish Ministry of Science and High Education and Apator S.A. Company under Contract 04409/C.ZR6-6/2009.

References

[1] IEEE Standards Association, *IEEE Guide for Smart Grid Interoperability of Energy Technology and Information Technology Operation with the Electric Power System (EPS), End-Use Applications, and Loads*, The Institute of Electrical and Electronics Engineers, 2011.

[2] M. Górczewska, S. Mroczkowska, and P. Skrzypczak, "Badanie wplywu barwy swiatla w oswietleniu drogowym na rozpoznawalnosc przeszkód (light color influence on obstacle recognition," *Electrical Engineering*, vol. 73, pp. 165–172, 2013.

[3] H. Schaffers, "Landscape and Roadmap of Future Internet and Smart Cities," 2012.

[4] S. Sun, B. Rong, and Y. Qian, "Artificial frequency selective channel for covert cyclic delay diversity orthogonal frequency division multiplexing transmission," *Security and Communication Networks*, vol. 8, no. 9, pp. 1707–1716, 2015.

[5] IEC 62386-102:2014, Digital addressable lighting interface - Part 102: General requirements - Control gear, 2014.

[6] EN 50065-1:2011, Signalling on low-voltage electrical installations in the frequency range 3 kHz to 148.5 kHz, General requirements, frequency bands and electromagnetic disturbances, 2011.

[7] M. A. Faisal, Z. Aung, J. R. Williams, and A. Sanchez, "Datastream-based intrusion detection system for advanced metering infrastructure in smart grid: a feasibility study," *IEEE Systems Journal*, vol. 9, no. 1, pp. 31–44, 2015.

[8] P. Kiedrowski, B. Dubalski, T. Marciniak, T. Riaz, and J. Gutierrez, "Energy greedy protocol suite for smart grid communication systems based on short range devices," in *Image Processing and Communications Challenges 3*, vol. 102 of *Advances in Intelligent and Soft Computing*, pp. 493–502, Springer, Berlin, Germany, 2011.

[9] P. Kiedrowski, "Errors nature of the narrowband plc transmission in smart lighting LV network," *International Journal of Distributed Sensor Networks*, vol. 2016, Article ID 9592679, 9 pages, 2016.

[10] A. S. Elmaghraby and M. M. Losavio, "Cyber security challenges in smart cities: Safety, security and privacy," *Journal of Advanced Research*, vol. 5, no. 4, pp. 491–497, 2014.

[11] M. H. Bhuyan, D. K. Bhattacharyya, and J. K. Kalita, "Network anomaly detection: methods, systems and tools," *IEEE Communications Surveys & Tutorials*, vol. 16, no. 1, pp. 303–336, 2014.

[12] M. Esposito, C. Mazzariello, F. Oliviero, S. P. Romano, and C. Sansone, "Evaluating pattern recognition techniques in intrusion detection systems," in *Proceedings of the 5th International Workshop on Pattern Recognition in Information Systems (PRIS'05), in Conjunction with ICEIS 2005*, pp. 144–153, Miami, FL, USA, May 2005.

[13] R. Mitchell and I.-R. Chen, "Behavior-rule based intrusion detection systems for safety critical smart grid applications," *IEEE Transactions on Smart Grid*, vol. 4, no. 3, pp. 1254–1263, 2013.

[14] V. Chandola, A. Banerjee, and V. Kumar, "Anomaly detection: a survey," *ACM Computing Surveys*, vol. 41, no. 3, article 15, 2009.

[15] T. Andrysiak and Ł. Saganowski, *Network Anomaly Detection Basedon ARFIMA Model, Image Processing & Communications Challenges 6, Advances in Intelligent Systems and Computing*, vol. 313, Springer, 2015.

[16] E. H. M. Pena, M. V. O. De Assis, and M. L. Proença, "Anomaly detection using forecasting methods ARIMA and HWDS," in *Proceedings of the 32nd International Conference of the Chilean Computer Science Society, SCCC 2013*, pp. 63–66, November 2013.

[17] G. Galvas, "Time series forecasting used for real-time anomaly detection on websites," 2016, https://beta.vu.nl/nl/Images/stageverslag-galvas_tcm235-801861.pdf.

[18] M. Xie, S. Han, B. Tian, and S. Parvin, "Anomaly detection in wireless sensor networks: a survey," *Journal of Network and Computer Applications*, vol. 34, no. 4, pp. 1302–1325, 2011.

[19] P. Cheng and M. Zhu, "Lightweight anomaly detection for wireless sensor networks," *International Journal of Distributed Sensor Networks*, vol. 2015, Article ID 653232, 2015.

[20] K. Ord and S. Lowe, "Automatic forecasting," *The American Statistician*, vol. 50, no. 1, pp. 88–94, 1996.

[21] V. Garcia-Font, C. Garrigues, and H. Rifà-Pous, "A comparative study of anomaly detection techniques for smart city wireless sensor networks," *Sensors*, vol. 16, no. 6, article 868, 2016.

[22] EFT/Burst generator Teseq, http://www.teseq.com/products/NSG-3060.php.

[23] N. Zhou, J. Wang, and Q. Wang, "A novel estimation method of metering errors of electric energy based on membership cloud and dynamic time warping," *IEEE Transactions on Smart Grid*, vol. 8, no. 3, pp. 1318–1329, 2017.

[24] V. J. Hodge and J. Austin, "A survey of outlier detection methodologies," *Artificial Intelligence Review*, vol. 22, no. 2, pp. 85–126, 2004.

[25] Y. Wang, T. T. Gamage, and C. H. Hauser, "Security Implications of Transport Layer Protocols in Power Grid Synchrophasor Data Communication," *IEEE Transactions on Smart Grid*, vol. 7, no. 2, pp. 807–816, 2016.

[26] M. Mahoor, F. R. Salmasi, and T. A. Najafabadi, "A hierarchical smart street lighting system with brute-force energy optimization," *IEEE Sensors Journal*, vol. 17, no. 9, pp. 2871–2879, 2017.

[27] C. Liao, C.-W. Ten, and S. Hu, "Strategic FRTU deployment considering cybersecurity in secondary distribution network," *IEEE Transactions on Smart Grid*, vol. 4, no. 3, pp. 1264–1274, 2013.

[28] S. M. Rinaldi, J. P. Peerenboom, and T. K. Kelly, "Identifying, understanding, and analyzing critical infrastructure interdependencies," *IEEE Control Systems Magazine*, vol. 21, no. 6, pp. 11–25, 2001.

[29] Y. Wu, C. Shi, X. Zhang, and W. Yang, "Design of new intelligent street light control system," in *Proceedings of the 2010 8th IEEE International Conference on Control and Automation, ICCA 2010*, pp. 1423–1427, June 2010.

[30] T. Macaulay and B. L. Singer, *ICS vulnerabilities. In:*

Cybersecurity industrial control systems SCADA, DCS, PLC, HMI, SIS [Internet], CRC PRESS: Taylor & Francis Group, 2012, https://www.crcpress.com/Cybersecurity-for-Industrial-Control-Systems-SCADA-DCS-PLC-HMI-and/Macaulay-Singer/9781439801963 [Google Scholar].

[31] R. Smoleński, *Conducted Electromagnetic Interference (EMI) in Smart Grids*, Springer, London, UK, 2012.

[32] J. Liu, Y. Xiao, S. Li, W. Liang, and C. L. P. Chen, "Cyber security and privacy issues in smart grids," *IEEE Communications Surveys & Tutorials*, vol. 14, no. 4, pp. 981–997, 2012.

[33] D. M. Hawkins, *Identification of Outliers*, Chapman and Hall, London, UK, 1980.

[34] M. J. Healy, "Multivariate Normal Plotting," *Journal of Applied Statistics*, vol. 17, no. 2, p. 157, 1968.

[35] P. J. Rousseeuw, "Least median of squares regression," *Journal of the American Statistical Association*, vol. 79, no. 388, pp. 871–880, 1984.

[36] P. Filzmoser, R. Maronna, and M. Werner, "Outlier identification in high dimensions," *Computational Statistics & Data Analysis*, vol. 52, no. 3, pp. 1694–1711, 2008.

[37] R. L. Goodrich, "The Forecast Pro methodology," *International Journal of Forecasting*, vol. 16, no. 4, pp. 533–535, 2000.

[38] R. J. Hyndman, A. B. Koehler, R. D. Snyder, and S. Grose, "A state space framework for automatic forecasting using exponential smoothing methods," *International Journal of Forecasting*, vol. 18, no. 3, pp. 439–454, 2002.

[39] E. S. Gardner, "Exponential smoothing: the state of the art," *Journal of Forecasting*, vol. 4, no. 1, pp. 1–28, 1985.

[40] E. S. Gardner Jr., "Exponential smoothing: the state of the art-part II," *International Journal of Forecasting*, vol. 22, no. 4, pp. 637–666, 2006.

[41] B. C. Archibald, "Parameter space of the holt-winters' model," *International Journal of Forecasting*, vol. 6, no. 2, pp. 199–209, 1990.

[42] J. Durbin and S. J. Koopman, *Time series analysis by state space methods*, vol. 24, Oxford University Press, Oxford, UK, 2001.

[43] R. J. Hyndman and Y. Khandakar, "Automatic time series forecasting: the forecast package for R," *Journal of Statistical Software*, vol. 27, no. 3, pp. 1–22, 2008.

[44] H. Bozdogan, "Model selection and Akaike's information criterion (AIC): the general theory and its analytical extensions," *Psychometrika*, vol. 52, no. 3, pp. 345–370, 1987.

[45] J. Ramsey and D. Wiley, "Book Reviews : exploratory data analysis John W. Tukey Reading, Mass: Addison-Wesley, 1977, Pps. xvi +688. $17.95," *Applied Psychological Measurement*, vol. 2, no. 1, pp. 151–155, 1978.

[46] National Fund for Environmental Protection and Water Management under the realized GEKON program (project no. 214093).

[47] IEC 61000-4-4, http://www.iec.ch/emc/basic_emc/basic_emc_immunity.htm.

[48] S. McLaughlin, B. Holbert, A. Fawaz, R. Berthier, and S. Zonouz, "A multi-sensor energy theft detection framework for advanced metering infrastructures," *IEEE Journal on Selected Areas in Communications*, vol. 31, no. 7, pp. 1319–1330, 2013.

[49] Y. Liu, S. Hu, and T.-Y. Ho, "Leveraging strategic detection techniques for smart home pricing cyberattacks," *IEEE Transactions on Dependable and Secure Computing*, vol. 13, no. 2, pp. 220–235, 2016.

[50] C.-H. Lo and N. Ansari, "CONSUMER: a novel hybrid intrusion detection system for distribution networks in smart grid," *IEEE Transactions on Emerging Topics in Computing*, vol. 1, no. 1, pp. 33–44, 2013.

7

An Edge Correlation based Differentially Private Network Data Release Method

Junling Lu,[1,2] Zhipeng Cai,[3] Xiaoming Wang,[1,2] Lichen Zhang,[1,2] and Zhuojun Duan[3]

[1]*Key Laboratory for Modern Teaching Technology, Ministry of Education, Xi'an 710062, China*
[2]*School of Computer Science, Shaanxi Normal University, Xi'an 710119, China*
[3]*Department of Computer Science, Georgia State University, Atlanta, GA 30303, USA*

Correspondence should be addressed to Zhipeng Cai; zcai@gsu.edu

Academic Editor: Houbing Song

Differential privacy (DP) provides a rigorous and provable privacy guarantee and assumes adversaries' arbitrary background knowledge, which makes it distinct from prior work in privacy preserving. However, DP cannot achieve claimed privacy guarantees over datasets with correlated tuples. Aiming to protect whether two individuals have a close relationship in a correlated dataset corresponding to a weighted network, we propose a differentially private network data release method, based on edge correlation, to gain the tradeoff between privacy and utility. Specifically, we first extracted the Edge Profile (PF) of an edge from a graph, which is transformed from a raw correlated dataset. Then, edge correlation is defined based on the PFs of both edges via Jenson-Shannon Divergence (JS-Divergence). Secondly, we transform a raw weighted dataset into an indicated dataset by adopting a weight threshold, to satisfy specific real need and decrease query sensitivity. Furthermore, we propose ϵ-correlated edge differential privacy (CEDP), by combining the correlation analysis and the correlated parameter with traditional DP. Finally, we propose network data release (NDR) algorithm based on the ϵ-CEDP model and discuss its privacy and utility. Extensive experiments over real and synthetic network datasets show the proposed releasing method provides better utilities while maintaining privacy guarantee.

1. Introduction

Recently, social networking such as cooperation networks, online/mobile social networks, and software defined vehicular network [1] is becoming increasingly prevalent. Accompanied with the growth of the networks, mass of network data is released for analytical decisions or scientific researches. However, direct publication of these data, including sensitive information, leads to privacy leakage of individuals. For example, whether two individuals in a social network have a close relationship may be expected to be kept a secret. Therefore, privacy concerns have been raised in increasingly emerging technologies [2–9].

In general, a dataset corresponding to such a network, usually modeled as a graph, is considered as correlated data; that is, tuples in this dataset are dependent. Clearly, privacy preserving in such correlated settings is more difficult because an adversary can infer the relationship of two individuals from their associated friends. Accordingly, our concern is preventing, whether the relationship of two individuals appears in a network dataset, from being unveiled.

Differential privacy (DP), a privacy preserving model originated from statistical database, has currently drawn considerable attentions in research communities [10–17] due to (i) its rigorous and provable privacy guarantee and (ii) its assumption of adversaries' arbitrary background knowledge. However, DP actually assumes that the tuples in databases are independent [18]. In other words, DP cannot provide claimed privacy guarantees over correlated (nonindependent) data [19]. Therefore, the application of DP over correlated data is a challenge, and how to achieve a differentially private correlated data release method deserves to be further explored.

The focus of our work is on hiding the affinity degree of two individuals in a correlated dataset corresponding to a weighted network, that is, protecting whether the affinity degree of two individuals exceeds a given weight threshold, in a differentially private manner. Toward this end, we first transform a weighted network dataset into a corresponding

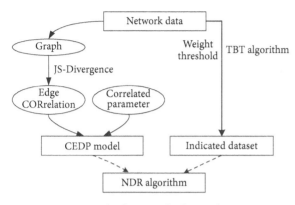

FIGURE 1: The framework of our solution.

weighted graph and define the correlation of both edges via Jenson-Shannon Divergence (JS-Divergence). For satisfying specific query need in spite of some utility loss, we utilize Threshold Based Transformation (TBT) algorithm to transform a weighted dataset, by adopting a weight threshold, into an indicated dataset, which also decreases query sensitivity. Finally, we present the notion of ϵ-correlated edge differential privacy (CEDP), by combining the correlation analysis and the correlated parameter, that is, the maximal number of correlated tuples, with traditional DP, and design differentially private network data release (NDR) algorithm to obtain better utilities while maintaining DP guarantee. Experimental results over real and synthetic network datasets also show the advantages of the proposed method. The framework of our solution is shown in Figure 1.

The contributions of our work are as follows.

First, we extract the Edge Profile (PF) vectors of edges in a weighted graph corresponding to a network dataset and then define the correlation of both edges via JS-Divergence. The inferred correlation analysis is more reasonable for datasets corresponding to such networks, since the typical Pearson correlation coefficient assumes that sample data follows normal distribution; however, the degree and weight distributions in such networks are often not so.

Second, we propose the ϵ-CEDP model based on our result of correlation analysis and the introduction of the correlated parameter, which makes DP over correlated datasets applicable and flexible. Furthermore, the NDR algorithm, based on correlated sensitivity and Laplace mechanism, is proposed, which also satisfies ϵ-CEDP and achieves the tradeoff of privacy and utility.

Third, we utilize TBT algorithm to transform a raw weighted dataset into an indicated dataset; that is, a weight value is equal to 1 or 0, by adopting a weight threshold, to satisfy specific real need and decrease query sensitivity. Admittedly, some utility loss exists in such transformation. However, many queries in real world only need Boolean values indicated by one and zero instead of accurate numeric answers. Therefore, this solution provides a feasible way for decreasing query sensitivity while maintaining real query need.

The rest of this paper is organized as follows. Section 2 discusses related literature. Section 3 provides the preliminaries. In Section 4, correlation analysis of both edges in a weighted graph is presented, and the ϵ-CEDP model and sensitivity calculation are proposed. Furthermore, a differentially private NDR algorithm, including TBT algorithm, to obtain the tradeoff between privacy and utility over correlated data is proposed in Section 5. The extensive experiments are illustrated in Section 6. Finally, Section 7 concludes the paper.

2. Related Work

Compared with previous works in privacy preserving, DP proposed by Dwork [20] provides a probabilistic formulation, which represents that adversaries learn little from both databases differing in one tuple even if adversaries know about all tuples except the target one. In other words, the inference abilities of adversaries about the presence or absence of a tuple are bounded regardless of adversaries' knowledge; that is, the presence or absence of a tuple is probabilistically indistinguishable for adversaries.

Currently, DP has drawn much attention in privacy preserving work needed in many fields. Wang et al. [10] considered a unified privacy distortion framework, where the distortion is defined to be the expected Hamming distance between the input and output databases, and investigated the relation between three different notions of privacy: identifiability, differential privacy, and mutual-information privacy. To provide personalized recommendation in big data resulting from social networks and maintain user privacy, a cloud-assisted differentially private video recommendation system based on distributed online learning was proposed [11]. The work in [12] proposed a new privacy preserving smart metering scheme for smart grid, which supports data aggregation, differential privacy, fault tolerance, and range-based filtering simultaneously. To et al. [13] introduced a novel privacy-aware framework for spatial crowdsourcing, which enables the participation of workers without compromising their location privacy. Focusing on the privacy protection of sensitive information in body area networks, the authors in [14, 15] proposed different privacy preserving schemes, based on differential privacy model, via a tree structure and dynamic noise thresholds, respectively. The work in [16] proposed a novel differentially private frequent sequence mining algorithm by leveraging a sampling-based candidate pruning technique, which satisfies ϵ-differential privacy and can privately find frequent sequences with high accuracy. In order to protect users' privacy in ridesharing services, a jointly differentially private scheduling protocol has been proposed [17], which aims to protect riders' location information and minimize the total additional vehicle mileage in the ridesharing system.

However, existing works have found that DP provides weaker privacy guarantee over nonindependent data; that is, DP needs more noise added to the output query result to cancel out the impact of correlations among tuples on privacy guarantee. Undoubtedly, how to analyze correlations among tuples and apply them into DP are desired to be further explored. For example, Kifer and Machanavajjhala [19] first explicitly doubted the privacy guarantee of DP in correlated settings, for example, social networks, and then adopted the subsequently proposed privacy framework, that is, Pufferfish, to formalize and prove that DP assumes independence between tuples [18]. Inspired by the Pufferfish framework, Blowfish privacy [21] was proposed to achieve the tradeoff between privacy and utility using policies specifying secrets and constraints. Similarly, the authors in [22] proposed Bayesian DP to evaluate the level of private information leakage even when data is correlated and prior knowledge is incomplete. The work in [23] regarded the correlation among tuples as complete correlation and multiplied the query sensitivity with the number of correlated tuples in publishing correlated network data, which leaves room for fine-grained correlation analysis in the following work. Aiming to decrease the noise amount, Zhu et al. [24] depicted the correlation between tuples via Pearson correlation coefficient, including complete correlation, partial correlation, and independence. Liu et al. [25] inferred the dependence coefficient, distributed in interval [0, 1], to evaluate the probabilistic correlation between two tuples in a more fine-grained manner, thus reducing the query sensitivity which results in less noise. Considering temporal correlations of a moving user's locations, the work in [26] leveraged a hidden Markov model to establish a location set and proposed a variant of DP to protect location privacy. Wu et al. [27] proposed the definition of correlated differential privacy to evaluate the real privacy level of a single dataset influenced by the other datasets when multiple datasets are correlated. The work in [28] formalized the privacy preservation problem to an optimization problem by modeling the temporal correlations among contexts and further proposed an efficient context-aware privacy preserving algorithm. Cao et al. [29] modeled the temporal correlations using Markov model and investigated the privacy leakage of a traditional DP mechanism under temporal correlations in the context of continuous data release. The work in [30] quantified the location correlation between two users through the similarity measurement of two hidden Markov models and applied differential privacy via private candidate sets to achieve the multiuser location correlation protection.

As seen from the above discussions, correlation analysis plays an important role in privacy preserving mechanisms, which directly influences the tradeoff between privacy protection and service utility. Obviously, the more accurate the correlation analysis, the better the balance of both aspects. Therefore, we attribute the underestimated privacy guarantee of DP over correlated data to the lack of data knowledge, and our work starts from data correlation analysis.

In this paper, we focus on correlated datasets corresponding to weighted cooperation networks. Different from the existing methods of correlation analysis, for example, simple multiplication in [23], Pearson correlation coefficient in [24], and the maximal information coefficient in [31], we extract the PF vectors of edges in a weighted graph corresponding to a correlated dataset and then define the correlation of both edges via JS-Divergence, which is more accurate and reasonable. Specifically, the work in [23] assumes both tuples are completely correlated; however, our proposed correlation

results lie in interval [0, 1] representing multiple correlation including complete correlation. In addition, the work in [24] assumes sample data follows normal distribution, while our method is not the case. Also, the maximal information coefficient proposed in [31] satisfies two heuristic properties including generality and equitability, and we will consider it in our future work.

3. Preliminaries

3.1. Differential Privacy.
Differential privacy provides the privacy guarantee for an individual in the probabilistic sense [20]. It is defined as follows.

Definition 1 (ϵ-differential privacy). A randomized mechanism $\mathcal{A}$ satisfies ϵ-differential privacy if, for any pair of databases D and D' differing in only one tuple and for any output $S \in O(\mathcal{A})$ representing the possible output set of $\mathcal{A}$,

$$\Pr\left[\mathcal{A}(D) = S\right] \le \exp(\epsilon) \cdot \Pr\left[\mathcal{A}(D') = S\right], \qquad (1)$$

where ϵ is the privacy budget depicting the probabilistic difference between the same outputs of $\mathcal{A}$ over D and D'.

Generally, DP is achieved via two mechanisms: Laplace mechanism [32] and exponential mechanism [33]. Both mechanisms include a concept of global sensitivity [20], which reveals DP's preferable choice of protecting the extreme case.

Definition 2 (global sensitivity). For any query function $f : D \to \mathbb{R}^d$, where D is a dataset and $\mathbb{R}^d$ is a d-dimension real-valued vector, the global sensitivity of f is defined as

$$\Delta f = \max_{D, D'} \left\| f(D) - f(D') \right\|_1, \qquad (2)$$

where D and D' denote any pair of databases differing in only one tuple and $\| \cdot \|_1$ denotes l_1 norm.

Laplace mechanism, used in this paper, is formally presented as follows.

Theorem 3 (Laplace mechanism). *Given any query function $f : D \to \mathbb{R}^d$, where D is a dataset and $\mathbb{R}^d$ is a d-dimension real-valued vector, the global sensitivity Δf of f, and privacy budget ϵ, a randomized mechanism $\mathcal{A}$*

$$\mathcal{A}(D) = f(D) + Laplace\left(\frac{\Delta f}{\epsilon}\right) \qquad (3)$$

provides the ϵ-differential privacy, where $Laplace(\cdot)$ denotes Laplace noise.

3.2. Weighted Adjacency Matrix.
In this paper, we model a correlated dataset as a weighted undirected simple graph $G = (V, E, W)$, where $V = \{v_1, \ldots, v_n\}$ is the set of vertices and $n = |V|$ is the number of vertices, $E = \{e_{ij}\}$ is the set of edges and $e_{ij} = (v_i, v_j)$, $v_i \in V$, $i = 1, \ldots, n$, $v_j \in V$, $j = 1, \ldots, n$, and $W = \{w_{ij}\}$ is the set of weights where weight w_{ij} corresponds

TABLE 1: A raw weighted dataset.

V_i	V_j	w_{ij}
1	2	2
2	3	4
2	4	8
2	5	1
4	5	5
4	6	3

Note. V_i and V_j denote two individuals, and weight w_{ij} denotes the relation strength between them.

with edge e_{ij}. Then, the weighted adjacency matrix A^w of G can be denoted as

$$A_{ij}^w = \begin{cases} w_{ij}, & e_{ij} \in E \\ 0, & \text{otherwise,} \end{cases} \tag{4}$$

where w_{ij} represents the affinity degree between two individuals. Obviously, the weighted adjacency matrix A_{ij}^w is symmetric.

Example 4. Suppose a raw weighted dataset D_W is listed in Table 1. Then, the corresponding weighted adjacency matrix A^w of D_W can be denoted as

$$\begin{pmatrix} 0 & 2 & 0 & 0 & 0 & 0 \\ 2 & 0 & 4 & 8 & 1 & 0 \\ 0 & 4 & 0 & 0 & 0 & 0 \\ 0 & 8 & 0 & 0 & 5 & 3 \\ 0 & 1 & 0 & 5 & 0 & 0 \\ 0 & 0 & 0 & 3 & 0 & 0 \end{pmatrix}. \tag{5}$$

3.3. Correlation Metric. Motivated by the entropy in information theory, we adopt JS-Divergence, inferred from Kullback-Leibler Divergence (KL-Divergence) [23], to depict the difference of two distributions, which can be transformed to depict the correlation of two tuples in a correlated dataset.

Definition 5 (KL-Divergence). Suppose $P = \{p_1, p_2, \ldots, p_n\}$ and $Q = \{q_1, q_2, \ldots, q_n\}$ are the probability distributions of random variables $X = \{x_1, x_2, \ldots, x_n\}$ and $Y = \{y_1, y_2, \ldots, y_n\}$; then the KL-Divergence of P and Q is defined as follows:

$$\text{KLD}(P \parallel Q) = \sum_{i=1}^{n} p_i \ln\left(\frac{p_i}{q_i}\right). \tag{6}$$

Here $0 \log 0 = 0$ is required. Based on KL-Divergence, we can obtain JS-Divergence as follows.

Definition 6 (JS-Divergence). Suppose $P = \{p_1, p_2, \ldots, p_n\}$ and $Q = \{q_1, q_2, \ldots, q_n\}$ are the probability distributions of random variables $X = \{x_1, x_2, \ldots, x_n\}$ and $Y =$

$\{y_1, y_2, \ldots, y_n\}$, and $M = (1/2)(P + Q)$; then the JS-Divergence of P and Q is defined as follows:

$$\text{JSD}(P \parallel Q) = \frac{1}{2}(\text{KLD}(P \parallel M) + \text{KLD}(Q \parallel M))$$

$$= \frac{1}{2}\sum_{i=1}^{n}\left(p_i \ln\frac{2p_i}{p_i + q_i} + q_i \ln\frac{2q_i}{p_i + q_i}\right). \tag{7}$$

4. Correlation Analysis of Weighted Edges

In this section, we first discuss how to define the correlation of both edges in a weighted graph corresponding to a network dataset and then introduce why and how we conduct dataset transformation based on a given weight threshold. Finally, we define the ϵ-CEDP model and calculate the correlated sensitivity for smaller added noise.

4.1. Correlation Definition. For achieving the correlation of tuples in a raw weighted dataset D_W, we first obtain a weighted graph G, whose weighted adjacency matrix is denoted by A^w. Then, the correlation problem is changed to seeking the correlation of edges in G. To this end, we first describe the PF vector of a weighted edge from the perspectives of relational strength and network structure and then define the correlation of both edges via JS-Divergence instead of Pearson correlation coefficient.

For a weighted edge e_{ij}, suppose $V_i = \{v \mid (v, v_i) \in E, v \neq v_i\}$ represents the set of vertices connected with v_i and $V_j = \{v \mid (v, v_j) \in E, v \neq v_j\}$ represents the set of vertices connected with v_j; we extract the PF vector of e_{ij}, denoted by $\text{PF}(e_{ij})$, from the perspectives of relational strength and network structure simultaneously. Specifically, we obtain $w_{ij}/\max_{e_{ij} \in E}(w_{ij}) \in [0, 1]$ from the global weights of all edges. In addition, we get $w_{ij}/\sum_{v \in V_i} w_{iv} \in [0, 1]$ and $w_{ij}/\sum_{v \in V_j} w_{jv} \in [0, 1]$ from the local weights of edge e_{ij}. On the other hand, similar to the representation of relational strength, $\text{Deg}(v_i)/\max_{v \in V}(\text{Deg}(v)) \in [0, 1]$ and $\text{Deg}(v_j)/\max_{v \in V}(\text{Deg}(v)) \in [0, 1]$ are constructed, by introducing the node degree $\text{Deg}(\cdot)$, to depict the global active degree for both vertices of edge e_{ij}. Also, $|V_i \cap V_j|/|V_i \cup V_j| \in [0, 1]$ is adopted, via the set similarity, to depict the ratio of the number of common vertices connecting v_i and v_j to that of V_i and V_j. Meanwhile, $\text{Deg}(v_i)/\sum_{v \in V_i} \text{Deg}(v) \in [0, 1]$ and $\text{Deg}(v_j)/\sum_{v \in V_j} \text{Deg}(v) \in [0, 1]$ are used to depict the local active degree for both vertices of edge e_{ij}. Combining the above factors, we obtain $\text{PF}(e_{ij})$ as follows:

$$\text{PF}(e_{ij}) = \left(\frac{w_{ij}}{\max_{e_{ij} \in E}(w_{ij})}, \frac{w_{ij}}{\sum_{v \in V_i} w_{iv}}, \frac{w_{ij}}{\sum_{v \in V_j} w_{jv}}, \right.$$

$$\frac{\text{Deg}(v_i)}{\max_{v \in V}(\text{Deg}(v))}, \frac{\text{Deg}(v_j)}{\max_{v \in V}(\text{Deg}(v))}, \frac{|V_i \cap V_j|}{|V_i \cup V_j|}, \tag{8}$$

$$\left. \frac{\text{Deg}(v_i)}{\sum_{v \in V_i} \text{Deg}(v)}, \frac{\text{Deg}(v_j)}{\sum_{v \in V_j} \text{Deg}(v)} \right).$$

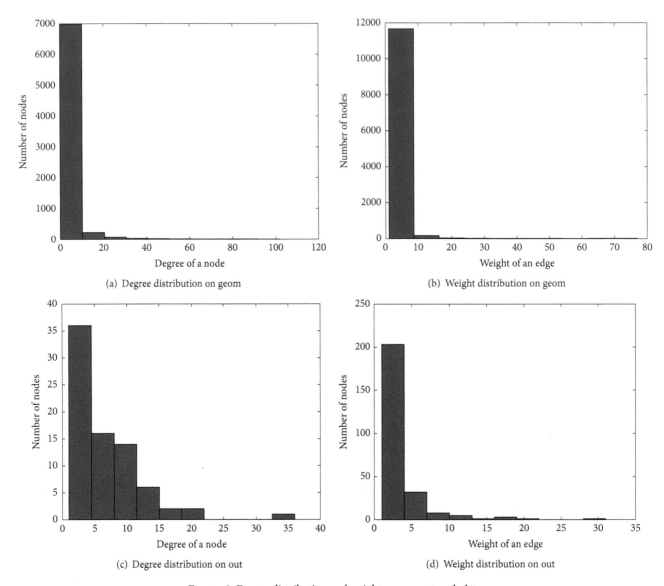

FIGURE 2: Degree distribution and weight one on network data.

Similarly, for any other edge e_{mn}, according to (8), we define $PF(e_{mn})$ as follows:

$$PF\left(e_{mn}\right) = \left(\frac{w_{mn}}{\max_{e_{mn} \in E}\left(w_{mn}\right)}, \frac{w_{mn}}{\sum_{v \in V_m} w_{mv}}, \frac{w_{mn}}{\sum_{v \in V_n} w_{nv}}, \right.$$
$$\frac{\text{Deg}\left(v_m\right)}{\max_{v \in V}\left(\text{Deg}\left(v\right)\right)}, \frac{\text{Deg}\left(v_n\right)}{\max_{v \in V}\left(\text{Deg}\left(v\right)\right)}, \frac{\left|V_m \cap V_n\right|}{\left|V_m \cup V_n\right|}, \quad (9)$$
$$\left. \frac{\text{Deg}\left(v_m\right)}{\sum_{v \in V_m} \text{Deg}\left(v\right)}, \frac{\text{Deg}\left(v_n\right)}{\sum_{v \in V_n} \text{Deg}\left(v\right)} \right).$$

Note that Pearson correlation coefficient assumes that sample data follows normal distribution. However, in social networks, the weight and degree distributions do not follow such distribution, which is also verified by our experiments shown in Figure 2, where geom and out are the abbreviations

of geom.net [34–36] and out.moreno_lesmis_lesmis [37–39] for simplicity. Specifically, (i) geom.net is the authors collaboration network in Computational Geometry based on the file geombib.bib, and the reduced simple network contains 7343 vertices and 11898 edges. Two authors are linked with an edge, iff they wrote a common work. The value of an edge is the number of common works. (ii) out.moreno_lesmis_lesmis is the characters cooccurrences network in Victor Hugo's novel "Les Misérables," and it contains 77 vertices and 254 edges. A node represents a character and an edge between two nodes shows that these two characters appeared in the same chapter of the book. The weight of each link indicates how often such a coappearance occurred.

Since our constructed PF vectors of edges do not satisfy the assumption of normal distribution, we adopt JS-Divergence, instead of Pearson correlation coefficient, to measure the CORrelation (COR) of any two edges e_{ij}, e_{mn} in a weighted graph. To this end, we normalize $PF(e_{ij})$ and

PF(e_{mn}) as PN(e_{ij}) and PN(e_{mn}), which are two probability distributions. Therefore, we have

$$PN\left(e_{ij}\right) = \frac{PF\left(e_{ij}\right)}{S_{ij}}, \tag{10}$$

where $S_{ij} = w_{ij}/\max_{e_{ij}\in E}(w_{ij}) + w_{ij}/\sum_{v\in V_i} w_{iv} + w_{ij}/\sum_{v\in V_j} w_{jv}$
$+ \text{Deg}(v_i)/\max_{v\in V}(\text{Deg}(v)) + \text{Deg}(v_j)/\max_{v\in V}(\text{Deg}(v)) + |V_i \cap V_j|/|V_i \cup V_j| + \text{Deg}(v_i)/\sum_{v\in V_i} \text{Deg}(v) + \text{Deg}(v_j)/\sum_{v\in V_j} \text{Deg}(v)$
and

$$PN\left(e_{mn}\right) = \frac{PF\left(e_{mn}\right)}{S_{mn}}, \tag{11}$$

where $S_{mn} = w_{mn}/\max_{e_{mn}\in E}(w_{mn}) + w_{mn}/\sum_{v\in V_m} w_{mv} + w_{mn}/\sum_{v\in V_n} w_{nv} + \text{Deg}(v_m)/\max_{v\in V}(\text{Deg}(v)) + \text{Deg}(v_n)/\max_{v\in V}(\text{Deg}(v)) + |V_m \cap V_n|/|V_m \cup V_n| + \text{Deg}(v_m)/\sum_{v\in V_m} \text{Deg}(v) + \text{Deg}(v_n)/\sum_{v\in V_n} \text{Deg}(v)$.

Meanwhile, we consider the distance of both edges as follows.

Definition 7 (edge distance). Suppose $e_{ij} = (v_i, v_j)$ and $e_{mn} = (v_m, v_n)$ are two edges in graph G, $d(v_1, v_2)$ denotes the length of the shortest path between nodes v_1 and v_2, and I is the index of the smallest value in vector $[d(v_i, v_m), d(v_i, v_n), d(v_j, v_m), d(v_j, v_n)]$; then the distance of e_{ij} and e_{mn} is defined as follows:

$$\text{dis}\left(e_{ij}, e_{mn}\right) = \begin{cases} d\left(v_i, v_m\right) + d\left(v_j, v_n\right), & I = 1 \\ d\left(v_i, v_n\right) + d\left(v_j, v_m\right), & I = 2 \\ d\left(v_j, v_m\right) + d\left(v_i, v_n\right), & I = 3 \\ d\left(v_j, v_n\right) + d\left(v_i, v_m\right), & I = 4. \end{cases} \tag{12}$$

Specifically, we first calculate the distances including $d(v_i, v_m)$, $d(v_i, v_n)$, $d(v_j, v_m)$, and $d(v_j, v_n)$ and then determine the smallest one among these distances and its index I, complete the calculation of the distance of another pair of nodes, and finally obtain the distance of two edges e_{ij} and e_{mn}.

Based on Definitions 6 and 7, we define the CORrelation (COR) of two probability distributions via JS-Divergence as follows.

Definition 8 (CORrelation). Suppose $P = \{p_1, p_2, \ldots, p_n\}$ and $Q = \{q_1, q_2, \ldots, q_n\}$ are the probability distributions of random variables $X = \{x_1, x_2, \ldots, x_n\}$ and $Y = \{y_1, y_2, \ldots, y_n\}$; then the CORrelation of P and Q is defined as follows:

$$COR\left(P, Q\right) = \frac{1 - JSD\left(P \parallel Q\right)}{1 + \text{dis}\left(e_{ij}, e_{mn}\right)}. \tag{13}$$

According to (10)–(13) and Definition 6, we adopt the normalized PN vectors of edges e_{ij}, e_{mn} to measure their correlation as

$$COR\left(e_{ij}, e_{mn}\right) = \frac{1}{1 + \text{dis}\left(e_{ij}, e_{mn}\right)} \left(1 \right.$$
$$- \frac{1}{2}\sum_{k=1}^{8} PN\left(e_{ij}\right)_k \ln \frac{PN\left(e_{ij}\right)_k}{PN\left(M\right)_k} \tag{14}$$
$$\left. - \frac{1}{2}\sum_{k=1}^{8} PN\left(e_{mn}\right)_k \ln \frac{PN\left(e_{mn}\right)_k}{PN\left(M\right)_k} \right),$$

where PN$(\cdot)_k$ denotes the k element of vector PN$(\cdot)$ and

$$PN\left(M\right)_k = \frac{1}{2}\left(PN\left(e_{ij}\right)_k + PN\left(e_{mn}\right)_k\right). \tag{15}$$

Substituting (15) into (14), we obtain

$$COR\left(e_{ij}, e_{mn}\right) = \frac{1}{1 + \text{dis}\left(e_{ij}, e_{mn}\right)} \left(1 \right.$$
$$- \frac{1}{2}\sum_{k=1}^{8} PN\left(e_{ij}\right)_k \ln \frac{2PN\left(e_{ij}\right)_k}{PN\left(e_{ij}\right)_k + PN\left(e_{mn}\right)_k} \tag{16}$$
$$\left. - \frac{1}{2}\sum_{k=1}^{8} PN\left(e_{mn}\right)_k \ln \frac{2PN\left(e_{mn}\right)_k}{PN\left(e_{ij}\right)_k + PN\left(e_{mn}\right)_k} \right).$$

In our opinion, the proposed correlation definition, extracted from two aspects of relational strength and network structure, is more reasonable. The rationale is (i) graph models, commonly abstracted from networks, reflect inherent dependent relations of individuals, which naturally form edge correlations and (ii) the weights of edges in weighted graphs describe the affinity degree of individuals' relations, which also influence the variances of edge correlations.

Example 9. Take e_{24} and e_{25} in D_W as an example to demonstrate the calculation of COR(e_{24}, e_{25}). According to (8) and (9), we have

$$PF\left(e_{24}\right) = \left(\frac{8}{8}, \frac{8}{15}, \frac{8}{16}, \frac{4}{4}, \frac{3}{4}, \frac{1}{6}, \frac{4}{7}, \frac{3}{7}\right),$$
$$PF\left(e_{25}\right) = \left(\frac{1}{8}, \frac{1}{15}, \frac{1}{6}, \frac{4}{4}, \frac{2}{4}, \frac{1}{5}, \frac{4}{7}, \frac{2}{7}\right). \tag{17}$$

Furthermore, according to (10) and (11), we get

$$PN\left(e_{24}\right) = (0.2020, 0.1077, 0.1010, 0.2020, 0.1515, 0.0337, 0.1154, 0.0866), \tag{18}$$

$$PN\left(e_{25}\right) = (0.0429, 0.0229, 0.0572, 0.3430, 0.1715, 0.0686, 0.1960, 0.0980). \tag{19}$$

Input: Weighted dataset D_W, weight threshold T.
Output: Indicated dataset D_I.
(1) **for** (Each tuple $(i, j) \in D_W$) **do**
(2)   **if** $(w_{ij} > T)$ **then**
(3) $w_{ij} = 1$;
(4)   **else**
(5) $w_{ij} = 0$;
(6)   **end if**
(7) **end for**
(8) **return** D_I with indicated values.

ALGORITHM 1: TBT algorithm.

Finally, according to (16), we obtain

$$COR(e_{24}, e_{25}) = 0.4679. \qquad (20)$$

4.2. Dataset Transformation. We consider some real world situations that do not need exact query answers. For example, people sometimes only want to learn about whether two individuals have an intimate relationship or not, rather than the specific number of communication or cooperation. So the privacy concern at this time is to avoid the leakage of close relationship, that is, yes or no. Therefore, the first thing we focus on is to transform a weighted dataset D_W to an indicated dataset D_I, based on a given weight threshold T. In other words, we consider replacing query "Select SUM(weight) from D_W where $w_{ij} > T$" with query "Select COUNT(∗) from D_W where $w_{ij} > T$", which satisfies some specific situations and decreases the query sensitivity simultaneously. Note that this method aims to avoid the leakage of whether an edge satisfying the given threshold condition exists and not to avoid the weights of edges satisfying the one exposed. In our opinion, this solution is reasonable and suitable for achieving privacy protection via DP in spite of some utility loss.

To this end, we propose the TBT algorithm to modify raw weight values w_{ij} in D_W as an indicated value; that is, $w_{ij} = 1$ if $w_{ij} > T$; otherwise, $w_{ij} = 0$, thus transforming D_W to D_I. The TBT algorithm is presented in Algorithm 1.

4.3. Correlated Edge Differential Privacy. As discussed above, we only consider the situations: the query answers responding to a correlated weighted data are yes or no, which indicates whether two individuals have close relationship. That is, the privacy concern herein is to avoid the leakage of whether there is a close relationship between two individuals, in a weighted dataset whose at most z tuples are correlated, where z is the correlated parameter. To this end, we first define correlated neighboring databases as follows.

Definition 10 (correlated neighboring databases). Any pair of databases $D_{COR,z}$ and $D'_{COR,z}$ are correlated neighboring databases, if the weight change of a tuple in $D_{COR,z}$ results in the weight changes of at most $z - 1$ other correlated tuples in D' based on the correlation $COR(\cdot, \cdot)$ of both tuples.

Note that the neighboring databases in Definition 10 are described by two parameters: the correlation $COR(\cdot, \cdot)$ aforementioned and the correlated parameter z. Specifically, we have the following.

(i) Based on JS-Divergence, we have the following conclusion about the correlation $COR(\cdot, \cdot)$.

Theorem 11. *For any two edges e_{ij} and e_{mn} in the weighted graph G corresponding to a network dataset D_W, $0 \le COR(e_{ij}, e_{mn}) \le 1$ holds.*

Proof. For the ease of exposition, we denote the last two items in the numerator of (16) as follows.

$$JSD\left(e_{ij} \parallel e_{mn}\right) = \frac{1}{2}$$

$$\cdot \sum_{k=1}^{8} \left(PN\left(e_{ij}\right)_k \ln \frac{2PN\left(e_{ij}\right)_k}{PN\left(e_{ij}\right)_k + PN\left(e_{mn}\right)_k} \right. \qquad (21)$$

$$\left. + PN\left(e_{mn}\right)_k \ln \frac{2PN\left(e_{mn}\right)_k}{PN\left(e_{ij}\right)_k + PN\left(e_{mn}\right)_k} \right).$$

Since $PN(\cdot)$ denotes a probability distribution, we have

$$\sum_{k=1}^{8} PN\left(e_{ij}\right)_k = 1,$$
$$\qquad (22)$$
$$\sum_{k=1}^{8} PN\left(e_{mn}\right)_k = 1;$$

we consider two cases separately.

Case 1 $(COR(e_{ij}, e_{mn}) \le 1)$. Since $\ln(x) \le x - 1$ when $x > 0$, we have

$$\sum_{k=1}^{8} PN\left(e_{ij}\right)_k \ln \frac{2PN\left(e_{ij}\right)_k}{PN\left(e_{ij}\right)_k + PN\left(e_{mn}\right)_k}$$

$$\le \sum_{k=1}^{8} PN\left(e_{ij}\right)_k \left(\frac{2PN\left(e_{ij}\right)_k}{PN\left(e_{ij}\right)_k + PN\left(e_{mn}\right)_k} - 1 \right)$$

$$= \sum_{k=1}^{8} PN\left(e_{ij}\right)_k \frac{PN\left(e_{ij}\right)_k - PN\left(e_{mn}\right)_k}{PN\left(e_{ij}\right)_k + PN\left(e_{mn}\right)_k} \qquad (23)$$

$$\le \sum_{k=1}^{8} PN\left(e_{ij}\right)_k.$$

Substituting (22) into (23), we have

$$\sum_{k=1}^{8} PN\left(e_{ij}\right)_k \ln \frac{2PN\left(e_{ij}\right)_k}{PN\left(e_{ij}\right)_k + PN\left(e_{mn}\right)_k} \le 1. \qquad (24)$$

Similarly, we obtain

$$\sum_{k=1}^{8} PN\left(e_{mn}\right)_k \ln \frac{2PN\left(e_{mn}\right)_k}{PN\left(e_{ij}\right)_k + PN\left(e_{mn}\right)_k} \le 1. \qquad (25)$$

Combining (21), (24), and (25), we have

$$\text{JSD}\left(e_{ij} \parallel e_{mn}\right) \le 1. \tag{26}$$

Case 2 $(\text{COR}(e_{ij}, e_{mn}) \ge 0)$. Since $\ln(x) \ge 1 - 1/x$ when $x > 0$, we have

$$\sum_{k=1}^{8} \text{PN}\left(e_{ij}\right)_k \ln \frac{2\text{PN}\left(e_{ij}\right)_k}{\text{PN}\left(e_{ij}\right)_k + \text{PN}\left(e_{mn}\right)_k}$$

$$\ge \sum_{k=1}^{8} \text{PN}\left(e_{ij}\right)_k \left(1 - \frac{\text{PN}\left(e_{ij}\right)_k + \text{PN}\left(e_{mn}\right)_k}{2\text{PN}\left(e_{ij}\right)_k}\right) \tag{27}$$

$$= \sum_{k=1}^{8} \frac{\text{PN}\left(e_{ij}\right)_k - \text{PN}\left(e_{mn}\right)_k}{2}.$$

Similarly, we obtain

$$\sum_{k=1}^{8} \text{PN}\left(e_{mn}\right)_k \ln \frac{2\text{PN}\left(e_{mn}\right)_k}{\text{PN}\left(e_{ij}\right)_k + \text{PN}\left(e_{mn}\right)_k}$$

$$\ge \sum_{k=1}^{8} \frac{\text{PN}\left(e_{mn}\right)_k - \text{PN}\left(e_{ij}\right)_k}{2}. \tag{28}$$

Combining (21), (27), and (28), we have

$$\text{JSD}\left(e_{ij} \parallel e_{mn}\right) \ge 0. \tag{29}$$

Combining (26) with (29), then we have

$$0 \le \text{JSD}\left(e_{ij} \parallel e_{mn}\right) \le 1. \tag{30}$$

Note that $\text{dis}(e_{ij}, e_{mn}) \ge 0$ due to (12). Finally, according to (16) and (30), we have

$$0 \le \text{COR}\left(e_{ij}, e_{mn}\right) \le 1. \tag{31}$$

$\square$

Clearly, $\text{COR}(e_{ij}, e_{mn}) = 0$ denotes e_{ij} is independent of e_{mn}; that is, the corresponding tuples in a dataset are independent. $\text{COR}(e_{ij}, e_{mn}) = 1$ denotes e_{ij} is fully dependent to e_{mn}; that is, the corresponding tuples in a dataset are fully correlated. $0 < \text{COR}(e_{ij}, e_{mn}) < 1$ denotes e_{ij} is partially dependent on e_{mn}; that is, the corresponding tuples in a dataset are partially correlated.

(ii) Similar to [23–25], we introduce the correlated parameter z representing that there are at most z correlated tuples in a dataset. In other words, a tuple is correlated with at most $z - 1$ other tuples; that is, an edge in a graph is correlated with at most $z - 1$ other edges. Obviously, $z = 1$ represents the independent case of tuples in a dataset, $z = n$ represents the fully correlated case of tuples in a dataset, and $1 < z < n$ represents the partially correlated case of tuples in a dataset. Therefore, the variance of z increases the flexibility of Definition 10.

Furthermore, we define the ϵ-CEDP model as follows.

Definition 12 (ϵ-correlated edge differential privacy). A randomized mechanism $\mathcal{M}$ satisfies ϵ-differential privacy if, for any neighboring databases $D_{\text{COR},z}$ and $D'_{\text{COR},z}$ and for any output $S \in O(\mathcal{M})$ representing the possible output set of $\mathcal{M}$,

$$\Pr\left(\mathcal{M}\left(D_{\text{COR},z}\right) = S\right) \le \exp\left(\epsilon\right)$$

$$\cdot \Pr\left(\mathcal{M}\left(D'_{\text{COR},z}\right) = S\right), \tag{32}$$

where ϵ is the privacy budget depicting the probabilistic difference between the same outputs of $\mathcal{M}$ over $D_{\text{COR},z}$ and $D'_{\text{COR},z}$ and $\text{COR}(\cdot, \cdot)$ and z are the correlation of two tuples and the correlated parameter representing the maximal number of correlated tuples, respectively.

4.4. Sensitivity Calculation. After transforming weighted dataset D_W to indicated dataset D_I, we add Laplace noise to query answers based on the ϵ-CEDP model. Laplace noise is determined by two factors: privacy budget ϵ and the global sensitivity of a query, and the latter refers to the maximal change of query result due to the modification of only one tuple. Here, for a query f, assume the global sensitivity of f, resulting from the change of tuple t_j, in independent settings is Δf_j. Clearly, $\Delta f_j = 1$. However, for dataset D_I with n tuples where at most z tuples are correlated, the query sensitivity resulted from modifying tuple t_i, called Edge Sensitivity denoted by ES_i, is more complex. Specifically, (i) if $\text{COR}(t_i, t_j) = 0$, that is, $z = 1$, denoting the independent case, $\text{ES}_i = 1$, (ii) if $\text{COR}(t_i, t_j) = 1$ and $2 \le z \le n$, denoting the fully correlated case, $\text{ES}_i = z$, and (iii) if $0 < \text{COR}(e_{ij}, e_{mn}) < 1$ and $2 \le z \le n$, denoting the partially correlated case, ES_i is defined as follows.

$$\text{ES}_i = \sum_{j=1}^{n} \left|\text{COR}\left(t_i, t_j\right)\right| \Delta f_j. \tag{33}$$

Since the change of a tuple only affects at most other $z - 1$ correlated tuples, ES_i can be rewritten as

$$\text{ES}_i = \sum_{j=1}^{z} \left|\text{COR}\left(t_i, t_j\right)\right| \Delta f_j. \tag{34}$$

Finally, we have the correlated sensitivity denoted by CS, that is, the maximal ES_i in dataset D_I, as follows:

$$\text{CS} = \max_{i \in D_I} \text{ES}_i. \tag{35}$$

Note that the CS is also suitable for the independent and fully correlated cases. Based on the CS, we can achieve ϵ-CEDP, which is shown as follows.

Theorem 13. *Given any query function* $f : D_{\text{COR},z} \to \mathbb{R}^d$, *where* $D_{\text{COR},z}$ *is a correlated dataset with the correlation definition* $\text{COR}(\cdot, \cdot)$ *and the correlated parameter* z *and* $\mathbb{R}^d$ *is a d-dimension real-valued vector, the correlated sensitivity CS of* f, *and privacy budget* ϵ, *a randomized mechanism* $\mathcal{M}$,

$$\mathcal{M}\left(D_{\text{COR},z}\right) = f\left(D_{\text{COR},z}\right) + Laplace\left(\frac{\text{CS}}{\epsilon}\right), \tag{36}$$

provides ϵ-CEDP, *where* $Laplace(\cdot)$ *denotes Laplace noise.*

Input: Original dataset D_W, privacy budget ϵ, correlated parameter z, threshold T and query set Q.
Output: Noisy query result $\mathcal{M}(D_W)$.
(1) Calculate the correlation $\text{COR}(\cdot, \cdot)$ of any two edges in D_W according to Eq. (16);
(2) Call Algorithm $\text{TBT}(D_W, T)$, return D_I;
(3) Calculate the correlated sensitivity CS according to Eq. (35);
(4) **for** (Each $f \in Q$) **do**
(5) $\mathcal{M}(D_I) = f(D_I) + \text{Laplace}\left(\dfrac{\text{CS}}{\epsilon}\right)$;
(6) **end for**
(7) **return** Noisy query result $\mathcal{M}(D_I)$ as $\mathcal{M}(D_W)$.

ALGORITHM 2: NDR algorithm.

Proof.

$$\frac{\Pr\left(\mathcal{M}\left(D_{\text{COR},z}\right) = S\right)}{\Pr\left(\mathcal{M}\left(D'_{\text{COR},z}\right) = S\right)}$$

$$= \frac{\exp\left(-\epsilon\left|\mathcal{M}\left(D_{\text{COR},z}\right) - f\left(D_{\text{COR},z}\right)\right|/\text{CS}\right)}{\exp\left(-\epsilon\left|\mathcal{M}\left(D'_{\text{COR},z}\right) - f\left(D'_{\text{COR},z}\right)\right|/\text{CS}\right)} \quad (37)$$

$$\leq \exp\left(\frac{\epsilon\left|f\left(D_{\text{COR},z}\right) - f\left(D'_{\text{COR},z}\right)\right|}{\text{CS}}\right).$$

According to (35), the following holds:

$$\frac{\left|f\left(D_{\text{COR},z}\right) - f\left(D'_{\text{COR},z}\right)\right|}{\text{CS}} \leq 1. \quad (38)$$

Finally, combining (37) with (38), we have

$$\frac{\Pr\left(\mathcal{M}\left(D_{\text{COR},z}\right) = S\right)}{\Pr\left(\mathcal{M}\left(D'_{\text{COR},z}\right) = S\right)} \leq \exp(\epsilon). \quad (39)$$

□

For indicated dataset D_I with weight $w_{ij} \in \{0, 1\}$ and the correlated parameter z, we can easily infer the global sensitivity is equal to z. Due to $0 \leq \text{COR}(\cdot, \cdot) \leq 1$, we have $\text{CS} < z$. Therefore, CS is less than the global sensitivity. In other words, added noise via CS is less than that via the global sensitivity; hence the utility of the mechanism $\mathcal{M}$ based on CS is better.

5. Network Data Release Method

Based on indicated dataset D_I and the CS discussed in Section 4, we proposed a network data release method in special cases, which achieves the ϵ-CEDP model. Furthermore, the theoretical analysis of privacy and utility is elaborated.

5.1. NDR Algorithm. The goal of NDR algorithm is to achieve the tradeoff between privacy and utility under correlated settings. To this end, three phases are taken into account: (i) for achieving the correlation of two tuples in D_W, we transform dataset D_W into the corresponding graph and

calculate the correlation $\text{COR}(\cdot, \cdot)$ of both edges via the JS-Divergence, (ii) based on a given weight threshold T, we convert D_W into D_I via TBT algorithm. In other words, the sensitivity in independent settings is 1, irrelevant to the weights. Furthermore, we implement the calculation of CS, and (iii) combining the affordable privacy budget ϵ with CS, we calculate the added Laplace noise and finally obtain the noisy query result $\mathcal{M}(D_I)$ for query f in query set Q. The NDR algorithm is presented in Algorithm 2.

5.2. Utility Analysis. Clearly, NDR algorithm satisfies the ϵ-CEDP model. To conduct utility analysis, we adopt the (α, δ)-useful definition in [40] to depict the utility of NDR as follows.

Definition 14. A mechanism NDR is (α, δ)-useful for a query f in all queries Q, if, with probability at least $1 - \delta$, for any query f and dataset D, NDR satisfies $\max_{f \in Q}|\text{NDR}(D) - f(D)| \leq \alpha$.

Based on Definition 14, we obtain the following utility analysis.

Theorem 15. *For any query $f \in Q$ and dataset D, a mechanism NDR satisfies (α, δ)-useful if NDR can obtain $\max_{f \in Q}|\text{NDR}(D) - f(D)| \leq \alpha$ with at least probability $1 - \delta$ when $\delta \geq \exp(-\epsilon\alpha/\text{CS})$.*

Proof. By Definition 14, we have

$$\Pr\left(\max_{f \in Q}\left|\text{NDR}(D) - f(D)\right| \leq \alpha\right)$$

$$= \Pr\left(\max_{f \in Q}\left|\text{Laplace}\left(\frac{\text{CS}}{\epsilon}\right)\right| \leq \alpha\right)$$

$$= \int_{-\alpha}^{\alpha} \frac{\epsilon}{2\text{CS}} \exp\left(-\frac{\epsilon x}{\text{CS}}\right) dx \quad (40)$$

$$= \int_{0}^{\alpha} \frac{\epsilon}{\text{CS}} \exp\left(\frac{-\epsilon x}{\text{CS}}\right) dx = 1 - \exp\left(-\frac{\epsilon\alpha}{\text{CS}}\right).$$

If $\delta \geq \exp(-\epsilon\alpha/\text{CS})$, then the following holds:

$$1 - \exp\left(-\frac{\epsilon\alpha}{\text{CS}}\right) \leq 1 - \delta. \quad (41)$$

According to (40) and (41), we obtain

$$\Pr\left(\max_{f\in\mathbb{Q}}|\text{NDR}(D) - f(D)| \le \alpha\right) \le 1 - \delta. \quad (42)$$

Therefore, mechanism NDR satisfies (α, δ)-useful. □

6. Experiment

Generally, the goal of privacy preserving is to achieve maximal utilities while maintaining required privacy guarantees; that is, the tradeoff between privacy and utility is desired. In this section, we first present the better privacy guarantees and utilities of Algorithm NDR based on the definition of (α, δ)-useful and then further demonstrate its better utilities in terms of mean absolute error (MAE). Here the Baseline algorithm adopts the multiplication in [23] to handle with the correlated tuples in a network dataset. Considering the constraint of applying Pearson correlation coefficient, we do not adopt the method using Pearson correlation coefficient as comparison reference in the following experiments. To verify the advantages of Algorithm NDR concerning privacy and utility, we conduct NDR and Baseline algorithms on three datasets: geom, out explained in Section 4, and randomly generated dataset (rgd), which is a randomly generated weighted network containing 100 vertices and 1645 edges. The weight of each edge is uniformly distributed in interval $[1, 50]$. Such doing can also show the better adaption of the proposed correlation metric and algorithm over real world and synthetic datasets. Without loss of generality, threshold T here is set as 0, and the selection of its value is to be investigated in future work.

6.1. Privacy and Utility. We analyzed privacy and utility of NDR and Baseline algorithms in terms of (α, δ)-useful when the correlated parameter is set to the size of the whole dataset. In terms of privacy, we evaluate the consumption of privacy budget ϵ under the same accuracy α and the same possibility $1 - \delta$. Clearly, the smaller the consumed privacy budget, the better the performance of algorithm.

Figures 3(a), 3(c), and 3(e) present the variation of privacy budget, consumed by algorithms NDR and Baseline based on datasets geom, out, and rgd, with the increase of α from 1 to 40 when δ equals 0.1 and 0.5, respectively. From Figures 3(a), 3(c), and 3(e), we can see that privacy budgets decrease in all cases with the increase of α. The reason is that, with the relaxation of α, larger noise can be allowed when δ stays fixed; therefore algorithm can consume smaller privacy budget. Meanwhile, we also see that privacy budgets decrease with the increase of δ from 0.1 to 0.5 when α stays fixed. Because the possibility of satisfying accuracy requirement decreases with the increase of δ, which means that algorithms can have more chances to add larger noise; that is, algorithms can use smaller privacy budget. Such advantage of both algorithms especially in the case of $\alpha = 1$ is more obvious than that of other ones. In fact, when δ stays constant, the higher the accuracy presented by α, the more the privacy budget needed by algorithms.

On the other hand, Figures 3(b), 3(d), and 3(f) demonstrate the variation of δ of algorithms NDR and Baseline

based on datasets geom, out, and rgd, with the increase of α from 0 to 10000 when ϵ equals 0.1 and 1.0, respectively. We can see that δ decreases in all cases with the increase of α; that is, the possibility increases with the increase of α. Note that this trend varies from dataset to dataset; for example, the possibility and accuracy of algorithm NDR over datasets geom and out are evidently different when $\epsilon = 1$. Clearly, when ϵ is determined, the possibility increases with the relaxation of α. In addition, we find that algorithm NDR can have larger possibility, that is, smaller δ, than the Baseline algorithm to achieve the same accuracy α under the same level of privacy budget ϵ. Also, when ϵ increases from 0.1 to 1.0, algorithms also have possibility to achieve the same accuracy α, which is easily understood from (40).

6.2. Utility. We adopt MAE, that is, $(1/|\mathbb{Q}|)\sum_{f\in\mathbb{Q}}|\hat{f}(t) - f(t)|$, to depict the performance of algorithms NDR and Baseline. Obviously, the smaller the MAE value, the better the utility. For each dataset, 10000 queries are randomly generated, and each query result ranges from 0 to the maximal number of tuples.

Figures 4(a), 4(c), and 4(e) show the variances of MAEs of NDR and Baseline algorithms, over datasets geom, out, and rgd, under various privacy budgets when the correlated parameter z is 10. From Figures 4(a), 4(c), and 4(e), we can see that the MAEs of both algorithms decrease with the increase of privacy budget ϵ from 0.1 to 1. Because larger privacy budget leads to smaller noise added to raw data, the downtrends always hold. More importantly, algorithm NDR can obtain better accuracy, that is, smaller MAE, under various ϵ. Furthermore, the smaller the privacy budget ϵ, the more obvious such advantage. The reason is that algorithm NDR adopts the more reasonable correlation metric compared with the Baseline algorithm.

Figures 4(b), 4(d), and 4(f) show the variances of MAEs of NDR and Baseline algorithms, over datasets geom, out, and rgd, under various correlated parameters when privacy budget ϵ is 0.5. In Figures 4(b), 4(d), and 4(f), we find that the MAEs of both algorithms increase with the increase of correlated parameter z from 1 to 40. Undoubtedly, with the increase of the number of correlated tuples in a dataset, larger noise needs to be injected to eliminate the effect of tuple correlation, which necessarily results in the increase of MAE. In addition, we also note that algorithm NDR can obtain better accuracy, that is, smaller MAE, under various correlated parameters compared with the Baseline algorithm. Also, the larger the correlated parameter, the larger such advantage. All these advantages are due to the more reasonable correlation metric, which is proposed in Section 4 and adopted by algorithm NDR.

7. Conclusion

In this paper, we focus on adopting differential privacy model to avoid the leakage of close relationship between two individuals in a network. To this end, we first extract the PF vector from both aspects of node degree and edge weight to depict an edge in a network dataset and then design the correlation metric of two edges via JS-Divergence to avoid the

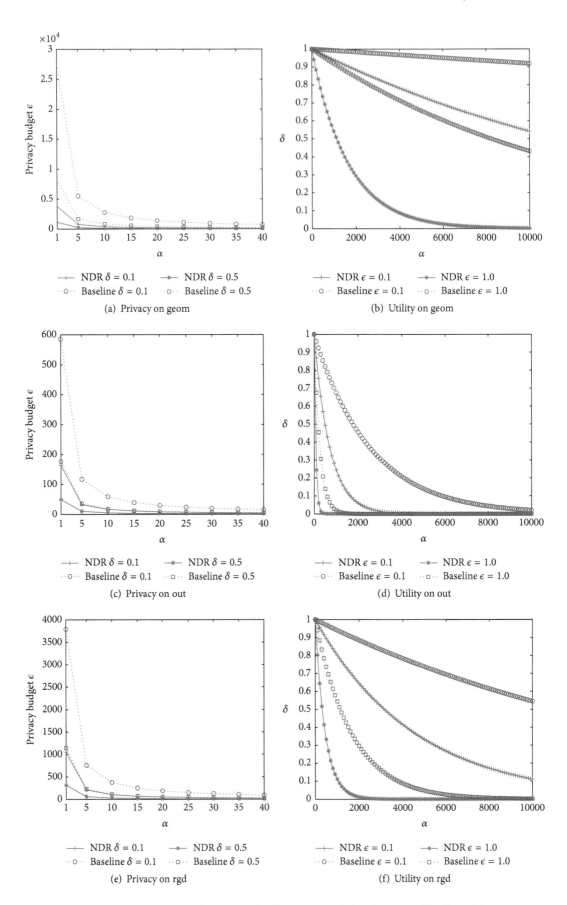

FIGURE 3: Comparison of privacy and utility on network data in terms of (α, δ)-useful.

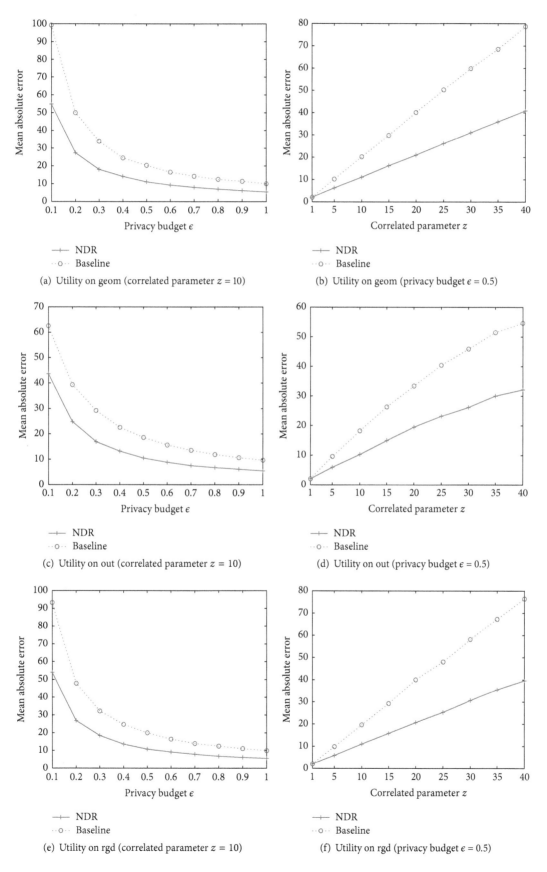

FIGURE 4: Comparison of utility on network data in terms of mean absolute error.

constraint of adopting Pearson correlation coefficient. Next, we proposed the ϵ-CEDP model to deal with the correlated dataset by introducing two parameters including our correlation metric and the correlated parameter. Furthermore, we present the NDR algorithm based on the ϵ-CEDP and discuss its privacy and utility in terms of the definition of (α, δ)-useful. Extensive experiments on real and synthetic network datasets verify the advantages of our proposed privacy preserving model and algorithm concerning privacy and utility. Admittedly, the proposed solution is currently appropriate for weighted network datasets, and other datasets are out of the scope of this paper. In future work, we will discuss the impacts of choosing weight threshold on algorithm performances, explore more appropriate correlation metrics, and investigate privacy preserving algorithms in different applications.

Acknowledgments

This work is partly supported by the Fundamental Research Funds for the Central Universities of China under Grant no. GK201703061, the National Natural Science Foundation of China under Grants nos. 61402273 and 61373083, the National Science Foundation (NSF) under Grants nos. CNS-1252292, 1741277, and 1704287, and the Natural Science Basic Research Plan in Shaanxi Province of China under Grants nos. 2017JM6060 and 2017JM6103.

References

[1] J. Liu, J. Wan, B. Zeng, Q. Wang, H. Song, and M. Qiu, "A scalable and quick-response software defined vehicular network assisted by mobile edge computing," *IEEE Communications Magazine*, vol. 55, no. 7, pp. 94–100, 2017.

[2] P. Hu, H. Ning, T. Qiu, H. Song, Y. Wang, and X. Yao, "Security and privacy preservation scheme of face identification and resolution framework using fog computing in internet of things," *IEEE Internet of Things Journal*, vol. 4, no. 5, pp. 1143–1155, 2017.

[3] Z. He, Z. Cai, and J. Yu, "Latent-data privacy preserving with customized data utility for social network data," *IEEE Transactions on Vehicular Technology*, vol. PP, no. 99, pp. 1-1, 2017.

[4] X. Zheng, Z. Cai, J. Yu, C. Wang, and Y. Li, "Follow but no track: privacy preserved profile publishing in cyber-physical social systems," *IEEE Internet of Things Journal*, vol. PP, no. 99, pp. 1-1, 2017.

[5] Z. Cai, Z. He, X. Guan, and Y. Li, "Collective data-sanitization for preventing sensitive information inference attacks in social networks," *IEEE Transactions on Dependable and Secure Computing*, vol. 99, pp. 1-1, 2017.

[6] Y. Liang, Z. Cai, Q. Han, and Y. Li, "Location privacy leakage through sensory data," *Security and Communication Networks*, vol. 2017, Article ID 7576307, 12 pages, 2017.

[7] X. Zheng, Z. Cai, J. Li, and H. Gao, "Location-privacy-aware review publication mechanism for local business service systems," in *Proceedings of the IEEE INFOCOM 2017 - IEEE Conference on Computer Communications*, pp. 1–9, Atlanta, GA, USA, May 2017.

[8] L. Zhang, Z. Cai, and X. Wang, "FakeMask: a novel privacy preserving approach for smartphones," *IEEE Transactions on Network and Service Management*, vol. 13, no. 2, pp. 335–348, 2016.

[9] Y. Wang, Z. Cai, G. Yin, Y. Gao, X. Tong, and G. Wu, "An incentive mechanism with privacy protection in mobile crowdsourcing systems," *Computer Networks*, vol. 102, Supplement C, pp. 157–171, June 2016.

[10] W. Wang, L. Ying, and J. Zhang, "On the relation between identifiability, differential privacy, and mutual-information privacy," *Institute of Electrical and Electronics Engineers Transactions on Information Theory*, vol. 62, no. 9, pp. 5018–5029, 2016.

[11] P. Zhou, Y. Zhou, D. Wu, and H. Jin, "Differentially Private Online Learning for Cloud-Based Video Recommendation with Multimedia Big Data in Social Networks," *IEEE Transactions on Multimedia*, vol. 18, no. 6, pp. 1217–1229, 2016.

[12] J. Ni, K. Zhang, K. Alharbi, X. Lin, N. Zhang, and X. S. Shen, "Differentially private smart metering with fault tolerance and range-based filtering," *IEEE Transactions on Smart Grid*, vol. 8, no. 5, pp. 2483–2493, 2017.

[13] H. To, G. Ghinita, L. Fan, and C. Shahabi, "Differentially private location protection for worker datasets in spatial crowdsourcing," *IEEE Transactions on Mobile Computing*, vol. 16, no. 4, pp. 934–949, 2017.

[14] C. Lin, P. Wang, H. Song, Y. Zhou, Q. Liu, and G. Wu, "A differential privacy protection scheme for sensitive big data in body sensor networks," *Annals of Telecommunications-Annales des Télécommunications*, vol. 71, no. 9-10, pp. 465–475, 2016.

[15] C. Lin, Z. Song, H. Song, Y. Zhou, Y. Wang, and G. Wu, "Differential privacy preserving in big data analytics for connected health," *Journal of Medical Systems*, vol. 40, no. 4, article no. 97, pp. 1–9, 2016.

[16] S. Xu, S. Su, X. Cheng, K. Xiao, and L. Xiong, "Differentially private frequent sequence mining," *IEEE Transactions on Knowledge and Data Engineering*, vol. 28, no. 11, pp. 2910–2926, 2016.

[17] W. Tong, J. Hua, and S. Zhong, "A jointly differentially private scheduling protocol for ridesharing services," *IEEE Transactions on Information Forensics and Security*, vol. 12, no. 10, pp. 2444–2456, 2017.

[18] D. Kifer and A. Machanavajjhala, "A rigorous and customizable framework for privacy," in *Proceedings of the 31st Symposium on Principles of Database Systems (PODS '12)*, pp. 77–88, Scottsdale, Arizona, USA, May 2012.

[19] D. Kifer and A. Machanavajjhala, "No free lunch in data privacy," in *Proceedings of the 2011 ACM SIGMOD and 30th PODS 2011 Conference on Management of Data (SIGMOD)*, pp. 193–204, Athens, Greece, June 2011.

[20] C. Dwork, "Differential privacy," in *Proceedings of the 33rd International Conference on Automata, Languages and Programming - Volume Part II (ICALP '06)*, pp. 1–12, Venice, Italy, 2006.

[21] X. He, A. Machanavajjhala, and B. Ding, "Blowfish privacy: Tuning privacy-utility trade-offs using policies," in *Proceedings of the 2014 ACM SIGMOD International Conference on Management of Data, (SIGMOD '14)*, pp. 1447–1458, Snowbird, Utah, USA, June 2014.

[22] B. Yang, I. Sato, and H. Nakagawa, "Bayesian differential privacy on correlated data," in *Proceedings of the ACM SIGMOD International Conference on Management of Data, (SIGMOD '15)*, pp. 747–762, Melbourne, Victoria, Australia, June 2015.

[23] R. Chen, B. C. M. Fung, P. S. Yu, and B. C. Desai, "Correlated network data publication via differential privacy," *The VLDB Journal*, vol. 23, no. 4, pp. 653–676, 2014.

[24] T. Zhu, P. Xiong, G. Li, and W. Zhou, "Correlated differential

privacy: hiding information in Non-IID data set," *IEEE Transactions on Information Forensics and Security*, vol. 10, no. 2, article no. A2, pp. 229–242, 2015.

[25] C. Liu, S. Chakraborty, and P. Mittal, "Dependence makes you vulnerable: differential privacy under dependent tuples," in *Proceedings of the Network and Distributed System Security Symposium (NDSS '16)*, San Diego, Calif, USA.

[26] Y. Xiao and L. Xiong, "Protecting locations with differential privacy under temporal correlations," in *Proceedings of the 22nd ACM SIGSAC Conference on Computer and Communications Security, (CCS '15)*, pp. 1298–1309, Denver, Colorado, USA, October 2015.

[27] X. Wu, T. Wu, M. Khan, Q. Ni, and W. Dou, "Game theory based correlated privacy preserving analysis in big data," *IEEE Transactions on Big Data*, vol. PP, no. 99, pp. 1-1, 2017.

[28] L. Zhang, Y. Li, L. Wang, J. Lu, P. Li, and X. Wang, "An efficient context-aware privacy preserving approach for smartphones," *Security & Communication Networks*, vol. 2017, no. 2, pp. 1–11, 2017.

[29] Y. Cao, M. Yoshikawa, Y. Xiao, and L. Xiong, "Quantifying differential privacy under temporal correlations," in *Proceeding of the IEEE 33rd International Conference on Data Engineering (ICDE '17)*, pp. 821–832, San Diego, CA, USA, 2017.

[30] L. Ou, Z. Qin, Y. Liu, H. Yin, Y. Hu, and H. Chen, "Multi-user location correlation protection with differential privacy," in *Proceedings of the 2016 IEEE 22nd International Conference on Parallel and Distributed Systems (ICPADS '16)*, pp. 422–429, Wuhan, China, December 2016.

[31] D. N. Reshef, Y. A. Reshef, H. K. Finucane et al., "Detecting novel associations in large data sets," *Science*, vol. 334, no. 6062, pp. 1518–1524, 2011.

[32] C. Dwork, F. McSherry, K. Nissim, and A. Smith, "Calibrating noise to sensitivity in private data analysis," in *Proceedings of the Third Conference on Theory of Cryptography (TCC '06)*, vol. 3876, pp. 265–284, New York, NY, USA, March 2006.

[33] F. McSherry and K. Talwar, "Mechanism design via differential privacy," in *Proceedings of the 48th Annual Symposium on Foundations of Computer Science (FOCS '07)*, pp. 94–103, Providence, RI, USA, October 2007.

[34] V. Batagelj and A. Mrvar, "Pajek datasets," http://vlado.fmf.uni-lj.si/pub/networks/data/.

[35] N. H. F. Beebe and H. F. Nelson, "Beebe's bibliographies page," http://www.math.utah.edu/~beebe/bibliographies.html.

[36] B. Jones, "Computational geometry database," http://jeffe.cs.illinois.edu/compgeom/biblios.html.

[37] *Les misérables network dataset – KONECT*, 2016, http://konect.uni-koblenz.de/networks/moreno_lesmis.

[38] D. E. Knuth, *The stanford graph base: a platform for combinatorial computing*, vol. 37, Addison-Wesley Reading, Boston, Mass, USA, 1993.

[39] J. Kunegis, "KONECT — The koblenz network collection," in *Proceeding of the 22nd International Conference on World Wide Web Companion (WWW '13)*, pp. 1343–1350, Rio de Janeiro, Brazil, May 2013.

[40] A. Blum, K. Ligett, and A. Roth, "A learning theory approach to non-interactive database privacy," in *Proceedings of the Fortieth Annual ACM Symposium on Theory of Computing (STOC '08)*, pp. 609–618, ACM, New York, NY, USA, 2008.

8

ABS-TrustSDN: An Agent-Based Simulator of Trust Strategies in Software-Defined Networks

Iván García-Magariño[1,2] and Raquel Lacuesta[1,2]

[1]Department of Computer Science and Engineering of Systems, Escuela Universitaria Politécnica de Teruel, University of Zaragoza, c/Atarazana 2, 44003 Teruel, Spain
[2]Instituto de Investigación Sanitaria Aragón, University of Zaragoza, Zaragoza, Spain

Correspondence should be addressed to Iván García-Magariño; ivangmg@unizar.es

Academic Editor: Huaizhi Li

Software-defined networks (SDNs) have become a mechanism to separate the control plane and the data plane in the communication in networks. SDNs involve several challenges around their security and their confidentiality. Ideally, SDNs should incorporate autonomous and adaptive systems for controlling the routing to be able to isolate network resources that may be malfunctioning or whose security has been compromised with malware. The current work introduces a novel agent-based framework that simulates SDN isolation protocols by means of trust and reputation models. This way, SDN programmers may estimate the repercussions of certain isolation protocols based on trust models before actually deploying the protocol into the network.

1. Introduction

Software-defined networks (SDNs) allow separating control and data planes, offering better network management rather than traditional networks. In SDNs, programming does not need to be performed node by node, but in a centralized way. This provides more flexible, efficient, and scalable networks. This way, the network is implemented independently of manufacturers or component models. The SDN controller is responsible for acting as a centralized control point at a logical level. The controller has the task of coordinating communications between applications that interact with network elements. However, this centralized control scenario introduces some security challenges. In order to protect a network, one should secure data, controllers and devices, and communications. In the literature, some works increased security in SDNs including authentication mechanisms, controller replication schemes, and policy conflict resolution schemas. Alterations in the network's components and in their behavior need to be assessed to sustain network security. That way, the network's components trust and reputation become an important issue to deal with.

Due to the global network view that the SDNs provide, we can introduce a detection system to assess the devices' reputation and trustworthiness. Based on the analysis, the controller can reprogram the network operation. In this scenario, the SDN architecture is used to improve the network security using a security monitor that analyzes anomaly-detection behaviors of the network's components. This approach can improve the robustness of the network to detect attacks.

Monitoring systems have been proposed by some authors in order to protect networks from attacks. Some of them use a centralized scheme. For example, OpenSAFE system [1] was proposed to enable the arbitrary direction of traffic for security monitoring applications. A flow specification language named ALARMs was used for arbitrary route management through monitoring devices. Braga et al. [2] presented a lightweight method for DDoS attack detection. In the proposal, they monitored NOX switches at regular intervals to identify abnormal flows. In [3], an Intrusion Detection-Prevention System architecture was proposed for the cloud virtual networking environment. It inherited the detection capability from Snort and the flexible network reconfiguration from SDNs. CloudWatchers, a framework used in [4], monitored network flows for large and dynamic cloud networks.

Other authors presented distributed architecture models to distribute the security efforts among the network's devices. For instance, a distributed approach was presented in [5] where the control and trust were delegated to end hosts and users. Therefore, the network's devices participated in network security enforcement. In [6], Resonance, a dynamic access control system, was carried out by network devices. The system used programmable switches to manipulate traffic at lower layers, enforcing high-level security policies. A deep packet inspection module was proposed by Goodney et al. [7]. The proposed engine was used as a simple network intrusion detection system.

Trust and reputation models have been applied for achieving security in networks. Yan et al. [8] proposed a security and trust framework using fifth-generation (5G) wireless systems. That work proposed an adaptive trust evaluation for deploying certain trustworthy security services in both virtualized networks and SDNs. Michiardi and Molva [9] proposed a collaborative reputation mechanism for promoting the cooperation among network nodes, preventing selfish behaviors. Liu and Issarny [10] proposed a reputation mechanism for mobile ad hoc networks, in which agents shared the reputation about other agents. This system promoted honest recommendations, by including the notion of recommendation reputation. The reputations were also calculated about the recommendations of other agents.

In general, multiagent systems (MASs) have been considered a proper mechanism for implementing and simulating trust and reputation models. For instance, the Agent Reputation and Trust (ART) testbed [11] provided a framework for testing different policies about trust on agents (estimated from the direct interaction) and reputation of other agents (obtained from the recommendations of other agents). Their framework illustrated these concepts in the domain of appraisals of paintings. They organized competitions, in which each participant programmed an agent, and all the agents were executed together. Other works explored how to integrate different trust measures in MASs, like in the one by Rosaci et al. [12]. They introduced concepts such as the reliability about each reputation value. Furthermore, Jelenc et al. [13] proposed an agent-based mechanism for evaluating trust models. They used a testbed, but their mechanism separated the measurement of trust models from the repercussions of the decision-making mechanisms. In addition, Chen et al. [14] presented a MAS trust model for wireless sensor networks. In their system, they propagated encrypted reputation information about the different nodes. They tested their system under the bad mouthing attacks (spread of false reputation information), conflicting behavior attacks (an agent is malicious towards one node and honest to the others, for provoking conflicts about the reputation of certain nodes), and on-off attacks (a node behaves well and badly alternatively). They also presented some simulations with their models.

Agent-based simulators (ABSs) are a specific kind of MASs intended for making simulations and have been applied to implement trust testbed, like in the work of Kim

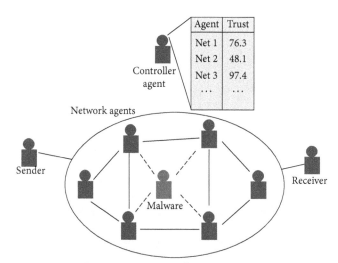

FIGURE 1: Overview of ABS-TrustSDN.

[15] in the domain of supply networks. That work tested adaptive behaviors based on trust and explored emergent outcomes such as self-organizing processes and macrolevel systems behaviors.

On the whole, the current literature shows the relevance of guaranteeing the security on SDNs. Trust models have been shown to be useful for this purpose. However, to the best of the authors' knowledge, the existing testbed for simulating trust strategies is not designed for simulating the repercussion of trust models specifically for SDNs. In this context, MASs have been shown to be useful for comparing and simulating trust models in several domains, especially when separating trust models from decision-making processes. ABSs may be a proper choice for developing trust testbeds and simulation frameworks.

In this context, the current work presents an Agent-Based Simulator of Trust strategies in SDNs (called ABS-TrustSDN). In this simulator, an agent represents the centralized controller of the SDN, and this agent builds a trust model regarding the history of the network's components based on the network packets that were properly transmitted or lost through that component. Other agents represent the network's components that can either work properly or malfunction. The underlying framework allows designers to test different isolation protocols based on trust models. This work explores different strategies of the SDN controller based on trust with the presented approach and compares their outcomes.

2. Materials and Methods

2.1. ABS-TrustSDN

2.1.1. Overview. The current work uses the novel ABS-TrustSDN tool as the main material of this research. This tool and its underlying framework have been developed specifically for the current work, which is one of its main contributions. In order to guarantee the reproducibility of the experiments, this tool has been made available on its website [16].

This tool is an ABS in which agents simulate the behaviors of the SNDs' components. Figure 1 introduces graphically

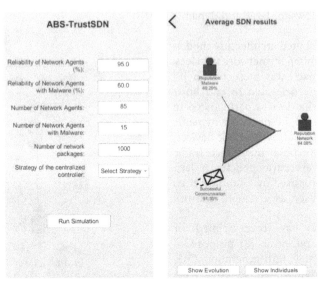

(a) Inputs of the UI   (b) Average results with a star plot

FIGURE 2: Main screens in the UI of ABS-TrustSDN.

an overview of this tool. The "network agents" represent the network's components such as groups of switches, and these can have different behaviors. Most of these work properly transmitting the network packages following the orders of the SDN centralized controller. However, a few of the network agents may have a malicious or nonproper behavior. This behavior can be intended for compromising the privacy and taking nonauthorized data. It can also be some malfunctioning that makes them lose a high rate of network packages. From this point forward, sometimes this kind of network agents will also be referred to as "malware agents" in order to distinguish them from all the other network agents that will be referred to as "normal network agents" in this context.

The "controller agent" represents the centralized controller of the SDN. It decides how to route the traffic of the network to avoid its saturation. In ABS-TrustSDN, this agent is mainly intended to incorporate the isolation protocol. This can be programmed by the SDN designer, in order to simulate several isolation protocols. The controller agent incorporates a table with its trust on each network agent as a percentage in the 0-to-100 interval.

The tool can simulate any number of messages from a sender to a receiver. In each simulated communication, the controller agent selects a route represented with several network agents. The receiver can report whether the message was properly received or whether it was lost. If lost, the controller agent can track in which point of the route the package was lost and decrease its trust in the corresponding network agent. Normally, if the transmission was correct, it slightly increases its trust on all the involved network agents.

The network agents with a nonproper behavior only perform malicious or error-prone actions sometimes in a certain percentage of times, so these can be difficult to detect without an accurate isolation protocol. This percentage of misbehavior can be configured as an input of the simulator.

2.1.2. Definition of Strategies with ABS-TrustSDN. This tool was developed following PEABS (a process for developing agent-based simulators) [17]. It considered the common guidelines for designing proper agent-oriented architectures [18] and integrating these with web-based systems [19]. The communications were designed considering the common recommendations in the area of MASs [20]. This process was adapted to develop the app with the Unity engine and the C# language.

In each simulation iteration, the controller agent selects the next network agent to transmit from the available ones with a nondeterministic decision based on probabilities. These probabilities are determined by its internal trust model. This way, normally, this agent selects more frequently the agents that it trusts more according to its model.

The controller agent receives feedback about whether the transmission was correct or not for each transmitted package in each network agent. The framework allows extending the controller agent to define exactly the way of updating the trust by overwriting the method "Update Trust." This method receives the previous trust of the agent, the positive or negative result of the communication, and the ID of the network agent. It must return the new trust. Designers can implement basic behaviors regarding only the previous trust and the communication result. They can also implement more elaborated trust models with data structures inside the extended class for taking into account the previous histories of the agents identified by their IDs. Section 2.2 introduces several examples of strategies that were defined with the current approach.

2.1.3. User Interface of ABS-TrustSDN. Figure 2 shows the main screens of the user interface (UI) of ABS-TrustSDN. More concretely, Figure 2(a) shows the screen in which the user enters the input values of the simulations. These include the reliabilities of, respectively, the normal network agents

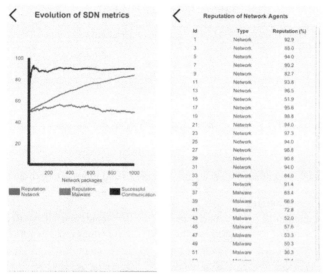

Evolution of SDN metrics

Id	Type	Reputation (%)
1	Network	92.9
3	Network	85.0
5	Network	94.0
7	Network	90.2
9	Network	82.7
11	Network	93.8
13	Network	96.5
15	Network	51.9
17	Network	95.6
19	Network	98.8
21	Network	94.0
23	Network	97.3
25	Network	94.0
27	Network	96.8
29	Network	90.8
31	Network	94.0
33	Network	84.0
35	Network	91.4
37	Malware	63.4
39	Malware	66.9
41	Malware	72.8
43	Malware	52.0
45	Malware	57.6
47	Malware	53.3
49	Malware	50.3
51	Malware	36.3

(a) Evolution of SDN metrics (%) (b) Reputation of network agents

FIGURE 3: Screens with the details of the simulation in the UI of ABS-TrustSDN.

and the ones with malware. Each reliability represents the percentage of times that a kind of network agents works properly. It is worth mentioning that even correct components can fail occasionally, and the network components with malware can work most of the times. Both aspects can be configured by the user with two percentages. The simulation can be set with different numbers of normal network agents and the ones with malware. The components with malware are usually a minority, but the user can simulate different scenarios about this.

The user can also set the number of transmitted network packages, to show both the short-term and the long-term repercussions of the different trust policies. Finally, the user can select one of the existing trust model strategies for the centralized controller. The user can easily define new strategies by using the underlying framework of ABS-TrustSDN, as previously introduced in Section 2.1.2. After entering the simulation inputs, the user can start running the simulation by pressing the corresponding "Run simulation" button.

After running the simulation, the ABS presents the average simulated outcomes with a star plot like the one in Figure 2(b). These outcomes include average reputations of, respectively, the normal network agents and the ones with malware. The star plot also includes the success rate of the transmitted network packages through the network agents in general. The user can also observe further details in the screens of the UI presented in Figure 3, by pressing any of the two bottom buttons in Figure 2(b).

The UI screen of Figure 3(a) shows the evolution of the average reputations of the two different kinds of network agents and the evolution of the success rate in the communications up to the corresponding time. The chart shows the evolution of these three variables evolving along the evolution time implicitly represented by the number of the network packages transmitted in the abscissa axis. In the UI screen of

Figure 3(b), the user can see the reputations of all the network agents alongside their IDs and their abbreviated types (i.e., "Network" for the normal network agents and "Malware" for the ones with malware). The reputation of each network agent is determined by the percentage that the centralized controller agent trusts on it.

2.2. Experimental Method. The current work followed an exploratory design, as commonly done in works about ABSs [21] or more generally in MASs [22], in order to test the utility of the novel ABS-TrustSDN tool and its underlying framework. We implemented three different strategies of conforming trust models. Then, we experienced the strategies in two different scenarios represented with certain input configurations. Each combination of strategy and configuration was executed 1,000 times for avoiding bias due to the nondeterministic behavior of the simulator. The results were compared by presenting and discussing the average results. The results were analyzed with a statistical test to determine the significance of the differences. We calculated the effect sizes to measure these differences. Furthermore, we analyzed the evolutions of the different combinations in order to provide possible explanations about the resulting outcomes.

In this experimental method, we defined the following strategies with the underlying framework of ABS-TrustSDN:

(i) *Fixed Strategy.* This strategy just considers the last time the controller agent interacted with a certain network agent. If the communication was successful, then it assigns a high fixed trust. Otherwise, it assigns a low fixed trust. The high fixed trust is 100%, while the low trust is 10%. It does not assign a 0% trust, as a normal network agent may have had an uncommon failure. This way, the network agent may be contacted eventually in the future and then it will recover the high trust if it does not fail again.

TABLE 1: Input configurations.

	Configuration 1	Configuration 2
Reliability of network agents (%)	95.0	95.0
Reliability of network agents with malware (%)	60.0	15.0
Number of network agents	85	85
Number of network agents with malware	15	15
Number of network packages	1000	1000

TABLE 2: Average results of the 1,000 simulations for each pair of strategies and input configuration with SDs between parentheses.

Strategy	Configuration 1			Configuration 2		
	Reputation network (%)	Reputation malware (%)	Successful communication (%)	Reputation network (%)	Reputation malware (%)	Successful communication (%)
Fixed	73.55 (4.63)	22.88 (8.04)	92.60 (0.76)	73.48 (4.46)	11.55 (3.04)	91.88 (0.81)
Tabsaond	84.51 (0.75)	55.18 (3.56)	90.84 (0.86)	85.08 (0.74)	28.32 (2.22)	88.18 (0.92)
History	99.52 (0.68)	39.94 (13.52)	91.12 (0.76)	99.53 (0.67)	3.70 (4.76)	89.03 (0.74)

(ii) *Tabsaond Strategy.* If the communication was correct with a network agent, the controller increases the trust on it. Otherwise, it decreases the trust. It updates the trust considering a ratio of the distance to the approaching limit, following the recommendations of TABSAOND (a technique for developing agent-based simulation apps and online tools with nondeterministic decisions) [23]. The controller agent decision can be either to increase its trust ($d = 1$), decrease its trust ($d = -1$), or keep the trust with a neutral trend ($d = 0$). In particular, the controller agent uses the following formula to calculate the variation for altering the trust on a network agent:

$$v = \begin{cases} K * (U_L - x), & \text{if } d > 0, \\ -K * (x - L_L), & \text{if } d < 0, \\ 0, & \text{otherwise,} \end{cases} \quad (1)$$

where x is the current trust on this agent, K represents the ratio to the approaching limit (in this work $K = 0.15$), and L_L and U_L, respectively, represent the lower and the upper limits (i.e., 0 and 100, as the trust is represented with percentages).

(iii) *History Strategy.* This strategy assigns a high trust value to all the network agents by default. In each interaction with a specific agent, it records the communication result. It does not change the trust until it has analyzed a minimum number of interactions that is established as an internal parameter named "analysis window." In this experiment, this parameter was set to 5 interactions. Once this limit is reached, this strategy calculates the ratio of successful transmissions with the corresponding agent. If this ratio is below a certain threshold (in this experiments set to 60%), then the agent is set to a low trust for isolating

the agent. In this case, the low trust was set to zero for the complete isolation, as it has made sure that its behavior is wrong for at least a certain number of interactions.

In order to experience the aforementioned strategies in different contexts, this work established two settings of the input parameters, which are referred to as input configurations. Table 1 shows the input values of these configurations. The difference between these two is that the rates of failures of the malware agents are different. This way, the strategies will be tested with different kinds of network agents with malware, represented with different reliability percentages (i.e., 60% versus 15%).

3. Results and Discussions

3.1. Comparison of the Final Simulated Outcomes of the Trust Strategies. As mentioned in the experimental method, the simulator was executed 1,000 times for each combination of strategy and input configuration. Table 2 presents the average results of these simulations with the SD between parentheses.

By observing the averages, one can extract several conclusions. First, when the input configuration varies considering different reliabilities of network agents with malware, the relative order of the strategies varies in the malware agents' reputation dependent variable. Thus, different strategies may be considered appropriate given the nature of the most expected kind of malware.

In addition, one can observe the results of the isolation of malware resources by observing the reputation of normal network agents and the reputation of the ones that got malware. An ideal strategy would trust network agents with 100% and would not rely on the ones with malware with trust of 0%. One can observe that History strategy is the one that gets closer to the ideal trust for isolating malware resources. When the agents with malware have a very low reliability

TABLE 3: Results of Welch's unequal variances t-test generalized for three samples. [a]Asymptotically F distributed. [**]Significant with a significance level of .001.

	Configuration 1			Configuration 2		
	Reputation network (%)	Reputation malware (%)	Successful communication (%)	Reputation network (%)	Reputation malware (%)	Successful communication (%)
Statistic[a]	119441.343	6993.621	1461.395	113571.231	17614.808	5368.600
df1	2	2	2	2	2	2
df2	1784.344	1613.377	1992.052	1783.826	1856.863	1983.274
Sig.	.000[**]	.000[**]	.000[**]	.000[**]	.000[**]	.000[**]

TABLE 4: Cohen's d effect sizes.

Configuration		Tabsaond			History		
		Reputation network (%)	Reputation malware (%)	Successful communication (%)	Reputation network (%)	Reputation malware (%)	Successful communication (%)
Fixed	1	2.34	3.67	−1.54	5.55	1.08	−1.39
	2	2.56	4.60	−3.02	5.77	−1.39	−2.59
Tabsaond	1				14.90	−1.09	0.24
	2				14.43	−4.78	0.72

(i.e., configuration 2), the history strategy assigns the highest reputation to network agents (i.e., 99.5%) compared to the other strategies and the lowest reputation to the agents with malware (i.e., 3.7%). In configuration 1 with malware agents with a higher reliability, Fixed strategy isolates them with a lower reputation, but it also isolates wrongly some normal network agents. Thus, even in this configuration, History strategy may be the most appropriate one for separating the trust values of network agents and malware agents.

Another relevant aspect is to analyze which strategy achieves the highest rate of successful communications. In this case, the Fixed strategy is the one that obtains the highest rate in both configurations. Notice that the rate of success in communications not only depends on the quality of the final trust model of the isolation protocol of malware resources, but also depends on how quick the isolation is taken. Slow isolation may cause the failure of many initial communications, and this will hinder the final communication rate. This may be the reason why the Fixed strategy got the highest rate, as it can start the isolation from the very first interaction with an agent.

The results were analyzed with Welch's unequal variances t-test generalized for more than two samples [24], in order to determine whether the differences were statistically significant. Table 3 shows the results of this statistical test. This test was selected as it is robust for comparing samples with unequal variances. The differences of the results between the different strategies were very significant with a significance level of .001 for all the dependent variables.

Table 4 analyzes Cohen's d effect sizes between each pair of strategies for each input configuration and dependent variable. Cohen's [25] guideline assigned .2, .5, and .8, respectively, to small, medium, and large effect sizes. According to this guideline, all the effect sizes of the current experiments were large between all the pairs of strategies and dependent variables, except in the case of the comparison of success rate in communications between Tabsaond and History strategies. In that case, the effect size was small and medium for, respectively, configurations 1 and 2.

On the whole, one can observe that ABS-TrustSDN has allowed comparing the repercussions of three different trust strategies on SDNs concerning two different kinds of attacks. These attack kinds were represented with their different ratios of communication failures implicitly indicated in the input configurations. The results presented significant differences. Hence, ABS-TrustSDN may be useful for selecting the right trust policy in an SDN when considering possible alternatives.

3.2. The Simulated Evolutions with the Trust Strategies. This section shows examples of evolutions of the simulations in each combination of strategy and input configuration, in order to understand some features of these simulations.

Figure 4 shows the evolution of the simulations of the Fixed strategy. One of the most relevant features is that it separates the reputation of network agents and malware agents very soon in the simulations (i.e., from the beginning). The drawback is that it starts decreasing the reputation of the normal network agents in the long term. The reason is that uncommon errors of these agents are taken seriously by this strategy, and wrongly isolating them enlarges the group of unfairly isolated network agents.

In Figure 5, one can observe that the most relevant aspect of simulations with the Tabsaond strategy is that the evolutions of strategies are smooth in comparison to the other strategies. In addition, Tabsaond strategy may reach stable states in different levels of reputations of malware regarding

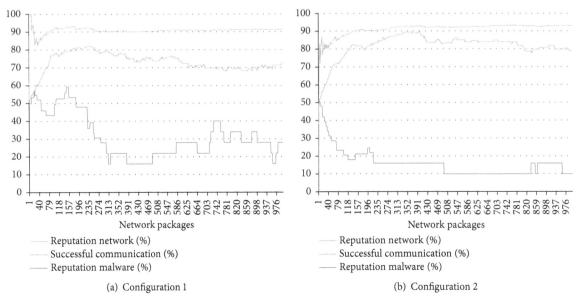

FIGURE 4: Evolution of SDN metrics with Fixed strategy.

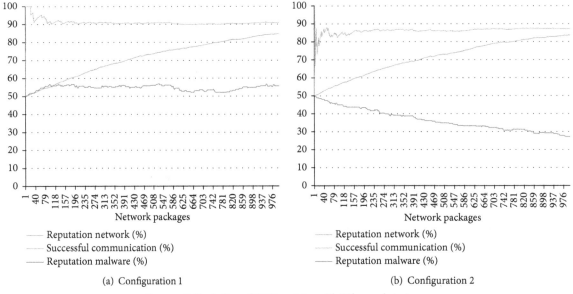

FIGURE 5: Evolution of SDN metrics with Tabsaond strategy.

the reliability of these agents, as suggested in the original TABSAOND approach.

Figure 6 shows the evolution of History strategy. One can observe that, in the beginning, it trusts almost the same malware agents and other agents, due to the minimum amount of interactions for analyzing an agent. Then, it almost separates perfectly the reputation of these two kinds of agents, getting really close to the ideal 0% and 100% trust for, respectively, malware agents and other agents in the second input configuration.

Therefore, ABS-TrustSDN presents detailed results of the simulations including their evolutions that have been useful for providing explanations to the outcomes of three different

trust strategies. In general, the results of this experimentation advocate that ABS-TrustSDN may be an appropriate framework for designing and comparing trust strategies in SDNs, providing an adequate testbed simulation environment for this comparison.

4. Conclusions

The current work has introduced a novel agent-based framework for defining strategies for conforming trust models about network components. This framework and the corresponding ABS tool allow SDN designers to simulate and estimate the repercussion of certain protocols regarding the

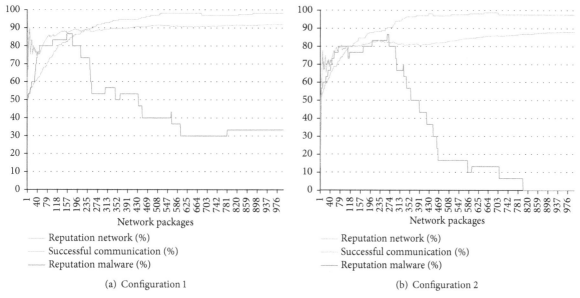

(a) Configuration 1   (b) Configuration 2

FIGURE 6: Evolution of SDN metrics with History strategy.

trust policy of the centralized controller of the SDN. This way, one can test several trust models in different contexts like short-term or long-term repercussions and the frequency of misbehavior of the network components with malware. This way, the current ABS supports the decision in selecting the most appropriate trust policy.

The current approach has assisted the definition of three different trust models. Each of these has been tested with two contexts with different frequencies of misbehavior of network components. Each case was simulated 1,000 times, and the results were compared. The results showed significant differences with a significance level of .001. In most cases, Cohen's d effect sizes were large according to Cohen's guidelines. Thus, the presented ABS approach was useful to find significant differences in the final simulated outcomes between different trust models for isolating problematic resources. The presented novel ABS-TrustSDN tool outputs several charts in its UI for analyzing the results not only at its final state but also in the evolution of the simulation. The evolution was crucial for understanding facts such as why the best isolation mechanism according to the final trust model does not necessarily imply the highest rate of success in the communications of the whole analyzed period.

The current work is planned to be enhanced by defining a higher number of trust policies in SDNs and simulating their repercussions. The presented approach will also be further experienced by simulating the repercussions of the variations of certain internal parameters of the strategies on the final simulated outcomes. The current approach will include the principles of model-driven development with (1) an agent-based metamodel [26] for supporting trust modeling and (2) model transformations for supporting the systems generation from their models [27]. The presented tool is planned to be tested with SDN designers as users to detect design opportunities related to aspects such as (a) improving the

usability of the tool, (b) including more functionalities, (c) adding new ways of presenting and analyzing the data, and (d) supporting more primitives for supporting the definition of trust strategies.

Acknowledgments

The authors would like to acknowledge "Desarrollo Colaborativo de Soluciones AAL" project (Ref. TIN2014-57028-R) supported by the Spanish Ministry of Economy and Competitiveness. This work was also supported by "Fondo Social Europeo" and the "Departamento de Tecnología y Universidad del Gobierno de Aragón" (Ref-T81).

References

[1] J. R. Ballard, I. Rae, and A. Akella, "Extensible and scalable network monitoring using OpenSAFE," in *Proceedings of the 2010 Internet Network Management Conference on Research on Enterprise Networking, INM/WREN'10*, p. 8, April 2010.

[2] R. Braga, E. Mota, and A. Passito, "Lightweight DDoS flooding attack detection using NOX/OpenFlow," in *Proceedings of the Local Computer Networks (LCN), 2010 IEEE 35th Conference*, pp. 408–415, IEEE, October 2010.

[3] T. Xing, Z. Xiong, D. Huang, and D. Medhi, "SDNIPS: enabling software-defined networking based intrusion prevention system in clouds," in *Proceedings of the 10th International Conference on Network and Service Management, CNSM 2014*, pp. 308–311, IEEE, Rio de Janeiro, Brazil, November 2014.

[4] S. Shin and G. Gu, "CloudWatcher: Network security monitoring using OpenFlow in dynamic cloud networks (or: How to provide security monitoring as a service in clouds?)," in *Proceedings of the 2012 20th IEEE International Conference on Network Protocols, ICNP 2012*, IEEE, Austin, TX, USA, November 2012.

[5] J. Naous, R. Stutsman, D. Mazieres, N. McKeown, and N. Zel-

dovich, "Delegating network security with more information," in *Proceedings of the In Proceedings of the 1st ACM Workshop on Research on Enterprise Networking*, pp. 19–26, 2009.

[6] A. K. Nayak, A. Reimers, N. Feamster, and R. Clark, "Resonance: dynamic access control for enterprise networks," in *Proceedings of the In Proceedings of the 1st ACM Workshop on Research on Enterprise Networking*, pp. 11–18, August 2009.

[7] A. Goodney, S. Narayan, V. Bhandwalkar, and Y. H. Cho, "Pattern based packet filtering using NetFPGA in DETER infrastructure," in *Proceedings of the 1st Asia NetFPGA Developers Workshop*, Daejeon, Korea.

[8] Z. Yan, P. Zhang, and A. V. Vasilakos, "A security and trust framework for virtualized networks and software-defined networking," *Security and Communication Networks*, 2015.

[9] P. Michiardi and R. Molva, "Core: a collaborative reputation mechanism to enforce node cooperation in mobile ad hoc networks," in *Advanced Communications and Multimedia Security*, pp. 107–121, Springer, New York, NY, USA, 2002.

[10] J. Liu and V. Issarny, "Enhanced reputation mechanism for mobile ad hoc networks," in *Proceedings of the In International Conference on Trust Management*, pp. 48–62, Springer, Berlin, Germany, 2004.

[11] K. K. Fullam, T. B. Klos, G. Muller et al., "A specification of the agent reputation and trust (art) testbed: experimentation and competition for trust in agent societies," in *Proceedings of the Fourth International Joint Conference on Autonomous Agents and Multiagent Systems*, pp. 512–518, July 2005.

[12] D. Rosaci, G. M. L. Sarné, and S. Garruzzo, "Integrating trust measures in multiagent systems," *International Journal of Intelligent Systems*, vol. 27, no. 1, pp. 1–15, 2012.

[13] D. Jelenc, R. Hermoso, J. Sabater-Mir, and D. Trček, "Decision making matters: A better way to evaluate trust models," *Knowledge-Based Systems*, vol. 52, pp. 147–164, 2013.

[14] H. Chen, H. Wu, X. Zhou, and C. Gao, "Agent-based trust model in wireless sensor networks," in *Proceedings of the 8th ACIS International Conference on Software Engineering, Artificial Intelligence, Networking, and Parallel/Distributed Computing (SNPD '07)*, vol. 3, pp. 119–124, IEEE, Qingdao, China, July 2007.

[15] W. S. Kim, "Effects of a trust mechanism on complex adaptive supply networks: an agent-based social simulation study," *Journal of Guangxi Traditional Chinese Medical University*, vol. 12, no. 3, pp. 56–58, 2009.

[16] I. García-Magariño and R. Lacuesta, ABS-TrustSDN website. Available at http://webdiis.unizar.es/~ivangmg/abstrustsdn/ (last accessed July 28, 2017).

[17] I. García-Magariño, A. Gómez-Rodríguez, J. C. González-Moreno, and G. Palacios-Navarro, "PEABS: a process for developing efficient agent-based simulators," *Engineering Applications of Artificial Intelligence*, vol. 46, pp. 104–112, 2015.

[18] I. García-Magariño, M. Cossentino, and V. Seidita, "A metrics suite for evaluating agent-oriented architectures," in *Proceedings of the 25th Annual ACM Symposium on Applied Computing, SAC 2010*, pp. 912–919, Sierre, Switzerland, March 2010.

[19] R. Fuentes-Fernández, I. García-Magariño, J. J. Gómez-Sanz, and J. Pavón, "Integration of web services in an agent-oriented methodology," in *Proceedings of the Integration of Web Services in an Agent-Oriented Methodology*, vol. 3, pp. 145–161, 2007.

[20] C. Gutierrez and I. Garcia-Magariño, "A metrics suite for the communication of multi-agent systems," *Journal of Physical Agents*, vol. 3, no. 2, pp. 7–14, 2009.

[21] B. Desmarchelier and E. S. Fang, "National Culture and Innovation diffusion. Exploratory insights from agent-based modeling," *Technological Forecasting and Social Change*, vol. 105, pp. 121–128, 2016.

[22] I. García-Magariño, J. J. Gómez-Sanz, and J. R. Pérez-Agüera, "A multi-agent based implementation of a Delphi process," in *Proceedings of the 7th International Joint Conference on Autonomous Agents and Multiagent Systems, AAMAS 2008*, vol. 3, pp. 1543–1546, International Foundation for Autonomous Agents and Multiagent Systems, Estoril, Portugal, May 2008.

[23] I. García-Magariño, G. Palacios-Navarro, and R. Lacuesta, "TABSAOND: A technique for developing agent-based simulation apps and online tools with nondeterministic decisions," *Simulation Modelling Practice and Theory*, vol. 77, pp. 84–107, 2017.

[24] B. L. Welch, "On the comparison of several mean values: an alternative approach," *Biometrika*, vol. 38, no. 3/4, pp. 330–336, 1951.

[25] J. Cohen, *Statistical Power Analysis for the Behavioral Sciences*, Lawrence Earlbaum Associates, Hillsdale, NJ, USA, 2nd edition, 1988.

[26] I. García-Magariño, R. Fuentes-Fernández, and J. J. Gómez-Sanz, "A framework for the definition of metamodels for computer-aided software engineering tools," *Information and Software Technology*, vol. 52, no. 4, pp. 422–435, 2010.

[27] I. García-Magariño, S. Rougemaille, R. Fuentes-Fernández, F. Migeon, M. P. Gleizes, and J. Gómez-Sanz, "A tool for generating model transformations by-example in multi-agent systems," in *Proceedings of the In 7th International Conference on Practical Applications of Agents and Multi-Agent Systems PAAMS 2009*, vol. 55 of *Advances in Intelligent and Soft Computing*, pp. 70–79, Springer, Berlin, Germany, 2009.

9

Reliable Collaborative Filtering on Spatio-Temporal Privacy Data

Zhen Liu,[1,2] **Huanyu Meng,**[1] **Shuang Ren,**[1,2] **and Feng Liu**[1,2]

[1]*School of Computer and Information Technology, Beijing Jiaotong University, Beijing 100044, China*
[2]*Engineering Research Center of Network Management Technology for High Speed Railway of MOE, Beijing 100044, China*

Correspondence should be addressed to Huanyu Meng; huanyum@bjtu.edu.cn

Academic Editor: Zhiping Cai

Lots of multilayer information, such as the spatio-temporal privacy check-in data, is accumulated in the location-based social network (LBSN). When using the collaborative filtering algorithm for LBSN location recommendation, one of the core issues is how to improve recommendation performance by combining the traditional algorithm with the multilayer information. The existing approaches of collaborative filtering use only the sparse user-item rating matrix. It entails high computational complexity and inaccurate results. A novel collaborative filtering-based location recommendation algorithm called LGP-CF, which takes spatio-temporal privacy information into account, is proposed in this paper. By mining the users check-in behavior pattern, the dataset is segmented semantically to reduce the data size that needs to be computed. Then the clustering algorithm is used to obtain and narrow the set of similar users. User-location bipartite graph is modeled using the filtered similar user set. Then LGP-CF can quickly locate the location and trajectory of users through message propagation and aggregation over the graph. Through calculating users similarity by spatio-temporal privacy data on the graph, we can finally calculate the rating of recommendable locations. Experiments results on the physical clusters indicate that compared with the existing algorithms, the proposed LGP-CF algorithm can make recommendations more accurately.

1. Introduction

With proliferation of mobile phones and location-based services (LBS), the existing social networks are able to collect the users geographical position in real time. LBS is combined with the traditional social network to form the location-based social network (LBSN). Through use of location services, LBSN integrates the online virtual network with the offline real world, thereby enabling users to share and obtain information of their interest more easily. Due to this reason, LBSN is gaining more and more favor with users. In addition to the relationship information of the traditional social network and the self-labelled information of the user, LBSN encompasses the user-registered historical trajectory collected via GPS and the labelled information of relevant locations [1]. Furthermore, the users mobile behavior patterns and trajectory show some characteristics in terms of time frequency, geographical distance, social relationship, and content [2–5]. For example, friends are more likely to check in together at the same place.

The locations where the user checks in on a daily and weekly basis also show some characteristics.

LBSN makes it possible for location recommendation. Location or Point of Interest (POI) refers to a geographical point that is useful or interesting to the user, such as hotel, restaurant, museum, and supermarket. Location recommendation refers to the service where the user-location check-in record is used to predict the location that has never been visited by the user but might be of supreme interest to the user and then recommend this location to the user [6].

Examples of LBSN include Foursquare, Gowalla, and Google Latitude [7]. This type of services allows the user to publish information on the place where they are via check-in and share their experience. These services have attracted a myriad of users. Statistical data indicates that Foursquare has more than 55 million users by the end of 2014. About 600 thousands to 1 million users check in at Foursquare each day. Over 6 billion check-in data items have been collected [6], which involve multidimensions, including the geographical location (Geo) automatically collected by the users mobile devices, temporal data, and content data [8].

The increasing number of LBSN users is accompanied by the sharp rise in the amount of multidimensional LBSN check-in data, making it more difficult for users to filter the information. In this context, how to recommend custom location more accurately by combining the abundant spatio-temporal information of the LBSN check-in data and the behavior tracks with the traditional recommendation algorithms is an issue of great significance. Meanwhile, due to increase in the size of check-in data, the recommendation algorithm imposes higher demands on the backend computational ability. The traditional single-machine computation method and the open-source Hadoop-based computation method are more and more computationally inefficient and resource intensive [1]. How to provide the user with real-time location information by developing a new recommendation algorithm that can process big data efficiently is a fresh challenge to the social recommendation system [9]. After the advent of the distributed parallel graph framework proposed in recent years, the graph theories have been used by the academia and industry to model the relationship between social network data. Moreover, based on the efficient graph framework, the graph algorithm is used to support machine learning and data mining, enabling the problem to be solved much more quickly.

Based on our previous work [10], we propose a new collaborative filtering-based location recommendation algorithm for LBSN, LGP-CF, which is based on parallel graph calculation and clustering, using the spatio-temporal data of LBSN. Taking the users check-in behavior patterns into account, the proposed method segment the dataset and obtains the set of users similar to the target user using the clustering algorithm to reduce the range of choices for similar users. User-location bipartite graph is established via the check-in data. The users common trajectories in the graph are filtered based on propagation of message across the graph. Afterwards, the trajectory data of the set of similar users that can represent the spatio-temporal information is combined with the point data to compute the similarity between the target user and each of similar users. Finally, the locations are clustered using the longitude and latitude data. The shortest path algorithm is then used to determine the set of recommended locations quickly and reliably. The final rating of a location is computed using the temporal information regarding the visit of similar users to it.

The contribution of this paper can be summarized as follows:

(1) The graph theory is used to model the spatio-temporal information and the user trajectory information of LBSN, facilitating rapid location of users and check-in locations in the graph.

(2) Calculation of user and location similarity is optimized after combining with the spatio-temporal privacy information of LBSN and taking the point and trajectory data into account.

(3) In addition to the point and trajectory of data, we also consider the regional data to cluster users and locations and reduce the size of data that needs to be computed.

The rest of this paper is organized as follows. Section 2 discusses related work. In Section 3, LBSN data analysis is presented; then data representation and modeling are given. Based on the data model, this paper proposes users similarity calculation using point, trajectory, and regional data information in Section 4. Section 5 is the proposed algorithm and its parallel design and implementation, followed by the experiment and evaluation results in Section 6. Conclusion is finally given in Section 7.

2. Related Works

Generally, user check-in location involved in LBSN recommendation can be classified into the following categories [11].

(1) Point Data. It is the most common type of user check-in location. It is characterized by fixed longitude and latitude of the geographical location corresponding to the point data. This type of data is usually used to compute the physical distance between users and measure the interuser similarity. Many point data-based recommendation methods have been proposed for LBSN [12–14].

(2) Trajectory Data. With proliferation of smart phones capable of localization, the mobile trajectory that the user follows during a time period can be recorded and then used by the academia and industry to study the users continuous behavior. Many trajectory data-based algorithms have been proposed to recommend routes for navigation and tour [15–17].

(3) Regional Data. The geographical locations can be divided into different regions according to predefined criterion. Data analysis and feature extraction are performed on each of the regions to facilitate user recommendation. Alternatively, the clustering methods can be used to cluster the collected data and produce regional data before recommendation.

The above analysis of user mobility behavior performed using various types of data indicates that user mobility is usually constrained by geographical space and social relationship. Lian et al. [2] and Liu et al. [4] reported that the user is more inclined to move within a geographical space nearby rather than go to a distant place during a time period. The results obtained by mining and analyzing the Brightkite and Gowalla check-in data indicate that 20% of the continuous check-in behaviors happen within a radius of 1 km, 60% happen within a radius of 1 km to 10 km, and only 20% happen beyond a range of 10 km. Zhang and Wang [18] revealed that the geographical location and time of check-in behavior are very periodic for most users. According to the work by Lian et al. in [2], the range of user mobility is centered on two points, that is, home and work place, which means that the user seldom moves to a place beyond a range of the two centers. In [19], Aamir jointly considered user mobility trajectory, regional data, social popularity, and custom location recommendation. A tree-based layered classification model based on the trajectory data was established. The regional data was clustered in each layer. The popularity of a location during a time period was computed using the ratio of users who have checked in at the location to all users of the same class.

TABLE 1: Example of check-in data of Gowalla dataset.

User ID	Check-in time	Altitude	Longitude	Location ID
0	2010-10-19T23:55:27Z	30.2359091167	−97.7951395833	22847
0	2010-10-18T22:17:43Z	30.2691029532	−97.7493953705	420315
3353	2010-10-04T06:12:33Z	39.7478004013	−104.9992454052	1109125
4368	2010-02-21T03:11:51Z	37.7625977833	−122.4231266667	174904
29534	2010-04-01T03:42:08Z	31.10072965	−97.44364675	821666
80157	2010-05-31T13:51:11Z	48.199R39617	16.3874741445	57426

TABLE 2: Example of check-in data of Foursquare dataset.

User ID	Check-in time	Altitude	Longitude	Location ID
0	2011-01-01	41.727575	−88.031988	0
1	2011-01-01	51.31791	−0.588761	1
2	2011-01-01	33.767021	−84.352638	2
3	2011-01-01	40.774759	−73.982432	3
4	2011-01-01	40.77476	−73.9824	4
5	2011-01-01	26.93896	−82.0532	5

Most of the graph model-based algorithms are reliant on clustering. After assuming that there is correlation between users with similar preferences, the graph clustering algorithm classifies the nodes according to node property and correlation [20]. In [12], Yao et al. proposed a collaborative location recommendation framework CLR for LBSN. In their framework, GPS is first used to obtain user trajectory data in a three-layer (user-location-behavior) structure. Afterwards, a graph model is established that consists of three types of nodes (user, location, and behavior). Finally, the proposed algorithms are used for collaborative filtering and location recommendation. In [21], Jin et al. proposed a model based on link analysis and custom PageRank. The user in the dataset is regarded as the node in the directed graph; mutual following between users is regarded as the edge. The custom PageRank algorithm is used to compute the rank of recommendable locations for the target user during a time period. In [22], Cui et al. proposed a new location recommendation algorithm based on the graph model. In their method, the vertex consists of user vertex and location vertex, while the edge encompasses the friendly relationship between users and the user-location check-in relationship in the historical information. The user vertexes that have made friendship with the target user are sorted out according to their similarity with the target user. Afterwards, location is recommended by sorting out the location vertexes which have been visited by these friends but not visited by the target user.

3. Representation and Modeling of Check-In Data

3.1. Check-In Dataset Analysis. Gowalla is a LBSN website where users check in to share their current locations with friends. It consists of 196,591 nodes and 950,327 edges. The Gowalla dataset used in the experiment includes 6,442,890 records collected from February 2009 to October 2010. Examples of Gowalla user check-in data are given in Table 1.

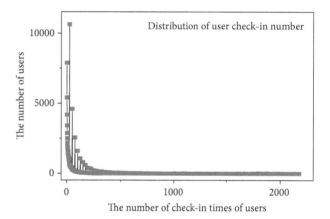

FIGURE 1: The distribution curve of user check-in numbers.

Foursquare is a LBSN service which encourages mobile phone users to check in and share their current locations with friends. It effectively combines the traditional social network with mobile Internet. Its dataset includes user check-in data, user social data, and user residence data. Foursquare includes 1,385,223 pieces of user check-in data. Examples of Foursquare user check-in data are given in Table 2.

The total number of checked-in users is 107,092 in the Gowalla dataset. The number of user check-in times is 60 in average, 2,175 at most, and 1 at least and mostly falls within the range [1, 300]. The number of corresponding users decreases with increase in the check-in times within this range. The distribution of all user check-in times is shown in Figure 1.

The number of Gowalla user check-in locations is also computed. It is indicated that there are 1,280,969 checked-in locations in Gowalla. The number of location check-in times is 5 in average, 5,811 at most, and 1 at least. The distribution of all location check-in times is shown in Figure 2. From this figure, it can be seen that most of the locations are seldom

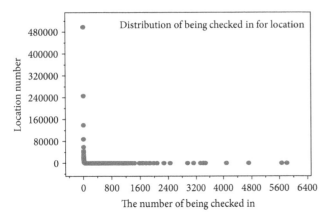

FIGURE 2: The distribution curve of the checked location numbers.

checked in. This means that the user check-in data is very sparse.

Performance of the recommendation system is closely related to data sparsity. Recommendation accuracy will be seriously affected if the data is very sparse. Therefore, we focus on the recommendation results of methods rather than the absolute value of performance metrics.

3.2. Check-In Data Representation. Let u, p, and t denote the user, location, and check-in time, respectively. Also let $U = \{u_1, u_2, \ldots, u_n\}$ denote the set of users in the user-location check-in data, $P = \{p_1, p_2, \ldots, p_m\}$ denote the set of locations, and $T = \{t_1, t_2, \ldots, t_l\}$ denote the set of check-in time. Hence, each of the location check-in data can be represented with a 5-dimension vector $\overrightarrow{d_{ijk}} = [u_i, p_j, p\text{Lng}_j, p\text{Lat}_j, t_k]$, where $i \in [1 \cdots n]$, $j \in [1 \cdots m]$, $k \in [1 \cdots l]$, t_k denotes the check-in time of the user u_i at the location p_j, $p\text{Lng}_j$ denotes the longitude of the location p_j, and $p\text{lat}_j$ denotes the latitude of the location p_j. If the user u_i has never visited the location p_j, the vector $\overrightarrow{d_{ijk}}$ does not exist. All vectors form the set of user-location check-in data, D. The recommendation algorithm is responsible for predicting the possibility that the user visits the location that he has never visited before using the dataset D.

3.3. Segmentation of the User Check-In Dataset. It can be learned that the geographical location and time of check-in behavior is very periodic for most users [18]. The range of user mobility is usually centered on two points, that is, home and work place, which means that the user seldom moves to a place beyond a range of the two centers [2]. Considering user needs for recommendation at different time periods, experiments are performed on the Gowalla and Foursquare datasets. Figures 3 and 4 show the ratio of the number of user check-in times at different time periods to the total number of check-in times in the Gowalla and Foursquare datasets, respectively.

In this paper, the check-in data is divided according to time periods. Demographic statistics analysis indicates that the location visited by the user during working days is

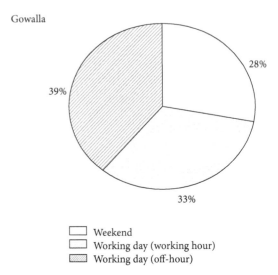

FIGURE 3: The distribution curve of user check-in number in a different period.

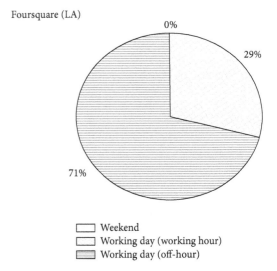

FIGURE 4: The distribution curve of user check-in number in a different period.

very different from the location visited during the weekend. Moreover, the checked in location by the user during the working hours differs greatly from that checked in after hours. Therefore, the dataset D is divided into three segments in this paper.

Weekend dataset DoffDay: it refers to the dataset whose check-in time is the weekend in the user check-in dataset, and DoffDay $= \{\overrightarrow{d_{ijk}} \mid t_k \in T$offDay$\}$, where ToffDay denotes the time set of weekend. Working hour dataset DofficeTime: it refers to the dataset whose check-in time is the working hour in the user check-in dataset, and DofficeTime $= \{\overrightarrow{d_{ijk}} \mid t_k \in T$officeTime$\}$, where TofficeTime denotes the time set of working hours. The time period from 8:00 a.m. to 7:00 p.m. is defined as the working hour in the demography. Off-hour dataset DNofficeTime: it refers to the dataset whose check-in time is the off-hour of working day in the user check-in dataset, and $DNofficeTime = \{\overrightarrow{d_{ijk}} \mid t_k \in TNofficeTime\}$, where $TNofficeTime$ denotes the set of off-hour during working day. The time period apart from working hours during the working day is defined as the off-hour in the demography.

The weekend dataset $DoffDay$, working hour dataset $DofficeTime$, and off-hour dataset $DNofficeTime$ are all the subsets of the user check-in dataset D: that is, $D = DoffDay \cup DofficeTime \cup DNofficeTime$. Moreover, the intersection set of any two of the three subsets is empty. Considering the request time period by the target user, we filter a subset D' from D: that is, $D' = DoffDay$ or $D' = DofficeTime$ or $D' = DNofficeTime$. Recommendation is made to the target user by performing data mining and analysis of D'.

3.4. Users Clustering on Temporal Pattern and Spatial Region.

Each user either has some or no similar preferences to the target user. Based on this observation, the selected check-in data subset is clustered into two classes according to the target user. The class of the target user consists of similar users.

There is correlation in two users who share similar preferences [23]. Based on this assumption, property vector is constructed for each member of the user set in the selected check-in data subset. And these users are clustered according to the property vector. The property vector involves the number of check-in times, time pattern, and spatial region. It can be written as

$$\overrightarrow{v_i} = \langle u_i, lMaxLng, lMaxLat, lNearLng, LNearLat, \tag{1}$$
$$lDistLng, LDistLat, lMaxWeek, lMaxTime \rangle,$$

where u_i denotes the ID of current user, $lMaxLng$ and $lMaxLat$ denote the longitude and latitude of the location $lMax$ most frequently checked in by the user u_i, $lMaxWeek$ denotes the day of a week that the user u_i most often checks in at the location $lMax$, and $lMaxTime$ denotes the hour of a day that the user u_i most often checks in at the location $lMax$. Describing user behavior in detail is helpful in identifying similar users more accurately. In addition to spatio-temporal description of the users mostly frequently registered location, we draw inspiration from the results in [2, 4], taking user mobility range into account. Let $lNearLng$ and $lNearLat$ denote the longitude and latitude of the location that the user has once checked in and has the shortest Euclidean distance to $lMax$. Also, let $lDistLng$ and $LDistLat$ denote the longitude and latitude of the location that the user has once checked in and has the longest Euclidean distance to $lMax$. After construction of the user property vector, the k-means algorithm is used to extract users from the class of the target user as the similar user set $SimU$.

3.5. Graph Modeling for User-Location Data.

After extracting the similar user set $SimU$ through clustering, we need to filter the user check-in data subset D' that is selected according to the recommendation request time. If u_i corresponding to the element $\overrightarrow{d_{ijk}}$ of D' does not belong to the similar user set $SimU$, the element should be deleted from D'. The filtered user check-in data subset is called D_1'. In this paper, we model

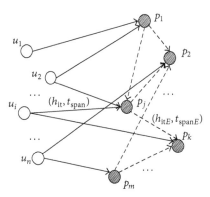

FIGURE 5: User-location bipartite graph.

the filtered subset D_1' as a user-item (location) bipartite graph. The graph G is shown in Figure 5. While clustering the similar users according to the regional data, we jointly consider the impact of point data and trajectory data on recommendation when we construct the graph model.

The user check-in data subset D_1' is represented with the graph G, and $G = \langle V, E \rangle$, where V denotes the set of vertexes, including user vertexes and location vertexes. $V = U_g \cup P_g$, where $U_g = \{u_1, u_2, \ldots, u_n\}$ denotes the user set in D_1' and $P_g = \{p_1, p_2, \ldots, p_m\}$ denotes the location set in D_1'. E denotes the set of edges, including the edge between the user and the registered location and the edge between locations. $E = E_v \cup E_t$, $\langle u_i, p_j \rangle \in E_v$ denotes the check-in behavior of the user u_i at the location p_j, and each edge $\langle u_i, p_j \rangle \in E_v$ has a weight (h_{it}, t_{span}), where h_{it} denotes the number of visits paid by the user u_i to the location p_j and t_{span} denotes the time of the latest visit paid by the user u_i to the location p_j. $\langle p_k, p_j \rangle \in E_t$ indicates a trajectory that a user checked in at the location p_k and then checks in at the location p_j. E_t denotes the set of directed edges between two locations. An edge exists between two locations if and only if a user has once checked in at the two locations and the time interval between the two visits is less than a threshold, which is set to one week in this paper. Each edge $\langle p_k, p_j \rangle \in E_t$ has a weight (h_{itE}, t_{spanE}), where h_{itE} denotes the number of times that the locations p_k and p_j are visited sequentially and the conditions are satisfied; t_{spanE} denotes the latest time that the locations p_k and p_j are visited sequentially and the conditions are satisfied. The problem of recommending location for the user u_i can be described as the problem of estimating the correlation between the target user vertex and the location vertexes that have no link before in the user-location bipartite graph.

From the temporal aspect of view, the graph is varying with time. Figure 6 shows graph G in time t_1 and t_2 ($t_1 < t_2$). In time t_2, there happens a check-in between user u_n and location p_k. It produces an edge between them. Thus, there is a common trajectory between user u_i and u_n, that is, edge $\langle p_j, p_k \rangle$.

In order to obtain two users' common locations and repeated check-in times quickly, this paper presents a method named GraPA based on the message propagation and aggregation on the graph to determine the common trajectory and repeated times.

```
Input: Graph G = ⟨V, E⟩
Output: Message list for each vertex in Graph G: List [(vid, L_i)]
(1)  for each v_i ∈ V do /*Initialization*/
(2)       L_i = vid_i
(3)  for each ⟨v_i, v_j⟩ ∈ E do /*Message Propagation*/
(4)       L_j ← L_i
(5)  for each v_i ∈ V do /*Message Aggregation*/
(6)       for k = 1 ··· m do
(7)            if k⟨⟩i then
(8)                 L_i = L_i ∪ L_k
(9)  return List [(vid, L_i)]
```

ALGORITHM 1: GraPA: message propagation and aggregation in graph.

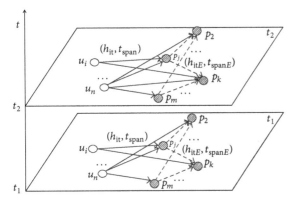

FIGURE 6: User-location bipartite graph with temporal information.

There are three states of vertices in a graph in GraPA method. The first state of the vertex is nonactivated, which is denoted as S_0. The second state of the vertex is activated, which is denoted as S_1, in which the vertex is propagating the message. The third state is denoted as S_2, in which the vertex is aggregating the received messages. Each vertex vi of the graph needs to maintain a message. The message of vertex v_i can be denoted as $vI = (vid_i, L_i)$, vid_i is the ID of vertex v_i, and L_i is the set of vertex ID which would arrive at the vertex v_i during the message propagating. L_i is initialized as vid_i itself. The states of all of the vertices alter among the three states according to time slot, so as to do message propagation and aggregation. The process of GraPA is depicted as Algorithm 1.

4. User Similarity Calculation

After the selected user check-in data subset is clustered into the regional data, the similar user set is extracted, and the user-location bipartite graph is constructed, we need to compute the similarity between target user and similar users. The point data and trajectory data in the user check-in data are jointly taken into account while computing the similarity.

4.1. Exploiting Spatio-Temporal Point Data.
Each user has his/her preferences. The basic idea of the user-based collaborative filtering algorithm is the observation that the level of

interuser similarity increases with the number of locations registered by the two users. The difference in the number of visits paid by the two users to the same location is taken into account in this paper, and the higher the difference, the lower the level of interuser similarity. Meanwhile, the check-in time is also considered. For two users who have once checked in at the same location, the longer the interval between their visits to the location, the lower the level of interuser similarity. Based on these observations, the interuser similarity can be computed as Formula (2):

$$
\text{sim}_{\text{point}}\left(u_i, u_j\right)
$$
$$
= \frac{-\sum_{i \in (P_{u_i} \cap P_{u_j})} th\left(\log\left(t_{\text{span}}(i) - \delta\right)\left(h_{\text{diff}}(i) - \beta\right)\right)}{\left|P_{u_i} \cap P_{u_j}\right|}, \quad (2)
$$

where P_{u_i} and P_{u_j} denote the set of locations once checked in by the target user u_i and the similar user u_j in the subset D_1', respectively; $t_{\text{span}}(i)$ denotes the time interval between the latest visits of the target user u_i and the similar user u_j to the same location i, δ denotes the preset threshold of time interval between visits in millisecond, $h_{\text{diff}}(i)$ denotes the difference in the number of visits paid by the target user u_i and the similar user u_j to the same location i, and β is the preset largest threshold of the difference in the number of visits. In this paper, the interuser similarity $\text{sim}_{\text{point}}(u_i, u_j)$ ranges from -1 to 1. The lower the value of $t_{\text{span}}(i)$ and $h_{\text{diff}}(i)$, the more closer the value of $\text{sim}_{\text{point}}(u_i, u_j)$ to 1. This means the interuser similarity is higher. The higher the value of $t_{\text{span}}(i)$ and $h_{\text{diff}}(i)$, the more closer the value of $\text{sim}_{\text{point}}(u_i, u_j)$ to -1. This means the interuser similarity is smaller. If the value of $t_{\text{span}}(i)$ is larger than the constant δ or the value of $h_{\text{diff}}(i)$ is larger than the threshold β, the data of this location belongs to negative feedback and the interuser similarity $\text{sim}_{\text{point}}(u_i, u_j)$ is less than 0.

4.2. Exploiting User Check-In Trajectories.
The trajectory in the user-location check-in data consists of a consecutive series of locations. It also includes the check-in time of different user locations, which is helpful in analyzing the mobility pattern of users at different time. The trajectory data is incorporated into the calculation of user similarity to

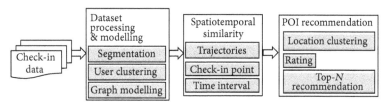

FIGURE 7: LGP-CF algorithm flowchart.

improve accuracy. If many of the trajectory data of one user is the same as the other user, it means that their mobility pattern is very similar and the interuser similarity is very high. Based on user trajectory data, the interuser similarity can be computed as Formula (3):

$$\text{sim}_{\text{traj}}\left(u_i, u_j\right) = th\left(\sum_{m,n \in (P_{u_i} \cap P_{u_j})} \text{weight}\,(m,n)\right), \quad (3)$$

where weight(m, n) is equal to 0 or 1. When the following three conditions are satisfied,

(i) the locations $m, n \in (P_{u_i} \cap P_{u_j})$,

(ii) users u_i and u_j visit the locations m and n in the same sequence,

(iii) the time interval between the visits of the same user to the two places is shorter than the threshold β, and we have weight$(m, n) = 1$.

Given a target user and the similar user set SimU, after the calculation of the spatio-temporal data-based user similarity $\text{sim}_{\text{point}}(u_i, u_j)$ and the trajectory data-based user similarity $\text{sim}_{\text{traj}}(u_i, u_j)$, the final user similarity can be computed as Formula (4):

$$\text{sim}\left(u_i, u_j\right) = \text{sim}_{\text{point}}\left(u_i, u_j\right) + \text{sim}_{\text{traj}}\left(u_i, u_j\right). \quad (4)$$

4.3. Rating for Recommendable Locations. The traditional collaborative filtering algorithm is characterized by data sparsity and operational inefficiency and does not take the selection of recommendable locations into account. While choosing the recommendable locations, we consider the mobility pattern of users and cluster the longitude and latitude of the location set P into two classes. Afterwards, the class which has more locations in common with the set of target user-registered locations is identified. And the set of locations in this class which have not been checked in by the target user is regarded as the set of recommendable locations for the target user. The rating of recommendable location p_k for u_i is then calculated as in Formula (5). Finally, the top-N locations are recommended to the user.

$$r\left(u_i, p_k\right) = \frac{\sum_{u_j \in \text{SimU}} \text{sim}\left(u_i, u_j\right)}{\left(1 + \left(T - \text{time}\left(u_j, p_k\right)\right)\right)}. \quad (5)$$

5. LGP-CF Algorithm and Its Parallel Design

5.1. LGP-CF Algorithm. Based on ideas above, we propose a new collaborative filtering-based spatio-temporal data-incorporated location recommendation algorithm LGP-CF

for LBSN. Algorithm flowchart is shown in Figure 7. The location check-in data of all users is divided into three dataset segments according to the time period. Next, the dataset corresponding to the recommendation request time of the target user is selected. The subsequently constructed cluster of regional data is used to obtain the set of users similar to the target user. Then we model the filtered subset D'_1 as a user-item (location) bipartite graph, over which we execute GraPA twice in order to find users' common locations and common trajectory between two common locations. These are the candidate similar users, locations, and trajectory of the target user. Then, the similarity between target user and each of the similar users is computed using the trajectory and point location. The locations are clustered using the longitude and latitude data. Finally, ratings are calculated and sorted using the location check-in time of similar users.

5.2. The Parallel Design of LGP-CF Algorithm. The pseudo code of LGP-CF is presented in Algorithm 2. The input of LGP-CF is the resilient distributed dataset (RDD) generated using the user-location check-in dataset and the parallel calculation framework Spark. RDD is not only an invariable partitioned set of records, but also a programming model of Spark. As in Hadoop, it submits the task at the two-stage of MapReduce and brings high delay between tasks. Different from Hadoop, Spark provides two RDD operations, that is, transformation and action. In Spark, a program actually constructs a directed acyclic graph (DAG) that consists of several interdependent RDDs. Various RDD operations are performed by submitting DAG as a task to Spark for execution. Hence, Spark tasks do not need to wait for each other, thereby improving the ability to process iterative data. Note that the data associated with each iteration of Spark is stored in the memory. This enables Spark to gain enormous performance improvement over Hadoop [24].

Each step of LGP-CF is parallelized and the data throughout the graph can thus be processed in a parallel manner. The first and second steps of Algorithm 2 are detailed here.

(1) In the first step, RDD needs to be converted into (user, location, latitude, longitude, hour, weekday) before the segmentation of the user-location check-in dataset according to time property, where hour denotes the hour of a day in the check-in time and weekday denotes the day of a week in the check-in time. Next, the converted RDD should be filtered based on the property (hour, weekday). RDD of the user check-in data subset that corresponds to the current time is obtained in this way.

(2) In the second step, RDD of the user check-in data subset needs to be converted to the user property RDD,

---

Input: user location check-in dataset: D; target user ID:TID.
Output: Recommended location list: List $[I_{id}]$
(1) Initialisation: $D' \leftarrow$ dataSetSplit (D); /*D' *is the subset of check-in dataset D according to the target user's request time.*/
(2) $U' = \{\vec{v_1}, \vec{v_2}, \ldots, \vec{v_n}\} \leftarrow$ userDataModel (D'); /*Construct users property vector exploiting the regional data.*/
(3) SimU $\leftarrow$ kMeansFilter (U'); /*Clustering similarity users as SimU set.*/
(4) $G = \langle V, E \rangle \leftarrow$ graphBuild (D'_1); /*Model the filtered subset D'_1 as a user-item (location) bipartite graph.*/
(5) **for** $i = 0$ to 1 **do**
(6)   GraPA (G); /*traverse the graph to find candidate similar users, locations and trajectory*/
(7) **for** each $u_i \in$ SimU **do**
(8) $\text{sim}(u_i, u_{TID}) = \text{sim}_{point} + \text{sim}_{traj}$
(9) $P' \leftarrow$ kMeansLocation (P); /*Clustering location to select candidate recommendable locations.*/
(10) **for** each $p_k \in P'$ **do**
(11)   **for** each $u_i \in$ SimU **do**
(12) $r(u_{TID}, p_k) = r(u_{TID}, p_k) + \text{sim}(u_i, u_{TID})/(1 + (T - \text{time}(u_{TID}, p_k)))$
(13) List$[I_{id}] \leftarrow$ sortByRating $(r_{pi}, r_{pj}, \ldots, r_{pk})$; /*Top-N recommendation.*/
(14) **return** List$[I_{id}]$

ALGORITHM 2: LGP-CF in LBSN.

---

that is, $(u_i$, lMaxLng, lMaxLat, lNearLng, lNearLat, lDistLng, lDistLat, lMaxWeek, lMaxDay), in order to construct the set of user properties. While constructing user property RDD, we need to first map the user check-in data subset RDD into ((user, location, longitude, latitude), 1) and name it user check-in RDD. Next, we compute the number of times that the user checked in at each of the registered locations through the key-based value processing operation reduceByKey. The combineByKey and mapping operations are performed to determine the location with the largest number of check-in times and the most registered location RDD (user, (lMaxLng, lMaxLat)). Afterwards, the mapping operation is done to convert the user check-in RDD into (user, longitude, latitude). Join and mapping operations are performed on it and the most registered location RDD, computing RDD of the distance between user check-in location and the most registered location. According to the distance property, we choose RDD of the location closest to the most registered location (user, lNearLng, lNearLat) and RDD of the location furthest from the most registered location (user, lDistLng, lDistLat). Similarly, the mapping operation, key-based value processing reduceByKey operation, and the clustering combineByKey operation are performed to determine RDD of the most frequent check-in hour in a day and RDD of the most frequent check-in day of a week. Finally, the join and mapping operations are performed to connect the most registered location RDD, RDD of the location closest to the most registered location, RDD of the location furthest from the most registered location, RDD of the most frequent check-in hour in a day, and RDD of the most frequent check-in day of a week. In this way, we finally obtain the user property RDD.

Each step of the Spark-based recommendation algorithm is parallelized and the calculation result of each step is stored in the buffer. After all tasks associated with the current step are completed, the buffered calculation result will be passed to the next step, resulting in fewer access to the disk, higher job execution efficiency, and improved algorithm performance.

6. Experiments and Evaluation

Experiment is conducted in this section to evaluate the recommendation performance of the proposed algorithm. Large-scale LBSN datasets from Gowalla and Foursquare are adopted in the experiment to evaluate algorithm performance. As in Section 3, the distribution of the number of user check-in times and the number of user check-in locations has been analyzed. And impact of different dataset segmentation on the recommendation results was discussed. In this section, LGP-CF is implemented and compared with other methods in the real-world physical cluster environment.

6.1. Experimental Environment. We use 6 servers in the experiment to build a cloud cluster. The Server OS is 64-bit Ubuntu14.04, cluster management platform is Spark1.1.0, and each server node includes a 4-core CPU and 8 GB memory. One server is configured as master and the other five as slave nodes. LGP-CF and other compared algorithms are implemented in a parallel manner in Spark.

6.2. Evaluation Results. Dataset segmentation of different time periods is used to evaluate the performance of the proposed algorithm in the experiment. Performance metrics include the predicted root-mean-square error (RMSE), precision, and recall.

Figures 8 and 9 compare precision and recall of LGP-CF on datasets of different time periods. From the two figures, it can be seen that the user check-in time concentrates in working days (after hours). Accuracy and recall of LGP-CF are very desirable. But algorithm performance is mediocre for time periods with a small number of user check-in times.

Based on this observation, we choose to compare LGP-CF with other algorithms on after-hour periods of working days. Because LGP-CF incorporates the spatio-temporal information, the traditional collaborative filtering algorithm L-CF is selected as a baseline algorithm for comparison. The aim is to

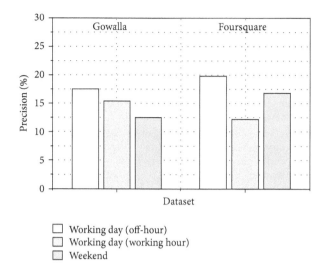

FIGURE 8: The precision in different periods.

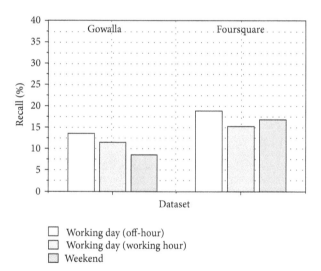

FIGURE 9: The recall in different periods.

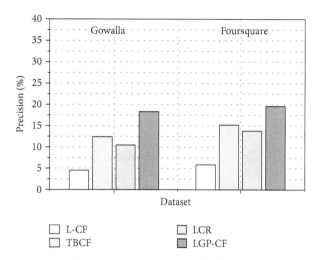

FIGURE 10: The precision comparison of different algorithms.

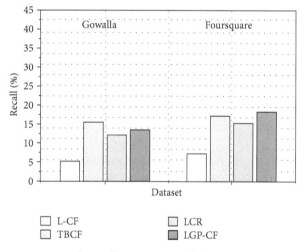

FIGURE 11: The recall comparison of different algorithms.

study the impact of incorporated spatio-temporal information on recommendation results. Afterwards, the time-based collaborative filtering algorithm TBCF is chosen to study the impact of combining temporal and spatial information on recommendation results. Finally, the LCR algorithm based on clustering of regional similarity is chosen to study the impact of combining spatio-temporal information with the clustering method on recommendation results.

Figures 10 and 11 show the comparison of all algorithms on the Gowalla and Foursquare datasets.

The comparison in Figures 10 and 11 indicates that LGP-CF is superior to L-CF in terms of precision and recall. This proves that LGP-CF achieves enormous performance gain in precision and recall, compared with the traditional collaborative filtering-based location recommendation algorithm for LBSN. While maintaining recall, LGP-CF produces higher accuracy than TBCF, because it incorporates both spatial and temporal information into recommendation, while TBCF only exploits the temporal information in its

recommendation. Meanwhile, comparison between LGP-CF with LCR also indicates that combining spatio-temporal information with the clustering method enables LGP-CF to achieve improvements in precision and recall.

7. Conclusions

In addition to processing a large amount of data, existing LBSN location recommendation algorithms are used to meet various user needs. However, most of these methods are not accurate and efficient enough to make high-quality recommendation. In this paper, a new collaborative filtering-based spatio-temporal data-incorporated recommendation algorithm LGP-CF is proposed. User-location check-in data is divided according to time periods. The dataset that corresponds to user recommendation request time is then selected to reduce the amount of data that needs to be computed. Regional data associated with user mobility ranges is used to cluster users, obtain the set of similar users, and narrow the scope of choices of similar users. The selected user-location check-in data subsets are modeled using the user-location bipartite graph. Therefore, the common visiting locations and the number of visits can be determined for two users by retrieving location edges in the directed graph. Afterwards, the trajectory data and point data corresponding to the set of similar users are used to compute the similarity between the target user and each of the similar users. The locations are then clustered using longitude and latitude data in order to obtain the set of recommendable locations accurately and reliably. Finally, the rating of a location is computed using the time of visits paid by similar users to it. Recommendation accuracy is improved in this way. Experiments on the real-world physical cluster are performed to compare with other LBSN recommendation algorithms. Results demonstrate superiority of LGP-CF in terms of precision and recall.

Acknowledgments

This work was supported in part by the National Key R&D Program of China under Grant no. 2016YFB1200100 and the Fundamental Research Funds for the Central Universities (2017JBM024).

References

[1] J. Bao, Y. Zheng, D. Wilkie, and M. Mokbel, "Recommendations in location-based social networks: a survey," *GeoInformatica*, vol. 19, no. 3, pp. 525–565, 2015.

[2] D. Lian, C. Zhao, X. Xie, G. Sun, E. Chen, and Y. Rui, "GeoMF: Joint geographical modeling and matrix factorization for point-of-interest recommendation," in *Proceedings of the 20th ACM SIGKDD International Conference on Knowledge Discovery and Data Mining, KDD 2014*, pp. 831–840, USA, August 2014.

[3] H. Gao, J. Tang, X. Hu, and H. Liu, "Modeling temporal effects of human mobile behavior on location-based social networks," in *Proceedings of the 22nd ACM International Conference on Information and Knowledge Management, CIKM 2013*, pp. 1673–1678, USA, November 2013.

[4] X. Liu, Y. Liu, and X. Li, "Exploring the context of locations for personalized location recommendations," in *Proceedings of the 25th International Joint Conference on Artificial Intelligence, IJCAI 2016*, pp. 1188–1194, New York, NY, USA, July 2016.

[5] H. Gao and H. Liu, "Data Analysis on Location-Based Social Networks," *Mobile Social Networking*, pp. 165–194, 2014.

[6] H. Gao, J. Tang, and H. Liu, "Personalized location recommendation on location-based social networks," in *Proceedings of the 8th ACM Conference on Recommender Systems, RecSys 2014*, pp. 399-400, USA, October 2014.

[7] O. Khalid, M. U. S. Khan, S. U. Khan, and A. Y. Zomaya, "OmniSuggest: A ubiquitous cloud-based context-aware recommendation system for mobile social networks," *IEEE Transactions on Services Computing*, vol. 7, no. 3, pp. 401–414, 2014.

[8] H. Abdel-Fatao, J. Li, and J. Liu, "Unifying spatial, temporal and semantic features for an effective GPS trajectory-based location recommendation," *Lecture Notes in Computer Science (including subseries Lecture Notes in Artificial Intelligence and Lecture Notes in Bioinformatics): Preface*, vol. 9093, pp. 41–53, 2015.

[9] S. Zhao, I. King, and M. R. Lyu, "A Survey of Point-of-interest Recommendation in Location-based Social Networks," https://arxiv.org/abs/1607.00647, 2016.

[10] M. Huanyu, L. Zhen, W. Fang, and X. Jiadong, "Towards Efficient Collaborative Filtering Using Parallel Graph Model and Improved Similarity Measure," in *Proceedings of the 18th IEEE International Conference on High Performance Computing and Communications, 14th IEEE International Conference on Smart City and 2nd IEEE International Conference on Data Science and Systems, HPCC/SmartCity/DSS 2016*, pp. 182–189, Sydney, Australia, December 2016.

[11] R. Levin, H. Abassi, and H. Uzi Cohen, "Guided walk: A scalable recommendation algorithm for complex heterogeneous social networks," in *Proceedings of the 10th ACM Conference on Recommender Systems, RecSys 2016*, pp. 293–300, Boston, Mass, USA, September 2016.

[12] L. Yao, Q. Z. Sheng, Y. Qin, X. Wang, A. Shemshadi, and Q. He, "Context-aware point-of-interest recommendation using Tensor Factorization with social regularization," in *Proceedings of the 38th International ACM SIGIR Conference on Research and Development in Information Retrieval, SIGIR 2015*, pp. 1007–1010, Chile, August 2015.

[13] R. Baral and T. Li, "MAPS: A multi aspect personalized POI recommender system," in *Proceedings of the 10th ACM Conference on Recommender Systems, RecSys 2016*, pp. 281–284, USA, September 2016.

[14] C. Yang, L. Bai, C. Zhang, Q. Yuan, and J. Han, "Bridging Collaborative Filtering and Semi-Supervised Learning," in *Proceedings of the the 23rd ACM SIGKDD International Conference*, pp. 1245–1254, Halifax, NS, Canada, August 2017.

[15] A. Noulas, S. Scellato, N. Lathia, and C. Mascolo, "A random walk around the city: New venue recommendation in location-based social networks," in *Proceedings of the 2012 ASE/IEEE International Conference on Social Computing, SocialCom 2012 and the 2012 ASE/IEEE International Conference on Privacy, Security, Risk and Trust, PASSAT 2012*, pp. 144–153, Netherlands, September 2012.

[16] Y. Zheng, "Trajectory data mining: an overview," *ACM Transactions on Intelligent Systems and Technology*, vol. 6, no. 3, article 29, 2015.

[17] Y. Wang, Y. Zheng, and Y. Xue, "Travel time estimation of a path using sparse trajectories," in *Proceedings of the 20th ACM SIGKDD International Conference*, pp. 25–34, ACM, August 2014.

[18] C. Zhang and K. Wang, "POI recommendation through cross-region collaborative filtering," *Knowledge and Information Systems*, vol. 46, no. 2, pp. 369–387, 2016.

[19] M. Aamir, "Dynamicity in Social Trends towards Trajectory Based Location Recommendation," in *Proceedings of the International Conference on Smart Homes and Health Telematics*, pp. 86–93, Singapore, Singapore, 2013.

[20] S. Shang, K. Zheng, C. S. Jensen et al., "Discovery of path nearby clusters in spatial networks," *IEEE Transactions on Knowledge and Data Engineering*, vol. 27, no. 6, pp. 1505–1518, 2015.

[21] Z. Jin, D. Shi, Q. Wu, H. Yan, and H. Fan, "LBSN Rank: personalized pagerank on location-based social networks," in *Proceedings of the the 2012 ACM Conference*, pp. 980–987, Pittsburgh, Penn, USA, September 2012.

[22] C. Cui, J. Shen, L. Nie, R. Hong, and J. Ma, "Augmented Collaborative Filtering for Sparseness Reduction in Personalized POI Recommendation," *ACM Transactions on Intelligent Systems and Technology*, vol. 8, no. 5, pp. 71–93, 2017.

[23] R. S. Xin, D. Crankshaw, A. Dave et al., "GraphX unifying data-parallel and graph-parallel analytics," *Computer Science Databases*, 2014, https://arxiv.org/abs/1402.2394.

10

Towards Large-Scale, Heterogeneous Anomaly Detection Systems in Industrial Networks: A Survey of Current Trends

Mikel Iturbe, Iñaki Garitano, Urko Zurutuza, and Roberto Uribeetxeberria

Department of Electronics and Computing, Mondragon Unibertsitatea, Goiru 2, 20500 Arrasate-Mondragón, Spain

Correspondence should be addressed to Mikel Iturbe; miturbe@mondragon.edu

Academic Editor: Javier Lopez

Industrial Networks (INs) are widespread environments where heterogeneous devices collaborate to control and monitor physical processes. Some of the controlled processes belong to Critical Infrastructures (CIs), and, as such, IN protection is an active research field. Among different types of security solutions, IN Anomaly Detection Systems (ADSs) have received wide attention from the scientific community. While INs have grown in size and in complexity, requiring the development of novel, Big Data solutions for data processing, IN ADSs have not evolved at the same pace. In parallel, the development of Big Data frameworks such as Hadoop or Spark has led the way for applying Big Data Analytics to the field of cyber-security, mainly focusing on the Information Technology (IT) domain. However, due to the particularities of INs, it is not feasible to directly apply IT security mechanisms in INs, as IN ADSs face unique characteristics. In this work we introduce three main contributions. First, we survey the area of Big Data ADSs that could be applicable to INs and compare the surveyed works. Second, we develop a novel taxonomy to classify existing IN-based ADSs. And, finally, we present a discussion of open problems in the field of Big Data ADSs for INs that can lead to further development.

1. Introduction

Industrial Networks (INs) refer to the networked environments where specialized, heterogeneous interconnected components, known collectively as Industrial Control Systems (ICSs), automate, control, and monitor physical processes. As such, they are responsible for running a wide range of physical processes, in different industrial sectors and in Critical Infrastructures (CIs) [1]. The European Council [2] defines a CI as "an asset, system or part thereof (...) which is essential for the maintenance of vital societal functions, health, safety, security, economic or social well-being of people, and the disruption or destruction of which would have a significant impact (...) as a result of the failure to maintain those functions." Examples of CIs include power generation and transport, water distribution, water waste treatment, and transportation systems.

Therefore, the correct functioning of CIs has a vital importance. Miller and Rowe [3] surveyed previous security incidents that affected CIs. Nowadays, there are two main specific concerns about the impact of IN related attacks:

(1) Successful attacks against INs may have an impact on the physical process the IN is monitoring, potentially leading to safety-threatening scenarios. Examples of such incidents include Aurora [4], Stuxnet [5], the Maroochy water breach [6], and the German steel mill incident [7].

(2) The proliferation of ICS-specific malware for conducting espionage: the aim of these pieces of malware is to gather information about the controlled process and/or company running it. The purpose can be twofold: stealing confidential information about the process (e.g., recipe for manufacturing a product) or to gather information to conduct attacks against a third party. Examples of such malware include Duqu [8] and Dragonfly [9].

As a consequence, the critical or confidential nature of some of the controlled processes and the potential impact of service malfunction, IN security is an active research field. As such, IN protection has received wide attention from both industry and the scientific community. Among the different fields of

IN security research, Intrusion Detection Systems (IDSs) and, particularly, Anomaly Detection Systems (ADSs) have an important role and there are many proposals in this direction [10–12].

Alternatively, since the birth of distributed computing frameworks such as MapReduce [13] and distributed file-systems such as the Hadoop File System (HDFS) [14], a new computing paradigm known as *Big Data Analytics* (BDA) has emerged. Big Data refers to the set of information that is too complex to process by traditional IT mechanisms within an acceptable scope [15]. Although no total consensus exists, this data complexity is generally expressed in at least three qualities: the amount of data (volume), data generation and transmission pace (velocity), and diversity of data, both structured and unstructured (variety) [16]. More recently, a fourth quality is also widely mentioned: the ability to search for valuable information on Big Data (veracity) [15]. However, the term Big Data has transcended the type of information and it is also used to refer to set of methodologies and mechanisms developed to work with this type of data. BDA aims to extract valuable knowledge from Big Data by analyzing or modeling it in a scalable manner.

Among the multiple applications BDA has, Cárdenas et al. [19] and Everett [20] discussed its potential for intrusion detection research. They conclude that using BDA can lead to more efficient IDSs. However, both works center on regular Information Technology (IT) networks and do not examine its applicability to INs. In this work, we analyze different existing Big Data ADSs that can be used in INs and extract insight from them in order to identify some possible future research areas.

Our contributions can be summarized as follows:

(i) A literature review of Big Data ADSs that can be applied to INs.

(ii) A novel taxonomy to classify IN-based ADSs.

(iii) A discussion of open problems in existing IN-oriented, large-scale, heterogeneous ADS research.

The rest of the paper is organized as follows. Section 2 introduces INs, ADSs, and Big Data Security Mechanisms. Section 3 presents the taxonomy used for ADS classification. Section 4 analyzes the most relevant proposals applicable to IN intrusion detection. Section 5 discusses the proposals and evaluates their suitability for their usage in INs. Section 6 points to some open research areas that have not been covered by previous approaches. Finally, Section 7 draws the final conclusions.

2. Background

In this section we provide the necessary background to support our argumentation.

2.1. Industrial Networks. Since the invention of the Programmable Logic Controller (PLC) in the 1960s, INs have evolved significantly from the initial primitive proprietary and isolated environments to the complex, standard interconnected networks that are today. Traditionally, INs

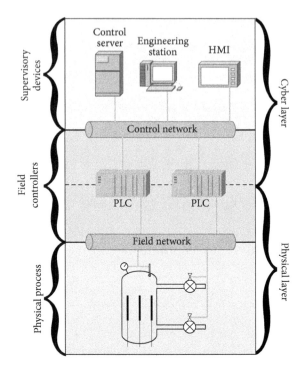

FIGURE 1: Example of a simple industrial network.

were isolated environments where communication was conducted through proprietary network protocols with limited or nonexistent interaction with external networks. However, since the 1990s, pushed by the increasing demand for location-independent access to network resources, INs became progressively interconnected with external networks such as the companies' internal IT network and even the Internet [21, 43].

On the one hand, this increased network standardization led to the start of using standard network protocols (TCP/IP) and commercial-off-the-shelf (COTS) software, laying behind proprietary, ad hoc hardware and software solutions [1]. On the other hand, this merge significantly increased the attack surface of INs, as it exposed them to simple remote attacks and exploitation by using known vulnerabilities of COTS software. Traditional isolation and obscure characteristics that INs had relied on for security did no longer exist.

Figure 1 shows the network architecture of a simple IN. INs have a vertical architecture. At the bottom lays the physical process that is being controlled. The physical process has a set of sensors and actuators that are used to gather information about the state of the process and to perform actions on it. These sensors and actuators are connected to field controllers, normally PLCs, through buses or direct connections in the so-called field network. Field controllers are the workhorse of INs. They read process data from the field sensors and, based on their stored control algorithm, send orders to the actuators to interact with the process, generally trying to keep process variables' values around a set of certain setpoints. Nevertheless, except for the simplest installations, field controllers are not enough to conduct all the required tasks. Consequently, additional devices, called

TABLE 1: Differences between industrial and IT networks [21, 22].

	Industrial networks	IT networks
Primary function	Control of physical equipment	Data processing and transfer
Applicable domain	Manufacturing, processing and utility distribution	Corporate and home environments
Hierarchy	Deep, functionally separated hierarchies with many protocols and physical standards	Shallow, integrated hierarchies with uniform protocol and physical standard utilization
Failure severity	High	Low
Reliability required	High	Moderate
Round trip times	250 μs–10 ms	50+ ms
Determinism	High	Low
Data composition	Small packets of periodic and aperiodic traffic	Large, aperiodic packets
Temporal consistency	Required	Not required
Operating environment	Hostile conditions, often featuring high levels of dust, heat and vibration	Clean environments, often specifically intended for sensitive equipment
System lifetime	Some tens of years	Some years
Average node complexity	Low (simple devices, sensors, actuators)	High (large servers/file systems/databases)
Primary security requirement	Availability	Confidentiality

supervisory devices, are necessary. These devices usually run on normal IT-based hardware and software. Examples include control servers, Human Machine Interfaces (HMIs), and engineering stations. Control servers store process data and, optionally, implement second-level control logic, usually involving data from different field controllers. HMIs are the graphical user interfaces operators used to interact with the process. Critical processes are monitored by human operators 24/7. Process engineers use engineering stations to develop and test new applications regarding control logic.

INs can be further divided according to different layers. According to the definition by Genge et al. [44], on the one hand, there is the physical layer, composed of the actuators and sensors that directly interact with the physical process. On the other hand, there is the cyber layer, composed of all the IT devices and software which acquire the data, elaborate low level process strategies, and deliver the commands to the physical layer. Field controllers act as the bridge between both layers, as they read field data and send local commands to the actuators, but they also forward field information to the cyber layer components while executing commands they receive from the supervisory devices.

Hence, ICSs can be considered a subset of Cyber Physical Systems, as they are able to process and communicate data while also interacting with their physical environment.

There are different types of INs, such as Supervisory Control and Data Acquisition (SCADA), Distributed Control Systems (DCSs), and Process Control Systems (PCS). However, differences are getting blurred, and they can often be considered as a single entity when designing security solutions [1, 22].

Although they share a common part of technology stack, INs are inherently different to commercial IT networks. Table 1 shows a summary of the main differences between both network types. The main difference resides in the purpose of each of the networks: whereas, in IT, the purpose

is the transfer and processing of data, in the case of INs the main objective is to control a physical process.

Additionally, security requirements in IT networks and INs differ in importance. There are three main security requirements that information systems or networks must fulfil in order to be considered secure: confidentiality, integrity, and availability [45, 46]. Dzung et al. [47] describe the requirements and relate them to INs.

Confidentiality. Prevention of information disclosure to unauthorized persons or systems: in the case of INs, this is relevant with respect to both domain specific information, such as product recipes or plant performance and planning data, and the secrets specific to the security mechanisms themselves, such as passwords and encryption keys.

Integrity. Prevention of undetected modification of information by unauthorized persons or systems: in INs, this applies to information such as product recipes, sensor values, or control commands. Violation of integrity may cause safety issues; that is, equipment or people may be harmed.

Availability. It refers to ensuring that unauthorized persons or systems cannot deny access or use to authorized users. In INs, it refers to all the devices of the plant, like control systems, safety systems, operator workstations, and so on, as well as the communication systems between these elements and to the outside world. Violation of availability, also known as Denial of Service (DoS), may not only cause economic damage but may also affect safety issues as operators may lose the ability to monitor and control the process.

On the one hand, IT networks, which are designed to store and transmit information, lean to keep the data confidential and information integrity and availability play a lesser role. On the other hand, in INs, availability is paramount, as losing control of a process or disrupting it can cause significant economic losses and, in the case of specially safety-critical INs, such as CIs, the consequences can be significantly more severe and potentially catastrophic [3].

These requirement differences mean that even when technically possible, blindly applying IT-based security mechanisms or procedures in industrial environments might lead to process malfunction or potentially safety-threatening scenarios, as they have been designed with different goals in mind. For instance, running antivirus software on PLCs might compromise the PLC's ability to perform real-time operations on a process, or conducting a penetration test can lead to dangerous scenarios [48].

However, these traits can also be leveraged to build security mechanisms for INs that would be impractical to use in IT networks. For instance, the deterministic nature of INs and its periodic traffic between different hosts makes them suitable candidates for using Anomaly Detection Systems [10].

2.2. Anomaly Detection Systems. Anomaly Detection Systems (ADSs) are a subset of Intrusion Detection Systems (IDSs) [49]. IDSs are security mechanisms that monitor network and/or system activities to detect suspicious events. IDSs are classified according to two main criteria: the detection mechanism they use (signature detection or anomaly detection) and their source of information (where they collect the events to analyze).

Signature-based IDSs compare monitored data to a database with known malicious patterns (signature database). If there is a match, an alert is raised, as the activity has been identified as suspicious. Their efficiency is directly related to the completeness and accuracy of the signature database they are working with, as attacks will go undetected if their signature is not available. Among their operational characteristics, they have a low number of false positives but they are unable to detect unknown attacks. ADSs, on the other hand, identify malicious patterns by measuring their deviation from normal activity. ADSs build a model of the normal behavior of the process (through automated learning or manual specifications) and detect deviations with respect to the model [21]. Many ADSs are built using machine learning methods [50]. As opposed to signature-based IDSs, ADSs are able to detect unknown attacks, but they often yield a higher number of false positives.

Regarding the source of information, IDSs traditionally have been classified into two main categories: network-level and host-level IDSs. Network-based IDSs monitor network traffic to detect suspicious activity (suspicious connections, malicious packet payloads, etc.), while host-based IDSs monitor local data stored in a device (system logs, file integrity, etc.). In the case of INs, the limited processing ability of industrial devices has limited the deployment of host-based ICSs [21]. Therefore, when considering IN IDSs, the source of information criterion can be set based on the IN layer they use to gather information from the cyber-level or the physical layer. Cyber-level IDSs are similar to their IT counterparts as they generally monitor network-level data. Physical-level IDSs monitor the physical quantities of the process (pressures, temperatures, currents, etc.) in order to

detect intrusions. Physical properties of the process are constantly monitored, often polling data every few milliseconds in the case of critical variables, which with large, continuous processes can lead to a scenario where it is necessary to use Big Data Analytics (BDA), covered in Section 1, in order to process field and control data. This is further confirmed by proposals that, outside the field of security research, point to this need and propose several BDA solutions focused on industrial applications, such as process monitoring [51–54], maintenance [55], fault detection [56], and fault diagnosis [57, 58].

Most IN ADSs work on the cyber layer (see surveys [10–12]). Physical-level ADSs can be divided into two main groups: ADSs where it is necessary to model the physical process [59, 60] or ADSs that do not need a specific model for the physical process [61, 62]. Few proposals combine data from both levels [63, 64].

2.3. Big Data Security Mechanisms. Modern and complex IT networks create and process vast amounts of data continuously. Analysis of the created data for security purposes is a daunting task, and, before the advent of Big Data processing tools, data was normally sampled or only subsets of it were analyzed (e.g., only metadata). Since MapReduce [13] was introduced, several Big Data frameworks have been proposed, which allow the processing of large, heterogeneous datasets.

Traditionally, Big Data frameworks have been divided into two main groups, according to the nature of the data they work with. On the one hand, there are batch processing technologies that work with data at rest and are usually used when doing Exploratory Data Analysis (EDA). Examples of technologies that use this approach would include Hadoop [65] and Disco [66]. On the other hand, there are stream processing technologies that are designed to work with flowing data. Gorawski et al. [67] reviewed different Big Data streaming proposals.

However, hybrid tools such as Apache Spark [68] or Apache Flink [69] are able to work on both streaming and resting data. Spark uses microbatches to process incoming data while Flink does batch processing as a special case of stream processing.

Extracting insight from the large amount of information that could be leveraged for security event detection (e.g., logs, network flows, or packets) in a network can be considered a Big Data problem [19, 20]. Consequently, different types of Big Data Security Mechanisms have been proposed:

(i) Intrusion detection (see survey [70]).

(ii) Botnet detection ([71–74]).

(iii) Malware detection ([75–78]) and analysis ([79, 80]).

(iv) Distributed Denial of Service (DDoS) detection ([81–85]).

(v) Spam detection ([86–88]).

On a related note, other resources have been developed that even if they are not security mechanisms per se, they have been designed to handle large volumes of network data and,

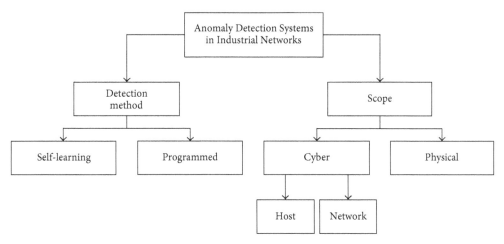

FIGURE 2: A taxonomy for Anomaly Detection Systems in Industrial Networks.

thus, can be useful in building security mechanisms on top of them:

(i) Frameworks for analyzing network flows ([89, 90]).

(ii) Frameworks for analyzing network packets ([91, 92]).

(iii) Frameworks for analyzing logs ([93, 94]).

However, in this paper we will limit the scope to Big Data ADSs that could potentially be applicable to the industrial domain.

3. Taxonomy

In this section, we describe the taxonomy or classification method that will be used in Section 4 for existing large-scale industrial ADSs. Figure 2 shows the created taxonomy tree. When classifying IDSs in general, two main criteria are used: the detection method and the scope of the IDS [10, 21, 49, 95]. We can apply these criteria to build an IN ADS classification method.

3.1. Detection Method. The main criterion to classify IDSs resides in the detection method. While the difference between signature-based IDSs and ADSs was already covered in Section 2.2, ADSs can be further classified based on their detection technique. According to Axelsson [95] and Mitchell and Chen [10] ADS detection techniques belong in two categories:

(1) Self-learning or behavior-based ADSs: the ADS detects anomalous features that are distinct from normal system behavior. Normal system behavior can be retrieved in an unsupervised (e.g., clustering historical data) or in a semisupervised manner (e.g., collection of training, generally attack-free, data).

(2) Programmed or behavior-specification-based ADSs: using expert knowledge, a human defines legitimate behaviors and implements them on the ADS. The ADS detects anomalies by detecting deviations from the specified behavior.

3.2. Scope. Apart from the detection method, the other main criterion for IDS and ADSs is their scope, that is, the source and nature of the data used for audit. In IT ADSs, there are two main types of ADSs depending on the data they use.

(1) Network ADSs: ADSs monitor a network without focusing on individual hosts. The most prominent data sources for these ADSs are network flows and packets.

(2) Host ADSs: the ADS monitors data from an individual host to check anomalies. Examples of host data include logs, files, or system calls.

While this split was conceived for IT-based ADSs, this classification has also held for IN ADSs [10, 21, 96]. And indeed, most IN ADS proposals can be classified in one of the two above categories. Nevertheless, due to the cyber physical nature of INs, this classification is not complete enough, as it only tackles the cyber part of INs, while not considering the physical dimension of INs that handles field data. Field data mainly consists of sensor signals that monitor physical quantities (temperature, pressure, etc.) although other process-based variables (counters, setpoint values, etc.) might be present. There are several examples of IN ADSs that leverage field-level data [59–62]. This data can come from logs on a control server, direct process measurements, and simulated data or can be scattered across different hosts or devices. Therefore, ADS proposes that leverage process data for anomaly detection do not fit well in the above classification. Consequently, we have created a novel taxonomy where the physical dimension of IN ADSs is taken into account as a proper data source. This taxonomy can be leveraged to classify IN ADSs, both conventional and Big Data proposals, as it encompasses more data sources and types that are present in INs than previous presented taxonomies that do not acknowledge the existence of ADSs based on the physical layer of INs.

4. Anomaly Detection Systems

In this section, we survey existing Big Data ADSs that could be used in INs. Proposals are divided according to the taxonomy described in Section 3.

4.1. Cyber-Level ADSs

4.1.1. Cyber-Level, Self-Learning ADSs. The proposal of Xu et al. [42] is an ADS based on host log mining. System logs are first parsed to provide a unified data-structure from different log formats, by getting log format templates from the application source code. Then, they build features from the extracted log data, focusing on state ratio vector (a vector representing a set of state variables on a time window) and the message count vector (a vector representing a set of related logs with different message types) features. These vector features are later mined using an algorithm based on Principal Component Analysis (PCA) for anomaly detection. The results are finally visualized in a decision tree to aid operators to find the root cause of an anomaly. The analysis is carried out in a Hadoop cluster to increase computing speed.

Yen et al. [23] introduce Beehive, a large scale log mining tool that uses Hive [97] to detect suspicious activities in corporate networks. For that purpose, Beehive mines logs coming from different sources and, specially, web proxy logs. Beehive clusters log data and identifies misbehaving hosts as cluster outliers, as they show a unique behavioral pattern. The clustering is done by an adapted version of the k-means algorithm. The incidents related to the outliers were labeled manually by using other system logs and showed that many of these outliers were not detected by traditional security mechanisms.

Ratner and Kelly [38] conduct a case study of network traffic anomalies in a corporate network. For this end, they extract packet metadata from a set of captured packets, and they perform specific queries in the gathered data to detect attacks, mainly IP scans. In order to process the large dataset, they use Apache Hadoop. They find a large number of IP scans and conclude that roughly half of the packets arriving from external IP addresses are anomalous. Those anomalies were found by comparing each packet's IP metadata to the average values for each day.

Therdphapiyanak and Piromsopa [98] expose an anomaly detection system based on host log analysis. First, the system parses log data and later clusters it by using k-means. Once the clusters are formed, the authors extract major characteristics from the clusters to examine differences and similarities. Minor clusters with important differences when compared to others are flagged as anomalous. While the system has been tested with Apache Web Server logs, the authors address aggregating logs from different network agents in future steps. Log parsing and clustering are performed in a Hadoop cluster.

Camacho et al. [17] use a PCA-based solution to detect anomalies in computer networks. The workflow of the approach can be seen in Figure 3. The anomaly detection is accomplished in two separate phases: a model building phase, where the ADS is tuned based on training data, and a monitoring phase, where the ADS analyzes incoming

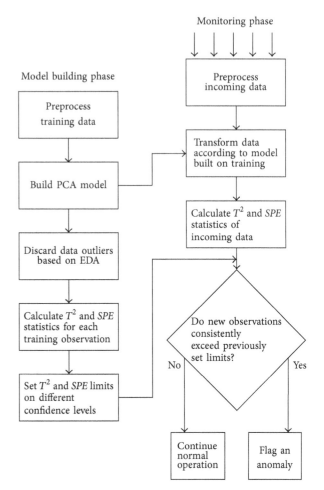

FIGURE 3: Anomaly Detection System proposed by Camacho et al. [17], based on Principal Component Analysis (PCA).

data and determines it as anomalous or legitimate based on the model built during the previous phase. In the first phase, incoming data (generally, IDS and Firewall logs) is preprocessed and converted into feature vectors. Later, this data is used to create a PCA model, where the original features are transformed into a new variable subspace. The dimensionality reduction helps to visually inspect the data and to identify outliers in it. These outliers can be considered as anomalies or attacks in training data, so this preliminary step cleans the data and allows building a more effective model, without requiring a completely attack-free initial dataset. The PCA model can also be used to create two different statistics that are widely used for process monitoring: Hotelling's T^2 [99], comprising the leverages of the PCA model, and the SPE [100], involving the residuals of the model. The proposed approach calculates the statistics for each of the observations in the training set and, based on it, calculates a control limit based on an arbitrary confidence level, where a given percentage of the training observations should be below the control limit. Once the control limits have been set, the training phase has ended and the ADS is now prepared to work in the monitoring phase. In this phase, incoming data is preprocessed and transformed using the previously created PCA model and it calculates the T^2 and SPE values for each incoming observation. If several consecutive observations surpass either of the set control limits (the necessary number of out-of-bounds observations depends on the confidence level), an anomaly is flagged. The process can be parallelized using hierarchical PCA and the workload shared through several slaves. The ability of PCA to work with high dimensional data ensures that the approach can be extended to a wide range of incoming data.

Hashdoop [31] is a MapReduce-based framework designed to run Anomaly Detection Systems in a distributed manner. It does not provide enhanced anomaly detection capacity to the original ADS but it speeds up its execution. First, it splits and hashes network traffic, preserving traffic structures. Later, each of the hashed traffic subsets is analyzed by an instance of the ADS to detect anomalies. Finally, the generated information about the subsets is summarized in a single output report. Results show that processing time is reduced when using Hashdoop-powered ADS compared to their single-node counterparts.

Marchal et al. [35] propose an intrusion detection system that uses honeypot data to detect similar intrusions in networks. First, it collects Domain Name System (DNS) replies, HTTP packets, and IP flow records from the network, along with honeypot data. Based on the collected data, three different scores are computed in order to quantify the maliciousness of the recorded DNS, HTTP, and flow communications. This quantification uses other gathered or publicly available data such as domain blacklists or the data compiled by the in-house honeypot. When one of these maliciousness indices reaches a certain threshold, a flag is raised to inform about the anomaly. The authors test different data-intensive frameworks that are designed to work with potentially very large data volumes. According to their tests, Apache Spark and its subproject, Shark, are faster than Hadoop, Hive, or Pig. However, several concerns arise with this mechanism: the performance of the proposed system is directly related to the performance of the honeypot. If an attacker does not interact with the honeypot and their domain is not explicitly blacklisted, the mechanism will not be able to raise an alert, even in the case of known attacks.

MATATABI [36] is a threat analysis platform that stores data from different sources (DNS captures and querylog, Network flows, and spam email) in a Hadoop cluster and organizes it in Hive [97] tables. Later, different modules query this data via a Javascript Object Notation (JSON) Application Programming Interface (API). Although the exact implementation details of each of the analysis modules are vague, each module queries the stored data looking for anomalous patterns, such as hosts receiving or sending a large number of packets, specific port scans by counting the number of packets to a specific port number, or botnet activity through abnormal DNS activity. While the gathered data is varied, the modules are designed to query a single type of data. If suspicious activity is detected, it is in the operator's hand to query other types of data to find additional evidence of the attack.

TADOOP [40] is a network flow ADS that implements an extension of the Tsallis Entropy [101] for anomaly detection, dubbed DTE-FP (Dual q Tsallis Entropy for flow Feature with Properties). In short, TADOOP gathers network flows and computes a pair of q values aiming to accentuate high and low probability feature distributions, usually linked to traffic anomalies. TADOOP is based on four main modules. (i) The *Traffic Collector* gathers network flow packets and decodes them. (ii) The *Entropy Calculation Module* extracts flow features from each flow and it computes the DTE-FP q values for each flow feature distribution. (iii) The *Semiautomatic Training Module* is responsible for setting optimal q pair detection thresholds for each of the distributions. The criterion is keeping false positive rate below an arbitrary maximal threshold. (iv) The *Detection module* calculates entropy values for all the flows in a given time window and compares them to the thresholds computed by the training module to detect anomalies. TADOOP uses Hadoop for storing and processing historical flow data. TADOOP is evaluated using the flow data of a university network.

Gonçalves et al. [29] present an approach for detecting misbehaving hosts by mining server log data. In the first phase, they extract features from DHCP, authentication, and firewall logs, and for each host a feature vector is created. These vectors are later clustered using the Expectation-Maximization (EM) algorithm which are later used to build a classification model. Smaller clusters in the set correspond to anomalous host behavior. In the second phase, once the classification model is built, incoming data is clustered in a similar way as in the first phase; however, these newly created clusters are classified with the previously created model in order to detect if they are anomalous. While the feature extraction from the log data is done in Hadoop, clustering and classification of the data are carried out with the Weka [102] data mining tool.

Dromard et al. [25] extend the UNADA [103] ADS to detect anomalies in Big Data network environments. UNADA is a three-step unsupervised ADS. (i) *Flow Change Detection*. Flows gathered in a given time window are aggregated on different levels defined by network masks. For each level, UNADA computes a simple metric or feature of the aggregated flows: number of bytes, number of packets, number of IP flows, and so on. Then, when a new set of flows is gathered, these metrics are recomputed for the new flow and compared to the previous set. If there is a change in the values, the time window is flagged and further computed. (ii) *Clustering*. In this phase, UNADA clusters the feature vectors from the previously flagged flow sets using DBSCAN [104]. Network flow feature vectors can have numerous variables and DBSCAN does not perform well in multivariate environments. In order to overcome this issue, UNADA splits the feature space into smaller, two-dimensional subspaces and computes DBSCAN independently on each of them. (iii) *Evidence Accumulation*. In the last phase, data from each of the subspaces is aggregated to identify anomalies. In each subspace, independently, data points that do not belong to a cluster are flagged as anomalous and UNADA records the distance to the nearest cluster centroid. A dissimilarity vector is built with the accumulated abnormality scores for each flow across all subspaces. To ease anomaly detection, dissimilarity vectors are later sorted and a threshold is defined to finally flag flows as anomalous. The authors evaluate the performance of UNADA over Apache Spark [68] to compute the ADS over the network data gathered on a core network of an Internet Service Provider. Results show that the approach is able to detect flow anomalies while speeding up execution time in regard to the original UNADA proposal.

The proposal of Rathore et al. [37] is a flow ADS built on four layers. (i) *Traffic capturing*. The traffic is captured from the network and forwarded to the next layer. (ii) *Filtration and load balancing*. This layer checks whether the flow has been previously registered as a legitimate or anomalous in a database. If it has not, data is forwarded to the next layer. (iii) *Hadoop layer*. This layer extracts the features from the gathered data. It uses Apache Spark [68] on top of Hadoop for faster computation. (iv) *Decision Server*. The extracted features are classified as legitimate or anomalous sets by a set of classifiers implemented in Weka. The authors use the well-known intrusion detection NSL-KDD dataset for result evaluation and conclude that the C4.5 and REPTree are the best performing classifiers for this task.

Wang et al. [41] propose a continuous, real-time flow ADS based on Apache Storm. For this end, they combine three different detection methods: (i) Network flows: They count the number of flows in a small enough time slot that allows online processing. Afterwards, they compute the standard deviation and mean of this count and calculate a confidence interval based on them. Later, they perform a set of operations over the flows involving hashing into groups and calculating Intergroup Flow Entropy [105]. In all steps, the system checks that the observations are inside the confidence interval; otherwise an alarm is raised. (ii) Intuitive Methods based on Traffic Volume: The system applies the same approach as in network flows but taking into account the number of packets in a time window instead the number of flows. (iii) Least-Mean-Square-based detection: The system uses a Least-Mean-Square-based (LMS) filtering method that aims to find inconsistencies between the intergroup flow and packet entropies, which should be strongly correlated. LMS also operates in an online manner. They evaluate the approach by replaying a capture of an Internet backbone while introducing in parallel two types of anomalies that were not present in the capture: an attack involving a large number of small network flows and an attack involving a small number of large flows.

Gupta and Kulariya [28] compare a set of feature extraction and classification algorithms for anomaly detection. They benchmark the different approaches using the popular intrusion detection KDD'99 and NSL-KDD datasets and the algorithms implemented in Spark's MLlib library. They evaluate correlation based feature selection and hypothesis based feature selection for feature extraction. For classification they measure the performance of Naïve Bayes, Logistic Regression, Support Vector Machines, Random Forests, and Gradient Boosted Decision Trees. They conclude that hypothesis based feature selection helps to achieve a better classification score. Among the classifiers, Random Forests and Gradient Boosted Decision Trees yield better results than the rest.

4.1.2. Cyber-Level, Programmed ADSs. The work presented by Giura and Wang [27] uses large-scale distributed computing to detect APTs. First, they model the APT using an Attack Pyramid, a multiplane extension of an attack tree [106, 107] where the top of the pyramid represents the asset to be protected. The planes of the pyramid represent different environments where attack events can be recorded (e.g., user plane, application plane, and physical plane). The detection method groups all potential security events from different planes and maps the relevant events that are related to a specific attack context. This context information is later leveraged to detect a security incident if some indicators surpass a set of user-defined thresholds. The method uses MapReduce to consider all the possible events and related contexts.

Bumgardner and Marek's approach [24] consists in a hybrid network analysis system that uses both stream and batch processing, capable of detecting some network anomalies. First, it uses a set of probes that collect network traffic to build and send network flows to the specified processing unit. Then, the created flows are stream processed through Storm to enrich it with additional data (e.g., known state of the internal network) and anomalies are detected based on previously defined event detection rules (bot activity, network scans). Once the flows have been processed, they are stored in a HBase table, a column oriented database, to perform EDA to get further insight that it is not explicitly stated in each of the flows. This batch data processing is executed on top of Hadoop. The main drawback of Bumgardner and Marek's approach is that the system's anomaly detection capability is directly related to the capability of describing network events or anomalies using rules when doing stream processing.

Iturbe et al. [33] propose a visual flow monitoring system for INs based on whitelisting and chord diagrams. In their approach, they detect flow-based anomalies (forbidden connections, missing hosts, etc.) based on a previously created set of whitelists. These whitelists can be created through network learning or established by a human operator. The proposed system's scalability is achieved through a distributed search server where data from different networks is sent to store it. Later, a visual application queries the relevant flow data and compares it to the corresponding whitelist. Based on the comparison, a chord diagram is built depicting the legitimate and anomalous flows.

4.2. Physical-Level ADSs. Hadžiosmanović et al. [30] present a log mining approach to detect process-related threats from legitimate users' unintentional mistakes. They identify unusual events in log data to detect these threats. In order to extract the unusual events from the potentially large log data, they first use a FP-growth algorithm to count matching log entries. Later, unusual events are defined as the ones whose number of occurrences is below of a user-set, absolute threshold. FP-growth algorithms do not use candidate generation and, thus, are able to effectively count occurrences in two data scans.

Difallah et al. [26] propose a scalable ADS for Water Distribution Networks. Specifically, they use Local Indicators of Spatial Association (LISA) [108] as a metric for anomaly detection, by extending the metric to consider temporal associations. In the proposal, wireless sensors send process data to a set of base stations that perform part of the anomaly detection process by computing a limited set of LISA calculations on the streaming data they receive. Thus, it uses a distributed approach for a first phase of anomaly detection. Later, data is sent to a central Array Database Management System (ADBMS). The ADBMS allows global analytics of the distribution network as a whole. Evaluation of the proposal is done using Apache Storm for the stream processing in the base stations and SciDB [109] as the ADBMS, analyzing data from a simulated environment created after the Water Distribution Network of a medium-sized city.

Hurst et al. [32] introduce a Big Data classification system for anomaly detection on CIs. They extract process data from a simulated nuclear power plant and extract relevant features from it, by selecting a number of variables that best describe the overall system behavior. However, this feature extraction relies on expert knowledge to identify the subset of variables that are most suitable. Moreover, the needed features will vary between different types of processes, even different installations, and, thus, the approach is process-dependent. They do not specify the used criteria for feature selection. After feature extraction, they perform anomaly detection using five different classifiers by splitting the gathered data into two halves for the training and testing. They demonstrate that increasing both dataset size and the number of features used for anomaly detection yields better classification results. They do not specify the framework they used for this large-scale classification.

Kiss et al.'s system [34] is designed to detect field-level anomalies in Industrial Networks. By leveraging the field data that sensors and actuators periodically send, they classify normal and abnormal operation cases. To this end, field parameters are used to build feature vectors that are later clustered using k-means to identify operation states and anomalous states of the physical process. In order to deal with the growing field data, the system uses Hadoop to create the different clusters. As the vectors to be clustered are built using field data, these feature vectors depend on process nature. Furthermore, in case of complex physical processes, building the features and identifying different operation states can be a challenging problem that can complicate the deployment of the proposal.

Wallace et al. [18] propose a Smart Grid ADS by mining Phasor Measurement Unit (PMU) data. The overview of their proposal is depicted in Figure 4. The system first models normal grid operation by measuring voltage deviation from each of the PMUs and creating a cumulative probability distribution to represent the likelihood for a signal to have a given voltage deviation. After the distribution function has been created, the likelihood of a given divergence of two voltage signals can be estimated. The system evaluates this calculated likelihood in order to classify an incoming observation as anomalous or legitimate. In detail, the system calculates the voltage deviation from two consecutive signals and then, using the probability distribution function constructed with the historical data, establishes an event as anomalous if this deviation is unlikely to happen. That is,

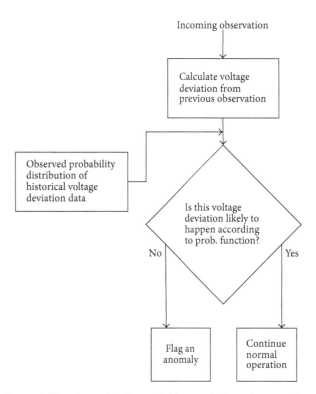

FIGURE 4: Flowchart of the Smart Grid anomaly detection procedure proposed by Wallace et al. [18].

consecutive signals with high discrepancies in voltage values are more unlikely to arise, and, therefore, when they happen they can be classified as anomalous situations in the grid. After an anomaly has been flagged, further analysis of the data can explain the nature of the anomaly. This anomaly identification is carried out by a classification decision tree algorithm that infers the type of anomaly based on three hand-coded events, developed with expert knowledge. The evaluation is done using real PMU data of an electrical grid and using Apache Spark for data computation.

5. Discussion

In this section, we discuss the proposals presented in Section 4, pointing to the advantages and disadvantages of the proposals, stressing their applicability to INs.

Table 2 shows a comparison of the presented works, according to different criteria:

(i) Domain refers to the network type the proposal has been defined to work in: IT or IN.

(ii) Granularity: Axelsson [95] defines granularity of data processing as a "category that contrasts systems that process data *continuously* with those that process data in *batches* at a regular interval."

(iii) Time of detection: Axelsson [95] defines this category by defining the two main groups that compose it: systems that give results in *real-time* or near real-time and those that process data with some delay (*nonreal*). Though related to the previous category,

TABLE 2: Comparison of the surveyed works.

Name	Ref.	Domain	Granul.	Time of detect.	Sources	Main Detect. technique
Beehive	[23]	IT	Batch	Nonreal	Proxy logs	k-means
Bumgardner and Marek	[24]	IT	Both	Real	Network flows	Established thresholds
Camacho et al.	[17]	IT	Both	Nonreal	Firewall & IDS logs	PCA
Dromard et al.	[25]	IT	Batch	Nonreal	Network flows	DBSCAN
Difallah et al.	[26]	IN	Both	Real	Process data	LISA
Giura and Wang	[27]	IT	Batch	Nonreal	Network and application data	Threshold establishing
Gupta and Kulariya	[28]	IT	Batch	Nonreal	Network captures	Several feature extraction and classification algorithms
Gonçalves et al.	[29]	IT	Batch	Nonreal	DHCP, Authentication and Firewall logs	EM
Hadžiosmanović et al.	[30]	IN	Batch	Nonreal	SCADA logs	FP-Graph
Hashdoop	[31]	IT	Batch	Nonreal	Network traffic (textual format)	None
Hurst et al.	[32]	IN	Batch	Nonreal	Process data	Multiple classification algs.
Iturbe et al.	[33]	IN	Batch	Nonreal	Network flows	Whitelisting
Kiss et al.	[34]	IN	Batch	Nonreal	Process data	k-means
Marchal et al.	[35]	IT	Batch	Nonreal	Honeypot, DNS, HTTP and Network flow data	Threshold establishing
MATATABI	[36]	IT	Batch	Nonreal	DNS records, Network flows, Spam email	Multiple
Rathore et al.	[37]	IT	Batch	Nonreal	Network flows	C4.5, RepTree
Ratner and Kelly	[38]	IT	Batch	Nonreal	Network packets	Manual data querying
Therdphapiyanak and Piromsopa	[39]	IT	Batch	Nonreal	Network logs	k-means
TADOOP	[40]	IT	Batch	Nonreal	Network flows	DTE-FP
Wallace et al.	[18]	IN	Continuous	Real	Process data	Cumulative Probability Distribution
Wang et al.	[41]	IT	Continuous	Real	Network flows	Intergroup entropy, LMS
Xu et al.	[42]	IT	Batch	Nonreal	Console logs	PCA

they do not overlap, as some real-time systems might process microbatches, thus giving real-time or almost real-time performance.

(iv) Source of information refers to the type of input data the ADS collects and audits for anomaly detection.

(v) Main detection technique refers to the main technique the ADS leverages to detect anomalies in the gathered information.

As Table 2 shows, most of the proposals are both batch and in non-real-time. Moreover, a similar set of proposals use a single type of data input as the source for audit information. Thus, it can be stated that the majority of these proposals focus on handling large, resting data volumes for anomaly detection (one of the V Big Data dimensions) while the other dimensions (mainly velocity and variety) are not as relevant.

Table 3 shows the Big Data adoption level of the proposals, by listing the following metrics:

(i) Locus of data collection (LDC): Axelsson [95] notes that "audit data can be collected from many different sources in a distributed fashion, or from a single point using the centralised approach."

(ii) Locus of data processing (LDP): similarly, Axelsson states that "audit data can either be processed in a central location, or is collected and collated from many different sources in a distributed fashion."

(iii) Underlying solution lists the underlying Big Data technology the ADS uses for Big Data computing.

(iv) Evaluation environment shows the nature of the evaluation data used to test the performance of the ADS.

Table 3 shows that most of the proposals use distributed computing for data processing. However, distributed data collection, where data from different sources is analyzed, is not as widespread. Hadoop and Spark are the most prominent Big Data frameworks that are used for anomaly detection. It is worth mentioning that, in some proposals, although Big Data mechanisms are used, they are only used in a part of the data pipeline. For instance, they use the Big Data tools for feature

TABLE 3: Big Data comparison of the surveyed works.

Name	Ref.	LDC	LDP	Solution	Eval. environ.
Beehive	[23]	Dist.	Dist.	Hadoop, Hive	Operational network
Bumgardner and Marek	[24]	Dist.	Dist.	Storm, HBase, Hadoop	Operational network
Camacho et al.	[17]	Dist.	Unknown	Custom	Public dataset
Dromard et al.	[25]	Dist.	Dist.	Spark	Operational network
Difallah et al.	[26]	Dist.	Dist.	Storm	Simulated process data
Giura and Wang	[27]	Dist.	Dist.	Hadoop	Operational network
Gupta and Kulariya	[28]	Cent.	Dist.	Spark	Public dataset
Gonçalves et al.	[29]	Dist.	Dist.	Hadoop, Weka	Operational network
Hadžiosmanović et al.	[30]	Cent.	Cent.	Custom	Operational network
Hashdoop	[31]	Cent.	Dist.	Hadoop	Public dataset
Hurst et al.	[32]	Cent.	Unknown	Custom	Simulated process data
Iturbe et al.	[33]	Cent.	Dist.	Elasticsearch	Operational network
Kiss et al.	[34]	Cent.	Dist.	Hadoop	Simulated process data
Marchal et al.	[35]	Dist.	Dist.	Hadoop, Hive, Pig, Spark	Operational network
MATATABI	[36]	Dist.	Dist.	Hive	Operational network
Rathore et al.	[37]	Cent.	Dist.	Spark, Weka	Public Dataset
Ratner and Kelly	[38]	Cent.	Dist.	Hadoop	Operational network
Therdphapiyanak and Piromsopa	[39]	Cent.	Dist.	Hadoop, Mahout	Public Dataset
TADOOP	[40]	Cent.	Dist.	Hadoop	Operational network
Wallace et al.	[18]	Dist.	Dist.	Spark	Operational network
Wang et al.	[41]	Dist.	Dist.	Storm	Operational network
Xu et al.	[42]	Cent.	Dist.	Hadoop	Operational network

TABLE 4: Suitability of IT-based solutions for their use in INs.

Name	Ref.	OSI layer	IN interoperability	Self-security
Beehive	[23]	7	Low	Medium
Bumgardner and Marek	[24]	3, 4	Medium	Medium
Camacho et al.	[17]	3, 4, 7	Medium	Unknown
Dromard et al.	[25]	3, 4	Medium	Medium
Giura and Wang	[27]	3, 4, 7	Medium	Medium
Gupta and Kulariya	[28]	3, 4, 7	Medium	Medium
Gonçalves et al.	[29]	3, 4, 7	Low	Medium
Hashdoop	[31]	Packet captures	Dependent on implementation	Medium
Marchal et al.	[35]	3, 4, 7	Medium	Medium
MATATABI	[36]	3, 4, 7	Medium	Medium
Rathore et al.	[37]	3, 4	Medium	Medium
Ratner and Kelly	[38]	Packet captures	Medium	Medium
Therdphapiyanak and Piromsopa	[39]	3, 4, 7	Medium	Medium
TADOOP	[40]	3, 4	Medium	Medium
Wang et al.	[41]	3, 4	Medium	Medium
Xu et al.	[42]	7	Medium	Medium

extraction, while once the features have been extracted into a smaller feature dataset, other conventional tools are used for the data classification.

Table 4 summarizes the suitability of the IT-based solutions to be used in INs. For that end, it defines the following metrics:

(i) OSI layer refers to the corresponding layer of the Open Systems Interconnection (OSI) model the network data belongs to. In the case of logs, it shows the layer of the network application that created the logs.

(ii) IN interoperability refers to the performance of running the IT ADS, out-of-the-box in an industrial environment. Low interoperability means that the ADS would not be usable. Medium means that the ADS is expected to run on INs and to detect anomalies to some extent. High means that the ADS is also tailored to work in IN environments.

(iii) Response type categorizes the ADSs in two categories, not related to the detection mechanism, but to their response when an anomaly is flagged. Passive responses consist of logging and sending alerts, without interacting with the traffic, while active responses try to tackle the source of the intrusion or anomaly. Active response mechanisms are often referred to as Intrusion Prevention Systems (IPSs). In this paper, all surveyed works have passive responses. The usage of active responses that fit well into the availability constraints of INs is still an undeveloped field [10].

(iv) Self-security: Zhu and Sastry [96] define self-security as "whether the proposed ADS itself is secure in the sense it will fail-safe." Availability is an important concern in INs. As such, redundant and fail-safe mechanisms are widespread in INs.

As Table 4 lists, most proposals, especially the ones that work with network flows, are able to work in INs, as, nowadays, IT networks and the cyber layer of IT networks share the same network stack at the OSI 3 and 4 layers (Network and Transport) and similar network infrastructure coexists in both types of networks (e.g., firewalls). However, even if technically possible, it is yet to be seen how they would perform.

It is worth mentioning that even if not listed in Table 4, the Time of Detection feature (covered in Table 2) becomes a relevant aspect of the ADSs when measuring their suitability for INs, as their real-time nature requires fast detection to raise alerts as fast as possible and to perform mitigation actions if necessary [10].

Furthermore, although Big Data ADSs listed were not designed for the availability constraints of INs, the usage of distributed file-systems for data storage and the distributed nature of Big Data processing give most solutions a relative defense against faults, as shown by the self-security field. However, this distributed approach might not be enough when considering the high availability requirements that ICSs and INs have and additional measures might be necessary to improve the availability of the ADS, but still, it makes Big Data ADSs better candidates in this aspect than their conventional counterparts.

6. Future Research Lines

There are several open research lines in the area of Big Data ADSs for INs. We categorize them based on the different Big Data dimensions.

6.1. Dealing with Volume. Most surveyed Big Data ADSs have dealt with large volumes of data, and in many cases it has been the main focus of the Big Data ADS. Indeed, some of the surveyed works go no further than applying conventional algorithms and approaches using Big Data mechanisms.

Therefore, the volume requirement for Big Data ADSs can be considered as partially fulfilled. However, there is still room for improvement that can lead to further research:

(i) No large-scale cyber-level ADSs for IN specific protocols: some IT counterparts deal with application-level data (7th OSI layer) but no proposals exist for INs. While lower OSI level proposals exist and could be applied to INs, these kind of mechanisms have been more studied and attackers expect related defensive measures [10]. Therefore, it is necessary to develop large-scale ADSs that will gather information from IN specific protocols, opening the way of analyzing packet payload information.

(ii) Big data IN storage: though process data has been traditionally stored in historian servers, novel approaches for the storage of IN related data are necessary: not only process readings, but wider types of data (network traces, process readings, alerts, etc.). This can help not only with anomaly detection but also for other fields of research regarding INs and Big Data.

6.2. Dealing with Velocity. As stated in Section 5, the vast majority of the proposals are neither continuous nor real-time. This presents the issue that the mentioned approaches are only capable of finding anomalies over historical data, and when new data arrives, a new, larger version of the original dataset that contains the new data is computed again in order to find anomalies. In some of the proposals historical data is divided in time bins and only data corresponding to an specific time bin is executed.

However, this is an impractical approach for a realistic ADS, more so in INs where, as previously stated, real-time detection is an important aspect. It is necessary to develop streaming models where incoming data is treated on arrival in order to detect anomalies. An issue regarding streaming models is that it is not possible to perform Exploratory Data Analysis (EDA) on them. EDA and the building of several models require data at rest, so relationships between different observations can be defined. Similarly, most streaming models need well-defined models for acting on incoming data.

A solution to this problem might lay in building hybrid models based on a two-phase approach where (i) a model is defined based on gathered historical data at rest. (ii) After building a model, this model is applied to compute incoming streaming data. INs have the advantage over IT networks that they are more static and deterministic by nature, so two-phase ADSs seem a viable solution, as once an ADS model is built, it will seldom require an update.

It is necessary to mention that, to encourage and compare different contributions in the area of real-time ADSs for INs, it is necessary to create and use a set of metrics where latency should be taken into account [10].

6.3. Dealing with Variety. ICSs are multivariate and heterogeneous by nature; they deal with very diverse types of data, both at the network level (packets, flows, logs, etc.) and, notably, at the field level where they keep track of a large number of different physical quantities simultaneously. However, existing large-scale ADSs do not leverage data from both levels and instead focus on a single or few data sources for anomaly detection. This issue is extensible to most conventional ADSs as well, as only a few proposals deal with both process-level and network-level data [63, 64] to detect anomalies.

Moreover, IN networks are also heterogeneous in the sense that various technologies coexist at a network and field level. INs are multivendor environments, where devices might be powered by different technologies and communicate using different protocols. This requires the development of different tools to extract data from devices belonging to different vendors. In addition, many of these devices might be limited in terms of computation, so, in order to avoid latencies and availability issues, it is necessary to extract ICS data out of the devices themselves in an unobtrusive manner, where it can later be computed in a cluster using a distributed computing framework, separate from the critical IN sections.

In this sense, analyzing and aggregating information sources from different levels can aid in the detection of complex attacks directed against INs [110]. BDA gives the opportunity to use this heterogeneous data and leverage it in a unified manner to detect anomalies. In this direction, the work of Camacho et al. [17, 111] gives promising insight. The usage of multivariate algorithms, such as PCA, can help to build a model where parametrized cyber and process data can be used to build a single ADS that leverages data from both levels. PCA-based techniques scale well horizontally and are used in fields such as genomics where they are used to handle massively dimensional data.

6.4. Dealing with Veracity. From our point of view, Big Data veracity for anomaly detection is not only related to correctly flagging a relevant anomaly on a large dataset, but also to communicating and alerting the anomaly correctly, instead of overwhelming the operator with too much alert noise. In a related note, we believe that properly testing different Big Data ADSs on neutral, relevant environments such as using public datasets is also ensuring the veracity of ADSs in Big Data. Therefore, we can identify the following research areas:

(i) Closing the semantic gap: Sommer and Paxson [112] define the semantic gap as the lack of actionable reports for the network operator. In other words, the ADS does not provide sufficient diagnosis information to aid decision making for the operator. In INs, it is necessary for an operator to know what is the cause for an anomaly, as successful attacks or serious disturbances could have potentially catastrophic outcomes. BDA can help to provide useful information about the cause of the anomaly. Big Data visualization techniques or Visual Analytics might play a significant role in this matter.

(ii) Necessity to have realistic, large-scale datasets: few datasets exist for anomaly detection evaluation in INs and existing datasets [113] are too small to evaluate Big Data ADSs. Therefore, it is necessary to have public, realistic, large-scale IN datasets that would allow the evaluation of the ADS performance independently.

(iii) Integration of honeypots: when trying to find anomalies in Big Data, it is important to keep the value of false positives and false negatives low. The task of finding anomalies is equivalent to finding a needle in a haystack. Trusted data sources can help in this endeavor. Honeypots can constitute such a trusted information source, as by definition they do not yield any false positives [114]. The field of IN-oriented honeypots is still maturing, though a few approaches have been proposed [114, 115], but the possibility of feeding and correlating IN honeypot data to a Big Data IN ADS, in a similar fashion as Marchal et al. [35], opens the way to a new field of research.

7. Conclusions

We have presented a survey paper comprising three main contributions: (i) a review of current proposals of Big Data ADSs that can be applied to INs, (ii) a novel taxonomy to classify existing IN-based ADSs, and (iii) a collection of possible future research areas in the field of large-scale, heterogeneous, and real-time ADSs for INs.

Big Data anomaly detection in Industrial Networks is still a developing field. Few proposals exist for INs exclusively, but some IT-based solutions show that it is possible to have similar counterparts on INs. Nevertheless, while most proposals focus on large-volume solutions for anomaly detection, other aspects, such as dealing with data with high velocity or variety, are still largely untackled. We finally have offered some future research work areas regarding these open issues.

Acknowledgments

This work has been developed by the Intelligent Systems for Industrial Systems group supported by the Department of Education, Language Policy and Culture of the Basque Government. This work has been partially funded by the European Union's Horizon 2020 research and innovation programme project PROPHESY, under Grant Agreement no. 766994.

References

[1] K. Stouffer, J. Falco, and K. Scarfone, "Guide to Industrial Control Systems (ICS) Security, Special publication 800-82," Tech. Rep., National Institute of Standards and Technology, June 2011.

[2] European Council, "Council Directive 2008/114/EC," Tech. Rep., Official Journal of the European Union, December 2008.

[3] B. Miller and D. C. Rowe, "A survey of SCADA and critical infrastructure incidents," in *Proceedings of the 1st Annual Conference on Research in Information Technology, RIIT 2012*, pp. 51–56, ACM, October 2012.

[4] M. Zeller, "Myth or reality - Does the Aurora vulnerability pose a risk to my generator?" in *Proceedings of the 64th Annual*

Conference for Protective Relay Engineers, pp. 130–136, April 2011.

[5] R. Langner, "Stuxnet: dissecting a cyberwarfare weapon," *IEEE Security and Privacy*, vol. 9, no. 3, pp. 49–51, 2011.

[6] J. Slay and M. Miller, *Lessons learned from the Maroochy Water Breach*, Springer, 2007.

[7] "Bundesamt für Sicherheit in der Informationstechnik," Tech. Rep., Die Lage der IT-Sicherheit in Deutschland, 2014.

[8] B. Bencsáth, G. Pék, L. Buttyán, and M. Félegyházi, "Duqu: Analysis, detection, and lessons learned," in *ACM European Workshop on System Security (EuroSec)*, 2012.

[9] Symantec Incident Response, "Dragonfly: Cyberespionage attacks against energy suppliers," Tech. Rep., July 2014.

[10] R. Mitchell and I.-R. Chen, "A survey of intrusion detection techniques for cyber-physical systems," *ACM Computing Surveys*, vol. 46, no. 4, article no. 55, 2014.

[11] B. Zhu, A. Joseph, and S. Sastry, "A taxonomy of cyber attacks on SCADA systems," in *Proceedings of the 2011 IEEE International Conference on Internet of Things, iThings 2011 and 4th IEEE International Conference on Cyber, Physical and Social Computing, CPSCom 2011*, pp. 380–388, October 2011.

[12] I. Garitano, R. Uribeetxeberria, and U. Zurutuza, "A review of SCADA anomaly detection systems," in *Proceedings of the6th International Conference Soft Computing Models in Industrial and Environmental Applications SOCO 2011*, vol. 87, pp. 357–366, Springer, 2011.

[13] J. Dean and S. Ghemawat, "MapReduce: simplified data processing on large clusters," *Communications of the ACM*, vol. 51, no. 1, pp. 107–113, 2008.

[14] D. Borthakur, "The hadoop distributed file system: Architecture and design," 2007.

[15] M. Chen, S. Mao, and Y. Liu, "Big data: A survey," *Mobile Networks and Applications*, vol. 19, no. 2, pp. 171–209, 2014.

[16] D. Laney, "3D data management: Controlling data volume, velocity and variety," *META Group Research Note*, vol. 6, 2001.

[17] J. Camacho, G. Macia-Fernandez, J. Diaz-Verdejo, and P. Garcia-Teodoro, "Tackling the big data 4 vs for anomaly detection," in *Proceedings of the IEEE Conference on Computer Communications Workshops, INFOCOM WKSHPS 2014*, pp. 500–505, May 2014.

[18] S. Wallace, X. Zhao, D. Nguyen, and K.-T. Lu, "Big data analytics on smart grid: Mining pmu data for event and anomaly detection," in *Big Data: Principles and Paradigms*, R. Buyya, R. N. Calheiros, and A. V. Dastjerdi, Eds., chapter 17, pp. 417–429, Morgan Kaufmann, 2016.

[19] A. A. Cárdenas, P. K. Manadhata, and S. P. Rajan, "Big Data Analytics for Security," *Security & Privacy, IEEE*, vol. 11, no. 6, pp. 74–76, 2013.

[20] C. Everett, "Big data - The future of cyber-security or its latest threat?" *Computer Fraud and Security*, vol. 2015, no. 9, pp. 14–17, 2015.

[21] M. Cheminod, L. Durante, and A. Valenzano, "Review of security issues in industrial networks," *IEEE Transactions on Industrial Informatics*, vol. 9, no. 1, pp. 277–293, 2013.

[22] B. Galloway and G. P. Hancke, "Introduction to industrial control networks," *IEEE Communications Surveys and Tutorials*, vol. 15, no. 2, pp. 860–880, 2013.

[23] T.-F. Yen, A. Oprea, K. Onarlioglu et al., "Beehive: Large-scale log analysis for detecting suspicious activity in enterprise networks," in *Proceedings of the 29th Annual Computer Security Applications Conference, ACSAC 2013*, pp. 199–208, December 2013.

[24] V. K. C. Bumgardner and V. W. Marek, "Scalable hybrid stream and hadoop network analysis system," in *Proceedings of the 5th ACM/SPEC International Conference on Performance Engineering, ICPE 2014*, pp. 219–224, Association for Computing Machinery, Dublin, Ireland, March 2014.

[25] J. Dromard, G. Roudire, and P. Owezarski, "Unsupervised network anomaly detection in real-time on big data," in *New Trends in Databases and Information Systems*, T. Morzy, P. Valduriez, and L. Bellatreche, Eds., vol. 539 of *Communications in Computer and Information Science*, pp. 197–206, Springer, Berlin, Germany, 2015.

[26] D. E. Difallah, P. Cudre-Mauroux, and S. A. McKenna, "Scalable anomaly detection for smart city infrastructure networks," *IEEE Internet Computing*, vol. 17, no. 6, pp. 39–47, 2013.

[27] P. Giura and W. Wang, "Using large scale distributed computing to unveil advanced persistent threats," *SCIENCE*, vol. 1, no. 3, pp. 93–105, 2012.

[28] G. P. Gupta and M. Kulariya, "A framework for fast and efficient cyber security network intrusion detection using apache spark," *Procedia Computer Science*, vol. 93, pp. 824–831, 2016.

[29] D. Gonçalves, J. Bota, and M. Correia, "Big data analytics for detecting host misbehavior in large logs," in *Proceedings of the 14th IEEE International Conference on Trust, Security and Privacy in Computing and Communications, TrustCom 2015*, pp. 238–245, fin, August 2015.

[30] D. Hadžiosmanović, D. Bolzoni, and P. H. Hartel, "A log mining approach for process monitoring in SCADA," *International Journal of Information Security*, vol. 11, no. 4, pp. 231–251, 2012.

[31] R. Fontugne, J. Mazel, and K. Fukuda, "Hashdoop: A MapReduce framework for network anomaly detection," in *Proceedings of the 2014 IEEE Conference on Computer Communications Workshops, INFOCOM WKSHPS 2014*, pp. 494–499, May 2014.

[32] W. Hurst, M. Merabti, and P. Fergus, "Big data analysis techniques for cyber-threat detection in critical infrastructures," in *Proceedings of the 28th IEEE International Conference on Advanced Information Networking and Applications Workshops, IEEE WAINA 2014*, pp. 916–921, May 2014.

[33] M. Iturbe, I. Garitano, U. Zurutuza, and R. Uribeetxeberria, "Visualizing Network Flows and Related Anomalies in Industrial Networks using Chord Diagrams and Whitelisting," in *Proceedings of the International Conference on Information Visualization Theory and Applications*, pp. 99–106, Rome, Italy, Feburary 2016.

[34] I. Kiss, B. Genge, P. Haller, and G. Sebestyen, "Data clustering-based anomaly detection in industrial control systems," in *Proceedings of the 2014 10th IEEE International Conference on Intelligent Computer Communication and Processing, ICCP 2014*, pp. 275–281, Cluj Napoca, Romania, September 2014.

[35] S. Marchal, X. Jiang, R. State, and T. Engel, "A big data architecture for large scale security monitoring," in *Proceedings of the 3rd IEEE International Congress on Big Data, BigData Congress*, pp. 56–63, IEEE Computer Society, Anchorage, Alaska, USA, July 2014.

[36] H. Tazaki, K. Okada, Y. Sekiya, and Y. Kadobayashi, "MAT-ATABI: Multi-layer Threat Analysis Platform with Hadoop," in *Proceedings of the 3rd International Workshop on Building Analysis Datasets and Gathering Experience Returns for Security, BADGERS 2014*, pp. 75–82.

[37] M. M. Rathore, A. Ahmad, and A. Paul, "Real time intrusion detection system for ultra-high-speed big data environments,"

The Journal of Supercomputing, vol. 72, no. 9, pp. 3489–3510, 2016.

[38] A. S. Ratner and P. Kelly, "Anomalies in network traffic," in *Proceedings of the 11th IEEE International Conference on Intelligence and Security Informatics, IEEE ISI 2013*, pp. 206–208, June 2013.

[39] J. Therdphapiyanak and K. Piromsopa, "An analysis of suitable parameters for efficiently applying K-means clustering to large TCPdump data set using Hadoop framework," in *Proceedings of the 2013 10th International Conference on Electrical Engineering/Electronics, Computer, Telecommunications and Information Technology, ECTI-CON 2013*, pp. 1–6, May 2013.

[40] G. Tian, Z. Wang, X. Yin et al., "TADOOP: Mining Network Traffic Anomalies with Hadoop," in *Security and Privacy in Communication Networks*, B. Thuraisingham, X. Wang, and V. Yegneswaran, Eds., vol. 164 of *Lecture Notes of the Institute for Computer Sciences, Social Informatics and Telecommunications Engineering*, pp. 175–192, Springer, 2015.

[41] Z. Wang, J. Yang, H. Zhang, C. Li, S. Zhang, and H. Wang, "Towards online anomaly detection by combining multiple detection methods and Storm," in *Proceedings of the 2016 IEEE/IFIP Network Operations and Management Symposium, NOMS 2016*, pp. 804–807, tur, April 2016.

[42] W. Xu, L. Huang, A. Fox, D. Patterson, and M. I. Jordan, "Detecting large-scale system problems by mining console logs," in *Proceedings of the 22nd ACM SIGOPS Symposium on Operating Systems Principles, SOSP'09*, pp. 117–131, October 2009.

[43] V. M. Igure, S. A. Laughter, and R. D. Williams, "Security issues in SCADA networks," *Computers & Security*, vol. 25, no. 7, pp. 498–506, 2006.

[44] B. Genge, C. Siaterlis, and M. Hohenadel, "Impact of network infrastructure parameters to the effectiveness of cyber attacks against Industrial Control Systems," *International Journal of Computers, Communications & Control*, vol. 7, no. 4, pp. 674–687, 2012.

[45] ISO, "EnglishInformation technology – Security techniques – Information security management systems – Requirements. ISO/IEC 27001:2013," Tech. Rep., International Organization for Standardization, 2013.

[46] M. Bishop, *Computer Security: Art and Science*, Addison-Wesley Professional, 2002.

[47] D. Dzung, M. Naedele, T. P. von Hoff, and M. Crevatin, "Security for industrial communication systems," *Proceedings of the IEEE*, vol. 93, no. 6, pp. 1152–1177, 2005.

[48] D. Duggan, M. Berg, J. Dillinger, and J. Stamp, "Penetration testing of industrial control systems," Tech. Rep. SAND2005-2846P, Sandia National Laboratories, 2005.

[49] H. Debar, M. Dacier, and A. Wespi, "Towards a taxonomy of intrusion-detection systems," *Computer Networks*, vol. 31, no. 8, pp. 805–822, 1999.

[50] A. L. Buczak and E. Guven, "A survey of data mining and machine learning methods for cyber security intrusion detection," *IEEE Communications Surveys & Tutorials*, vol. 18, no. 2, pp. 1153–1176, 2016.

[51] M. Obitko, V. Jirkovský, and J. Bezdíček, "Big Data Challenges in Industrial Automation," in *Industrial Applications of Holonic and Multi-Agent Systems*, V. Mařík, J. Lastra, and P. Skobelev, Eds., vol. 8062 of *Lecture Notes in Computer Science*, pp. 305–316, Springer, Berlin, Heidelberg, 2013.

[52] H. P. Zhu, Y. Xu, Q. Liu, and Y. Q. Rao, "Cloud service platform for big data of manufacturing," *Applied Mechanics and Materials*, vol. 456, pp. 178–183, 2014.

[53] S. Windmann, A. Maier, O. Niggemann et al., "Big data analysis of manufacturing processes," *Journal of Physics: Conference Series*, vol. 659, no. 1, Article ID 012055, 2015.

[54] M. Kezunovic, L. Xie, and S. Grijalva, "The role of big data in improving power system operation and protection," in *Proceedings of the 2013 IREP Symposium on Bulk Power System Dynamics and Control - IX Optimization, Security and Control of the Emerging Power Grid, IREP 2013*, August 2013.

[55] J. Wan, S. Tang, D. Li et al., "A Manufacturing Big Data Solution for Active Preventive Maintenance," *IEEE Transactions on Industrial Informatics*, vol. 13, no. 4, pp. 2039–2047, 2017.

[56] L. Stojanovic, M. Dinic, N. Stojanovic, and A. Stojadinovic, "Big-data-driven anomaly detection in industry (4.0): An approach and a case study," in *Proceedings of the 4th IEEE International Conference on Big Data, Big Data 2016*, pp. 1647–1652, December 2016.

[57] Y. Xu, Y. Sun, J. Wan, X. Liu, and Z. Song, "Industrial Big Data for Fault Diagnosis: Taxonomy, Review, and Applications," *IEEE Access*, 2017.

[58] W. Shi, Y. Zhu, T. Huang et al., "An Integrated Data Preprocessing Framework Based on Apache Spark for Fault Diagnosis of Power Grid Equipment," *Journal of Signal Processing Systems*, vol. 86, no. 2-3, pp. 221–236, 2017.

[59] N. Svendsen and S. Wolthusen, "Using Physical Models for Anomaly Detection in Control Systems," in *Critical Infrastructure Protection III*, vol. 311 of *IFIP Advances in Information and Communication Technology*, pp. 139–149, Springer, Berlin, Heidelberg, 2009.

[60] M. Krotofil, J. Larsen, and D. Gollmann, "The process matters: Ensuring data veracity in Cyber-physical systems," in *Proceedings of the 10th ACM Symposium on Information, Computer and Communications Security, ASIACCS 2015*, pp. 133–144, Singapore, April 2015.

[61] I. Kiss, B. Genge, and P. Haller, "A clustering-based approach to detect cyber attacks in process control systems," in *Proceedings of the 13th International Conference on Industrial Informatics, INDIN 2015*, pp. 142–148, July 2015.

[62] M. Iturbe, J. Camacho, I. Garitano, U. Zurutuza, and R. Uribeetxeberria, "On the Feasibility of Distinguishing between Process Disturbances and Intrusions in Process Control Systems Using Multivariate Statistical Process Control," in *Proceedings of the 46th IEEE/IFIP International Conference on Dependable Systems and Networks, DSN-W 2016*, pp. 155–160, France, July 2016.

[63] B. Genge, C. Siaterlis, and G. Karopoulos, "Data fusion-base anomaly detection in networked critical infrastructures," in *Proceedings of the 2013 43rd Annual IEEE/IFIP Conference on Dependable Systems and Networks Workshop (DSN-W)*, pp. 1–8, Budapest, Hungary, June 2013.

[64] W. Jardine, S. Frey, B. Green, and A. Rashid, "SENAMI: Selective non-invasive active monitoring for ICS intrusion detection," in *Proceedings of the 2nd ACM Workshop on Cyber-Physical Systems Security and PrivaCy, CPS-SPC 2016*, pp. 23–34, Vienna, Austria, October 2016.

[65] A. Bialecki, M. Cafarella, D. Cutting, and O. OMalley, "Hadoop: a framework for running applications on large clusters built of commodity hardware," AT Wiki, 2005, http://hadoop.apache.org.

[66] P. Mundkur, V. Tuulos, and J. Flatow, "Disco: A computing platform for large-scale data analytics," in *Proceedings of the 10th ACM SIGPLAN Erlang Workshop, Erlang 2011, Co-located with the Annual ACM SIGPLAN International Conference on Functional Programming, ICFP*, pp. 84–89, jpn, September 2011.

[67] M. Gorawski, A. Gorawska, and K. Pasterak, "A survey of data stream processing tools," in *Information Sciences and Systems 2014*, pp. 295–303, Springer International Publishing, Cham, 2014.

[68] M. Zaharia, M. Chowdhury, M. J. Franklin, S. Shenker, and I. Stoica, "Spark: cluster computing with working sets," in *Proceedings of the 2nd USENIX conference on Hot topics in cloud computing*, p. 10, 2010.

[69] P. Carbone, S. Ewen, S. Haridi, A. Katsifodimos, V. Markl, and K. Tzoumas, "Apache flink: Stream and batch processing in a single engine," *Data Engineering*, p. 28, 2015.

[70] R. Zuech, T. M. Khoshgoftaar, and R. Wald, "Intrusion detection and Big Heterogeneous Data: a Survey," *Journal of Big Data*, vol. 2, no. 1, pp. 1–41, 2015.

[71] J. François, S. Wang, W. Bronzi, R. State, and T. Engel, "Bot-Cloud: detecting botnets using MapReduce," in *Proceedings of the IEEE International Workshop on Information Forensics and Security (WIFS '11)*, pp. 1–6, Iguacu Falls, Brazil, December 2011.

[72] K. Singh, S. C. Guntuku, A. Thakur, and C. Hota, "Big data analytics framework for peer-to-peer botnet detection using random forests," *Information Sciences*, vol. 278, pp. 488–497, 2014.

[73] T.-W. Chiou, S.-C. Tsai, and Y.-B. Lin, "Network security management with traffic pattern clustering," *Soft Computing*, vol. 18, no. 9, pp. 1757–1770, 2014.

[74] Z. Luo, J. Shen, H. Jin, and D. Liu, "Research of Botnet Situation Awareness Based on Big Data," in *Web Technologies and Applications*, vol. 9461 of *Lecture Notes in Computer Science*, pp. 71–78, Springer International Publishing, 2015.

[75] L. Invernizzi, S. Miskovic, R. Torres et al., "Nazca: Detecting Malware Distribution in Large-Scale Networks," in *Proceedings of the Network and Distributed System Security Symposium*, San Diego, Calif, USA, 2014.

[76] D. H. Chau, C. Nachenberg, J. Wilhelm, A. Wright, and C. Faloutsos, "Polonium: Tera-Scale Graph Mining and Inference for Malware Detection," in *Proceedings of the SIAM International Conference on Data Mining (SDM) 2011*, Mesa, Ariz, USA, April 2011.

[77] S. T. Liu and Y. M. Chen, "Retrospective detection of malware attacks by cloud computing," *International Journal of Information Technology, Communications and Convergence*, vol. 1, no. 3, pp. 280–296, 2011.

[78] C. R. Panigrahi, M. Tiwari, B. Pati, and R. Prasath, "Malware Detection in Big Data Using Fast Pattern Matching: A Hadoop Based Comparison on GPU," in *Mining Intelligence and Knowledge Exploration*, vol. 8891 of *Lecture Notes in Computer Science*, pp. 407–416, Springer International Publishing, 2014.

[79] J. Jang, D. Brumley, and S. Venkataraman, "Bitshred: Fast, Scalable Malware Triage," Tech. Rep., Cylab, Carnegie Mellon University, Pittsburgh, Pa, USA, 2010.

[80] Z. Hanif, C. Telvis, and J. Trost, "BinaryPig: Scalable Static Binary Analysis Over Hadoop," in *Proceedings of the Blackhat USA*, Las Vegas, Nev, USA, 2013.

[81] M. Mizukoshi and M. Munetomo, "Distributed denial of services attack protection system with genetic algorithms on Hadoop cluster computing framework," in *Proceedings of the*

IEEE Congress on Evolutionary Computation, CEC 2015, pp. 1575–1580, May 2015.

[82] S. Tripathi, B. Gupta, A. Almomani, A. Mishra, and S. Veluru, "Hadoop Based Defense Solution to Handle Distributed Denial of Service (DDoS) Attacks," *Journal of Information Security*, vol. 04, no. 03, pp. 150–164, 2013.

[83] Y. Lee and Y. Lee, "Detecting DDoS attacks with Hadoop," in *Proceedings of the 2011 ACM CoNext Student Workshop, CoNEXT 2011*, ACM, December 2011.

[84] J. Choi, C. Choi, B. Ko, D. Choi, and P. Kim, "Detecting web based DDoS attack using MapReduce operations in cloud computing environment," *Journal of Internet Services and Information Security*, vol. 3, pp. 28–37, Nov 2013.

[85] T. Zhao, D. C.-T. Lo, and K. Qian, "A neural-network based DDoS detection system using hadoop and HBase," in *Proceedings of the 17th IEEE International Conference on High Performance Computing and Communications, IEEE 7th International Symposium on Cyberspace Safety and Security and IEEE 12th International Conference on Embedded Software and Systems, HPCC-ICESS-CSS 2015*, pp. 1326–1331, August 2015.

[86] G. Caruana, M. Li, and H. Qi, "SpamCloud: A mapreduce based anti-spam architecture," in *Proceedings of the 2010 7th International Conference on Fuzzy Systems and Knowledge Discovery, FSKD 2010*, pp. 3003–3006, August 2010.

[87] G. Caruana, M. Li, and M. Qi, "A MapReduce based parallel SVM for large scale spam filtering," in *Proceedings of the 2011 8th International Conference on Fuzzy Systems and Knowledge Discovery, FSKD 2011, Jointly with the 2011 7th International Conference on Natural Computation, ICNC'11*, pp. 2659–2662, July 2011.

[88] P. H. B. Las-Casas, V. S. Dias, W. Meira, and D. Guedes, "A Big Data Architecture for Security Data and Its Application to Phishing Characterization," in *Proceedings of the 2nd IEEE International Conference on Big Data Security on Cloud, IEEE BigDataSecurity 2016, 2nd IEEE International Conference on High Performance and Smart Computing, IEEE HPSC 2016 and IEEE International Conference on Intelligent Data and Security, IEEE IDS 2016*, pp. 36–41, April 2016.

[89] M. Thomas, L. Metcalf, J. Spring, P. Krystosek, and K. Prevost, "SiLK: A tool suite for unsampled network flow analysis at scale," in *Proceedings of the 3rd IEEE International Congress on Big Data, BigData Congress*, pp. 184–191, Anchorage, Alaska, USA, July 2014.

[90] Y. Lee, W. Kang, and H. Son, "An internet traffic analysis method with MapReduce," in *Proceedings of the IEEE/IFIP Network Operations and Management Symposium Workshops, NOMS 2010*, pp. 357–361, April 2010.

[91] M. Baker, D. Turnbull, and G. Kaszuba, "Finding Data Needles in Haystacks (the Size of Countries," in *Prooceedings of Blackhat Europe*, 2012.

[92] Y. Lee, W. Kang, and Y. Lee, "A hadoop-based packet trace processing tool," in *Traffic Monitoring and Analysis*, vol. 6613 of *Lecture Notes in Computer Science*, pp. 51–63, Springer, Berlin, Heidelberg, 2011.

[93] M. Kumar and M. Hanumanthappa, "Scalable intrusion detection systems log analysis using cloud computing infrastructure," in *Proceedings of the 2013 4th IEEE International Conference on Computational Intelligence and Computing Research, IEEE ICCIC 2013*, December 2013.

[94] S.-F. Yang, W.-Y. Chen, and Y.-T. Wang, "ICAS: An inter-VM IDS log cloud analysis system," in *Proceedings of the 2011 IEEE*

International Conference on Cloud Computing and Intelligence Systems, CCIS2011, pp. 285–289, September 2011.

[95] S. Axelsson, "Intrusion detection systems: A survey and taxonomy," Tech. Rep., Chalmers University of Technology, 2000.

[96] B. Zhu and S. Sastry, "SCADA-specific intrusion detection/prevention systems: a survey and taxonomy," in Proceedings of the in Proceedings of the 1st Workshop on Secure Control Systems (SCS' 10), 2010.

[97] A. Thusoo, J. S. Sarma, and N. Jain, "Hive: a warehousing solution over a map-reduce framework," Proceedings of the VLDB Endowment, vol. 2, no. 2, pp. 1626–1629, 2009.

[98] J. Therdphapiyanak and K. Piromsopa, "Applying hadoop for log analysis toward distributed IDS," in Proceedings of the 7th International Conference on Ubiquitous Information Management and Communication, ICUIMC 2013, January 2013.

[99] H. Hotelling, "Multivariate quality control," Techniques of Statistical Analysis, 1947.

[100] J. E. Jackson and G. S. Mudholkar, "Control procedures for residuals associated with principal component analysis," Technometrics, vol. 21, no. 3, pp. 341–349, 1979.

[101] A. Ziviani, A. T. A. Gomes, M. L. Monsores, and P. S. S. Rodrigues, "Network anomaly detection using nonextensive entropy," IEEE Communications Letters, vol. 11, no. 12, pp. 1034–1036, 2007.

[102] M. Hall, E. Frank, G. Holmes, B. Pfahringer, P. Reutemann, and I. H. Witten, "The WEKA data mining software: an update," ACM SIGKDD Explorations Newsletter, vol. 11, no. 1, pp. 10–18, 2009.

[103] P. Casas, J. Mazel, and P. Owezarski, "Unsupervised Network Intrusion Detection Systems: Detecting the Unknown without Knowledge," Computer Communications, vol. 35, no. 7, pp. 772–783, 2012.

[104] M. Ester, H.-P. Kriegel, J. Sander, and X. Xu, "A density-based algorithm for discovering clusters in large spatial databases with noise," in Proceedings of the 2nd International Conference on Knowledge Discovery and Data Mining (KDD '96), pp. 226–231, 1996.

[105] Z. Wang, J. Yang, and F. Li, "An on-line anomaly detection method based on LMS algorithm," in Proceedings of the 16th Asia-Pacific Network Operations and Management Symposium, APNOMS 2014, September 2014.

[106] B. Schneier, "Attack trees," Dr. Dobb's Journal, vol. 24, no. 12, pp. 21–29, 1999.

[107] E. J. Amoroso, Fundamentals of Computer Security, PTR Prentice Hall, Englewood Cliffs, NJ, USA, 1994.

[108] L. Anselin, "Local indicators of spatial association—LISA," Geographical Analysis, vol. 27, no. 2, pp. 93–115, 1995.

[109] P. G. Brown, "Overview of sciDB: large scale array storage, processing and analysis," in Proceedings of the ACM SIGMOD International Conference on Management of Data, pp. 963–968, ACM, 2010.

[110] E. Bompard, P. Cuccia, M. Masera, and I. N. Fovino, "Cyber vulnerability in power systems operation and control," in Critical Infrastructure Protection, vol. 7130, pp. 197–234, Springer, 2012.

[111] J. Camacho, R. Magán-Carrión, P. García-Teodoro, and J. J. Treinen, "Networkmetrics: multivariate big data analysis in the context of the internet," Journal of Chemometrics, vol. 30, no. 9, pp. 488–505, 2016.

[112] R. Sommer and V. Paxson, "Outside the closed world: on using machine learning for network intrusion detection," in Proceedings of the IEEE Symposium on Security and Privacy, pp. 305–316, IEEE Computer Society, 2010.

[113] T. Morris and W. Gao, "Industrial Control System Traffic Data Sets for Intrusion Detection Research," in Critical Infrastructure Protection VIII, vol. 441 of IFIP Advances in Information and Communication Technology, pp. 65–78, Springer, Berlin, Heidelberg, 2014.

[114] E. Vasilomanolakis, S. Srinivasa, C. G. Cordero, and M. Mühlhäuser, "Multi-stage attack detection and signature generation with ICS honeypots," in Proceedings of the IEEE/IFIP Network Operations and Management Symposium, NOMS 2016, pp. 1227–1232, April 2016.

[115] D. Antonioli, A. Agrawal, and N. O. Tippenhauer, "Towards high-interaction virtual ICS honeypots-in-a-box," in Proceedings of the 2nd ACM Workshop on Cyber-Physical Systems Security and PrivaCy, CPS-SPC 2016, pp. 13–22.

11

Efficient Asymmetric Index Encapsulation Scheme for Anonymous Content Centric Networking

Rong Ma,[1] Zhenfu Cao,[2] and Xingkai Wang[1]

[1]*Shanghai Jiao Tong University, Shanghai, China*
[2]*East China Normal University, Shanghai, China*

Correspondence should be addressed to Rong Ma; marong.sjtu@gmail.com

Academic Editor: Yacine Challal

Content Centric Networking (CCN) is an effective communication paradigm that well matches the features of wireless environments. To be considered a viable candidate in the emerging wireless networks, despite the clear benefits of location-independent security, CCN must at least have parity with existing solutions for confidential and anonymous communication. This paper designs a new cryptographic scheme, called Asymmetric Index Encapsulation (AIE), that enables the router to test whether an encapsulated header matches the token without learning anything else about both of them. We suggest using the AIE as the core protocol of anonymous Content Centric Networking. A construction of AIE which strikes a balance between efficiency and security is given. The scheme is proved to be secure based on the DBDH assumption in the random oracle with tight reduction, while the encapsulated header and the token in our system consist of only three elements.

1. Introduction

Conventional networking protocols designed to support end-to-end communications between nodes which are uniquely identified through an IP address may fail in wireless environments due to dynamic changes caused by the mobility. Content Centric Networking is an emerging networking architecture with the goal of becoming an alternative to the IP-based Internet. Communication in CCN adheres to the pull model. Its primary characteristic is that content and routable content in the network are always named. Interests represent the willingness of the consumer to retrieve certain content, independently of its location. A consumer who wishes to obtain content first issues an interest by name, which is then routed to the producer or router that is capable of satisfying the request. The corresponding content carrying the same name is then sent to the consumer along the reverse path.

The CCN architecture has some innate privacy friendly features; for example, the source addresses of contents are hard to trace. However, support for name privacy is not a standard feature. Names reveal significantly more information about content than IP addresses [1].

ANDaNA [2] and AC[3]N [3] are the initial attempt to provide anonymous communication in CCN. They are inspired by Tor, using onion-like encryption to wrap interests, and forwarded by participating anonymizing routers. However, caching mechanism as one of the most important features of CCN could not be used in these designs due to the lack of an cryptographic primitive keeping the name private while ensuring accessibility and routability.

In this paper we propose a new cryptographic scheme called Asymmetric Index Encapsulation (AIE) to hide the name except the entity which is given appropriate token. Token can be viewed as a kind of encrypted interest; it can only be generated from the authorized consumers and the functionality of the token kept secret even during the name and interest match procedure. We believe AIE is a positive answer to the open question raised in [1, 4]. AIE is proved to be secure based on the DBDH/CDH assumption in the random oracle with tight reduction, while the encapsulated header and the token in our system consist of only three elements. Moreover, AIE is applicable in any CCN incarnation, for example, CCNx and NDN [5].

1.1. Organization. The rest of this paper is organized as follows. The next section shows the related work of our paper. Section 3 gives an overview of CCN. The scheme description is presented in Section 4. Definitions of security model are given and discussed in Section 5. The reduction proofs are shown in Sections 6 and 7. Then we show implementation and provide an analysis of the performances of the proposed schema in Section 8. Finally, we conclude with related work and future work in Section 9.

2. Related Work

Symmetric searchable encryption with adaptive security against chosen-keyword attacks was first considered explicitly in [6], where symmetric index encapsulation was first considered explicitly by [7]. Unlike in asymmetric settings, securely encapsulating a single keyword/index is nearly trivial in symmetric settings. In these schemes and subsequent work [8–11], researchers focus on how to handle full text indices and try to improve efficiency. Another line of work uses deterministic encryption [8, 12]. It only provides security for data and queries that have high entropy.

Starting with the work of Boneh et al. [13–15], searchable encryption has also been considered in the public key setting [10, 16–19]. The early works lack function privacy until the first definition was suggested very recently by Boneh et al. [20].

One of the key goals of CCN projects is "security by design" [21]. In contrast to today's Internet, where security problems were identified along the way, the research community stresses both awareness of issues and support for features and countermeasures from the outset. To this end, a few of papers investigate various attacks and solutions in CCN or CON [1, 2, 5]. However, to the best of our knowledge, there is an absence of cryptographic perspective. The major contribution of our paper is in defining a new cryptographic primitive known as Asymmetric Index Encapsulation scheme.

A preliminary version of this paper [22], which concentrated on solving the related fundamental cryptographic problem, appeared at ProvSec 2016, while this paper focuses more on solving practical problem of CCN network. The extra contents mainly are shown in Sections 8 and 9.

3. CCN Overview

We now review the building blocks of Content Centric Networking. There are three types of entities in CCN:

  (i) Consumer which issues interests for content

  (ii) Producer which generates and publishes content to the network

  (iii) Routers which forward interest messages and content between consumers and producers

CCN supports two types of packets:

  (i) Named content: in CNN, contents are always named to facilitate data dissemination and search. A content name is a URI-like string composed of one or more variable-length segments.

  (ii) Interest: to obtain content, consumer issues a request, called an interest message, with the name of the desired content. This interest will be satisfied by either a router or the content producer.

Name and interest matching in CCN is exact, for example, an interest for "/2017/news.txt" can only be satisfied by a content object named "/2017/news.txt."

Each CCN entity should maintain the following components:

  (i) Forwarding Interest Base (FIB): this includes a lookup table used to determine entities for forwarding incoming interests.

  (ii) Pending Interest Table (PIT): this include a lookup table of outstanding pending interests and a set of corresponding incoming entities.

  (iii) Content Store (CS): this is a buffer used for content caching and retrieval. Each network entity can provide content caching, which is limited only by resource availability. Note that this is different from packet buffers in today's routers, as cache size is expected to be several orders of magnitude bigger in CCN.

All CCN communication is initiated by a consumer that sends an interest for a specific content [23]. When a router receives an interest, it looks up its PIT to determine whether an interest for the content is pending:

  (i) If the desired name in the PIT, the interest does not need to be forwarded further. If the arrival entity is new, the router just updates the PIT entry by adding a new incoming entity.

  (ii) Otherwise, the router looks up its CS for a matching content. If it succeeds, the cached content is returned and no new PIT entry is needed. If no matching content is found, the router creates a new PIT entry and forwards the interest using its FIB.

During receipting of the interest, the producer distributes requested content among the network, thus satisfying the interest. Then, the content is forwarded towards the consumer, by the path of the preceding interest, in reverse.

4. Scheme Description

Formally, AIE is specified by a quadruple of probabilistic polynomial-time algorithms:

  (i) The setup algorithm *Setup* is run by the central authority, takes a security parameter 1^λ, and outputs the public system parameters pp together with a master secret key mk. The system parameters will be publicly known, while the master key will be known only to the key generation algorithm.

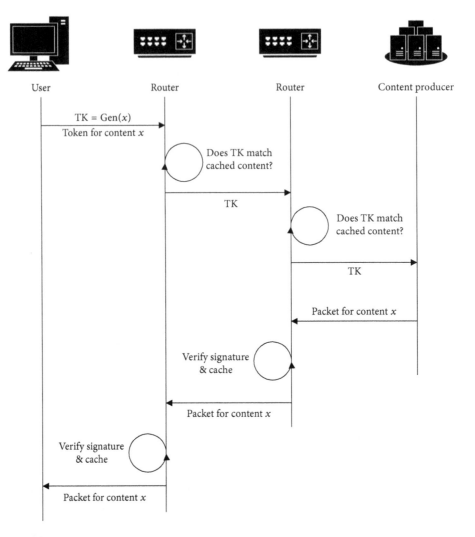

Packet for content x (EC, HD, SIG)
EC: encrypted content x
HD: encapsulated header: Enc(x)
SIG: signature (EC, HD)

FIGURE 1: Instantiating AIE in anonymous CCN.

(ii) The index (a.k.a. name) encapsulation algorithm *Enc* is run by the producer, takes as input an index x, and outputs encapsulated header hd_x.

(iii) The token generation algorithm *Gen* is run by the central authority, takes as input the master secret key mk and an interest y, and outputs a related token tk_y.

(iv) The test algorithm *Test* is run by the router, takes as input a header hd_x and a token tk_y, and outputs a value which indicates the matching relationship between tk_y and hd_x, "1" for matching and "0" on the contrary. Usage of this algorithm is to show the linkability between headers and tokens.

To deploy AIE in CCN, we should introduce a trusted central authority which is in charge of issuing token. As illustrated in Figure 1, if a consumer plans to request a content named x, instead of sending the plain interest packet, it should use the token issued by Gen(x) from the central

authority. Token is like a private key of public encryption scheme. However, its functionality is not decrypting but testing.

When a producer generates new content named y, it encrypts the content at first. The encryption algorithm used by consumers to conceal content should be secure against adaptive chosen ciphertext (CCA) attacks. Then, the producer runs encapsulation algorithm *Enc* to encapsulate the name y. We call the output of Enc(y) the encapsulated header of y. Finally, a signature binds the encrypted content with its encapsulated header and provides origin authentication no matter how or from where it is retrieved. For any adversary without the correct token, this signed and encrypted packet will lose no information under our security model (discussed in Section 5.4).

When a token is received and there are no same pending tokens in its cache, router runs *Test* algorithm to find an encapsulated header which matches the token. If there is no such encapsulated header, the router forwards this new token to the neighbor routers. When the desired content is returned or there is already an encapsulated header matching this token in the cache, the router forwards it out on all neighbors and flushes the corresponding cache entry.

Since adversary can mount a guessing attack, exhaustively testing the known token, we give a reasonable security model in Section 5.5 to ensure that there is no more obviously effective attack better than the brute force method.

4.1. Construction. Let *GroupGen* be a probabilistic polynomial-time algorithm taking 1^λ as security parameter and outputs $(\mathbb{G}, \mathbb{G}_T, p, g, e)$, where $\mathbb{G}$ and $\mathbb{G}_T$ are groups of prime order p, $2^\lambda < p < 2^{\lambda+1}$, g is a generator of group $\mathbb{G}$, and $e : \mathbb{G} \times \mathbb{G} \to \mathbb{G}_T$ is a nondegenerate efficiently computable bilinear map. See [24] for a description of the properties of such pairings. We present AIE scheme as follows; the design inspiration comes from [20, 25].

(i) Setup(1^λ): on input security parameter 1^λ, the setup algorithm works as follows:

    (1) Generate $(p, \mathbb{G}, \mathbb{G}_T, g, e) \leftarrow \text{GroupGen}(1^\lambda)$.

    (2) Randomly sample $a \leftarrow \mathbb{Z}_p^*$.

    (3) Compute $g_a \leftarrow g^a$.

    (4) Choose two cryptographic hash functions H and $F : \{0, 1\}^* \to \mathbb{G}$. The security analysis will view H, F as random oracles.

    (5) Output a as master key and (g, g_a) as public parameters.

(ii) Enc(pp, x): given x, the index encapsulation algorithm does the following:

    (1) Randomly sampling $r \leftarrow \mathbb{Z}_p^*$

    (2) Computing $c \leftarrow g^r$, $T \leftarrow e(g_a, H(x))^r$, and $R \leftarrow e(g_a, F(x))^r$

    (3) Outputting (c, T, R) as an encapsulated header

(iii) Gen(mk, y): on input master key a and an index y, the token generation algorithm does the following:

    (1) If the same query for y is repeated twice, then the same token is provided.

    (2) It randomly chooses $u, v \leftarrow \mathbb{Z}_p^*$.

    (3) It computes $d \leftarrow (H(y)^u F(y)^v)^a$.

    (4) It outputs and records (d, u, v) as the token of y.

(iv) Test(hd, tk): given an encapsulated header hd and a token tk, the test algorithm does the following:

    (1) It parses hd as (c, T, R) and tk_y as (d, u, v).

    (2) It checks if the following equation holds true:

$$e(c, d) = T^u \cdot R^v, \tag{1}$$

    and if it holds, output "1," meaning tk matches hd; else output "0."

Correctness. For any index x, we need to guarantee $\text{Test}(hd_x, tk_x) = 1$, where $hd_x \leftarrow \text{Enc}(x, pp)$ and $tk_x \leftarrow \text{Gen}(x, mk)$. Denoting $hd_x = (c, T, R)$ and $tk_x = (d, u, v)$, that is clear since

$$
\begin{aligned}
e(c, d) &= e\left(g^s, \left(H(x)^u F(x)^v\right)^a\right) \\
&= e\left(g^s, H(x)\right)^{au} e\left(g^s, F(x)\right)^{av} \\
&= \left(e\left(g^a, H(x)\right)^s\right)^u \left(e\left(g^a, F(x)\right)^s\right)^v = T^u \cdot R^v.
\end{aligned}
\tag{2}
$$

5. Security Models

We give the precise formal definitions based on the above discussion.

5.1. Notation. We denote by $\mathbf{X} = (X_1, X_2, \ldots, X_q)$ a joint distribution of q random variables, and by $\mathbf{x} = (x_1, x_2, \ldots, x_q)$ a sample drawn from $\mathbf{X}$. The min-entropy of a random variable X is $\mathbf{H}_\infty(X) = -\log_2(\max_x \Pr[X = x])$. A k-source is a random variable X with $\mathbf{H}_\infty(X) \geq k$. A (q, k)-block-source is a random variable $\mathbf{X} = (X_1, X_2, \ldots, X_q)$, where, for each $i \in \{1, 2, \ldots, q\}$, $(x_1, \ldots, x_{i-1})$ holds that $X_i|_{X_1=x_1,\ldots,X_{i-1}=x_{i-1}}$ is k-source. The statistical distance between two random variables X and Y over a finite domain S is defined as

$$\text{SD}(X, Y) = \frac{1}{2} \sum_{x \in S} |\Pr[X = x] - \Pr[Y = x]|. \tag{3}$$

5.2. DBDH and CDH Assumption. Decisional bilinear Diffie-Hellman (DBDH) problem is to distinguish two distributions $\mathcal{P}_{\text{BDH}} = (g^\alpha, g^\beta, g^\gamma, e(g, g)^{\alpha\beta\gamma})$ and $\mathcal{R}_{\text{BDH}} = (g^\alpha, g^\beta, g^\gamma, R)$ for random α, β, γ, and R. Computational Diffie-Hellman (CDH) problem is to compute $g^{\alpha\beta}$ given g^α and g^β. To state the assumption asymptotically we rely on the bilinear group generator algorithm GroupGen(1^λ).

Definition 1. Let GroupGen(1^λ) be a bilinear group generator. The DBDH assumption holds for GroupGen(1^λ) if, for all probabilistic polynomial-time algorithm $\mathcal{B}$, its BDDH advantage, denoted by

$$
\begin{aligned}
\text{Adv}_{\mathcal{B}}^{\text{DBDH}}(\lambda) = &\left| \Pr\left[\mathcal{B}\left(g^\alpha, g^\beta, g^\gamma, e(g, g)^{\alpha\beta\gamma}\right) = 1\right] \right. \\
&\left. - \Pr\left[\mathcal{B}\left(g^\alpha, g^\beta, g^\gamma, R\right) = 1\right] \right|,
\end{aligned}
\tag{4}
$$

is a negligible function of λ, where the probability is over $(\mathbb{G}, \mathbb{G}_T, p, g, e) \leftarrow \text{GroupGen}(1^\lambda)$, $\alpha, \beta, \gamma \leftarrow \mathbb{Z}_p^*$, $R \leftarrow \mathbb{G}_T$.

Definition 2. Let GroupGen(1^λ) be a bilinear group generator. The CDH assumption holds for GroupGen(1^λ) if, for all probabilistic polynomial-time algorithm $\mathcal{B}$, its CDH advantage, denoted by

$$\text{Adv}_{\mathcal{B}}^{\text{CDH}}(\lambda) = \Pr\left[\mathcal{B}\left(g^\alpha, g^\beta\right) = g^{\alpha\beta}\right], \tag{5}$$

is a negligible function of λ, where the probability is over $(\mathbb{G}, \mathbb{G}_T, p, g, e) \leftarrow \text{GroupGen}(1^\lambda)$, $\alpha, \beta \leftarrow \mathbb{Z}_p^*$.

5.3. The Leftover Hash Lemma

Definition 3 (universal hash function). A collection $\mathcal{H}$ of function H with form $U \to V$ is universal if for any $x, x' \in U$ such that $x \neq x'$ the following holds:

$$\Pr_{H \leftarrow \mathcal{H}} \left[H(x) = H(x') \right] = \frac{1}{|V|}. \quad (6)$$

Theorem 4 (leftover hash lemma for block-source; see [20]). *Let $\mathcal{H}$ be a universal collection of functions $H : U \to V$; let $\mathbf{X} = (X_1, X_2, \ldots, X_q)$ be (q, k)-block-source where $k \geq \log |V| + 2 \log(1/\epsilon) + \Theta(1)$. Then there exists the distribution*

$$\left(H_1, H_1(X_1), H_2, H_2(X_2), \ldots, H_q, H_q(X_q) \right), \quad (7)$$

where $(H_1, H_2, \ldots, H_q) \leftarrow \mathcal{H}^q$ is ϵq-close to the uniform distribution over $(\mathcal{H} \times V)^q$.

5.4. Security Model for Anonymity.
AIE is anonymous if $\mathrm{Enc}(pp, x)$ leaks no information about x. To capture the anonymity properties formally, a game between a challenger and an adversary $\mathcal{A}$ is defined as follows:

(i) Setup Phase: the challenger runs $\mathrm{Setup}(1^\lambda)$ and sends pp to adversary $\mathcal{A}$ and keeps mk to itself.

(ii) Prechallenge Phase: in this phase, adversary $\mathcal{A}$ is allowed to make token extraction query. The challenger responds to the query about index y by sending $\mathcal{A}$ to the output of $\mathrm{Gen}(mk, y)$.

(iii) Challenge Phase: $\mathcal{A}$ submits two indices x_0, x_1, which is restricted to the indices that he did not request in prechallenge phase. The challenger flips a fair binary coin b and returns $\mathrm{Enc}(pp, x_b)$ as challenge header.

(iv) Postchallenge Phase: this phase is repeat of prechallenge phase. The adversary issues additional adaptive queries with the restriction where it can not request token of x_0 or x_1.

(v) Guess Phase: finally, $\mathcal{A}$ submits a guess b' of b. The adversary wins if $b' = b$.

Definition 5 (anonymity of AIE). AIE is anonymous if, for any probabilistic polynomial-time algorithm $\mathcal{A}$, its ANON advantage, denoted by

$$\mathrm{Adv}_{\mathcal{A}}^{\mathrm{ANON}}(\lambda) = \left| \Pr\left[b' = b \right] - \frac{1}{2} \right|, \quad (8)$$

is a negligible function of λ, where the probability is over the random bits used by the challenger and the adversary.

5.5. Security Model for Function Privacy.
Formalizing such a notion is not straightforward since adversary can mount a guessing attack. If adversary has some knowledge that the token comes from a small set, it can encapsulate each candidate index and run the legitimate *Test* procedure to learn the function embedded inside the token. We adapt the notion from [20] which requires that $\mathrm{Gen}(mk, y)$ is

indistinguishable from a random token if y is chosen from a sufficiently high min-entropy distribution. The following security game parameterized by a distribution D helps us capture properties of function privacy:

(i) Setup Phase: the challenger runs $\mathrm{Setup}(1^\lambda)$ and sends both master secret key mk and public parameters pp to adversary $\mathcal{A}$.

(ii) Challenge Phase: in this phase, the challenger samples an indices vector $(x_1, x_2, \ldots, x_q)$ from the distribution $\mathbf{D}$ and then, for every $i \in \{1, 2, \ldots, n\}$, computes $tk_i = \mathrm{Gen}(mk, x_i)$ and returns $(tk_1, \ldots, tk_q)$ to $\mathcal{A}$.

(iii) Guess Phase: finally, $\mathcal{A}$ submits a guess of the distribution challenger has used. It outputs "0" standing for uniform distribution; otherwise it outputs "1."

Definition 6 (privacy of AIE). AIE says private function if, for any probabilistic polynomial-time algorithm $\mathcal{A}$ and any (q, k)-block-source distribution D where q, k is a polynomial of λ, its PRIV advantage, denoted by

$$\mathrm{Adv}_{\mathcal{A}}^{\mathrm{PRIV}}(\lambda) = \left| \Pr\left[\Psi_D(\lambda) = 1 \right] - \Pr\left[\Psi_R(\lambda) = 1 \right] \right|, \quad (9)$$

is a negligible function of λ where R stands for uniform distribution.

To gain reasonable high min-entropy in anonymous CCN, we suggest that data provider should assign a complicated name of the encrypted data. Since adversary can mount a guessing attack (exhaustively testing the token by using pairings), the definition of privacy actually guarantees that there is no more obviously effective attack better than the brute force method.

6. Proof of Anonymity

We use reduction to prove anonymity of our scheme under the DBDH assumption.

Lemma 7. *Suppose there is an adversary $\mathcal{A}$ that can win the anonymity game with advantage $\epsilon(\lambda)$. Then there is an algorithm $\mathcal{B}$ which solves the DBDH problem with advantage $\epsilon(\lambda)$.*

Given a tuple $(g_\alpha, g_\beta, g_\gamma, Z)$, which is either sampled from $\mathcal{P}_{\mathrm{BDH}}$ or from $\mathcal{R}_{\mathrm{BDH}}$, algorithm $\mathcal{B}$ interacts with adversary $\mathcal{A}$ as follows.

Setup Phase. $\mathcal{B}$ sets up public parameter $pp = g_\alpha$.

Programming the Random Oracle. $\mathcal{B}$ simulates the random oracle for $\mathcal{A}$ as follows.

If the same query is repeated twice, then the same return value is provided, on issuing a fresh query for $H(x)$, and $\mathcal{B}$

(1) samples $t_1 \leftarrow \mathbb{Z}_p^*, t_2 \leftarrow \mathbb{Z}_p^*$,
(2) stores tuple (x, t_1, t_2) in table L_H,
(3) returns $H(x) = (g_\beta)^{t_1} g^{t_2}$,

On issuing a fresh query for $F(x)$, $\mathcal{B}$

(1) samples $t_3 \leftarrow \mathbb{Z}_p^*, t_4 \leftarrow \mathbb{Z}_p^*$,
(2) stores tuple (x, t_3, t_4) in table L_F,
(3) returns $F(x) = (g_\beta)^{t_3} g^{t_4}$.

Prechallenge Phase. On $\mathcal{A}$ issuing a token for index y, algorithm $\mathcal{B}$ does the following:

(1) If the same query for y is repeated twice, then the same token is provided.
(2) If $\mathcal{A}$ has not made a query for $H(y)$ and/or $F(y)$, it programs $H(y)$ and/or $F(y)$ as mentioned above.
(3) It retrieves (y, t_1, t_2) from L_H and (y, t_3, t_4) from L_F.
(4) It samples $u \leftarrow \mathbb{Z}_p^*$ and computes $v \leftarrow -u \cdot t_1/t_3$. That is, it randomly samples u and v such that $u \cdot t_1 + v \cdot t_2 = 0$.
(5) It computes $d \leftarrow (g_\alpha)^{u t_2 + v t_4}$.
(6) It returns (d, u, v).

Correctness of Simulation. We argue that (d, u, v) is always a proper token corresponding to y since

$$\left(H(y)^u F(y)^v \right)^\alpha = \left(\left(g_\beta^{t_1} g^{t_2} \right)^u \left(g_\beta^{t_3} g^{t_4} \right)^v \right)^\alpha$$

$$= \left(\left(g_\beta^{u t_1 + v t_3} \right) g^{u t_2 + v t_4} \right)^\alpha = g_\alpha^{u t_2 + v t_4} \quad (10)$$

$$= d.$$

Challenge Phase. After $\mathcal{A}$ sends x_0 and x_1, algorithm $\mathcal{B}$ does the following:

(1) It picks a random bit $b \leftarrow \{0, 1\}$.
(2) If $\mathcal{A}$ has not made a query for $H(x_b)$ and/or $F(x_b)$, it programs $H(x_b)$ and/or $F(x_b)$ as mentioned above.
(3) It retrieves (x_b, s_1, s_2) from L_H and (x_b, s_3, s_4) from L_F.
(4) It computes $c \leftarrow g_\gamma$, $T \leftarrow Z^{s_1} e(g_\alpha, g_\gamma)^{s_2}$, $W \leftarrow Z^{s_3} e(g_\alpha, g_\gamma)^{s_4}$.
(5) It returns (c, T, W) as challenge header.

Postchallenge Phase. $\mathcal{B}$ responds as before in prechallenge phase.

Guess Phase. Finally $\mathcal{A}$ outputs a guess b' of b. $\mathcal{B}$ concludes its own game by outputting a guess as follows. if $b' = b$, $\mathcal{B}$ returns 1, else returns 0.

Analysis of $\mathcal{B}$'s Behavior. Denote $\gamma = \log_g g_\gamma$. If Z is sampled from $\mathscr{P}_{\text{BDH}}$, that is, $Z = e(g_\alpha, g_\beta)^\gamma$, then (c, T, W) is a perfectly legitimate header of x_b since

$$e(g_\alpha, H(x))^\gamma = e\left(g_\alpha, g_\beta^{s_1} g^{s_2} \right)^\gamma$$

$$= \left(e(g_\alpha, g_\beta)^\gamma \right)^{s_1} e(g_\alpha, g^{s_2})^\gamma$$

$$= Z^{s_1} e(g_\alpha, g_\gamma)^{s_2} = T,$$

$$e(g_\alpha, F(x))^\gamma = e\left(g_\alpha, g_\beta^{s_3} g^{s_4} \right)^\gamma$$

$$= \left(e(g_\alpha, g_\beta)^\gamma \right)^{s_3} e(g_\alpha, g^{s_4})^\gamma$$

$$= Z^{s_3} e(g_\alpha, g_\gamma)^{s_4} = W. \quad (11)$$

Therefore, $\mathcal{B}$ simulates a perfect environment of $\mathcal{A}$, and the probability of the event $\mathcal{A}$ winning the game is identical to ϵ. However, when Z is uniformly random, the challenge header will not be legitimate. This is not a problem, and indeed it is crucial to the proof of security.

Lemma 8. *If Z is sampled from uniform random, the distribution of b is independent of the adversary's view, so the probability of event $\mathcal{A}$ winning the game is identical to $1/2$.*

Proof. Consider the joint distribution of the adversary's view. Note that the adversary is not allowed to make a token query for x_0 and x_1; from his view, only $H(x_b), F(x_b), T$, and W may leak information about b. What we need to prove is that, for any fixed $g_\alpha, g_\beta, g_\gamma, T, W, H(x_0), F(x_0), H(x_1)$, and $F(x_1)$,

$$\Pr \begin{bmatrix} Z^{r_1} e(g_\alpha, g_\gamma)^{r_2} = T \\ Z^{r_3} e(g_\alpha, g_\gamma)^{r_4} = W \\ g_\beta^{r_1} g^{r_2} = H(x_0) \\ g_\beta^{r_3} g^{r_4} = F(x_0) \end{bmatrix}$$

$$= \Pr \begin{bmatrix} Z^{r_1} e(g_\alpha, g_\gamma)^{r_2} = T \\ Z^{r_3} e(g_\alpha, g_\gamma)^{r_4} = W \\ g_\beta^{r_1} g^{r_2} = H(x_1) \\ g_\beta^{r_3} g^{r_4} = F(x_1) \end{bmatrix}, \quad (12)$$

where the probability is over r_1, r_2, r_3, r_4, and Z. That is clear because the four equations are linearly independent since, for any fixed T, W, f, and h,

$$\Pr \begin{bmatrix} Z^{r_1} e(g_\alpha, g_\gamma)^{r_2} = T \\ Z^{r_3} e(g_\alpha, g_\gamma)^{r_4} = W \\ g_\beta^{r_1} g^{r_2} = h \\ g_\beta^{r_3} g^{r_4} = f \end{bmatrix} = \frac{1}{|\mathbb{G}|^2}. \quad (13)$$

That concludes that $\mathcal{A}$ learns nothing about b. $\square$

To summarize, when the input tuple is sampled from $\mathscr{P}_{\text{BDH}}$, then adversary's view is identical to its view in a real security game and therefore $\mathcal{A}$ satisfies $|\Pr[b' = b] - 1/2| \geq \epsilon$.

When the input tuple is sampled from $\mathscr{R}_{\mathrm{BDH}}$, then $\Pr[b' = b] = 1/2$. Therefore, we have that

$$
\begin{aligned}
\mathrm{Adv}_{\mathscr{B}}^{\mathrm{DBDH}}(\lambda) \\
= \left| \Pr\left[\mathscr{B}\left(\mathscr{P}_{\mathrm{BDH}}\right) = 1\right] - \Pr\left[\mathscr{B}\left(\mathscr{R}_{\mathrm{BDH}}\right) = 1\right] \right| \\
\geq \left| \left(\frac{1}{2} \pm \epsilon\right) - \frac{1}{2} \right| = \epsilon.
\end{aligned}
\tag{14}
$$

We present our conclusion as the following statement.

Theorem 9. *The AIE scheme one proposed is anonymous, assuming the DBDH assumption holds for the bilinear group generated by GroupGen.*

7. Proof of Function Privacy

Proof. Denote View_D by the distribution of $\mathscr{A}$'s view in the game $\Psi_D(\lambda)$ and View_R by the distribution of $\mathscr{A}$'s view in the game $\Psi_R(\lambda)$. We prove that View_D is statistically close to View_R even for arbitrary fixed public parameters.

Suppose $\mathscr{A}$ received tokens corresponding to $(x_1, x_2, \ldots, x_q)$ in the challenge phase. As $\mathscr{A}$ knows the master key and having fixed pp, we can assume that View_D is equivalent to

$$
\left(u_1, v_1, h_1^{u_1} f_1^{v_1}, u_2, v_2, h_2^{u_2} f_2^{v_2}, \ldots, u_q, v_q, h_q^{u_q} f_q^{v_q}\right), \tag{15}
$$

where $h_i = H(x_i)$ and $f_i = F(x_i)$ for each $i \in \{1, \ldots, q\}$.

Without loss of generality, we can assume that H and F are injective since they are modeled as random oracle. Assuming that H and F are injective guarantees that for any (q, k)-block-source X over $\{0, 1\}^{\lambda q}$ the fact that $((h_1, f_1), \ldots, (h_q, f_q))$ is also a (q, k)-block-source over $\mathbb{G}^{2q}$ holds.

Note that the collection of functions $\{g_{u,v} : \mathbb{G}^2 \to \mathbb{G}\}_{u,v \in \mathbb{Z}_p^*}$ defined by $g_{u,v}(h, f) = h^u f^v$ are universal (see [26]). This enables us to directly apply the leftover hash lemma on block-source, implying that the statistical distance between View_D and the uniform distribution is negligible in λ. The same holds also for View_R since R is a (q, k)-block-source in particular. This completes the proof of function privacy. $\square$

We present our conclusion as the following statement.

Theorem 10. *The AIE scheme one proposed is (computational) function privacy under random oracle model.*

8. Implementation and Performance

We implement our AIE schema by JPBC Library [27]. JPBC Library provides cryptographic interface to perform the mathematical operations underlying pairing-based cryptosystems. Our experiments were deployed on Intel Xeon E3-1231, a 4-core 3.40 GHz CPU, with 8 GB of RAM. We calculate the average time cost of each algorithm run on security parameters with different length. The result is shown in Table 1.

As we introduced in Section 3, *Setup* is run by the central authority only once, when deploying the environment. When

TABLE 1: Average time cost (ms) of each algorithm.

Length	Setup	Enc	Gen	Test
120	5.41	36.46	39.09	4.61
160	10.08	68.88	74.16	8.08
200	17.47	117.12	127.34	13.84
240	29.04	187.74	207.54	21.08

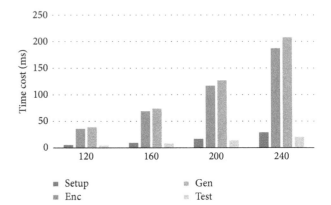

FIGURE 2: Comparison of time cost on 120-, 160-, 200- and 240-bit security parameter over AIE.

the producer generates new content, *Enc* is run by producer once. When a consumer plans to request a content, *Gen* is run by the central authority and *Test* is run by each router. Thus, the extra time a consumer would spend for AIE is no more than $\mathrm{Time}(\mathrm{Gen}) + n \cdot \mathrm{Time}(\mathrm{Test})$, where n represents the hop count. Taking 120-bit security parameter as an example, assuming the hop count is 5 on average [2], the total extra time cost for a consumer is $39.09 + 4.61 \times 5 = 62.14 \, \mathrm{ms}$ on average. AIE schema brings only less than 5 ms latency on each hop.

The relationship between time cost and the length of security parameter is shown in Figure 2. The comparison of four groups of data with different length of security parameter is shown in the graph horizontally. Each bar represents an algorithm in AIE, which is *Setup, Enc, Gen,* and *Test* from left to right. The vertical axis represents the average time cost of each experiment. It concludes that the performance of AIE is satisfying with small size of security parameter. But the time cost increases by a large margin with the increase of security parameter size. However, it is not necessary to choose too large security parameter since no one can break DBDH and CDH assumption up to the present.

Finally we turn to study the stability of our protocols run time. Figures 3 and 4 show time cost of each independent call of *Gen* and *Test* with 240-bit security parameter. x-axis represents the index of each call and y-axis represents the time cost. Each point in the graph represents a result of one experiment. As expected, the result shows most calls of *Gen* and *Test* are very close to the average time cost.

The experimental results are quite different from other approaches [2, 3]. The main time costs of [2, 3] are used in the transmission of data. But since our scheme decouples index from data, the run time costs are used in encapsulating the

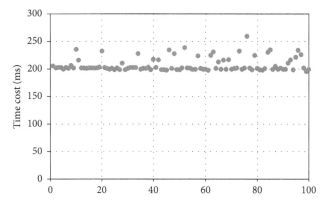

FIGURE 3: Time cost of 100 experiments for *Gen* on 240-bit security parameter.

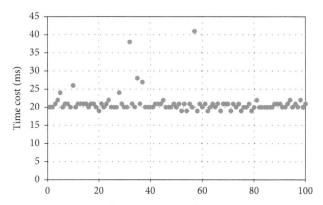

FIGURE 4: Time cost of 100 experiments for *Test* on 240-bit security parameter.

index, and the performance of our scheme can be seen as a negligible constant, which is uncorrelated with the data size.

9. Conclusion

This work presents an initial attempt to provide privacy and anonymity in CCN by cryptographic protocol. We embed AIE scheme in the CCN to provide comparable anonymity with lower relative overhead.

AIE is a new cryptographic primitive. There are at least two differences between Asymmetric Index Encapsulation and PEKS or identity based searchable encryption [13, 20]. Firstly, the goal of AIE scheme is to decouple index hiding and searching procedure from encryption scheme. There are independent application scenarios of index encapsulation. Identity based searchable encryption can be replaced by any combination of AIE and anonymous identity based encryption. Secondly, Asymmetric Index Encapsulation scheme does not imply public key encryption or identity based encryption. There is possibility of getting better security reduction and efficiency.

The security of our scheme relies on the DBDH/CDH assumption in prime-order groups and random oracle. An encapsulated header in our system consists of only three elements, while a token in our system also consists of only three elements. Besides the acceptable efficiency in practice, the scheme has tight security reduction against all kinds of adversaries. (A security reduction is said to be tight when breaking the scheme is exactly as hard as solving the underlying problem.)

We introduce new adversarial models for anonymous CCN. The anonymity model captures the intuitive notion that an adversary should not be able to distinguish between the encapsulated header of two challenge indices of his choice, even if it is allowed to obtain tokens for any other indices. The privacy model requires any token belonging to index x to be indistinguishable from a random token if x is chosen from a sufficiently high min-entropy distribution.

An interesting open problem is to construct AIE schemes for other classes of functions. A possible starting point is to consider simple functionalities, such as wildcard [28] and inner-product testing [29]. Another fascinating open problem is to design a scheme which is secure in the standard model as well as keeping the token size and header size constant. Finally, we leave it as an open problem to design an AIE scheme without pairing.

Disclosure

An extended abstract was presented at Provable Security 10th International Conference, ProvSec 2016 [22].

References

[1] A. Chaabane, E. De Cristofaro, M. A. Kaafar, and E. Uzun, "Privacy in content-oriented networking: threats and counter-measures," *ACM SIGCOMM Computer Communication Review*, vol. 43, no. 3, pp. 25–33, 2013.

[2] S. DiBenedetto, P. Gasti, G. Tsudik, and E. Uzun, "ANDaNA: Anonymous Named Data Networking Application," in *Proceedings of the Proceedings of the Network and Distributed System Security Symposium (NDSS' 12)*, San Diego, Calif, USA, 2012.

[3] G. Tsudik, E. Uzun, and C. A. Wood, "AC3N: Anonymous communication in Content-Centric Networking," in *Proceedings of the 13th IEEE Annual Consumer Communications and Networking Conference, CCNC 2016*, pp. 988–991, Las Vegas, Nev, USA, January 2016.

[4] C. Ghali, G. Tsudik, and C. A. Wood, "(The futility of) data privacy in content-centric networking," in *Proceedings of the 15th ACM Workshop on Privacy in the Electronic Society, WPES 2016*, pp. 143–152, Vienna, Austria, 2016.

[5] P. Gasti, G. Tsudik, E. Uzun, and L. Zhang, "DoS and DDoS in named data networking," in *Proceedings of the 2013 22nd International Conference on Computer Communication and Networks, ICCCN 2013*, Nassau, Bahamas, August 2013.

[6] R. Curtmola, J. Garay, S. Kamara, and R. Ostrovsky, "Searchable symmetric encryption: improved definitions and efficient constructions," *Journal of Computer Security*, vol. 19, no. 5, pp. 895–934, 2011.

[7] E.-J. Goh, *Secure Indexes*, 2004.

[8] S. Kamara, C. Papamanthou, and T. Roeder, "Dynamic searchable symmetric encryption," in *Proceedings of the 2012 ACM Conference on Computer and Communications Security, CCS 2012*, pp. 965–976, USA, October 2012.

[9] D. Cash and S. Tessaro, "The locality of searchable symmetric

encryption," in *Advances in Cryptology – EUROCRYPT 2014*, vol. 8441 of *Lecture Notes in Computer Science*, pp. 351–368, 2014.

[10] J. G. Li, Y. R. Shi, and Y. C. Zhang, "Searchable ciphertext-policy attribute-based encryption with revocation in cloud storage," *International Journal of Communication Systems*, 2015.

[11] J. G. Li, X. N. Lin, Y. C. Zhang, and J. G. Han, "KSF-OABE: outsourced attribute-based encryption with keyword search function for cloud storage," *IEEE Transactions on Services Computing*, vol. PP, no. 99, p. 1, 2016.

[12] M. Bellare, A. Boldyreva, and A. O'Neill, "Deterministic and efficiently searchable encryption," in *Advances in Cryptology - CRYPTO 2007*, vol. 4622 of *Lecture Notes in Computer Science*, pp. 535–552, 2007.

[13] D. Boneh, G. Di Crescenzo, R. Ostrovsky, and G. Persiano, "Public key encryption with keyword search," in *Advances in Cryptology - EUROCRYPT 2004*, vol. 3027 of *Lecture Notes in Computer Science*, pp. 506–522, 2004.

[14] J. Li, Y. Guo, Q. Yu, Y. Lu, and Y. Zhang, "Provably secure identity-based encryption resilient to post-challenge continuous auxiliary input leakage," *Security and Communication Networks*, vol. 9, no. 10, pp. 1016–1024, 2016.

[15] J. Li, M. Teng, Y. Zhang, and Q. Yu, "A leakage-resilient CCA-secure identity-based encryption scheme," *Computer Journal*, vol. 59, no. 7, pp. 1066–1075, 2016.

[16] M. Abdalla, M. Bellare, D. Catalano et al., "Searchable encryption revisited: consistency properties, relation to anonymous IBE, and extensions," *Journal of Cryptology*, vol. 21, no. 3, pp. 350–391, 2008.

[17] J. Camenisch, M. Kohlweiss, A. Rial, and C. Sheedy, "Blind and anonymous identity-based encryption and authorised private searches on public key encrypted data," in *Public Key Cryptography – PKC 2009*, vol. 5443 of *Lecture Notes in Computer Science*, pp. 196–214, 2009.

[18] J. Baek, R. Safavi-Naini, and W. Susilo, "Public key encryption with keyword search revisited," in *Computational Science and Its Applications—ICCSA 2008*, vol. 5072 of *Lecture Notes in Computer Science*, pp. 1249–1259, Springer, Berlin, Germany, 2008.

[19] T. H. Yuen, Y. Zhang, S. M. Yiu, and J. K. Liu, "Identity-based encryption with post-challenge auxiliary inputs for secure cloud applications and sensor networks," in *Computer Security - ESORICS 2014*, vol. 8712 of *Lecture Notes in Computer Science*, pp. 130–147, 2014.

[20] D. Boneh, A. Raghunathan, and G. Segev, "Function-private identity-based encryption: hiding the function in functional encryption," in *Advances in Cryptology – CRYPTO 2013*, vol. 8043 of *Lecture Notes in Computer Science*, pp. 461–478, 2013.

[21] A. Compagno, M. Conti, P. Gasti, and G. Tsudik, "Poseidon: Mitigating interest flooding DDoS attacks in named data networking," in *Proceedings of the 38th Annual IEEE Conference on Local Computer Networks, LCN 2013*, pp. 630–638, Sydney, NSW, Australia, October 2013.

[22] R. Ma and Z. Cao, "Efficient asymmetric index encapsulation scheme for named data," in *Provable Security*, vol. 10005 of *Lecture Notes in Computer Science*, pp. 191–203, 2016.

[23] C. Ghali, A. Narayanan, D. Oran, G. Tsudik, and C. A. Wood, "Secure fragmentation for content-centric networks," in *Proceedings of the IEEE 14th International Symposium on Network Computing and Applications (NCA '15)*, pp. 47–56, Cambridge, Mass, USA, September 2015.

[24] D. Boneh and M. Franklin, "Identity-based encryption from the Weil pairing," *SIAM Journal on Computing*, vol. 32, no. 3, pp. 586–615, 2003.

[25] J.-S. Coron, "A variant of Boneh-Franklin IBE with a tight reduction in the random oracle model," *Designs, Codes and Cryptography*, vol. 50, no. 1, pp. 115–133, 2009.

[26] J. L. Carter and M. N. Wegman, "Universal classes of hash functions," *Journal of Computer and System Sciences*, vol. 18, no. 2, pp. 143–154, 1979.

[27] A. de Caro and V. Iovino, "jPBC: Java pairing based cryptography," in *Proceedings of the 16th IEEE Symposium on Computers and Communications (ISCC '11)*, pp. 850–855, July 2011.

[28] M. Abdalla, J. Birkett, D. Catalano et al., "Wildcarded identity-based encryption," *Journal of Cryptology*, vol. 24, no. 1, pp. 42–82, 2011.

[29] J. Katz, A. Sahai, and B. Waters, "Predicate encryption supporting disjunctions, polynomial equations, and inner products," *Journal of Cryptology*, vol. 26, no. 2, pp. 191–224, 2013.

12

GA-DoSLD: Genetic Algorithm based Denial-of-Sleep Attack Detection in WSN

Mahalakshmi Gunasekaran[1] and Subathra Periakaruppan[2]

[1]Department of Computer Science and Engineering, NPR College of Engineering and Technology, Tamil Nadu 624001, India
[2]Department of Information Technology, Kamaraj College of Engineering & Technology, Tamil Nadu, India

Correspondence should be addressed to Mahalakshmi Gunasekaran; mahalakshmiit15@hotmail.com

Academic Editor: Qing Yang

Denial-of-sleep (DoSL) attack is a special category of denial-of-service attack that prevents the battery powered sensor nodes from going into the sleep mode, thus affecting the network performance. The existing schemes used for the DoSL attack detection do not provide an optimal energy conservation and key pairing operation. Hence, in this paper, an efficient Genetic Algorithm (GA) based denial-of-sleep attack detection (GA-DoSLD) algorithm is suggested for analyzing the misbehaviors of the nodes. The suggested algorithm implements a Modified-RSA (MRSA) algorithm in the base station (BS) for generating and distributing the key pair among the sensor nodes. Before sending/receiving the packets, the sensor nodes determine the optimal route using Ad Hoc On-Demand Distance Vector Routing (AODV) protocol and then ensure the trustworthiness of the relay node using the fitness calculation. The crossover and mutation operations detect and analyze the methods that the attackers use for implementing the attack. On determining an attacker node, the BS broadcasts the blocked information to all the other sensor nodes in the network. Simulation results prove that the suggested algorithm is optimal compared to the existing algorithms such as X-MAC, ZKP, and TE$_2$P schemes.

1. Introduction

Wireless Sensor Network (WSN) contains a collection of self-governing sensors that monitors the conditions such as sound, temperature, pressure, and vibration [1]. The sensor nodes in the WSN are energized using the batteries. But, one of the major issues of WSN is energy loss. It is caused due to the following reasons [2]:

(i) Collisions

(ii) Overhearing

(iii) Idle listening

(iv) Control packet overhead

In the collision loss, the collision of data packets in the wireless medium introduces the energy loss. In the overhearing loss, the maintenance of radios in the receiving mode during data packet transmission introduces the energy loss. The idle listening loss is created by a node's radio in just monitoring the channel. As the control packets may have to be received by all the nodes in the transmission range, the control packet overhead is introduced. Generally, the WSN is prone to two types of attacks such as invasive attack and noninvasive attack. The noninvasive attacks affect the power, frequency, and timing of the channel, whereas the invasive attacks affect the information transmission, routing process, and service availability [3]. Among the attacks of WSN, the denial-of-service attacks make the system or service inaccessible. The important properties of the DoSL attacks are

(i) malicious,

(ii) disruptive,

(iii) remote.

When the denial-of-service attack is performed intentionally, it is termed as malicious. When the DoSL attack is successful, the capability or service in WSN is affected. Thus, disrupting the affected service is not the only goal of the attacker.

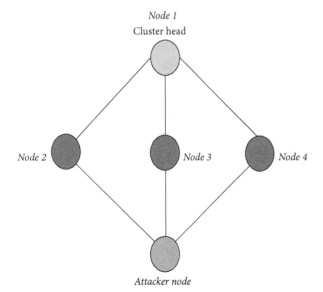

Node 1
Cluster head

Node 2   *Node 3*   *Node 4*

Attacker node

FIGURE 1: Denial-of-sleep attack [2].

As the physical presence of the attacker is uncomfortable for launching multiple types of DoSL attacks, the attack is performed from a remote place. One of the special categories of denial-of-service attack is DoSL attack.

An example of the DoSL attack is represented in Figure 1. In this attack, the energy consumption of the sensor nodes is increased by preventing them from sleeping. The attacker node can forward the fake data packets to the authorized nodes, thus resulting in unnecessary transmissions. On receiving the data packets, if the receiver could not identify the source, it will process the data obtained from the attacker nodes.

This makes the receiver node to be awake till the data transmission gets completed, thus exhausting the battery power of the nodes. Further, the attacker nodes can transmit a false acknowledgment and make the source node transmit all the services, thus maximizing the power consumption. The existing components used for defending the DoSL attack are as follows [2]:

(i) Strong link-layer authentication

(ii) Antireplay protection

(iii) Jamming identification

(iv) Broadcast attack protection

The strong layer authentication is a key component of the DoSL defense. On integrating this component to the WSN, the DoSL attacks can be prevented efficiently. The antireplay protection component is used for preventing the replay attacks that force the nodes to forward the old traffic information. The jamming identification component is used for preventing the jamming attack that prevents the sensor nodes from accessing the wireless medium. This component integrates the sensor nodes with the simple radios. Generally, the MAC protocols are prone to unauthenticated broadcast attacks. The broadcast attack protection technique

differentiates the legitimate traffic from the malicious traffic for minimizing the energy consumption. But, the demerits of the existing DoSL defense mechanisms are nonoptimal energy conservation and lack of key pairing operations for preventing the attacker from implementing the attack. Thus, to address the issues in the existing DoSL defense schemes, an efficient GA-DoSLD algorithm is suggested.

Objectives. The key objectives of the suggested GA-DoSLD are as follows:

(i) To analyze the neighbor information for creating the population

(ii) To perform the key pairing using MRSA algorithm

(iii) To deploy the AODV protocol for determining the optimal route

(iv) To determine the behavior of the already existing attacker by estimating the fitness value

(v) To provide an alert message to the base station regarding the behavior of the neighbor node

(vi) To broadcast the blocked information to other sensor nodes in the network

The rest of the paper is organized as follows. Section 2 discusses the existing techniques used for detecting the DoSL attacks, energy draining attacks, and soft computing algorithms exploited for addressing the energy draining attacks. Section 3 provides a detailed description of the proposed GA-DoSLD algorithm. Section 4 discusses the experimental analysis of the proposed method and the study is concluded in Section 5.

2. Related Works

This section illustrates the existing techniques used for DoS attack detection, energy draining attacks, and soft computing algorithms used for addressing the energy draining attacks.

2.1. Detection of DoS Attacks in WSN. Mansouri et al. [4] proposed a clustering technique for addressing the DoS attacks. The suggested technique exploited the energy consumption of the nodes. Mansouri et al. [5] detected the compromised nodes in WSN using energy-preserving solution. The suggested algorithm detected the controlled nodes (Cnode) using a hierarchical clustering technique. Experimental results proved that the suggested technique achieved optimal energy balance, throughput, detection coverage, and delay between the packet transmissions. Chen et al. [6] proposed a time-division secret key protocol for detecting the DoS attack. The simulation results proved that the cipher function was optimal for WSN. Further, the detection jamming scheme increased the network lifetime of the WSN. He et al. [7] suggested a distributed code dissemination protocol, namely, DiCode, for detecting the DoS attacks. The demerits of the suggested protocol were nonoptimal security properties and consequences on the network availability. Han et al. [8] proposed an Intrusion Detection System based Energy Prediction (IDSEP) for the cluster-based WSN. The suggested scheme exploited the energy consumption of the sensor nodes for detecting the malicious nodes. Further, based on the energy consumption thresholds, the categories of the DoS attacks were determined. Simulation results proved that the suggested IDSEP efficiently detected the malicious nodes. Ram Pradheep Manohar [9] proposed the Slowly Increasing and Decreasing under Constraint DoS Attack Strategy (SIDCAS) for detecting the Stealthy DoS (S-DoS) attacks in WSN. In addition to providing security, the suggested approach also decreased the resource maintenance cost. Tan et al. [10] suggested a Deluge based multihop code dissemination protocol for enhancing the confidentiality of the WSN. Experimental results proved that the suggested approach provided optimal latency, dissemination rate, and energy consumption.

2.2. Energy Draining Attacks. Nam and Cho [11] suggested a Statistical En-Route Filtering (SEF) scheme for detecting the false reports in the intermediate nodes. Further, the false report injection attack was defended using three types of keys such as individual key, pairwise key, and cluster key. The comparison of SEF with the suggested method proved that the proposed method enhanced the energy savings than the SEF in sensor networks. Manju et al. [1] suggested three steps such as network organization, malicious node detection, and selective authentication for detecting the denial-of-sleep attack in WSN. Experimental results proved that the suggested method was optimal for defending the attacker from performing the task. Naik and Shekokar [12] addressed the denial-of-sleep attack using zero knowledge protocol and interlock protocol. Experimental results proved that the suggested protocols prevented the replay attack and man-in-the-middle attack and also minimized the resource consumption. Hsueh et al. [13] suggested a cross-layer design of secure scheme with MAC protocol for minimizing the energy consumption of the sensor nodes. Analysis results proved that the suggested protocol efficiently defended the replay attacks and forge attacks. Further, the security requirements and energy conservation were coordinated. Kaur and Ataullah [14] suggested a hierarchical clustering based isolation of nodes for addressing the denial-of-sleep attack. The suggested approach enhanced the network lifetime, but the idle listening problem was unaddressed. Hsueh et al. [13] proposed a cross-layer design of secure scheme integrated with MAC protocol for defending against the replay attack and forge attack. Experimental results proved that the suggested protocol coordinated the energy conservation and security requirements.

2.3. Soft Computing Algorithms Used for Addressing the Energy Draining Attack. Shamshirband et al. [15] proposed a Density-Based Fuzzy Imperialist Competitive Clustering Algorithm (D-FICCA) for detecting the intruders in WSN. When compared to the existing algorithms, the proposed algorithm produced 87% detection accuracy and 0.99 clustering quality. Shamshirband et al. [16] suggested a cooperative Game-Based Fuzzy Q-Learning (G-FQL) approach for detecting the intrusions in the WSN. The suggested model deployed the cooperative defense counterattack scenario for

the sink node and game theory strategy for the base station nodes. When compared to the Low Energy Adaptive Clustering Hierarchy (LEACH), the suggested model produced optimal detection accuracy, counterdefense, energy consumption, and network lifetime. Further, when compared to the existing machine learning methods, the suggested model provided enhanced detection and defense accuracy. Sreelaja and Vijayalakshmi Pai [17] suggested an Ant Colony Optimization Attack Detection (ACO-AD) algorithm for detecting the sinkhole attacks in WSN. The keys were distributed among the alerted nodes using Ant Colony Optimization Boolean Expression Evolver Sign Generation (ABXES) algorithm. Experimental results proved that when compared to the existing LIDeA architecture, the suggested architecture minimized the false positives and also minimized the storage in the sensor nodes. Keerthana and Padmavathi [18] suggested an Enhanced Particle Swarm Optimization (EPSO) technique for detecting the sinkhole attacks in WSN. When compared to the existing ACO and PSO algorithms, the suggested algorithm provided optimal packet delivery ratio, message drop, average delay, and false alarm rate. Saeed et al. [19] suggested a Random Neural Network based IDS for detecting the attackers. Experimental results proved that the suggested IDS provided higher accuracy and reduced performance overhead.

From the analysis of the existing techniques, it is clear that they do not address the idle listening problem. Further, the solutions suggested for preventing the DoSL attacks are unrealistic. Thus, to address the issues in the existing techniques, an efficient GA-DoSLD algorithm is proposed.

3. Proposed Method

This section describes the proposed GA-DoSLD algorithm for analyzing the misbehaviors of the sensor nodes in WSN. The overall flow of the suggested algorithm is represented in Figure 2.

From the figure, it is clear that the key steps involved in the suggested algorithm are as follows:

   (i) WSN initialization

   (ii) Population generation

   (iii) Generation and distribution of key pair

   (iv) Route discovery

   (v) Behavior monitoring

A detailed description of every step is provided in the following sections.

3.1. WSN Initialization. The initial step involved in the suggested approach is WSN initialization. By exploiting the NS2 tool, the WSN is initialized with 100 numbers of sensor nodes that have random waypoint mobility model. The transmission range of the WSN is 250 meters. Further, the initialized WSN poses the specifications listed in Table 1.

3.2. Population Generation and BS Configuration. Once the WSN environment is initialized, the suggested GA-DoSLD

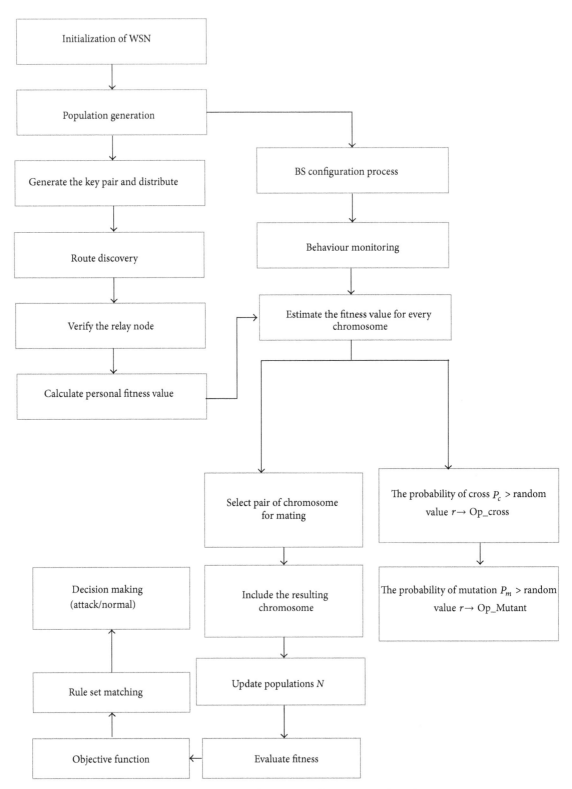

FIGURE 2: Overall flow of the proposed GA-DoSLD algorithm.

TABLE 1: System specifications.

Simulation parameters	Values
Packet size	1024 Kbps
Packet rate	Random packets/sec
Routing protocol	AODV
Channel bit rate	10 MB/s
Initial power	25 J
Sensor node sensing power	5×10^{-8} J
Transmission range	150–250 meters
Duty cycle	20-time slots

algorithm generates the population using population generation algorithm. The suggested algorithm initially loads the two-hop neighbor information to the base station; then for every member in the neighbor list, the next-of-neighbor is initialized as the population. The steps involved in the suggested algorithm are illustrated as follows.

Algorithm 1 (population generation algorithm).

Step 1. Load the two-hop neighbor information with the base station.

Step 2

 for (member in the neighbor list)

  {

   Population ← Load_Individual (new neighbor (next-of-neighbor))

  }

During the implementation of the population generation algorithm, the BS configuration process is performed in parallel for analyzing the behavior of the nodes in the WSN.

3.3. Generation and Distribution of Key Pair. After the generation of the population, the BS deploys the MRSA algorithm for generating a public key and private key pair. Among the keys, the public key is used for the BS and the private key is used for the sensor nodes. The main objective of this step is to prevent the attacker from implementing the DoSL attack. By deploying this step, the attacker node is blocked at the initial level before sending or receiving the packet, thus saving the energy of the sensor nodes. The steps involved in the suggested algorithm are illustrated as follows [20].

Algorithm 2 (MRSA algorithm).

Step 1. Choose the large prime numbers "n" and "r."

Step 2. Compute the modulus totient using

$$\Phi(a) = (n-1) * (r-1). \tag{1}$$

Step 3. Choose the public exponent "i" such that $1 < i < \Phi(n)$ and $GCD(i, \Phi(a)) = 1$.

Step 4. Estimate the private exponent "m" such that $m = i^{-1} \bmod \Phi(a)$.

Step 5. Estimate the private key as (m, a).

Step 6. Estimate the public key as (i, a).

The suggested MRSA algorithm has a key size of 512 bits. Among the total number of bits, 256 bits are used as the public key in the base station and the remaining 256 bits are used as the private key in the sensor nodes. The minimal key size provides the following advantages:

 (i) Minimal computational complexity

 (ii) Achieving memory optimization

3.4. Route Discovery and Relay Node Validation. Before initiating the packet transmission, the sensor nodes determine the optimal route using Ad Hoc On-Demand Distance Vector (AODV) routing protocol. An example of the route discovery process is represented in Figure 3. The suggested protocol has two key operations such as route discovery and route maintenance. When the source node demands a route to the destination node or when the lifetime of the existing route to the destination node has expired, the route discovery operation is initiated with the broadcast of the RREQ messages. On receiving the RREQ messages, the intermediate nodes provide an optimal route to the destination node. When the intermediate node is the destination node, the RREP packets are directly transferred to the source node.

The steps involved in the suggested AODV based route discovery are described as follows.

Algorithm 3 (AODV routing protocol).

Step 1. When a sensor node seeks a route, the RREQ packet is propagated through the entire network till the packet reaches the destination node.

Step 2. When the source node and destination nodes are placed at the corners of the network, the RREQ packets have to travel a maximum number of hops.

Step 3. On receiving the RREQ packets, the relay nodes broadcast it ahead till it reaches the destination.

Step 4. The overhead created due to the route request process is represented as follows:

$$R_{RREQ} = \sum_{a-1}^{N} (H) E^{N-1} \sum_{b=2}^{H} \left[(a-1-b) - \sum_{c=1}^{N-1} R_c \right] PC_b. \tag{2}$$

Step 5. Once the RREQ packet reaches the destination node, it replies back to the source node as RREP packet through the same sequence for reaching the source node.

Step 6. According to [21], the overhead created for the RREP packets is represented as follows:

$$R_{RREP} = N + \frac{N}{2}(a - h - 2)p. \tag{3}$$

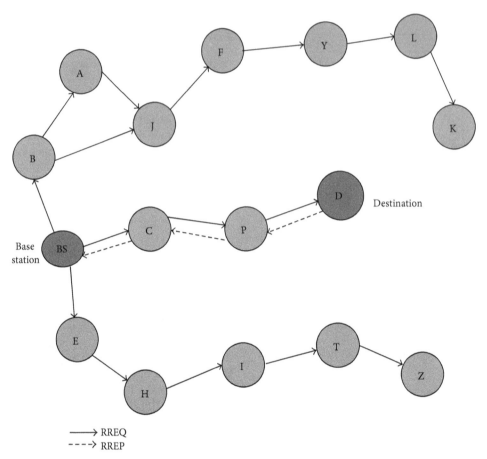

FIGURE 3: Example for the route discovery process using AODV.

Step 7. The overall overhead introduced for the route discovery process is

$$R_{\text{Overall}} = \text{RREQ} + \text{RREP},$$

$$R_{\text{Overall}} = \sum_{a-1}^{N} (H) E^{N-1} \sum_{b=2}^{H} \left[(a-1-b) - \sum_{c=1}^{N-1} R_c \right] PC_b \quad (4)$$

$$+ N + \frac{N}{2} (a - h - 2) p.$$

The merits of using the AODV routing protocol for the route discovery process are as follows:

(i) Loop-free routes

(ii) Faster response to link breakage

(iii) Minimal demand for the broadcast

After establishing an optimal route, the sensor nodes estimate the trustworthiness of the neighbor nodes using fitness evaluation function.

3.5. Behavior Monitoring. After ensuring the trustworthiness of the neighbor nodes, the sensor nodes forward the packets. During the transmission, if the sensor node suspects any

malicious behaviors as follows, it estimates the fitness value based on the information provided by the BS:

(i) Flooding of data packets

(ii) Transmission of large sized data packets that exceed the data capacity of the sensor nodes

By estimating the fitness value based on attacker ID, the chromosome of the already existing attacker is determined. After estimating the fitness value, the sensor nodes provide alert messages about the neighbor node behavior to the BS. On receiving the alert message, the BS performs the crossover and mutation operations on the chromosomes for identifying and analyzing the method that is used by the attacker for implementing the attack. The resultant chromosomes obtained from the crossover and mutation operation are added to the existing population. Finally, the BS confirms whether the particular neighbor node is a normal node or an attacker node. If the BS determines the neighbor node as an attacker node, then the BS broadcasts the blocked information to all the other sensor nodes in the WSN. By exploiting the suggested GA-DoSLD algorithm, the attacker nodes that introduce the DoSL attacks are eliminated from the communication, thus saving the energy of the sensor nodes. Notations describe the symbols used in Algorithm 4 for the proposed GA-DoSLD. The steps involved in the suggested GA-DoSLD algorithm are illustrated below.

Algorithm 4 (GA-DoSLD algorithm).

Input. Population.

Output. Optimal population with fitness value.

Step 1. Compute the index of individuals:

Individual ← Random member (population)

Initialize the array of fittest as empty

For (node in population)

{

If (Fittest.getFitness() = getIndividual(node).getFitness())

{

$$Fittest = getIndividual (node); \tag{5}$$

}

}

Individuals [index] = Fittest;

Step 2. Compute fitness function:

Load member, population

Compute the weight accuracy (W_{ac}) and relative accuracy (R_{ac})

Compute the occurrences of weight (W_{oc}) and relative weight (R_{oc})

$$Fitness = W_{ac} * accuracy \ of \ m \ hop + W_{oc}$$
$$* occurrence \ of \ m \ hop, \tag{6}$$
$$Fitness = (W_1 + W_2) * af + (-W_2) * R_{oc}.$$

Step 3. Execute reproduction:

Initialize the new_pop as an empty set

//select the random member in the input population based on fitness function

For (i = 1; i ≤ maximum size of population; i + +)

{

X ← Random selected member in population based on fitness function

Y ← Random selected member in population based on fitness function

Find the parent profiles of (X, Y)

Len. X ← length (X)

Len. Y ← length (Y)

c = Select random number between 1 and Len. X

new_chromosome
$$= (substring (X, 1, c), \ substring (Y, 1, c)) \tag{7}$$

Set offspring as new_chromosome

Step 4. Population Update:

If (random probability to mutate ≥ threshold)

off spring ⟵ Mutates (off spring)

Set new population
$$⟵ Union (new \ population, \{offspring\}) \tag{8}$$

End do

Population ← Union (new population, new_pop)

Return Best (Population, Fitness)

4. Performance Analysis

This section describes the performance results of the proposed GA-DoSLD algorithm for the following metrics:

(i) Normalized energy consumption

(ii) Effective packet number

(iii) End-to-end delay

(iv) Average energy consumption

(v) Packet delivery ratio

(vi) Throughput ratio versus packet rate

To prove the superiority of the proposed GA-DoSLD algorithm, it is compared with the existing algorithms such as zero knowledge protocol (ZKP) [22], X-MAC, and Two-Tier Energy-Efficient Secure (TE$_2$S) scheme [23] and their results are discussed in the following sections.

4.1. Normalized Energy Consumption. Normalized energy consumption is the amount of energy consumed for transferring 3 packets per second. The normalized energy consumption of the existing X-MAC algorithm, ZKP, TE$_2$P scheme, and the proposed GA-DoSLD algorithm is validated for multiple intervals of attack. The comparison result represented in Figure 4 depicts that, for all the attack intervals, the suggested GA-DoSLD algorithm consumes minimal energy.

4.2. Effective Packet Number. The effective packet number of the existing X-MAC algorithm, ZKP, TE$_2$S scheme, and the proposed GA-DoSLD algorithm is validated for the variable attack intervals. The comparison considers the packet sending rate as 1 packet every 3 seconds. The comparison result represented in Figure 5 shows that the suggested GA-DoSLD algorithm provides higher scores on effective packet number than the existing schemes.

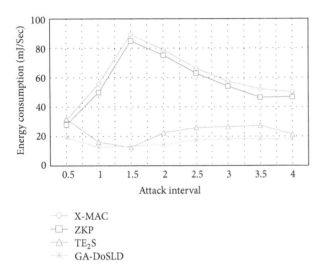

FIGURE 4: Comparison of normalized energy consumption for the existing and the proposed methods.

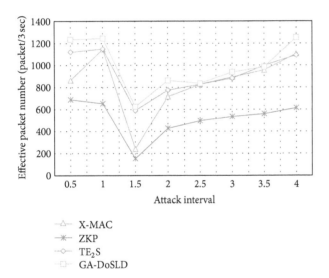

FIGURE 5: Comparison of packet number versus attack interval.

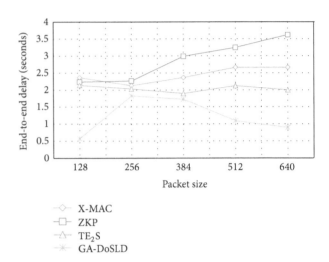

FIGURE 6: Comparison of end-to-end delay versus packet size for the existing and the proposed methods.

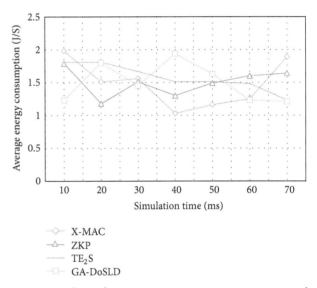

FIGURE 7: Analysis of average energy consumption versus simulation time for the existing and the proposed methods.

4.3. End-to-End Delay. The end-to-end delay is defined as the average time consumed for transmitting the packets. The analysis of end-to-end delay with respect to the packet size is represented in Figure 6. From the figure, it is clear that, when compared to existing X-MAC, ZKP, and TE$_2$S algorithms, the suggested GA-DoSLD algorithm provides a minimal end-to-end delay for the variable packet sizes.

4.4. Average Energy Consumption. The average energy consumption is the amount of energy consumed by the algorithms for transmitting the data packets. The comparison of average energy consumption for the existing X-MAC, ZKP, TE$_2$S schemes, and the proposed GA-DoSLD algorithm is represented in Figure 7. From the figure, it is clear that the suggested GA-DoSLD algorithm provides minimal energy consumption than the existing schemes.

4.5. Packet Delivery Ratio. The packet delivery ratio (PDR) is defined as the ratio of the number of data packets successfully delivered to the destination node to the number of data packets transmitted from the source. The estimation of the PDR is based on the following equation:

$$\text{PDR} = \frac{P_R * 100}{\sum_{a-1}^{n} P_{\text{Gen}_a}}, \tag{9}$$

where P_R represents the number of data packets received at the destination node, P_{Gen} is the total number of data packets generated by the source nodes, and n denotes the number of sensor nodes. The comparison of PDR with respect to simulation time is represented in Figure 8.

From the figure, it is analyzed that, when compared to the existing X-MAC, ZKP, and TE$_2$S schemes, the proposed GA-DoSLD algorithm provides higher PDR.

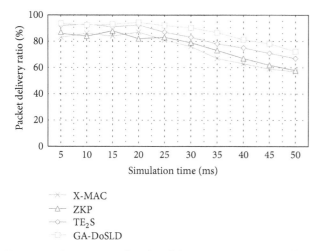

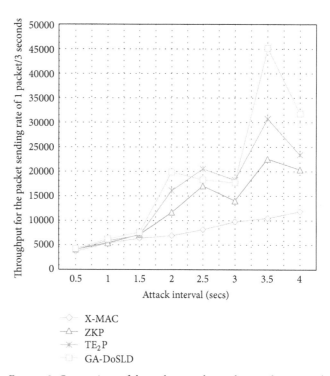

FIGURE 8: Comparison of packet delivery ratio versus simulation time for the existing and proposed schemes.

FIGURE 9: Comparison of throughput under packet sending rate of 1 packet/3 seconds versus attack interval.

4.6. Throughput Performance for Various Packet Sending Rates. The effectiveness of the protocol depends on the successful reception and transmission of data packets under the various sending rates such as 1 packet/3 seconds, 1 packet/5 seconds, and 1 packet/7 seconds [22]. In this paper, the packet sending rate of 1 packet/3 seconds is taken to validate the performance of proposed work. The estimation of the throughput ratio is based on the following equation:

$$\text{Throughput ratio} = \frac{P_{\text{NS}}}{P_{\text{NT}}}, \tag{10}$$

where P_{NS} denotes the packet number under simulation scenario and P_{NT} represents the packet number delivered under the theoretical scenario. The superiority of the suggested GA-DoSLD algorithm is validated against the existing algorithms such as X-MAC, ZKP, and TE$_2$P for a packer rate of 1 packet per 3 seconds. Figure 9 represents the comparison of the throughput ratio with respect to the variable attack interval.

From the figure, it is clear that the suggested GA-DoSLD algorithm provides higher throughput than the existing algorithms under the packet sending rate of 1 packet/3 seconds.

5. Conclusion and Future Work

In this paper, an efficient GA-DoSLD algorithm is proposed for generating the DoSL attack profiles from multiple sensor nodes such that the attacker nodes can be prevented from the communication process. Initially, a WSN is simulated with 100 numbers of static sensor nodes; then the BS performs the operations such as key pair generation and behavior monitoring in parallel. The base station monitors the behavior of the sensor nodes and initializes every behavior as a chromosome. The MRSA algorithm is implemented in the base station for generating and distributing the key pair among the sensor nodes. Before initiating the communication between the sensor nodes, the AODV routing protocol estimates the optimal route. To validate the trustworthiness of the relay nodes in the route, the fitness value is estimated for every chromosome. If the chromosome is determined as unusual, it is validated against the existing attack profiles. If there does not exist a match, the pair of chromosomes is subjected to the crossover and mutation operations. The resultant chromosomes are added to the existing chromosomes. Finally, the BS determines the attacker nodes broadcasting the blocked information to all the sensor nodes in the network. To prove the superiority of the suggested GA-DoSLD algorithm, it is compared against the existing X-MAC, ZKP, and TE$_2$S schemes for the metrics such as normalized energy consumption, effective packet number, end-to-end delay, average energy consumption, packet delivery ratio, and throughput ratio versus packet rate. The validation results prove that, when compared to the existing schemes, the proposed algorithm provides optimal results for all the metrics. The repeated execution of the GA-DoSLD algorithm in the sensor nodes consumes a considerable amount of energy. Thus, to achieve the energy optimization, a different soft computing algorithm other than GA can be used in future for detecting the denial-of-sleep attack in the WSN environment.

Notations

N: Expected number of hops
H: Number of hops between the source and destination
E: Number of neighbors at the higher tiers
R_c: Expected number of neighbors at cth hop
C_b: Additional coverage index of the node with b neighbors
W_{ac}:   Weight accuracy

R_{ac}: Accuracy relative
W_{oc}: Occurrence
R_{oc}: Relative weight of occurrence.

Competing Interests

The authors declare that there is no conflict of interests regarding the publication of this paper.

References

[1] V. C. Manju, S. L. Senthil Lekha, and M. Sasi Kumar, "Mechanisms for detecting and preventing denial of sleep attacks on wireless sensor networks," in *Proceedings of the IEEE Conference on Information and Communication Technologies (ICT '13)*, pp. 74–77, Tamil Nadu, India, April 2013.

[2] D. R. Raymond, R. C. Marchany, M. I. Brownfield, and S. F. Midkiff, "Effects of denial-of-sleep attacks on wireless sensor network MAC protocols," *IEEE Transactions on Vehicular Technology*, vol. 58, no. 1, pp. 367–380, 2009.

[3] R. P. Manohar and E. Baburaj, "Detection of Stealthy Denial of Service (S-DoS) attacks in wireless sensor networks," *International Journal of Computer Science and Information Security (IJCSIS)*, vol. 14, pp. 343–348, 2016.

[4] D. Mansouri, L. Mokddad, J. Ben-Othman, and M. Ioualalen, "Preventing denial of service attacks in wireless sensor networks," in *Proceedings of the IEEE International Conference on Communications (ICC '15)*, pp. 3014–3019, London, UK, June 2015.

[5] D. Mansouri, L. Mokdad, J. Ben-Othman, and M. Ioualalen, "Detecting DoS attacks in WSN based on clustering technique," in *Proceedings of the IEEE Wireless Communications and Networking Conference (WCNC '13)*, pp. 2214–2219, Shanghai, China, April 2013.

[6] J.-L. Chen, Y.-W. Ma, X. Wang, Y.-M. Huang, and Y.-F. Lai, "Time-division secret key protocol for wireless sensor networking," *Institution of Engineering and Technology Communications*, vol. 5, no. 12, pp. 1720–1726, 2011.

[7] D. He, C. Chen, S. Chan, and J. Bu, "DiCode: DoS-resistant and distributed code dissemination in wireless sensor networks," *IEEE Transactions on Wireless Communications*, vol. 11, no. 5, pp. 1946–1956, 2012.

[8] G. Han, J. Jiang, W. Shen, L. Shu, and J. Rodrigues, "IDSEP: a novel intrusion detection scheme based on energy prediction in cluster-based wireless sensor networks," *IET Information Security*, vol. 7, no. 2, pp. 97–105, 2013.

[9] E. B. Ram Pradheep Manohar, "Detection of stealthy denial of service (S-DoS) attacks in wireless sensor networks," *International Journal of Computer Science and Information Security (IJCSIS)*, vol. 14, 2016.

[10] H. Tan, D. Ostry, J. Zic, and S. Jha, "A confidential and DoS-resistant multi-hop code dissemination protocol for wireless sensor networks," *Computers & Security*, vol. 32, pp. 36–55, 2013.

[11] S. M. Nam and T. H. Cho, "Energy efficient method for detection and prevention of false reports in wireless sensor networks," in *Proceedings of the 8th International Conference on Information Science and Digital Content Technology (ICIDT '12)*, pp. 766–769, Jeju Island, South Korea, June 2012.

[12] S. Naik and N. Shekokar, "Conservation of energy in wireless sensor network by preventing denial of sleep attack," *Procedia Computer Science*, vol. 45, pp. 370–379, 2015.

[13] C.-T. Hsueh, C.-Y. Wen, and Y.-C. Ouyang, "A secure scheme against power exhausting attacks in hierarchical wireless sensor networks," *IEEE Sensors Journal*, vol. 15, no. 6, pp. 3590–3602, 2015.

[14] S. Kaur and M. Ataullah, "Securing the wireless sensor network from denial of sleep attack by isolating the nodes," *International Journal of Computer Applications*, vol. 103, no. 1, pp. 29–33, 2014.

[15] S. Shamshirband, A. Amini, N. B. Anuar, M. L. Mat Kiah, Y. W. Teh, and S. Furnell, "D-FICCA: a density-based fuzzy imperialist competitive clustering algorithm for intrusion detection in wireless sensor networks," *Measurement*, vol. 55, pp. 212–226, 2014.

[16] S. Shamshirband, A. Patel, N. B. Anuar, M. L. M. Kiah, and A. Abraham, "Cooperative game theoretic approach using fuzzy Q-learning for detecting and preventing intrusions in wireless sensor networks," *Engineering Applications of Artificial Intelligence*, vol. 32, pp. 228–241, 2014.

[17] N. K. Sreelaja and G. A. Vijayalakshmi Pai, "Swarm intelligence based approach for sinkhole attack detection in wireless sensor networks," *Applied Soft Computing Journal*, vol. 19, pp. 68–79, 2014.

[18] G. Keerthana and G. Padmavathi, "Detecting sinkhole attack in wireless sensor network using enhanced particle swarm optimization technique," *International Journal of Security and Its Applications*, vol. 10, no. 3, pp. 41–54, 2016.

[19] A. Saeed, A. Ahmadinia, A. Javed, and H. Larijani, "Random neural network based intelligent intrusion detection for wireless sensor networks," *Procedia Computer Science*, vol. 80, pp. 2372–2376, 2016.

[20] D. Management, "RSA Algorithm," 2016, http://www.di-mgt.com.au/rsa_alg.html.

[21] M. Zhao, Y. Li, and W. Wang, "Modeling and analytical study of link properties in multihop wireless networks," *IEEE Transactions on Communications*, vol. 60, no. 2, pp. 445–455, 2012.

[22] C.-T. Hsueh, C.-Y. Wen, and Y.-C. Ouyang, "A secure scheme against power exhausting attacks in hierarchical wireless sensor networks," *IEEE Sensors Journal*, vol. 15, no. 6, pp. 3590–3602, 2015.

[23] D. N. S. Swapna Naik, "Conservation of energy in wireless sensor network by preventing denial of sleep attack," in *Proceedings of the International Conference on Advanced Computing Technologies and Applications (ICACTA '15)*, pp. 370–379, Mumbai, India, March 2015.

13

Secure and Privacy-Preserving Data Sharing and Collaboration in Mobile Healthcare Social Networks of Smart Cities

Qinlong Huang,[1,2] Licheng Wang,[1,2] and Yixian Yang[1,2]

[1]*Information Security Center, State Key Laboratory of Networking and Switching Technology,*
 Beijing University of Posts and Telecommunications, Beijing 100876, China
[2]*National Engineering Laboratory for Disaster Backup and Recovery, Beijing University of Posts and Telecommunications,*
 Beijing 100876, China

Correspondence should be addressed to Qinlong Huang; longsec@bupt.edu.cn

Academic Editor: Qing Yang

Mobile healthcare social networks (MHSN) integrated with connected medical sensors and cloud-based health data storage provide preventive and curative health services in smart cities. The fusion of social data together with real-time health data facilitates a novel paradigm of healthcare big data analysis. However, the collaboration of healthcare and social network service providers may pose a series of security and privacy issues. In this paper, we propose a secure health and social data sharing and collaboration scheme in MHSN. To preserve the data privacy, we realize secure and fine-grained health data and social data sharing with attribute-based encryption and identity-based broadcast encryption techniques, respectively, which allows patients to share their private personal data securely. In order to achieve enhanced data collaboration, we allow the healthcare analyzers to access both the reencrypted health data and the social data with authorization from the data owner based on proxy reencryption. Specifically, most of the health data encryption and decryption computations are outsourced from resource-constrained mobile devices to a health cloud, and the decryption of the healthcare analyzer incurs a low cost. The security and performance analysis results show the security and efficiency of our scheme.

1. Introduction

As an emerging paradigm, smart cities leverage a variety of promising techniques, such as Internet of Things, mobile communications, and big data analysis, to enable intelligent services and provide a comfortable life for local residents [1]. The smart city is an urbanized area where multiple sectors cooperate to achieve sustainable outcomes through the analysis of contextual, real-time information, which would produce massive opportunities for mobile healthcare social network (MHSN) [2]. MHSN extends the traditional centralized healthcare system, in which the patients stay at home or in hospital environment and the professional physicians in the healthcare center take responsibility of generating medical treatment. With the considerable development of wearable devices and body sensors in the smart city, MHSN serving as a mobile community platform for healthcare purposes improves healthcare efficiency and places great emphasis on social interactivities [3] and assists patients in dealing with certain emergency situations or helps in forwarding data and sharing patients' feelings.

Compared to traditional hospital-centric healthcare which not only lacks efficiency when dealing with identifying some serious diseases in early stages but also suffers from limited healthcare information [4], MHSN enables continuous health monitoring and timely diagnosis to the patients in the smart city. It relies on wearable devices and medical sensors to measure the patients' health conditions and sends health data to the processing unit for doctors' further diagnosis and analysis and provides easy access to a patient's historical comprehensive health information. Additionally, the patients wearing body sensors continuously monitoring their health conditions are assumed to walk outside, moving from time to time and place to place [5]. However, MHSN may suffer from a series of security and privacy threats due to the vulnerabilities of personal health and social data. The collected private information is stored and processed in the honest but curious health and social cloud servers, which may be directly revealed during the storage and processing phases [6, 7]. Moreover, the adversary can intercept the sessions between patients to get their health and social data. Hence, the underlying security and privacy requirements, including confidentiality and access control, should be satisfied in MHSN [8–10].

Intelligent healthcare is another functionality that can be realized in MHSN, which would provide efficient diagnosis and health condition warning by analyzing the infectiousness in real time, such as infectious diseases analysis [11]. As we know, infectious diseases could be rapidly spread in the population via human-to-human contact. An old-fashioned approach to prevent the spread of disease is to isolate the susceptible people for a certain period. However, this approach is always not satisfactory, since people having frequent contact or strong social relationships with a patient are more easily infected from the perspectives of biomedicine and sociology. In general, the spread of infectious diseases depends on users' social contacts and health conditions in a high probability. Specifically, the effective infectious diseases analysis could take several key factors into consideration, that is, susceptibility of the infected patient and immunity strength of contacted user. However, the health and social data of patients are collected by multiple independent service providers, such as hospitals and social network vendors. Hence, the collaboration of these service providers is the key challenge of enabling this enhanced infection analysis in MHSN.

1.1. Our Techniques. In order to preserve the patient's data privacy and achieve data availability, encryption techniques must be adopted to make both health and social data invisible to the untrusted cloud servers. Any users without the authorization of the data owner should not be able to access the personal health and social data, and the collaboration of different untrusted cloud servers should be achieved via an authorized entity. Otherwise, patients may not be willing to share their health and social data such that the infection analysis would be disabled. In fact, attribute-based encryption (ABE) and identity-based broadcast encryption (IBBE) are widely adopted encryption algorithms [12]. Particularly, CP-ABE is conceptually closer to traditional access control models, to enforce fine-grained access control of encrypted data. By using CP-ABE, health data can be protected with access policy, and only the people who possess a set of attributes that satisfy the access policy can access data. IBBE scheme is a cryptographic mechanism in which data owners could broadcast their encrypted data to multiple receivers at one time and the public key of the user can be regarded as any valid strings, such as the email, unique ID, and username. In combination, these two mechanisms can be used to implement data protection in healthcare systems and social networks. In this paper, we propose a secure health and social data sharing and collaboration scheme in MHSN. The main contributions of our scheme are as follows:

(1) We realize secure and privacy-preserving health data and social data sharing with attribute-based encryption and identity-based broadcast encryption

techniques, respectively, which protects the private data confidentiality.

(2) We provide a secure data collaboration construction from different independent cloud servers based on proxy reencryption (PRE), which allows the healthcare analyzers authorized by the data owner to access the reencrypted health data and social data for enhanced data analysis.

(3) We outsource most of the health data encryption and decryption computations from resource-constrained mobile devices to a health cloud, and the decryption of the healthcare analyzer incurs low cost. The extensive security and performance analysis results show that our scheme is secure and efficient.

1.2. Organization. This paper is structured as follows: we review related work in Section 2. We introduce the preliminaries in Section 3 and provide the system model, system definition, and security definition in Section 4. The detailed construction is given in Section 5. Then, we analyze the security and performance of our scheme in Sections 6 and 7, respectively. Finally, we conclude this paper in Section 8.

2. Related Work

Personal health records (PHRs) are the electronic records containing health and medical information of patients, which involves privacy information that patients are unwilling to disclose. Thus, the security and protection of PHR have been of great concern and a subject of research over the years [13]. Zhang et al. [14] proposed a PHR security and privacy preservation scheme by introducing consent-based access control, where the consent can only be generated by an authorized user based on PRE. Currently, there has been an increasing interest in applying ABE to protect PHR. ABE is a promising one-to-many cryptographic technique to realize flexible and fine-grained access control for sharing data [15], which was first introduced by Sahai and Waters as a new method for fuzzy identity-based encryption (IBE) [16]. It features a mechanism that enables access control over encrypted data using access policies and ascribed attributes among private keys and ciphertexts [17]. Narayan et al. [18] proposed an attribute-based infrastructure for PHR systems, where each patient's PHR files are encrypted using a broadcast variant of ciphertext-policy ABE. Li et al. [19] proposed a novel ABE-based framework for patient-centric secure sharing of PHRs in cloud computing environments. Au et al. [20] designed a general framework for secure sharing of PHR in cloud with CP-ABE, and it deploys attribute-based PRE (ABPRE) mechanism so that the ciphertext for doctor A can be transformed to the ciphertext for doctor B. However, the main complaint in CP-ABE scheme is the high computation overhead brought about by its complex computation. This problem will become even worse in the face of resource-limited wearable devices or mobile sensors in MHSN, since it needs to perform burdensome computation tasks for fine-grained data access control when adopting the ABE algorithm. In order to reduce the computational overheads, Liu et al. [21] proposed an outsourced healthcare record access control system by moving the encryption computation offline and keeping online computation task very low. Yeh et al. [22] proposed a decryption outsourcing framework for health information access control in the cloud by utilizing CSP to check whether the attributes satisfy the access policy in ciphertext, which induces the outsourced encryption and decryption scheme introduced by Zhang et al. [23].

Intelligent healthcare, which is one of the intelligent services in the smart city, contains various health-related applications in MHSN, such as home care and emergency alarm [24]. Wang et al. [25] designed a secure health cloud system framework based on IBE, in which the assistant doctor can access the health data for enhanced analysis with authorization from the data owner based on identity-based PRE (IBPRE). In particular, by analyzing the collected social data together with real-time health data, accurate infection analysis can be achieved. The secure collaboration of healthcare and social network service providers is the key challenge of intelligent healthcare, since different service providers may adopt different techniques to protect data privacy. Zhang et al. [11] introduced some challenges of security and privacy in MHSN of smart cities and proposed the first secure data collaboration framework of healthcare and social network service providers. However, this scheme does not give the implementation construction. Liang et al. [26] proposed PEC, an ABE-based emergency call scheme for MHSN, which combines location data with health data to guarantee that emergency information is sent to nearby physicians. Jiang et al. [27] proposed EPPS, a personal health information sharing scheme based on ABE by combining the mobile social network with a healthcare center. Patients with geographical proximity can constitute a group to exchange health conditions, healthcare experiences, and medical treatments with the authorized physician. But in this scheme, the physicians in the healthcare center must have many attribute secret keys for each attribute to dock with patients in different groups. Moreover, these two schemes above do not consider the data collaboration (e.g., infectious diseases analysis) with health and social data.

3. Preliminaries

3.1. Bilinear Pairing. Let $\mathbb{G}_0$ and $\mathbb{G}_T$ be two multiplicative groups of prime order p. A bilinear map is a function $e : \mathbb{G}_0 \times \mathbb{G}_0 \to \mathbb{G}_T$ with the following properties:

(1) *Computability.* There is an efficient algorithm to compute $e(g,h) \in \mathbb{G}_T$, for any $g, h \in \mathbb{G}_0$.

(2) *Bilinearity.* For all $g, h \in \mathbb{G}_0$ and $a, b \in \mathbb{Z}_p$, we have $e(g^a, h^b) = e(g,h)^{ab}$.

(3) *Nondegeneracy.* If g is a generator of $\mathbb{G}_0$, then $e(g,g)$ is also a generator of $\mathbb{G}_T$.

3.2. Ciphertext-Policy Attribute-Based Encryption. The CP-ABE is a cryptography prototype for one-to-many secure communication, which consists of the following algorithms [17].

(1) *Setup(1^λ).* The setup algorithm takes as input the security parameter λ and outputs a public key PK and a master secret key MK.

(2) *KeyGen(PK, MK, S).* The key generation algorithm takes as input the public key PK, the master secret key MK, and a set S of attributes and outputs an attribute key AK.

(3) *Enc(PK, M, T).* The encryption algorithm takes as input the public key PK, a message M, and an access policy T and outputs a ciphertext CT.

(4) *Dec(PK, AK, CT).* The decryption algorithm takes as input the public key PK, an attribute key AK, and a ciphertext CT with an access policy T. If $S \in T$, it outputs the message M.

3.3. Identity-Based Broadcast Encryption. The IBBE can be seen as an extension of the IBE, by allowing one to encrypt a message once for many receivers. The definition of IBBE is as follows [28].

(1) *Setup($1^\lambda, N$).* The setup algorithm takes as input a security parameter λ and the maximal size N of a set of receivers and outputs a pair of public key PK and master secret key MK.

(2) *KegGen(PK, MK, ID).* The key generation algorithm takes as input the public key PK, the master secret key MK, and a user's identity ID and outputs a secret key SK_{ID} for the user.

(3) *Enc(PK, M, U).* The encryption algorithm takes as input the public key PK, a message M, and a set U of receivers' identities; the algorithm outputs a ciphertext CT for U.

(4) *Dec(PK, CT, SK_{ID}, ID).* The decryption algorithm takes as input the public key PK, a ciphertext CT, a secret key SK_{ID}, and an identity ID; the algorithm outputs the message M if ID $\in U$.

4. The Proposed Scheme

4.1. System Model. In MHSN, the fusion of health data and social data facilitates a novel paradigm of authorized infection analysis. Our scheme focuses on the secure sharing and collaboration of these data. As shown in Figure 1, the system model of our scheme consists of central authority, health cloud, social cloud, users, healthcare provider, and healthcare analyzer.

(1) *Central Authority.* The central authority is a fully trusted party which is in charge of generating system parameters as well as private keys for each user.

(2) *Health Cloud.* The health cloud is a semitrusted party which provides health data storage service. It is also responsible for helping encrypt health data for mobile healthcare sensors and decrypt the ciphertext for healthcare providers and reencrypt ciphertext for healthcare analyzers.

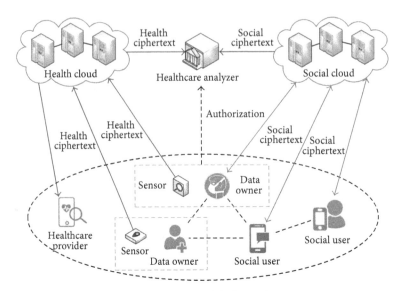

FIGURE 1: System model of our scheme.

(3) *Social Cloud*. The social cloud is also a semitrusted party which provides social data storage service and is in charge of reencrypting social ciphertext for healthcare analyzers.

(4) *Data Owner*. The data owners generate a great amount of health data through the mobile healthcare sensors and upload them to the health cloud by defining access policy and also upload their social data to the social cloud for sharing.

(5) *User*. The user is the ciphertexts' receiver and is able to decrypt the ciphertexts if he is the intended receiver defined by the data owners.

(6) *Healthcare Provider*. The healthcare providers are the intended receivers of health ciphertext stored in the health cloud. If a healthcare provider's attribute set satisfies the access policy in the ciphertext, he is able to decrypt the patient's health data from the ciphertext.

(7) *Healthcare Analyzer*. The healthcare analyzer is the authorized receiver of both health ciphertext and social ciphertext for data collaboration and analysis.

4.2. System Definition. Based on the system model, our scheme consists of the following algorithms.

(1) $Setup(1^\lambda, N)$. The central authority takes as input a security parameter λ and the maximal size of receiver set N and outputs a system public key PK and a master secret key MK.

(2) $AKeyGen(PK, MK, S)$. The central authority takes as input PK and MK and a set of attributes S of user or healthcare provider and outputs the attribute key AK.

(3) $SKeyGen(PK, MK, ID)$. The central authority takes as input PK and MK and an identity ID of user or healthcare analyzer and outputs the secret key of user SK.

(4) $Cloud.Encrypt(PK, T)$. The health cloud takes as input PK and an access policy T and outputs an outsourced health ciphertext CT'.

(5) $Health.Encrypt(PK, m_h, CT')$. The health data owner takes as input PK, health data m_h, and an outsourced health ciphertext CT' and outputs a health ciphertext CT_h.

(6) $Cloud.Decrypt(PK, CT_h, AK')$. The health cloud takes as input PK, a health ciphertext CT_h, and an outsourced attribute key AK' and outputs a partial decrypted health ciphertext CT_r if the attributes in AK' satisfy the access policy in the ciphertext.

(7) $Health.Decrypt(CT_r, AK)$. The healthcare provider takes as input a partial decrypted health ciphertext CT_r and an attribute key AK and outputs the health data m_h.

(8) $Social.Encrypt(PK, m_c, U)$. The social data owner takes as input PK, social data m_c, and a set U of receivers' identities and outputs a social ciphertext CT_c.

(9) $Social.Decrypt(PK, CT_c, ID, SK)$. The social receiver takes as input PK, a social ciphertext CT_c, a receiver's identity ID, and its secret key SK and outputs the social data m_c if ID and SK are valid.

(10) $Health.ReKeyGen(PK, AK, ID')$. The health data owner takes as input PK, attribute key AK, and a healthcare analyzer's identity ID' and outputs a health reencryption key RK_h.

(11) $Health.ReEnc(CT_h, RK_h)$. The health cloud takes as input a health ciphertext CT_h and a heath reencryption key RK_h and outputs a reencrypted health ciphertext RT_h.

(12) $Social.ReKeyGen(PK, SK, ID')$. The social data owner takes as input PK, a secret key SK, and a healthcare

analyzer's identity ID' and outputs a social reencryption key RK_c.

(13) *Social.ReEnc*(CT_c, RK_c). The social cloud takes as input a social ciphertext CT_c and a social reencryption key RK_c and outputs a reencrypted social ciphertext RT_c.

(14) *Analyzer.Decrypt*(RT_h, RT_c, SK'). The healthcare analyzer takes as input a reencrypted health ciphertext RT_h, a reencrypted social ciphertext RT_c, and a secret key SK' and outputs health data m_h and social data m_c.

In the registration phase, the central authority runs *Setup* algorithms to generate system public key and master secret key. Meanwhile, it also uses *AKeyGen* and *SKeyGen* algorithm to generate attribute keys and secret keys of users in the system. For the health data, the health cloud first runs *Cloud.Encrypt* algorithm to encrypt data with an access policy, and then the data owner runs *Health.Encrypt* algorithm to finish the encryption. When accessing the health data, the health cloud first uses the *Cloud.Decrypt* algorithm to partially decrypt the ciphertext, and then the user can use the *Health.Decrypt* algorithm to recover the data. For the social data, the data owner runs *Social.Encrypt* algorithm to encrypt data for a set of receivers, and the user can use the *Social.Decrypt* algorithm to recover the social data. Furthermore, the data owner could run *Health.ReKeyGen* and *Social.ReKeyGen* algorithms, respectively, to generate reencryption keys containing their own attribute keys and secret keys. Receiving the reencryption keys, the health cloud and social cloud would run *Health.ReEnc* and *Social.ReEnc* algorithms to transform the initial ciphertexts to the reencrypted ciphertexts. Hence, the healthcare analyzer can run *Analyzer.Decrypt* algorithm to decrypt the reencrypted health and social ciphertexts.

4.3. Security Definition. In our scheme, we assume that the health cloud and social cloud are honest but curious, which means they carry out computation and storage tasks but may try to learn information about the private data [29]. Specifically, the security model covers the following aspects.

(1) *Data Confidentiality.* The unauthorized users that are not the intended receivers defined by the data owner should be prevented from accessing the health and social data. The healthcare analyzer should not be able to access the reencrypted data without the authorization of the data owner.

(2) *Fine-Grained Access Control.* The data owner can customize an expressive and flexible access policy so that the health data only can be accessed by the healthcare providers whose attributes satisfy these policies.

(3) *Collusion Resistance.* If each of the users' attributes in the set cannot satisfy the access policy in the ciphertexts alone, the access of ciphertext should not successful.

5. Construction

5.1. System Setup. The central authority runs *Setup* algorithm to select a bilinear map $e : \mathbb{G}_0 \times \mathbb{G}_0 \rightarrow \mathbb{G}_T$, where $\mathbb{G}_0$ and $\mathbb{G}_T$ are two multiplicative groups with prime order p and g is the generator of $\mathbb{G}_0$. Then, the central authority chooses the maximum number of receivers N, randomly chooses $g, h, u, v, w \in \mathbb{G}_0$ and $\alpha, \beta \in \mathbb{Z}_p$, chooses cryptographic hash function $H_1 : \{0, 1\}^* \rightarrow \mathbb{Z}_p^*$, $H_2 : \mathbb{G}_T \rightarrow \mathbb{G}_0$, and finally outputs a system public key PK $= (g, g^\beta, e(g, g)^\alpha, h, u^\alpha, v, v^\alpha, \dots, v^{\alpha^N}, e(u, v), w)$ and a master secret key MK $= (u, \alpha, \beta)$.

5.2. Key Generation. The central authority runs *AKeyGen* algorithm to select a random $\gamma \in \mathbb{Z}_p$, which is a unique secret assigned to each user. Then, the central authority chooses random $\varepsilon, \varphi \in \mathbb{Z}_p$ and random r_j for each attribute $j \in S$, where S is the attribute set of the user, and outputs the attribute key AK.

$$AK = \Big(D = g^{(\alpha+\gamma)/\beta}, \ D_1 = g^\gamma h^\varepsilon, \ D_2 = g^\varepsilon, \ D_3$$

$$= g^{1/\varphi}, \ D_4 = g^{\varphi\alpha}, \ D_5 \tag{1}$$

$$= w^{\varphi\alpha}, \ \Big\{ \widetilde{D}_j = g^\gamma H_1(j)^{r_j}, \ \widetilde{D}'_j = g^{r_j} \Big\}_{j \in S} \Big).$$

For each user in the system, the central authority runs *SKeyGen* algorithm to select a random $\pi \in \mathbb{Z}_p$ and output the secret key SK for the user with identity ID.

$$SK = \Big(K = g^{1/(\alpha+H_1(ID))}, \ K_1 = u^{1/\pi}, \ K_2 = v^\pi, \ K_3$$

$$= w^\pi \Big). \tag{2}$$

5.3. Secure Health Data Sharing

5.3.1. Health Data Encryption. The mobile healthcare sensors of the data owner could collect a wide range of real-time health data (e.g., blood pressure, heart rate, and pulse), for further diagnosis or specialist analysis. Before uploading the data to the health cloud, the data owner first chooses a random HK $\in \mathbb{Z}_p$ and encrypts the health data m_h with HK using a symmetric encryption algorithm, denoted as $C = SE_{HK}(m_h)$. Then, the data owner defines an access policy T, to ensure that only users satisfying this policy can access data, and then sends to the health cloud.

Then, the health cloud runs *Cloud.Encrypt* algorithm to perform the outsourced encryption. For each node x in the access policy tree T, the health cloud chooses a polynomial p_x. These polynomials are chosen in the following way in a top-down manner, starting from the root node R. For each node x in the tree, set the degree d_x of the polynomial p_x to be one less than the threshold value k_x of that node; that is, $d_x = k_x - 1$. Starting with the root node R, the algorithm chooses a random $s \in \mathbb{Z}_p$ and sets $p_R(0) = s$. Then, it chooses d_R other points of the polynomial p_R randomly to define it completely. For any other node x, it sets $p_x(0) = p_{\text{parent}(x)}(\text{index}(x))$ and chooses d_x other points randomly to completely define p_x.

Let Y be the set of leaf nodes in T; the health cloud outputs an outsourced ciphertext CT' as

$$CT' = \left(T, \; C_3' = g^s, \; C_4' = h^s, \; C_7 \right.$$

$$\left. = \left\{ \widetilde{C}_y = g^{p_y(0)}, \; \widetilde{C}_y' = H_1\left(attr_y\right)^{p_y(0)} \right\}_{y \in Y} \right). \tag{3}$$

The health cloud returns CT' to the data owner. The data owner runs *Health.Encrypt* algorithm to select $t \in \mathbb{Z}_p$ at random and computes $C_1 = HK \cdot e(g,g)^{\alpha t}$ with HK and computes $C_2 = g^{\beta t}$, $C_3 = C_3' \cdot g^t$, $C_4 = C_4' \cdot h^t$, $C_5 = (D_4)^t$, $C_6 = (D_5)^t$. Finally, the data owner outputs the ciphertext CT_h as

$$CT_h = \left(T, \; C = SE_{HK}(m_h), \; C_1 = HK \cdot e(g,g)^{\alpha t}, \; C_2 \right.$$

$$= g^{\beta t}, \; C_3 = g^{s+t}, \; C_4 = h^{s+t}, \; C_5 = g^{\varphi \alpha t}, \; C_6$$

$$= w^{\varphi \alpha t}, \; C_7 \tag{4}$$

$$\left. = \left\{ \widetilde{C}_y = g^{p_y(0)}, \; \widetilde{C}_y' = H_1\left(attr_y\right)^{p_y(0)} \right\}_{y \in Y} \right).$$

5.3.2. Health Data Decryption. If the attributes of the healthcare provider satisfy the access policy T, he can decrypt CT_h successfully by informing health cloud and obtaining the symmetric key. The health cloud runs *Cloud.Decrypt* algorithm with the ciphertext and outsourced attribute key $AK' = (D_1, D_2, \{\widetilde{D}_j, \widetilde{D}_j'\}_{j \in S})$ from the healthcare provider. The health cloud first runs *DecryptNode* algorithm which can be described as a recursive algorithm. This algorithm takes the ciphertext CT_h, AK', and a node x from the access tree T as input.

(1) If the node x is a leaf node, then we let $z = attr_x$ and compute as follows. If $z \in S$, then

$$DecryptNode\left(CT_h, AK', x\right) = \frac{e\left(\widetilde{D}_z, \widetilde{C}_x\right)}{e\left(\widetilde{D}_z', \widetilde{C}_x'\right)}$$

$$= \frac{e\left(g^\gamma H_1(z)^{r_z}, g^{p_x(0)}\right)}{e\left(g^{r_z}, H_1(attr_x)^{p_x(0)}\right)} = e(g,g)^{\gamma p_x(0)}. \tag{5}$$

If $z \notin S$, then $DecryptNode(CT_h, AK', x) = \bot$.

(2) If the node x is a nonleaf node, the algorithm $DecryptNode(CT_h, AK', x)$ proceeds as follows: for all nodes n that are children of x, it calls $DecryptNode(CT_h, AK', n)$ and stores output as F_n. Let S_x be an arbitrary k_x-sized set of child nodes n such that $F_n \neq \bot$. If no such set exists, then the node is not satisfied and the function returns $\bot$. Otherwise,

the function defines $j = index(n)$ and $S_x' = \{index(n) : n \in S_x\}$ and returns the result.

$$F_x = \prod_{n \in S_x} F_n^{\Delta_{j,S_x'}(0)}$$

$$= \prod_{n \in S_x} \left(e(g,g)^{r \cdot p_{parent(n)}(index(n))} \right)^{\Delta_{j,S_x'}(0)} \tag{6}$$

$$= \prod_{n \in S_x} e(g,g)^{r \cdot p_x(j) \cdot \Delta_{j,S_x'}(0)} = e(g,g)^{r p_x(0)}.$$

If the access policy tree T is satisfied by S, we set the result of the entire evaluation for the access tree T as F, such that

$$F = DecryptNode\left(CT_h, AK', R\right) = e(g,g)^{\gamma p_R(0)} \tag{7}$$

$$= e(g,g)^{\gamma s}.$$

Then, the health cloud computes

$$B = \frac{e(D_1, C_3)}{e(D_2, C_4)} = \frac{e(g^\gamma h^\varepsilon, g^{s+t})}{e(g^\varepsilon, h^{s+t})} = e(g,g)^{\gamma(s+t)},$$

$$\tag{8}$$

$$A = \frac{B}{F} = \frac{e(g,g)^{\gamma(s+t)}}{e(g,g)^{\gamma s}} = e(g,g)^{\gamma t}.$$

Finally, the health cloud sends the partial decrypted health ciphertext $CT_r = (C = SE_{HK}(m_h), \; C_1 = HK \cdot e(g,g)^{\alpha t}, \; C_2 = g^{\beta t}, \; A = e(g,g)^{\gamma t})$ to the healthcare provider. After receiving CT_r from the health cloud, the healthcare provider runs *Health.Decrypt* algorithm to obtain the symmetric key.

$$HK = \frac{C_1 \cdot A}{e(C_2, D)} = \frac{HK \cdot e(g,g)^{\alpha t} \cdot e(g,g)^{\gamma t}}{e(g^{\beta t}, g^{(\alpha+\gamma)/\beta})}. \tag{9}$$

Thus, $SE_{HK}(m_h)$ can be decrypted with HK by applying the symmetric decryption algorithm, and the healthcare provider can access the data owner's health data for diagnosis.

5.4. Secure Social Data Sharing

5.4.1. Social Data Encryption. For the private social data denoted as m_c, the data owner runs *Social.Encrypt* algorithm to encrypt it and then outsource the ciphertext to the social cloud. First, the data owner chooses a set U of receivers' identities (where $|U| \leq N$) and a random $CK \in \mathbb{Z}_p$ which is used to encrypt the data based on the symmetric encryption algorithm. The data owner randomly picks $k \in \mathbb{Z}_p^*$ and outputs a social ciphertext CT_c.

$$CT_c = \left(C = SE_{CK}(m_c), \; C_1 = CK \cdot e(u,v)^k, \; C_2 \right.$$

$$= v^{k \cdot \prod_{ID_i \in U}(\alpha + H_1(ID_i))}, \; C_3 = v^{\pi k}, \; C_4 = w^{\pi k}, \; C_5 \tag{10}$$

$$\left. = u^{-\alpha k} \right).$$

5.4.2. Social Data Decryption. The user with identity ID runs *Social.Decrypt* algorithm to decrypt the social ciphertext. If

$\text{ID} \in U$, the user computes

$$I = \left(e\left(C_5, v^{\Delta_\alpha(\text{ID},U)}\right) \cdot e\left(K, C_2\right)\right)^{1/\prod_{\text{ID}_i \in U \wedge \text{ID}_i \neq \text{ID}} H_1(\text{ID}_i)} = \left(e\left(u^{-\alpha k}, v^{\Delta_\alpha(\text{ID},U)}\right) \cdot e\left(u^{1/(\alpha+H_1(\text{ID}))}, v^{k\cdot\prod_{\text{ID}_i \in U}(\alpha+H_1(\text{ID}_i))}\right)\right)^{1/\prod_{\text{ID}_i \in U \wedge \text{ID}_i \neq \text{ID}} H_1(\text{ID}_i)}$$

$$= \left(e\left(u^{-\alpha k}, v^{\alpha^{-1}\cdot\left(\prod_{\text{ID}_i \in U \wedge \text{ID}_i \neq \text{ID}}(\alpha+H_1(\text{ID}_i)) - \prod_{\text{ID}_i \in U \wedge \text{ID}_i \neq \text{ID}} H_1(\text{ID}_i)\right)}\right) \cdot e(u,v)^{k\cdot\prod_{\text{ID}_i \in U \wedge \text{ID}_i \neq \text{ID}}(\alpha+H_1(\text{ID}_i))}\right)^{1/\prod_{\text{ID}_i \in U \wedge \text{ID}_i \neq \text{ID}} H_1(\text{ID}_i)} \tag{11}$$

$$= \left(e\left(u^k, v\right)^{\prod_{\text{ID}_i \in U \wedge \text{ID}_i \neq \text{ID}} H_1(\text{ID}_i) - \prod_{\text{ID}_i \in U \wedge \text{ID}_i \neq \text{ID}}(\alpha+H_1(\text{ID}_i)) + \prod_{\text{ID}_i \in U \wedge \text{ID}_i \neq \text{ID}}(\alpha+H_1(\text{ID}_i))}\right)^{1/\prod_{\text{ID}_i \in U \wedge \text{ID}_i \neq \text{ID}} H_1(\text{ID}_i)} = e(u,v)^k,$$

where

$$\Delta_\alpha(\text{ID},U) = \alpha^{-1} \cdot \left(\prod_{\text{ID}_i \in U \wedge \text{ID}_i \neq \text{ID}}(\alpha + H_1(\text{ID}_i))\right. \tag{12}$$

$$\left. - \prod_{\text{ID}_i \in U \wedge \text{ID}_i \neq \text{ID}} H_1(\text{ID}_i)\right).$$

Then, the user computes CK with I.

$$\text{CK} = \frac{C_1}{I} = \frac{\text{CK} \cdot e(u,v)^k}{e(u,v)^k}. \tag{13}$$

Finally, the user recovers message m_c with CK using the symmetric encryption algorithm.

5.5. Authorized Data Analysis

5.5.1. Health Data Reencryption.
In order to analyze the healthcare data, the health data owner runs *Health.ReKeyGen* algorithm to choose a healthcare analyzer's identity ID', randomly pick $t', b \in \mathbb{Z}_p$, and compute the following with attribute key AK:

$$R_1 = D_3 \cdot w^b = g^{1/\varphi} \cdot w^b,$$

$$R_2 = v^{t'\cdot(\alpha+H_1(\text{ID}'))}, \tag{14}$$

$$R_3 = H_2\left(e(u,v)^{t'}\right) \cdot g^b.$$

Then, the health data owner outputs the health reencryption key $\text{RK}_h = (R_1, R_2, R_3)$. When receiving the reencryption key, the health cloud runs *Health.ReEnc* algorithm to reencrypt the initial health ciphertext. The health cloud computes

$$C_1' = \frac{C_1}{e(R_1, C_5)} = \frac{\text{HK} \cdot e(g,g)^{\alpha t}}{e(g^{1/\varphi} \cdot w^b, g^{\varphi\alpha t})} \tag{15}$$

$$= \text{HK} \cdot e\left(w^b, g^{-\varphi\alpha t}\right).$$

Finally, the health cloud outputs a reencrypted health ciphertext.

$$\text{RT}_h = \left(C' = C = \text{SE}_{\text{HK}}(m_h), \ C_1' = \text{HK}\right.$$

$$\cdot e\left(w^b, g^{-\varphi\alpha t}\right), \ C_2' = R_2 = v^{t'\cdot(\alpha+H_1(\text{ID}'))}, \ C_3' = R_3 \tag{16}$$

$$\left. = H_2\left(e(u,v)^{t'}\right) \cdot g^b, \ C_4' = C_6 = w^{\varphi\alpha t}\right).$$

5.5.2. Social Data Reencryption.
The social data is also used to analyze healthcare, such as infectious diseases. The data owner runs *Social.ReKeyGen* algorithm to choose a healthcare analyzer's identity ID', randomly pick $k', l \in \mathbb{Z}_p$, and compute the following with secret key SK:

$$R_1 = K_1 \cdot w^l = u^{1/\pi} \cdot w^l,$$

$$R_2 = v^{k'\cdot(\alpha+H_1(\text{ID}'))}, \tag{17}$$

$$R_3 = H_2\left(e(u,v)^{k'}\right) \cdot v^l.$$

Then, the data owner outputs the social reencryption key $\text{RK}_c = (R_1, R_2, R_3)$. Then, receiving the reencryption key, the social cloud runs *Social.ReEnc* algorithm to reencrypt the initial social ciphertext. The social cloud computes

$$C_1' = \frac{C_1}{e(R_1, C_3)} = \frac{\text{CK} \cdot e(u,v)^k}{e(u^{1/\pi} \cdot w^l, v^{\pi k})} \tag{18}$$

$$= \text{CK} \cdot e\left(w^l, v^{-\pi k}\right).$$

Finally, the social cloud outputs a reencrypted social ciphertext.

$$\text{RT}_c = \left(C' = C = \text{SE}_{\text{CK}}(m_c), \ C_1' = \text{CK}\right.$$

$$\cdot e\left(w^l, v^{-\pi k}\right), \ C_2' = R_2 = v^{k'\cdot(\alpha+H_1(\text{ID}'))}, \ C_3' = R_3 \tag{19}$$

$$\left. = H_2\left(e(u,v)^{k'}\right) \cdot v^l, \ C_4' = C_4 = w^{\pi k}\right).$$

5.5.3. Authorized Decryption.
For the reencrypted health and social ciphertext, the healthcare analyzer with identity ID' runs *Analyzer.Decrypt* algorithm to decrypt. For the health data, the healthcare analyzer first computes

$$K' = e\left(K, C_2'\right) = e\left(u^{1/(\alpha+H_1(\text{ID}'))}, v^{t'\cdot(\alpha+H_1(\text{ID}'))}\right) \tag{20}$$

$$= e(u,v)^{t'}.$$

Then, the healthcare analyzer computes

$$Z = \frac{C_3'}{H_2(K')} = \frac{H_2\left(e(u,v)^{t'}\right) \cdot g^b}{H_2\left(e(u,v)^{t'}\right)} = g^b. \tag{21}$$

Finally, the healthcare analyzer computes the HK and recovers the health data m_h.

$$
\begin{aligned}
\text{HK} &= C_1' \cdot e\left(Z, C_4'\right) \\
&= \text{HK} \cdot e\left(w^b, g^{-\varphi \alpha t}\right) \cdot e\left(g^b, w^{\varphi \alpha t}\right).
\end{aligned}
\tag{22}
$$

For the social data, the healthcare analyzer can compute v^l with secret key and then compute CK and recover the social data m_c.

$$
\text{CK} = C_1' \cdot e\left(v^l, C_4'\right) = \text{CK} \cdot e\left(w^l, v^{-\pi k}\right) \cdot e\left(v^l, w^{\pi k}\right). \tag{23}
$$

Therefore, the healthcare analyzers can access both the reencrypted health data and the social data for collaboration and analysis with authorization from the data owner.

6. Security Analysis

The sharing data in our scheme is encrypted with CP-ABE and IBBE techniques, which are secure against chosen plaintext attack since the DBDH assumption holds [23, 28]. We analyze the security properties of our scheme as follows [29].

(1) *Data Confidentiality.* The health data is encrypted using access policy, and the confidentiality of health data can be guaranteed against users who do not hold a set of attributes that satisfy the access policy. In the encryption phase, though the health cloud performs encryption computation for the data owner, it still cannot access the data without the attribute key. During the decryption phase, since the set of attributes cannot satisfy the access policy in the ciphertext, the health cloud server cannot recover the value $A = e(g, g)^{yt}$ to further get the desired value HK. Therefore, only the users with valid attributes that satisfy the access policy can decrypt the health ciphertext. The social data is encrypted with a random symmetric key CK, and then CK is protected by IBBE. Since the symmetric encryption and IBBE scheme are secure, the confidentiality of outsourced social data can be guaranteed against unauthorized users whose identities are not in the set of receivers' identities defined by the data owner.

(2) *Fine-Grained Access Control.* The fine-grained access control allows flexibility in specifying differential access policies of individual health data. To enforce this kind of access control, we utilize CP-ABE to escort the symmetric encryption key of health data. In the health data encryption phase of our scheme, the data owner is able to enforce an expressive and flexible access policy and encrypt the symmetric key which is used to encrypt the health data. Specifically, the access policy of encrypted data defined in access tree supports complex operations including both AND and OR gate, which is able to represent any desired access conditions.

(3) *Collusion Resistance.* The users may intend to combine their attribute keys to access the data which they cannot access individually. In our scheme, the central authority generates attribute keys for different users; the attribute key is associated with random γ, which is uniquely related to each user and makes the combination of components in different attribute keys meaningless. Suppose two or more users with different attributes combine together to satisfy the access policy; they cannot compute $F = e(g, g)^{ys}$ in the outsourced decryption phase. Thus, the proposed scheme is collusion-resistant.

7. Performance Analysis

7.1. Functionality Comparisons. We list the key features of our scheme in Table 1 and make a comparison of our scheme with several data sharing schemes in MHSN in terms of health data confidentiality, health data access control, outsourced encryption and decryption, data authorization, and social data collaboration. In order to achieve fine-grained access control, most of these schemes adopt the ABE technique. From the comparison, we can see that only EPPS [27] and our scheme achieve health data outsourced decryption considering the low computing power of resource-constrained mobile devices or healthcare sensors. Zhang et al. [14], Wang et al. [25], Au et al. [20], and our scheme support data authorization by deploying PRE mechanism so that the semitrusted server could reencrypt the ciphertext to data requester for research and analysis purposes without acquiring any plaintext. Further, PEC [26] combines social data with healthcare record for emergency call, and EPPS [27] divides the mobile patients into different groups according to social data. However, both PEC [26] and EPPS [27] only utilize location information of social data and ignore other valuable data in social networks, which makes extensive social data needed in-depth healthcare analysis (e.g., infectious diseases analysis) impossible.

Moreover, the health and social data may be collected and protected by different independent service providers adopting different encryption techniques, such as ABE and IBBE. Thus, to achieve data collaboration of these service providers, data authorization in these different service providers must be supported. Our scheme proposes an efficient CP-ABE construction with outsourced encryption and decryption to achieve efficient fine-grained access control of health data and provides a secure solution for the collaboration of different service providers by transforming the ABE-encrypted health data and IBBE-encrypted social data into an IBE-encrypted one that can only be decrypted by an authorized healthcare analyzer such as specialists, since IBE is more suitable to be employed on resource-constrained mobile devices in MHSN.

7.2. Performance Comparisons. We analyze the performance efficiency of health data encryption, decryption, reencryption key generation, and reencryption by comparing our scheme with several secure health data sharing schemes; the result is shown in Table 2. Let T_r be the computation cost of a single pairing, T_0 be the computation cost of an exponent

TABLE 1: Functionality comparison of data sharing schemes in MHSN.

	Zhang et al. [14]	Wang et al. [25]	Au et al. [20]	PEC [26]	EPPS [27]	Our scheme
Health data confidentiality	PKE	IBE	CP-ABE	CP-ABE	CP-ABE	CP-ABE
Health data access control	Consent-based	Identity-based	Attribute-based	Attribute-based	Attribute-based	Attribute-based
Outsourced encryption	—	No	No	No	No	Yes
Outsourced decryption	—	No	No	No	Yes	Yes
Data authorization	Yes	Yes	Yes	No	No	Yes
Social data collaboration	No	No	No	Yes	Yes	Yes

TABLE 2: Comparison of computation overhead for health data sharing.

Schemes	Data encryption	Data decryption	Data reencryption key generation	Data reencryption
Yeh et al. [22]	$T_r + (2N_c + 1)T_0 + T_t$	$2T_r + T_t$	—	—
EPPS [27]	$(3N_c + 1)T_0 + T_t$	T_t	—	—
Au et al. [20]	$(3N_c + 2)T_0 + T_t$	$(2N_c + 1)T_r + N_cT_t$	$(3N_r + 1)T_0 + T_t$	$(2N_r + 2)T_r + N_rT_t$
Wang et al. [25]	$2T_0 + 2T_t$	$2T_r$	$3T_0$	$T_r + T_0$
Our scheme	$5T_0 + T_t$	T_r	$3T_0 + T_t$	T_r

TABLE 3: Computation overhead of social data sharing.

Data encryption	Data decryption	Data reencryption key generation	Data reencryption	Data authorized decryption
$(N_u + 4)T_0 + T_t$	$2T_r + (N_u - 1)T_0 + T_t$	$4T_0 + T_t$	T_r	$2T_r$

operation in $\mathbb{G}_0$, T_t be the time for an exponent operation in $\mathbb{G}_T$, N_c be the number of attributes in a ciphertext, N_r be the number of attributes in a reencrypted ciphertext, and N_u be the total number of receivers in social networks. We ignore the simple multiplication, hash, and symmetric encryption and decryption operations.

First, we discuss the computation cost of health data encryption and decryption. Since Yeh et al. [22], EPPS [27], and Au et al. [20] all perform standard ABE algorithm locally in the encryption phase, their encryption computation costs are $T_r + (2N_c + 1) T_0 + T_t$, $(3N_c + 1) T_0 + T_t$, and $(3N_c + 2) T_0 + T_t$, respectively, which grow linearly with the number of attributes in access policy. In our scheme, the users with mobile sensors only need to perform $5T_0 + T_t$ to encrypt the data, which is constant, the same as Wang et al. [25] and less than these schemes. In the data decryption phase, receivers in Au et al.'s study [20] use secret keys corresponding to matched attributes to recursively decrypt the health ciphertext, and the computation cost is $(2N_c + 1)T_r + N_cT_t$. In Yeh et al.'s study [22], EPPS [27], and our scheme, most of the decryption computations are outsourced to the cloud server. In particular, users in our scheme only need to perform one pairing operation to decrypt the ciphertext.

Further, in the data authorization phase, Au et al. [20] adopted ABPRE to reencrypt ciphertext for authorized users, and the computation costs of reencryption key generation and data reencryption are both related to the number of attributes of new access policy. Our scheme transforms ABE-encrypted health data to IBE-encrypted health data for analysis purposes, and the computation costs in these two phases are $3T_0 + T_t$ and T_r, which is constant and efficient as in Wang et al.'s study [25].

We also evaluate the computation overhead of social data sharing when the ciphertexts in different service providers need to collaborate together. From Table 3, we can observe that the social data encryption cost on the data owner is $(N_u + 4)T_0 + T_t$ based on IBBE. If the user is one of the desirable receivers, he can perform $2T_r + (N_u - 1)T_0 + T_t$ cost to decrypt ciphertext. Moreover, our scheme also has high efficiency for the social data authorized phase, in which the IBBE-encrypted social data can be reencrypted to IBE-encrypted one by semitrusted social cloud with reencryption key generated by the data owner. The computation cost of generating reencryption key is $4T_0 + T_t$, and the semitrusted social cloud needs to take T_r cost to finish the social data reencryption. At last, the authorized healthcare analyzer needs to perform $2T_r$ to obtain the social data or health data which are both protected by IBE.

7.3. Experimental Evaluation. We conduct experiments on a Linux system with an Intel Core 2 Duo CPU with 2.53 GHz processor and 4 GB memory. The experimental prototype is written in C language with the assistance of cpabe toolkit and pairing-based cryptography library [30]. We use a pairing-friendly type A 160-bit elliptic curve group based on the supersingular curve over a 512-bit finite field. The Advanced Encryption Standard (AES) is chosen as the symmetric key encryption scheme.

We analyze the time cost of the data encryption and decryption by comparing our scheme with Yeh et al. [22], EPPS [27], Au et al. [20], and Wang et al. [25]. In the data encryption phase, the data owner in these schemes encrypts a file with an access policy and posts the encrypted file to the cloud server. Figure 2 shows the computation time on data owners during this phase. The encryption time on data

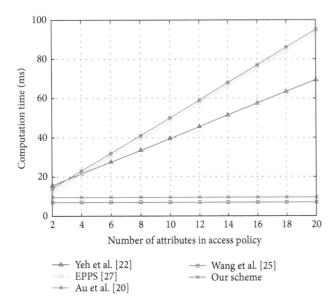

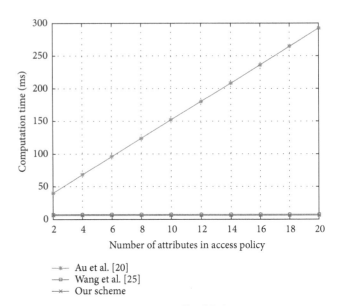

FIGURE 2: Computation cost of health data encryption.

FIGURE 4: Computation cost of health data reencryption.

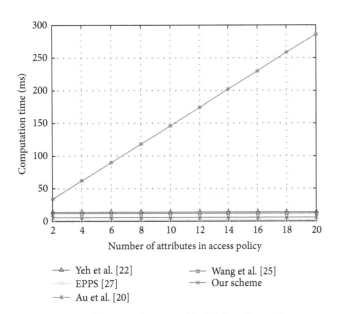

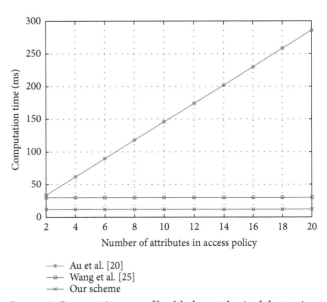

FIGURE 3: Computation cost of health data decryption.

FIGURE 5: Computation cost of health data authorized decryption.

owners grows with the number of attributes in access policy in Yeh et al. [22], EPPS [27], and Au et al. [20], while it stays constant in our scheme. In the data decryption phase, Figure 3 shows the computation time on healthcare providers for decryption versus the number of attributes in access policy of ciphertext. Compared to Au et al. [20], we can see that the decryption times of Yeh et al. [22], EPPS [27], and our scheme are almost the same, which are constant since most of the laborious decryption operations are delegated to the cloud server.

Furthermore, we evaluate the computation time cost in health data reencryption phase and health data authorized decryption phase, and the results are shown in Figures 4 and 5, respectively. We compare our scheme with that of

Au et al. [20] which utilizes ABPRE to support a general framework for secure sharing of PHR and that of Wang et al. [25] which adopts IBPRE. We can observe that the experimental results in Au et al. [20] approximately follow a linear relationship as the number of attributes increases. In our scheme, the data owner generates reencryption keys for authorized healthcare analyzers so that the ABE-based ciphertext can be reencrypted to an IBE-based one and then be decrypted with a secret key, which is independent of the number of attributes in access policy as in Wang et al. [25].

8. Conclusion

In this paper, we focus on the secure health data and social data sharing and collaboration in MHSN for smart cities and propose a detailed construction based on ABE and

IBBE. Our scheme allows the data owner to authorize the healthcare analyzers to access data by reencrypting both ABE-protected health data and IBBE-protected social data to IBE-protected one, which provides a solution for the collaboration of different service providers. In order to reduce the computation overhead of resource-constrained mobile devices, outsourced encryption and decryption construction is adopted in our scheme, which can delegate most of the computation cost to a cloud server. Finally, we analyze the performance of our scheme with the existing schemes in MHSN and conduct experiments. The results have shown that our scheme is secure and efficient.

Acknowledgments

This work was supported by the National Key Research and Development Program of China under Grant no. 2016YFB0800605, the National Natural Science Foundation of China under Grant no. 61572080, and the CCF and Venustech Research Program under Grant no. 2016012.

References

[1] M. S. Hossain, G. Muhammad, W. Abdul, B. Song, and B. Gupta, "Cloud-assisted secure video transmission and sharing framework for smart cities," *Future Generation Computer Systems*, 2017.

[2] B. Tang, Z. Chen, G. Hefferman et al., "Incorporating intelligence in fog computing for big data analysis in smart cities," *IEEE Transactions on Industrial Informatics*, no. 99, 2017.

[3] J. Zhou, Z. Cao, X. Dong, X. Lin, and A. Vasilakos, "Securing m-healthcare social networks: challenges, countermeasures and future directions," *IEEE Wireless Communications*, vol. 20, no. 4, pp. 12–21, 2013.

[4] K. Zhang, K. Yang, X. Liang, Z. Su, X. Shen, and H. H. Luo, "Security and privacy for mobile healthcare networks: from a quality of protection perspective," *IEEE Wireless Communications*, vol. 22, no. 4, pp. 104–112, 2015.

[5] H. Huang, T. Gong, N. Ye, R. Wang, and Y. Dou, "Private and secured medical data transmission and analysis for wireless sensing healthcare system," *IEEE Transactions on Industrial Informatics*, vol. 13, no. 3, pp. 1227–1237, 2017.

[6] X. Liang, M. Barua, R. Lu, X. Lin, and X. Shen, "HealthShare: achieving secure and privacy-preserving health information sharing through health social networks," *Computer Communications*, vol. 35, no. 15, pp. 1910–1920, 2012.

[7] J. Zhou, Z. Cao, X. Dong, N. Xiong, and A. V. Vasilakos, "4S: a secure and privacy-preserving key management scheme for cloud-assisted wireless body area network in m-healthcare social networks," *Information Sciences*, vol. 314, pp. 255–276, 2015.

[8] L. Chen, Z. Cao, R. Lu, X. Liang, and X. Shen, "EPF: an event-aided packet forwarding protocol for privacy-preserving mobile healthcare social networks," in *Proceedings of the 54th Annual IEEE Global Telecommunications Conference (GLOBECOM '11)*, Kathmandu, Nepal, December 2011.

[9] L. Guo, C. Zhang, J. Sun, and Y. Fang, "A privacy-preserving attribute-based authentication system for mobile health networks," *IEEE Transactions on Mobile Computing*, vol. 13, no. 9, pp. 1927–1941, 2014.

[10] W. Yu, Z. Liu, C. Chen, B. Yang, and X. Guan, "Privacy-preserving design for emergency response scheduling system in medical social networks," *Peer-to-Peer Networking and Applications*, vol. 10, no. 2, pp. 340–356, 2017.

[11] K. Zhang, J. Ni, K. Yang, X. Liang, J. Ren, and X. S. Shen, "Security and privacy in smart city applications: challenges and solutions," *IEEE Communications Magazine*, vol. 55, no. 1, pp. 122–129, 2017.

[12] A. Lounis, A. Hadjidj, A. Bouabdallah, and Y. Challal, "Healing on the cloud: secure cloud architecture for medical wireless sensor networks," *Future Generation Computer Systems*, vol. 55, pp. 266–277, 2016.

[13] T.-L. Chen, Y.-T. Liao, Y.-F. Chang, and J.-H. Hwang, "Security approach to controlling access to personal health records in healthcare service," *Security and Communication Networks*, vol. 9, no. 7, pp. 652–666, 2016.

[14] A. Zhang, A. Bacchus, and X. Lin, "Consent-based access control for secure and privacy-preserving health information exchange," *Security and Communication Networks*, vol. 9, no. 16, pp. 3496–3508, 2016.

[15] Q. Huang, Y. Yang, and M. Shen, "Secure and efficient data collaboration with hierarchical attribute-based encryption in cloud computing," *Future Generation Computer Systems*, vol. 72, pp. 239–249, 2017.

[16] A. Sahai and B. Waters, "Fuzzy identity-based encryption," in *Proceedings of the 24th Annual International Conference on the Theory and Applications of Cryptographic Techniques (EUROCRYPT '05)*, pp. 457–473, Springer, Aarhus, Denmark, May 2005.

[17] J. Bethencourt, A. Sahai, and B. Waters, "Ciphertext-policy attribute-based encryption," in *Proceedings of the IEEE Symposium on Security and Privacy (SP '07)*, pp. 321–334, Berkeley, Calif, USA, May 2007.

[18] S. Narayan, M. Gagné, and R. Safavi-Naini, "Privacy preserving ehr system using attribute-based infrastructure," in *Proceedings of the ACM Workshop on Cloud Computing Security Workshop (CCSW '10)*, pp. 47–52, Chicago, Ill, USA, October 2010.

[19] M. Li, S. Yu, Y. Zheng, K. Ren, and W. Lou, "Scalable and secure sharing of personal health records in cloud computing using attribute-based encryption," *IEEE Transactions on Parallel and Distributed Systems*, vol. 24, no. 1, pp. 131–143, 2013.

[20] M. H. Au, T. H. Yuen, J. K. Liu et al., "A general framework for secure sharing of personal health records in cloud system," *Journal of Computer and System Sciences*, 2017.

[21] Y. Liu, Y. Zhang, J. Ling, and Z. Liu, "Secure and fine-grained access control on e-healthcare records in mobile cloud computing," *Future Generation Computer Systems*, 2017.

[22] L.-Y. Yeh, P.-Y. Chiang, Y.-L. Tsai, and J.-L. Huang, "Cloud-based fine-grained health information access control framework for lightweight IoT devices with dynamic auditing and attribute revocation," *IEEE Transactions on Cloud Computing*, no. 99, 2015.

[23] P. Zhang, Z. Chen, J. K. Liu, K. Liang, and H. Liu, "An efficient access control scheme with outsourcing capability and attribute update for fog computing," *Future Generation Computer Systems*, 2016.

[24] A. Zanella, N. Bui, A. P. Castellani, L. Vangelista, and M. Zorzi, "Internet of things for smart cities," *IEEE Internet of Things Journal*, vol. 1, no. 1, pp. 22–32, 2014.

[25] X. A. Wang, J. Ma, F. Xhafa, M. Zhang, and X. Luo, "Cost-

effective secure E-health cloud system using identity based cryptographic techniques," *Future Generation Computer Systems*, vol. 67, pp. 242–254, 2017.

[26] X. Liang, R. Lu, L. Chen, X. Lin, and X. Shen, "PEC: a privacy-preserving emergency call scheme for mobile healthcare social networks," *Journal of Communications and Networks*, vol. 13, no. 2, pp. 102–112, 2011.

[27] S. Jiang, X. Zhu, and L. Wang, "EPPS: Efficient and privacy-preserving personal health information sharing in mobile healthcare social networks," *Sensors*, vol. 15, no. 9, pp. 22419–22438, 2015.

[28] Y. Zhou, H. Deng, Q. Wu, B. Qin, J. Liu, and Y. Ding, "Identity-based proxy re-encryption version 2: making mobile access easy in cloud," *Future Generation Computer Systems*, vol. 62, pp. 128–139, 2016.

[29] Q. Huang, L. Wang, and Y. Yang, "DECENT: secure and fine-grained data access control with policy updating for constrained IoT devices," *World Wide Web*, pp. 1–17, 2017.

[30] B. Lynn, The pairing-based cryptography library, http://crypto.stanford.edu/pbc/.

14

Detecting Web-Based Botnets using Bot Communication Traffic Features

Fu-Hau Hsu,[1] Chih-Wen Ou,[1] Yan-Ling Hwang,[2] Ya-Ching Chang,[1] and Po-Ching Lin[3]

[1]*Department of Computer Science and Information Engineering, National Central University, Taoyuan, Taiwan*
[2]*School of Applied Foreign Languages, Chung Shan Medical University, Taichung, Taiwan*
[3]*Department of Computer Science and Information Engineering, National Chung Cheng University, Chiayi, Taiwan*

Correspondence should be addressed to Chih-Wen Ou; chihwen.frankou@gmail.com

Academic Editor: Steffen Wendzel

Web-based botnets are popular nowadays. A Web-based botnet is a botnet whose C&C server and bots use HTTP protocol, the most universal and supported network protocol, to communicate with each other. Because the botnet communication can be hidden easily by attackers behind the relatively massive HTTP traffic, administrators of network equipment, such as routers and switches, cannot block such suspicious traffic directly regardless of costs. Based on the clients constituent of a Web server and characteristics of HTTP responses sent to clients from the server, this paper proposes a traffic inspection solution, called Web-based Botnet Detector (WBD). WBD is able to detect suspicious C&C (Command-and-Control) servers of HTTP botnets regardless of whether the botnet commands are encrypted or hidden in normal Web pages. More than 500 GB real network traces collected from 11 backbone routers are used to evaluate our method. Experimental results show that the false positive rate of WBD is 0.42%.

1. Introduction

A botnet is a group of compromised computers, namely, bots, controlled by one or multiple controllers [1–3]. These botnet controllers, also named bot masters, provide commands to their bots through C&C (Command-and-Control) servers so that the bots can perform actions for their bot masters. There are several criteria to categorize botnets, including the attacking behavior, C&C model, communication channel, rallying mechanism, and the evasion technique. We firstly focus on the centralized C&C model and discuss details about it in this study.

For a botnet with a centralized C&C model, each bot connects to its C&C server to retrieve commands or to deliver data. There are many advantages to use such an architecture to organize C&C servers and their bots compared to the decentralized and randomized models. The first advantage is the low cost to construct such a botnet, because bot masters can easily create this kind of botnets using many off-the-shelf open resources and applications. Meanwhile, the centralized model allows a bot master to quickly rally a large number of its bots by commanding few C&C servers. Such efficiency

obviously facilitates cybercriminals to use botnets to conduct malicious activities, such as DDoS attacks and spamming [4].

According to the communication protocols used by botnets, botnets can be classified into several categories. These categories include the IRC- (Internet Relay Chat-) based botnet, the IM- (Instant Message-) based botnet, and the Web-based botnet. This paper focuses on the Web-based botnet, also named *HTTP botnet*, whose communication channel between the C&C server and its bot clients is via the HTTP. A C&C server of a Web-based botnet works like a normal Web server, and bot clients of a Web-based botnet work as normal Web clients. We call the C&C server of a Web-based botnet a *botnet Web server* hereafter. Two botnets, Spyeye [5] and Zeus [6], are well-known HTTP-based botnets. According to previous studies on these two botnets, there are several reasons why the HTTP is attractive to botnet owners. First, HTTP traffic is the most popular Internet traffic nowadays so that Web-based botnet traffic can be easily disguised as normal HTTP traffic, making the botnets more difficult to be discovered than those that use less popular protocols. Second, most network firewalls/proxies allow hosts behind them to access Internet via the HTTP. As a result,

Web-based botnets can easily provide stable and qualified client-to-server connectivity. Third, many promising solutions [1, 7–9] have been developed to precisely detect traditional IRC-based botnets instead of Web-based botnets. Therefore, the HTTP gradually becomes an ideal alternative protocol for botnet owners to use as the communication channel in recent years, and our study focuses on this kind of botnets.

1.1. Web-Based Botnet Detection. Bot clients are trojans, executable programs, or scripts running on compromised hosts. Hence, their behavior is different from human user behavior. Besides, their activity pattern, sizes, and transferred content are also different from human users. As programs generate the communication traffic automatically, the Web-based botnet communication has some prominent characteristics. According to our preliminary survey on a botnet taxonomy study [2], a typical bot client of a centralized C&C botnet often needs to synchronize with its botnet Web server to retrieve commands or deliver execution results. Such synchronization is often scheduled when bot clients are effectively controlled by botnet Web servers. Hence, we think that this phenomenon of synchronization can be utilized as a hint to indicate whether Web clients are controlled by human users or by bot clients. Besides, we also found that if a group of Web clients associated with a Web server consists of human users, each of them often has a different access pattern to the Web server. For example, these human clients may visit the Web server at different times of a day, or these clients may visit the Web server different numbers of times each day. On the contrary, if these Web clients are bot clients, which run programs or scripts, they may act together and behave similarly. Therefore, they may contact their botnet Web server repeatedly according to a predefined time interval to access commands from their botnet Web server. Such repeated contact to certain botnet Web servers may continue for several days, which is apparently different from normal human behavior. In addition, the same group of bot clients usually tends to communicate with the same botnet Web server. Based on the long-term repeated contact phenomenon and similar access pattern of the clients of a Web server, we use a metric named *Total Host Repetition Rate*, or *THR* in short, as one of our criteria to examine whether a Web server is a suspicious botnet C&C server.

Instead of THR, we also found that the payload inside the traffic between bot clients and their botnet Web server usually contains short and simple commands. Furthermore, all bot clients commanded by a certain C&C server tend to receive commands at the same time. This similarity of payloads among the bot clients controlled by the same botnet Web server is also described as the command-response pattern by BotProbe [7]. A normal Web server usually contains many Web pages and different users accessing different Web pages. Hence, unless the Web server contains only one Web page, the probability that its users retrieve the same Web page from the Web server simultaneously is low, and different Web pages usually have different sizes. As a result, during a period of time, the sizes of responding payloads of different Web clients accessing the same Web server are supposed to be different,

while a botnet Web server often dispatches similar commands to its bot clients at the same time. Thus, we utilize the payload size difference as a metric called the *payload size similarity*, or *PSS* in short, to judge whether a Web server is a suspicious botnet C&C server or not. The formalization for these two metrics will be discussed later in Section 2.2.

In our prototype implementation, we designed an automatic mechanism based on the above two metrics and integrated this mechanism into our prototype system, named *Web-based Botnet Detector*, or *WBD* in short, to perform the inspection. WBD is attached to a network traffic monitoring system which is able to generate traffic logs from the online network stream and analyzes these logs simultaneously. Only few arithmetic calculations are required by WBD while performing runtime inspection on those monitored traffic logs. Such calculation brings significant overhead to other similar approaches during traffic inspection.

1.2. Contributions. The solution of this paper contains the following characteristics: (1) Compared to mainstream machine learning approaches which often rely heavily on tens or even hundreds of features, an approach with only few features can reduce notable overhead. WBD requires only several deterministic calculations which are easily extracted and calculated from monitored network traffic. (2) WBD inspects traffic of backbone networks. It does not require any program installed on network end-hosts and servers. (3) WBD does not use features based on traffic content mining. It does not rely on particular protocol-parsing as well. In summary, the contributions of WBD include the following.

(1) WBD requires only several deterministic calculations, which means that it is ideal to cooperate with heavy-loading backbone equipment.

(2) We conducted large-scale backbone data inspection for this study. It reveals those IP addresses and timestamps of Web servers that generate suspicious Web-based botnet communications across the global Internet.

(3) Due to the low correlation between the content itself, our solution can target the HTTPS protocol theoretically. Also, botnet owners may deliberately embed their botnet commands into some normal traffic, such as universal Web contents, to bypass the potential inspection along the traffic path. Our solution can work for this situation, because the calculation on THR and PSS requires the source and destination IP addresses of the packets in the traffic, which are not encrypted by most secure protocols.

This paper includes six sections. Section 2 will explain how we use features calculated from these criteria for the datagram-like network traffic logs. Sections 3 and 4 evaluate our approach and discuss issues including comparison with other similar approaches and the accuracy. Section 5 describes previous studies aiming at botnet related issues. Section 6 summaries this study.

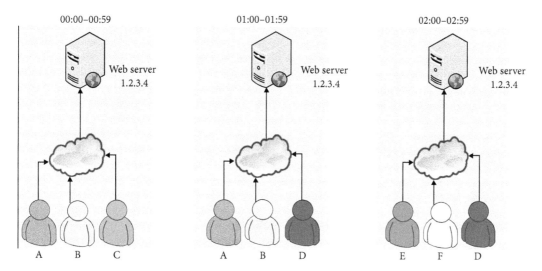

FIGURE 1: A communication pattern between 6 Web clients and a Web server during a three-hour monitoring period.

2. Methodology

In order to develop a traffic inspection approach, several issues have to be considered. These issues include the involved scale of monitoring, the volume of the traffic, and the feasibility to obtain such traffic. If an approach has to monitor the user-side traffic, an appropriate inspecting location may be at a gateway, a router, or a proxy (if it is mandatory for each network user) of the target user-side network. If an approach requires to monitor the server-side network, a possible location to do this work may be located at the intrusion detection equipment or firewall equipment of the target server-side network. These two deployments are commonly selected by many traffic inspection approaches because of their deployment feasibility and the affordable traffic volume. Different from these two categories, our approach aims at monitoring the global Internet as much as possible. The possible inspecting locations for such kind of approach should include backbone equipment that routes and processes large amount of IP packets. In our study, we are allowed to obtain the traffic from several online backbone routers in Taiwan so that we can develop a solution that is not specifically restricted by user-side or server-side networks.

Even though we are able to obtain logs from actual backbone routers, these routers are so important for our Internet service provider and they are always full-loaded. Hence, directly running inspecting procedures on them is certainly impractical so we adopted offline analyzing-after-recording method to make our experiments. We collected log samples from these backbone routers for several times and analyzed them. The detailed information about this will be described in Section 3. Due to many security and privacy concerns, all these actions were conducted and completed in an office of an Internet service provider. We cannot see the content of IP packet payloads and we cannot take any log-out from the office. Information about the recorded data from the traffic will be described later in Section 3.1.

2.1. A Case Study. To provide a clear understanding of our approach, considering an input case extracted from our logs depicted in Figure 1, there are six Web clients named from A to F requesting, respectively, a Web server with an IP address denoted as 1.2.3.4 hereafter. The three-hour long monitoring period is separated into three consecutive time intervals, as shown in Figure 1, and the length of each time interval is one hour. If clients A, B, and C make requests to the Web server in the first time interval, there will be arrows connecting them to the Web server, as shown in the left time interval marked with 00:00–00:59. Similarly, clients A and B repeat requesting and D makes the request in the second time interval. Client D repeats requesting, and clients E and F make requests in the third time interval in this case. A graphic representation of this case is shown in Figure 2. A Web server is denoted as an S-vertex, and a Web client is denoted as a C-vertex. The communication between a Web server and a client is denoted as an undirected edge connecting these two vertexes, as an example shown in Figure 2. There is no edge between two different C-vertexes because we do not need to consider the case when a Web client also runs a Web service. After all, we only focus on centralized botnets. We can also ignore edges between two S-vertexes because we only focus on communication made by Web clients. A graph is used to describe the communication patterns between Web clients and a Web server in a time interval. These graphs will not be used directly for graph computation. How these graphs are used will be described in Section 2.2.

2.2. Features Formulation. We use graphic representation only for conceptive discussion. For actual calculation conducted by WBD, equivalent formulas calculation is adopted after obtaining traffic logs. Such a design ensures that related calculation is theoretically light-weight, and such an approach is suitable for working with existing Internet backbone equipment. As we have mentioned in Section 1.1, two metrics are used to determine whether there exists botnet

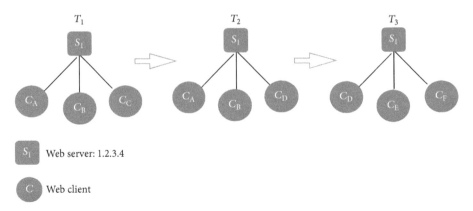

FIGURE 2: Graph representations of communication patterns between Web clients and their Web server at different monitoring time intervals.

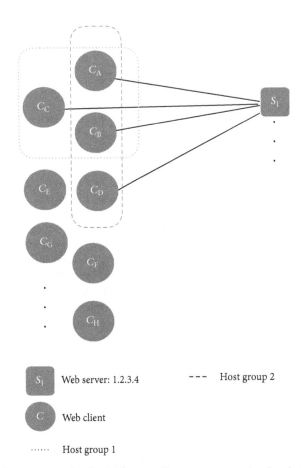

FIGURE 3: Two host groups related to Web server S_1 at two consecutive time intervals T_1 and T_2.

communication in the monitored HTTP traffic. In this paper, we call the group of Web clients that communicate with a Web server in a time interval a *host group*, as two groups of this case shown in Figure 3 show two host groups appearing at two different time intervals. If a Web server is a botnet Web server, the associated host groups are called *bot groups*. According to the previous studies [2, 10] and observation, the hosts of a bot group tend to communicate with the same botnet Web server all the time. Even though the constituent members of a bot group may change due to some technical

issues or management reasons, such a change does not occur dramatically in a short period of time.

Two host groups, which are associated with the same Web server appearing in successive time intervals, are called *adjacent host groups*. We use two scores, *Access (AC)* score and *Total Host Repeat (THR)* score, to evaluate the THR feature of a Web server. Equation (1) defines these two scores, respectively. Score AC_s represents the number of total hosts communicating with Web server s in these n time intervals. For a certain time interval, the *HR* score is defined as the proportion of the number of hosts appearing in both the current host group and its previously adjacent host group to the number of hosts in the current host group. The intersection of hostgroup$_{s_{t-1}}$ and hostgroup$_{s_t}$ denotes the set of hosts appearing in both the adjacent host groups. Score THR$_s$ is an average of n Host Repeat (HR) scores, denoting the similarity of the host groups of Web server s in n time intervals.

$$AC_s = \sum_{t=1}^{n} \left| hostgroup_{s_t} \right|$$

$$THR_s = \frac{1}{n} \sum_{t=1}^{n} \frac{\left| hostgroup_{s_{t-1}} \cap hostgroup_{s_t} \right|}{\left| hostgroup_{s_t} \right|}. \tag{1}$$

Assume the host group of Web server s is hostgroup$_{s_t}$ in time interval t and there are k_t different total responding payload sizes, $PS_{t_{k_1}}, PS_{t_{k_2}}, \ldots, PS_{t_{k_t}}$, for the $|hostgroup_{s_t}|$ hosts. $|PS_{t_{k_i}}|$ represents the number of hosts whose payload size is $PS_{t_{k_i}}$ in time interval t. Score *payload size similarity (PSS)* defined in (2) is used to evaluate the payload similarity feature of a Web server. Equation (2) gives its definition.

$$PSS_s = \frac{\sum_{t=1}^{n} \max_{i=1}^{k_t} \left(\left| PS_{t_i} \right| \right)}{\sum_{t=1}^{n} \left| hostgroup_{s_t} \right|} = \frac{\sum_{t=1}^{n} \max_{i=1}^{k_t} \left(\left| PS_{t_i} \right| \right)}{AC_s}. \tag{2}$$

2.3. WBD Classifier. After quantification of features for each input Web server, we can distinguish between normal Web servers and suspicious botnet Web server by comparing their THR, AC, and PSS scores to thresholds. In order to find the proper thresholds, we extracted the HTTP traffic traces of Alexa top 20 Websites in Taiwan from 11 backbone routers. The traffic related to these popular Websites is supposed to be nonbotnet traffic. However, when botnet traffic is hidden in the traffic of a social network Website, the social network traffic may contain botnet traffic. Hence, when collecting nonbotnet traffic, we can filter out social network related traffic first to avoid the above problem. However, in our traces, except Facebook which continues detecting and removing fake or malicious accounts, almost all of the top 20 Websites are nonsocial network Websites. Therefore, we consider the traffic associated with these popular Websites as benign. We calculated the THR score and AC score of each Web server and then selected the maximum THR score and AC score as the thresholds. Equation (3) shows the equations. THR$_i$ represents the THR score of Web server i, and AC$_i$ represents the AC score of Web server i.

$$THR_{thershold} = \max_{i \in top\_20\_benign\_servers} (THR_i)$$

$$AC_{thershold} = \max_{i \in top\_20\_benign\_servers} (AC_i). \tag{3}$$

WBD uses the thresholds to examine Web servers appearing in the HTTP traffic traces and uses (4) to check whether Web server i exhibits the THR feature denoted by HR$_{Susp\_Server}(i)$.

$$HR_{Susp\_Server}(i)$$
$$= \begin{cases} True, & THR_i > THR_{thershold} \wedge AC_i < AC_{thershold} \\ False, & otherwise. \end{cases} \tag{4}$$

WBD uses (5) to check whether Web server i exhibits the similar payload size feature denoted by notation PSS$_{Susp\_Server}(i)$. PSS$_{threshold}$ in (5) is defined as 0.5 because if in average the payload sizes of 50% hosts of each host group of a Web server during a time interval are similar to each other, the Web server is unlikely to be a normal Web server.

$$PSS_{Susp\_Server}(i) = \begin{cases} True, & PSS_i > PSS_{threshold} \\ False, & otherwise. \end{cases} \tag{5}$$

Based on the values determined by (4) and (5) for Web server i, WBD uses (6) to determine whether Web server i is a suspicious botnet Web server. All hosts which connect to it more than once are supposed to be its bot clients.

$$Susp\_C\&C(i)$$
$$= \begin{cases} True, & HR_{Susp\_Server}(i) == True \vee PSS_{Susp\_Server}(i) == True \\ False, & otherwise. \end{cases} \tag{6}$$

WBD is built based on the above equations. There are four components in our prototype system. The first is to collect the raw data. The second is a module able to calculate THR and AC. The third is a module able to calculate PSS. The last is a combination of a report generator and a classifier operating according to the output from the second and the third modules.

3. Evaluation

The evaluation of WBD has two purposes. The first purpose is to discover appropriate thresholds of our solutions. The second purpose is to estimate the effectiveness of WBD. In order to evaluate the effectiveness of WBD, we need to know the number of botnet Web servers whose network traffic is recorded in our datasets. However, according to the phishing domain survey reports made by McGrath et al. [9] and Aaron et al. [11], attackers usually do not use a compromised host for more than a couple of days. Hence, we are not able to check all the Web servers in our collected datasets before attackers stop using some botnet Web servers that are hidden inside these large numbers of Web servers. Instead of checking all Web servers for entire datasets, we can only perform manual check on malicious hosts identified by WBD to determine whether they are truly malicious, so that we can at least calculate the false positive rate of WBD in our evaluation.

We collected network traces three times from 11 backbone routers in Taiwan. These routers belong to one of the three largest Internet service providers in Taiwan. Each collection generates a dataset. Each collection lasts for 48 hours to generate a dataset. Hence, we obtained 3 datasets. These routers

TABLE 1: Fields of a NetFlow V5 record.

Content	Bytes offset	Description
srcaddr	0–3	Source IP address
dstaddr	4–7	Destination IP address
dPkts	16–19	Packets in the flow
srcport	32-33	Source port number
dstport	34-35	Destination port number
prot	38	Protocol (6 = TCP, 17 = UDP)

TABLE 2: Information of our training phase dataset.

Time period	Size of the raw file	Number of Web servers
2013/03/16 00:00–2013/03/17 23:59	About 200 GB	9933

TABLE 3: Information of our testing phase datasets.

Index	Time period	Size of the raw file	Number of Web servers
1	2013/06/01 00:00–2013/06/02 23:59	About 140 GB	156294
2	2013/01/18 00:00–2013/01/19 23:59	About 160 GB	170920

TABLE 4: Results of the testing phase.

Index	False positive	Number of suspicious Web servers
1	3 (0.28%)	1047
2	9 (0.83%)	1085
Total	12 (0.42%)	2132

are Cisco routers equipped with NetFlow [12]. Therefore, these datasets were recorded in the NetFlow V5 compatible format. Our experiments include two phases. The first is the training phase which is used to determine the thresholds using the first dataset. The second is the testing phase which uses the other two datasets.

3.1. NetFlow. NetFlow is able to record all traffic passing through a Cisco router. It fetches data from IP packets and generates flow records. Those flow records can be transferred to other devices for further analysis. The source address field *srcaddr*, destination address field *dstaddr*, source port field *srcport*, destination port field *dstport*, and protocol field *prot* of a NetFlow V5 record specify a session between a certain source host and a destination host via the HTTP, as shown in Table 1. The *dPkts* field contains the raw packet data, so that we can calculate the payload size of a packet and the total payload size of an HTTP session.

3.2. Threshold and Training Phase. The first part of our experiments is to calculate the thresholds and perform training. The training data were collected from March 16 to 17 in 2013. The number of backbone routers involved in this phase is less than the number of routers in the testing phase because we chose the routers which forward packets to popular Web servers in this phase. As shown in Table 2, the total raw data size in this phase is about 200 GB which consists of the IP addresses of 9,933 Web servers. The THR scores of Alexa top 20 popular Websites in Taiwan are all less than 0.521. We also

used a browser to manually connect to the 9,933 Web servers to check which of them are normal Web servers and which of them are abnormal. The THR scores of the above normal Web servers are almost all less than 0.521. In contrast, the THR scores of the above abnormal Web servers are almost all greater than 0.521. Therefore, we set $THR_{threshold}$ as 0.521 and set $AC_{threshold}$ as 12,000. Besides, $PSS_{threshold}$ is set to 0.5 as described in previous subsection. We also calculated the average Web page size for these top 20 Websites, and the size is 47,087 bytes.

3.3. Testing Phase. In the testing phase, two datasets were used. Table 3 shows the information of these samples. More than 300 GB data were used in our analysis. These two datasets contain network traces of 156,294 and 170,920 Web servers, respectively. Among these Web servers, WBD found 1,047 suspicious botnet Web servers from testing dataset 1 and 1,085 suspicious servers from testing dataset 2. For each of these 2,132 suspicious botnet Web servers, we use a browser to manually check their content. If a suspicious botnet Web server replies to a normal Web page, we treat this case as a false positive case. Besides, bot clients usually retrieve commands from their botnet Web server, and the sizes of the commands are supposed to be smaller than the size of normal Web pages. Therefore, if the size of data returning from a Web server is greater than 47,087 bytes, we will deem the Web server as a normal one and also treat this case as a false positive case. The result of the testing phase is shown in Table 4. To calculate the false negative rate, we need to

TABLE 5: Features and classifiers used by four similar approaches.

Approaches	Features	Classifier
Venkatesh and Nadarajan	ORT, RIO, PT, SYN, FIN, PSH	Neural network
Zhao et al.	PX, PPS, NR, APL, FPS, PV, FPH, TBP	Decision tree
Cai and Zou	SHH, CC, SCL, BIC, PR, DWS	Multilayer filter
WBD	AC, THR, PSS	Decision tree

TABLE 6: Comparisons of features used by four approaches.

Calculations	Venkatesh and Nadarajan	Zhao et al.	Cai and Zou	WBD
Counting specific packets	ORT, RIO, PT, SYN, FIN, PSH	PX, PPS, NR	—	—
Arithmetic based on packet size	—	APL, FPS, PV	SHH, CC, SCL	PSS
Arithmetic based on numbers of hosts	—	FPH	BIC	AC, THS
Arithmetic based on interpacket timing	—	TBP	PR	—
Host fingerprinting	—	—	DWS	—

manually check 327,214 Web servers to confirm the botnet Web servers within them. However, according to the phishing domain survey reports made by McGrath et al. [13] and Aaron et al. [14], attackers usually do not use a compromised host for more than a couple of days. Because we are not able to check all the 327,214 Web servers before attackers stop using some botnet Web servers that are hidden inside these 327,214 Web servers, currently we are not able to calculate the false negative rate of WBD. However, when comparing with a malicious IP list provided by ICST [15], we found that the majority of the botnet Web servers we found are not in the list, which shows that WBD provides a list of originally unknown botnet Web servers to system administrators.

4. Discussion

Some approaches aiming at detecting HTTP botnets were also proposed in recent years. These approaches use various features to inspect network traffic to detect HTTP botnets. Three of such approaches are selected and compared with WBD. Table 5 lists these approaches with their features and classifiers. Venkatesh and Nadarajan [16] proposed a multi-layer feedforward neural network solution with six features, including one-way ratio of TCP packets (ORT), ratio of incoming to outgoing TCP packets (RIO), the proportion of TCP packets in the flow (PT), and TCP flags counting on SYN, FIN, and PSH flags. These features require only counting specific packets, so that they increase relatively slight performance overhead compared to other complex features used by the rest of the approaches. Such counting-based features are simple and can be manipulated by communicators, so that botnet owners who are aware of such features can bypass the detection by specifically changing their forms of communication packets. Zhao et al. [17] proposed a solution with eight features. Three of them are related to counting-based features including the number of packets exchanged (PX), the number of packets exchanged per second in short time interval (PPS), and the number of reconnections (NR). Three of them are related to arithmetic operations based on the packet payload size, including the average payload packet

length (APL), the variance of the payload packet length (PV), and the size of the first packet (FPS). One of the two remaining features involves arithmetic calculations for the number of flows from this address over the total number of flows generated per hour (FPH), and the other feature calculates the average time interval between two consecutive packets (TBS). This approach has higher accuracy than the previous study of Venkatesh and Nadarajan, and its performance overhead is certainly increased due to involving more complicated features compared to the previous study. Cai and Zou [10] proposed a solution with six features. Three of them require arithmetic operations based on the packet payload size, including short HTTP header (SHH), constant content (CC), and short content length (SCL). One feature is related to the bot IP clustering (BIC), one focuses on the periodical request (PR), and the last one requires the host fingerprinting among Web servers to estimate the extent of diversified Web services (DWS). Although this approach has the comprehensive discussion about the features of HTTP botnet and comes up with a set of complicated features that is suitable for determining the existence of botnet communication precisely, the performance overhead is still a significant issue. Many complex features, especially the DWS feature, are involved in this approach for traffic inspection.

Based on the above discussion, we discovered that some kinds of calculations are commonly required by some of these four approaches. Table 6 describes the summarization. Both the study of Venkatesh and Nadarajan and the study of Zhao et al. count specific packets. Both the study of Zhao et al. and the study of Cai and Zou have features which require performing arithmetic operations based on the packet payload size or based on interpacket timing. Three approaches, including WBD, have features requiring execution of arithmetic operations based on the numbers of hosts and the packet size. However, WBD uses only three features requiring execution of arithmetic operations based on numbers of hosts and the packet payload size. Compared to the study of Venkatesh and Nadarajan and the study of Zhao et al., WBD does not need to count specific packets, so that botnet owners have fewer opportunities to bypass WBD. Besides,

TABLE 7: Comparison among false positive rates of four similar approaches.

Approaches	False positive rates of various test datasets
Venkatesh and Nadarajan	Spyeye-1 (0.97%), Spyeye-2 (0.98%), Zeus-1 (0.99%), Zeus-2 (0.96%)
Zhao et al.	BlackEnergy (0%), Weasel (82%)
Cai and Zou	SJTU1 (17.6%), SJTU2 (26.3%), QingPu (13.6%)
WBD	0.42%

unlike the study of Cai and Zou, WBD does not apply time consuming features such as features of interpacket timing and host fingerprinting so that WBD has limited performance overhead and is able to complete classification in time.

To evaluate the effectiveness of their approaches, each of these four similar approaches used their own datasets to obtain the false positive rates of the chosen datasets. Table 7 lists test datasets and respective false positive rates of these four similar approaches. Four datasets were used by Venkatesh and Nadarajan, and all false positive rates of these datasets are under 1%. For the false positive rates of Zhao et al., the false positive rate of test dataset BlackEnergy is 0%. Dataset BlackEnergy is a pure botnet traffic dataset. The false positive rate of test dataset Weasel is 82%. Dataset Weasel contains normal traffic. The authors analyzed these 82% false positives (2902 false alerts) and discovered that all of these false alerts belong to six applications. They claimed that once a whitelist is adopted for their approach, these false positives would be reduced. The study of Cai and Zou used three datasets to test their approach. The false positive rates range from 13.6% to 26.3%. WBD used logs directly captured from backbone routers and the false positive rate is 0.42%. Compared to other three approaches, WBD is better than the study of Venkatesh and Nadarajan and the study of Cai and Zou. WBD does not need a prebuilt whitelist to remove normal applications before detection.

4.1. False Positives. The total false positive rate of our study is 0.42%. This excellent accuracy results from the adoption of THS and PSS. In fact, many existing front-end Web applications may repeat contacting a Web server. The Web-based instant messenger is one of the typical examples where Web clients contact their Web servers repeatedly. However, as mentioned in previous paragraph, other related approaches may not distinguish the differences between a botnet and a Web server functioning as a Web-based instant messenger.

4.2. False Negatives. Due to the reasons described in this subsection, currently we are not able to discuss the false negative of our work. According to the phishing domain survey reports made by McGrath et al. [13] and Aaron et al. [14], attackers usually do not use a comprised host for more than a couple of days. Apparently, we are not able to check all the Web servers classified as benign in our datasets in time before most attackers stop using botnet Web servers that are hidden inside these large amounts of Web servers. Compared to several previous similar studies [10, 16, 17], most of them evaluate their solution by the datasets containing specific botnets of Spyeye [5] and Zeus [6] instead of real live traffic from Internet. This means that these similar approaches

may be accurate when they are applied for detecting those botnets which have similar characteristics to Spyeye and Zeus, but the accuracy is not evaluated for other Web-based botnets. However, most botnet owners keep changing attributes and characteristics of their botnets to avoid being detected. Another reason why false negatives sometimes are impractical is that the Web-based botnets may provide legal online Web services simultaneously. Mostly they may act like normal Web services, and it is very difficult, if not impossible, to enumerate all Internet Web servers having such a characteristic. All issues listed here lead to the uncertainty of the discussion about the false negatives. We will keep discussing this issue in our future work.

4.3. Detection Evasion. Experimental results show that WBD is an ideal solution for Web-based botnet detection. However, current Web-based botnets may change their designs to bypass the detection of WBD. For example, bot clients may connect to their C&C server at nonadjacent time intervals, or various lengths of gibberish bytes may be added to the response payloads of different bot clients to diversify the response lengths. However, such evasion methods may create several drawbacks in the modified botnets. First, this makes the design and operation of a botnet much more complicated because a botnet needs to coordinate the action of each bot client. Second, gibberish bytes increase network traffic. Besides, if different bot clients use the same URL but get Web pages with different lengths, this may be a sign that the related server is not a normal Web server. Besides, C&C servers may apply fast-flux domain technique to change their IP addresses frequently in a very short period of time. Botnets with such ability theoretically possibly bypass WBD deliberately with the price that all bots need to connect and disconnect different hosts frequently, which makes them much more detectable by system/network administrators. In the literature of fast-flux research, an approach proposed by Hsu et al. [18] has been developed to detect fast-flux domains from a single host without using router traces. Hence, by integrating both kinds of approaches, we can create an effective method to detect various Web server-based botnets.

The goal of this paper is to find the botnet Web servers. However, during the detection, we can also obtain the hosts, that is, bot clients, that connect to the botnet Web servers. Hence, in our future work, we will make more detailed survey to find the properties of bot clients. Moreover, this study also works for detecting botnet Web servers communicating with their bot clients via the HTTPS channel because the detection relies only on unencrypted parts of IP packets instead of inspecting the payload content. The unencrypted parts include the information of the source host and

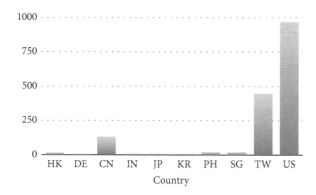

FIGURE 4: C&C server locations.

destination host and the payload size. Furthermore, the THR feature and the PSS feature will not be changed by modifying the content that a botnet Web server sends to its bot clients. Hence, even if a bot master hides its command inside a normal-looking Web page, WBD is still able to detect it. After detecting a list of C&C servers, we also survey the distribution of the locations of these C&C servers. Figure 4 shows the locations of the 1,085 C&C servers that WBD detects from testing dataset 2. The majority of them are located in the USA and Taiwan. Some of them are located in China, Singapore, Philippines, and so on.

5. Related Work

Most previous studies aim at generic botnet detection. Gu et al. proposed several correlation-based detection solutions: BotMiner [19], BotSniffer [3], BotProbe [7], and BotHunter [20]. BotMiner is a well-known network level correlation-based and protocol-structure independent solution. It performs the connection behavior (C-Plane) and attack behavior (A-Plane) clustering and then performs cross-plane correlation to build a model for botnet C&C servers. BotMiner requires some real-world C&C server network traces in the training phase. However, such reliable C&C traces are not always available in practice. BotSniffer is also a correlation-based solution able to detect C&C servers in a port-independent manner. It is composed of a protocol matcher, an activity/message response detector, and a correlation engine. The correlation engine runs group activity/message response analysis based on the outputs from this protocol matcher and response detectors without requiring other prior knowledge of these botnet C&C servers. Only few packets are needed for training BotSniffer, and it also works well at detecting small botnets. BotProbe is a behavior-based solution, specifically focusing on the command-response pattern of the botnet and its deterministic behavior (for the stateless bot client). BotMiner, BotSniffer, and BotProbe have some problems when the botnet attempts to avoid such detection. The possible evasions include using strong encryption, using atypical response, and injecting random noise packets. Especially for BotMiner, the botnet can create a specific evasion for bypassing the C-plane and A-plane clustering. BotProbe has assumptions that the input has to be perspective and the chat

protocol between bots has to be available for the detection engine. BotHunter detects botnets based on the bot-specific heuristics and the IDS dialog-based correlation. The IDS dialogs represent different stages of a botnet life cycle. Such correlation can produce signatures for IDS systems. This IDS-driven strategy has a problem when detecting encrypted botnet communications. Furthermore, this solution also has weaknesses similar to IDS, and the signature generation and update problems must be overcome to reach ideal detection performance.

Yu et al. proposed the SBotMiner [21], an approach based on large-scale network traffic filtering aiming at detecting search bots, which often perform suspicious search activities on the Internet, and SBotMiner uses PCA (Principle Component Analysis) to separate the bot traffic from the benign user traffic. This approach suffers from noise-queries because the search bots can generate lots of meaningless search activities to decrease the detection performance considerably. Karasaridis et al. proposed a wide network traffic correlation solution [9]. However, it only focuses on IRC-based botnet and needs many kinds of prior knowledge before performing the correlation. Zand et al. proposed an approach [22] to automatically extract Command-and-Control signatures for detecting botnets. Since the signature generation is based on the extraction of frequent communication patterns, it is also not applicable to encrypted communication. Wang et al. proposed a fuzzy pattern-based filtering algorithm [23]. This algorithm depends on the DNS query patterns, so that the botnet, especially for the Web-based botnet, can easily avoid the filtering by directly using IP address to communicate.

Some recent research aims at detecting the decentralized peer-to-peer (P2P) botnets. Zhang et al. proposed an approach [24] aiming at detecting P2P botnets. Using decentralized architecture greatly increases the survivability because most botnet takedown actions target C&C servers. However, the decentralized architecture also has some critical disadvantages. P2P botnets often have a complex architecture. Hence, maintaining a P2P network always demands significant technical efforts. In addition, its non-client-server architecture makes it inappropriate to be integrated into existing Web services. Other early studies discussed and evaluated the scale and the takedown techniques of a botnet. Both Dagon et al. [2] and Khattak et al. [25] discussed how different kinds of botnets are organized and what activities they may have. Abu Rajab et al. focused on botnet scale evaluation [1], and Stone-Gross et al. addressed detailed issues of taking down a botnet [26]. Honeypots are often used to collect or observe malicious network traffic in early botnet research. However, honeypots usually do not provide outgoing communication. Therefore, they are not suitable for collecting botnet traffic. Nadji et al. proposed a system for the botnet takedowns [27]. Such botnet takedown solution aims at stopping those DNS servers from functioning in the botnet communication. However those C&C servers are able to reorganize using other DNS servers rapidly, since this approach targets deactivating the botnet communication, not removing botnet C&C servers.

Most approaches mentioned so far may be able but not specifically designed to detect Web-based botnet. Since the majority of botnet owners seldom use their own hosts as the C&C servers, they often use compromised hosts instead. In other words, there must be the HTTP-supported malware on those compromised hosts performing C&C server-like operations. According to the study [28] proposed by Perdisci et al., they addressed the concrete relationship between HTTP-supported malware and Web-based botnets. They also proposed an approach to detect the HTTP-supported malware by using malicious network traces. This approach uses behavioral clustering of these HTTP-supported malware samples by finding their structural similarities among the sequences of HTTP requests. The results of behavioral clustering are used for generating signatures for an IDS system. Since they look into the sequences of HTTP requests, it means that this approach cannot be used for HTTPS-based malware. In addition, this approach still suffers from similar evasions mentioned so far, including injecting noise sequences of HTTP requests and implementing HTTP requests in a time triggering oriented approach.

Many recent botnet studies focus on problems brought by new types of botnets which utilize currently popular Internet applications. For example, some of these papers aim at detecting botnets running on social networks. Kartaltepe et al. proposed a study focusing on the social network-based botnet [11]. Wang et al. proposed an approach [29] to detect the DGA botnet by utilizing social network analysis. Venkatesh and Nadarajan proposed a survey of Stegobot [30], which is a kind of botnets using steganography to mask crucial information in digital images and then transmitting the images over social networks. Ferrara et al. addressed the rise of botnets running on social networks in a recent article [31]. Botnets utilizing IoT and mobile devices were also addressed by several prestigious conferences and projects recently. Bertino and Islam addressed the issues related to botnets and Internet of Things (IoT) security [32]. Project [33], conducted in 2017, is also motivated by Bertino and Islam to analyze the DDoS attack via IoT botnets. Mobile devices suffer from vulnerabilities as well as untrusted firmware and are also vulnerable to botnet owners. Eslahi et al. unveiled MoBots [34], which represent those botnets on mobile devices and networks. MoBots may use some existing services, such as SMS, to communicate with their bot masters. Such issue is critical to the telecommunication industry. Therefore, there is a related patent [35], which has been filed in 2016, disclosing a method for SMS-based botnet detection. Social network-based botnets, IoT botnets, or even mobile device-based botnets are not typical Web-based botnets. To be able to communicate in multiple mechanisms, they are more complicated than traditional Web-based botnets.

6. Conclusion

This study proposes a solution called WBD to detect suspicious Web-based botnets, no matter whether the botnet communication is encrypted or hidden in normal Web pages. We propose three features, two of them related to robot-like repeated contact clustering and one of them related to similar payload size, to detect the existence of botnet Web servers within the network communication. Applying our solutions

to 500 GB practical network traces, we found the false positive rate of WBD is only 0.42%.

Acknowledgments

This work was funded by the projects of Ministry of Science and Technology of Taiwan under no. 105-2221-E-008-074-MY3 and no. 106-3114-E-002-005.

References

[1] M. Abu Rajab, J. Zarfoss, F. Monrose, and A. Terzis, "A multifaceted approach to understanding the botnet phenomenon," in *Proceedings of the 6th ACM SIGCOMM on Internet Measurement Conference, IMC 2006*, pp. 41–52, Brazil, October 2006.

[2] D. Dagon, O. Gu, C. P. Lee, and W. Lee, "A taxonomy of botnet structures," in *Proceedings of the 23rd Annual Computer Security Applications Conference, ACSAC 2007*, pp. 325–338, Miami Beach, Fla, USA, December 2007.

[3] G. Gu, J. Zhang, and W. Lee, Botsniffer: Detecting botnet command and control channels in network traffic. In NDSS. The Internet Society, 2008.

[4] FBI. Botnets 101 What They Are and How to Avoid Them, 2013.

[5] A. K. Sood, R. J. Enbody, and R. Bansal, "Dissecting spyeye-understanding the design of third generation botnets," *Computer Networks*, vol. 57, no. 2, pp. 436–450, 2013.

[6] H. Binsalleeh, T. Ormerod, A. Boukhtouta et al., "On the analysis of the Zeus botnet crimeware toolkit," in *Proceedings of the 2010 8th International Conference on Privacy, Security and Trust, PST 2010*, pp. 31–38, Canada, August 2010.

[7] G. Gu, V. Yegneswaran, P. Porras, J. Stoll, and W. Lee, "Active botnet probing to identify obscure command and control channels," in *Proceedings of the 25th Annual Computer Conference Security Applications, ACSAC 2009*, pp. 241–253, Honolulu, Hawaii, USA, December 2009.

[8] C. Livadas, R. Walsh, D. Lapsley, and W. T. Strayer, "Using machine learning techniques to identify botnet traffic," in *Proceedings of the 31st Annual IEEE Conference on Local Computer Networks (LCN '06)*, pp. 967–974, Tampa, Fla, USA, November 2006.

[9] A. Karasaridis, B. Rexroad, and D. Hoeflin, "Wide-scale botnet detection and characterization," in *Proceedings of the First Conference on First Workshop on Hot Topics in Understanding Botnets, HotBots'07*, 7 pages, USENIX Association, Berkeley, Calif, USA, 2007.

[10] T. Cai and F. Zou, "Detecting HTTP botnet with clustering network traffic," in *Proceedings of the 8th International Conference on Wireless Communications, Networking and Mobile Computing (WiCOM '12)*, pp. 1–7, September 2012.

[11] E. J. Kartaltepe, J. A. Morales, S. Xu, and R. Sandhu, "Social network-based botnet command-and-control: emerging threats and countermeasures," *Lecture Notes in Computer Science (including subseries Lecture Notes in Artificial Intelligence and Lecture Notes in Bioinformatics): Preface*, vol. 6123, pp. 511–528, 2010.

[12] Cisco. NetFlow Services Solutions Guide, 2007.

[13] Behind Phishing: An Examination of Phisher Modi Operandi.

[14] Global Phishing Survey: Trends and Domain Name Use in 2H2009.

[15] Information and Communication Security Technology Center.

[16] G. K. Venkatesh and R. A. Nadarajan, "HTTP botnet detection using adaptive learning rate multilayer feed-forward neural network," *Lecture Notes in Computer Science (including subseries Lecture Notes in Artificial Intelligence and Lecture Notes in Bioinformatics): Preface*, vol. 7322, pp. 38–48, 2012.

[17] D. Zhao, I. Traore, B. Sayed et al., "Botnet detection based on traffic behavior analysis and flow intervals," *Computers & Security*, vol. 39, pp. 2–16, 2013.

[18] F.-H. Hsu, C.-S. Wang, C.-H. Hsu, C.-K. Tso, L.-H. Chen, and S.-H. Lin, "Detect fast-flux domains through response time differences," *IEEE Journal on Selected Areas in Communications*, vol. 32, no. 10, pp. 1947–1956, 2014.

[19] G. Gu, R. Perdisci, J. Zhang, and W. Lee, "Botminer: Clustering analysis of network traffic for protocol- and structure-independent botnet detection," in *Proceedings of the 17th Conference on Security Symposium, SS'08*, pp. 139–154, USENIX Association, Berkeley, Calif, USA, 2008.

[20] G. Gu, P. Porras, V. Yegneswaran, M. Fong, and W. Lee, "Bothunter: Detecting malware infection through ids-driven dialog correlation," in *Proceedings of 16th USENIX Security Symposium on USENIX Security Symposium, SS'07*, pp. 12:1–12:16, Berkeley, Calif, USA, 2007.

[21] F. Yu, Y. Xie, and Q. Ke, "SBotMiner: Large scale search bot detection," in *Proceedings of the 3rd ACM International Conference on Web Search and Data Mining, WSDM 2010*, pp. 421–430, USA, February 2010.

[22] A. Zand, G. Vigna, X. Yan, and C. Kruegel, "Extracting probable command and control signatures for detecting botnets," in *Proceedings of the 29th Annual ACM Symposium on Applied Computing, SAC 2014*, pp. 1657–1662, Republic of Korea, March 2014.

[23] K. Wang, C. Huang, S. Lin, and Y. Lin, "A fuzzy pattern-based filtering algorithm for botnet detection," *Computer Networks*, vol. 55, no. 15, pp. 3275–3286, 2011.

[24] J. Zhang, R. Perdisci, W. Lee, X. Luo, and U. Sarfraz, "Building a scalable system for stealthy P2P-botnet detection," *IEEE Transactions on Information Forensics and Security*, vol. 9, no. 1, pp. 27–38, 2014.

[25] S. Khattak, N. R. Ramay, K. R. Khan, A. A. Syed, and S. A. Khayam, "A Taxonomy of botnet behavior, detection, and defense," *IEEE Communications Surveys & Tutorials*, vol. 16, no. 2, pp. 898–924, 2014.

[26] B. Stone-Gross, M. Cova, L. Cavallaro et al., "Your botnet is my botnet: Analysis of a botnet takeover," in *Proceedings of the 16th ACM Conference on Computer and Communications Security, CCS'09*, pp. 635–647, New York, NY, USA, November 2009.

[27] Y. Nadji, M. Antonakakis, R. Perdisci, D. Dagon, and W. Lee, "Beheading hydras: Performing effective botnet takedowns," in *Proceedings of the 2013 ACM SIGSAC Conference on Computer and Communications Security, CCS 2013*, pp. 121–132, Germany, November 2013.

[28] R. Perdisci, W. Lee, and N. Feamster, "Behavioral clustering of http-based malware and signature generation using malicious network traces," in *Proceedings of the 7th USENIX Conference on Networked Systems Design and Implementation, NSDI'10*, 26 pages, Berkeley, Calif, USA, 2010.

[29] T.-S. Wang, C.-S. Lin, and H.-T. Lin, "DGA botnet detection utilizing social network analysis," in *Proceedings of the 2016 IEEE International Symposium on Computer, Consumer and Control, IS3C 2016*, pp. 333–336, China, July 2016.

[30] N. Venkatachalam and R. Anitha, "A multi-feature approach to detect Stegobot: a covert multimedia social network botnet," *Multimedia Tools and Applications*, vol. 76, no. 4, pp. 6079–6096, 2017.

[31] E. Ferrara, O. Varol, C. Davis, F. Menczer, and A. Flammini, "The rise of social bots," *Communications of the ACM*, vol. 59, no. 7, pp. 96–104, 2016.

[32] E. Bertino and N. Islam, "Botnets and internet of things security," *The Computer Journal*, vol. 50, no. 2, Article ID 7842850, pp. 76–79, 2017.

[33] R. Hallman, J. Bryan, G. Palavicini, J. Divita, and J. Romero-Mariona, Ioddos the internet of distributed denial of sevice attacks, 2017.

[34] M. Eslahi, R. Salleh, and N. B. Anuar, "MoBots: A new generation of botnets on mobile devices and networks," in *Proceedings of the 2012 IEEE Symposium on Computer Applications and Industrial Electronics, ISCAIE 2012*, pp. 262–266, Malaysia, December 2012.

[35] C. Adams, Sms botnet detection on mobile devices, May 24 2016. US Patent 9, 351, 167.

15

How to Share Secret Efficiently over Networks

Lein Harn,[1] **Ching-Fang Hsu,**[2] **Zhe Xia,**[3,4] **and Junwei Zhou**[3,4]

[1]*Department of Computer Science Electrical Engineering, University of Missouri-Kansas City, Kansas City, MO 64110, USA*
[2]*Computer School, Central China Normal University, Wuhan 430079, China*
[3]*Department of Computer Science, Wuhan University of Technology, Wuhan 430071, China*
[4]*Hubei Key Laboratory of Transportation Internet of Things, Wuhan University of Technology, Wuhan, China*

Correspondence should be addressed to Ching-Fang Hsu; cherryjingfang@gmail.com

Academic Editor: Pedro Peris-Lopez

In a secret-sharing scheme, the secret is shared among a set of shareholders, and it can be reconstructed if a quorum of these shareholders work together by releasing their secret shares. However, in many applications, it is undesirable for nonshareholders to learn the secret. In these cases, pairwise secure channels are needed among shareholders to exchange the shares. In other words, a shared key needs to be established between every pair of shareholders. But employing an additional key establishment protocol may make the secret-sharing schemes significantly more complicated. To solve this problem, we introduce a new type of secret-sharing, called *protected secret-sharing* (PSS), in which the shares possessed by shareholders not only can be used to reconstruct the original secret but also can be used to establish the shared keys between every pair of shareholders. Therefore, in the secret reconstruction phase, the recovered secret is only available to shareholders but not to nonshareholders. In this paper, an information theoretically secure PSS scheme is proposed, its security properties are analyzed, and its computational complexity is evaluated. Moreover, our proposed PSS scheme also can be applied to threshold cryptosystems to prevent nonshareholders from learning the output of the protocols.

1. Introduction

Secret-sharing schemes, first introduced by Shamir [1] and Blakley [2] in 1979, are very important techniques to ensure secrecy and availability of sensitive information. Moreover, they are widely used as building blocks in various cryptographic protocols, such as threshold cryptosystems, attribute-based encryption, and multiparty computation. In a (t, n) threshold secret-sharing scheme, the secret is divided into n shares so that it can only be recovered with t or more than t shares, but fewer than t shares cannot reveal any information of the secret. In the past few decades, many secret-sharing schemes have been proposed in the literature, and three major approaches can be used to design them: Shamir's approach [1] based on the univariate polynomial, Blakely's approach [2] based on the hyperplane geometry, and Mignotte/Asmuth-Bloom approach [3, 4] based on the Chinese Remainder Theorem (CRT).

In the majority of existing secret-sharing schemes, it is simply assumed that shares are released by the shareholders in the secret reconstruction phase, and then anyone can reconstruct the secret using these revealed shares. But, in many cases, it is undesirable for nonshareholders to learn the secret. Considering the scenario where a famous billionaire sets up the will and shares it among his children using secret-sharing, the children are told that the will should not be read when the billionaire is alive and its contents should be kept strictly private among the family members. However, some paparazzi may want to learn the will after the billionaire passes away to make some head news. In this case, traditional secret-sharing schemes may not provide sufficient protection. To solve this problem, shareholders can use pairwise secure channels to exchange the shares so that the recovered secret is only available to shareholders but not to nonshareholders. If these secure channels are built using cryptographic methods, a shared key is required to be established between every pair of shareholders beforehand. However, employing an additional key establishment protocol may make the secret-sharing schemes significantly more complicated.

The same problem also arises if secret-sharing schemes are used as building blocks in some other cryptographic protocols. For example, threshold cryptography, first introduced by Desmedt [5], is the application of secret-sharing with public-key algorithms. Among various threshold cryptosystems, some are based on ElGamal [6, 7], some are based on RSA [8–11], some are based on Elliptic Curves [12, 13], and some are based on Pairing [14]. In these protocols, shares are either used to generate a digital signature or used to decrypt a ciphertext. To prevent any nonshareholder from learning the outputs of the protocol, a shared key is also needed between every pair of shareholders. Similarly, employing an additional key establishment protocol in threshold cryptosystems can complicate the process significantly.

In this paper, we use bivariate polynomials to propose a new type of secret-sharing scheme, called *protected secret-sharing* (PSS), in which shareholders can use their shares to achieve two purposes simultaneously: one is to reconstruct the original secret and the other is to establish a shared key between every pair of shareholders. Using these shared keys, shareholders can build pairwise secure channels among them to exchange the shares in the secret reconstruction phase. Therefore, PSS provides an efficient solution to protect the original secret from nonshareholders. Our proposed scheme is information theoretically secure, and it can be easily extended to threshold cryptosystems for the same purpose.

Note that although bivariate polynomials have been used to design many different types of secret-sharing schemes in the literature, for example, verifiable secret-sharing (VSS) [15–17], pairwise key distribution [18–21], and dynamic secret-sharing [22], the purpose of this work is different from the previous ones, and the types of employed bivariate polynomials are different as well.

The rest of paper is organized as follows. In Section 2, we review some secret-sharing schemes based on polynomials. In Section 3, we present the models for PSS, including the system model, the adversary model, and the security goals. Our proposed (t, n) PSS scheme based on bivariate polynomials is introduced in Section 4. Its security and complexity analysis is described in Section 5. Finally, we conclude the paper in Section 6.

2. Review of Secret-Sharing Schemes Based on Polynomials

Shamir's (t, n) secret-sharing scheme [1] is based on univariate polynomials. The dealer first randomly selects a polynomial $f(x)$ over $\mathbb{Z}_p$ with degree at most $t - 1$, where $s = f(0)$ is the secret. Then the dealer evaluates the polynomial $f(x)$ at different points w_i to generate the shares $f(w_i)$ for $i = 1, 2, \ldots, n$. Here, p is a large prime with $p > s$, and w_i is some public information associated with each shareholder. In what follows in this paper, we assume that all computations are modulo p unless otherwise stated.

In 1985, Chor et al. [23] have extended the notion of secret-sharing and they have proposed the first verifiable secret-sharing (VSS) scheme. The verifiability property allows shareholders to verify the validity of their received shares. If invalid shares were found, shareholders can request the

dealer to regenerate new shares. In the literature, several (t, n) VSS schemes [15, 16, 24–27] are designed using bivariate polynomials. A bivariate polynomial with degree at most $t - 1$ can be represented as

$$F(x, y) = a_{0,0} + a_{1,0}x + a_{0,1}y + \cdots + a_{t-1,t-1}x^{t-1}y^{t-1}, \quad (1)$$

where $a_{i,j} \in \mathbb{Z}_p, \forall i, j \in [0, t-1]$. If the coefficients satisfy $a_{i,j} = a_{j,i}, \forall i, j \in [0, t - 1]$, such a polynomial is called a symmetric bivariate polynomial. Otherwise, it is called an asymmetric bivariate polynomial. In these VSS schemes, the dealer uses a symmetric bivariate polynomial $F(x, y)$ to generate shares $F(w_i, y)$ for the shareholders, where $i = 1, 2, \ldots, n$. Each share $F(w_i, y)$ is a univariate polynomial with degree at most $t - 1$. Note that since $F(w_i, w_j) = F(w_j, w_i), \forall i, j \in [1, n]$, a pairwise key $k_{ij} = F(w_i, w_j) = F(w_j, w_i)$ can be established between the shareholders U_i and U_j. Therefore, a symmetric bivariate polynomial can enable two shareholders to establish a pairwise shared key.

3. Models for Protected Secret-Sharing

3.1. System Model

Definition 1 (protected secret-sharing (PSS)). In a PSS, the received shares by shareholders can be used to serve two purposes simultaneously: (a) reconstruct the original secret and (b) establish pairwise shared keys among shareholders (note that these pairwise shared keys are used to build a secure channel between every pair of shareholders in order to exchange the shares in the secret reconstruction phase. Therefore, the reconstructed secret can be protected from any nonshareholder).

The players in our proposed scheme include a trusted dealer $\mathcal{D}$, n shareholders $\{U_1, U_2, \ldots, U_n\}$, and some insider or outsider adversaries. We assume that all these players have unlimited computational power. Among the n shareholders, at least a portion ϵ of them are assumed to be honest.

We assume that there exists a secure channel between the dealer and every shareholder, so that the shares can be securely distributed to shareholders. Moreover, we assume that every player is connected to a common authenticated broadcast channel $\mathcal{C}$, so that any message sent through $\mathcal{C}$ can be heard by the other players. The adversaries cannot modify messages sent by an honest player through $\mathcal{C}$, and they cannot prevent honest players from receiving messages from $\mathcal{C}$. Note that these assumptions are widely used in existing secret-sharing schemes. With these assumptions, we can focus our discussion on the key aspects of PSS without digging into the low level of technical details. Our purpose is to provide an efficient way to establish additional pairwise secret channels among shareholders without invoking a separate key establishment protocol.

Our proposed PSS scheme consists of two phases: (i) share generation and distribution by the dealer and (ii) secret reconstruction by shareholders. During the share generation and distribution phase, the dealer selects a random asymmetric bivariate polynomial to generate the shares for each shareholder, and every share consists of two univariate polynomials. These shares are sent to shareholders through the secure channels. During the secret reconstruction phase, each shareholder first uses her share to compute pairwise shared keys with the other shareholders. With these shared keys, pairwise secure channels can be established among the shareholders. After receiving the shares from the other shareholders through these secure channels, each shareholder can recover the original secret without leaking it to any nonshareholder.

3.2. Adversary Model. We consider two types of adversaries in the proposed PSS scheme.

(i) Insider Adversary. The insider adversary is a legitimate shareholder who owns a share generated by the dealer. An insider adversary may work alone or collude with some other insider adversaries to learn the secret before it is supposed to be reconstructed or to recover invalid secret using fake shares. Note that when the secret is reconstructed, we assume that the insider adversaries can learn the secret, but they will not leak the secret to nonshareholders, for example, the outsider adversaries.

(ii) Outsider Adversary. The outsider adversary is an attacker who does not own any share generated by the dealer, but she may try to learn the secret that she is unauthorized to access. Note that this attack is possible in many existing secret-sharing schemes when the shares are exchanged in an insecure fashion during the secret reconstruction phase.

3.3. Security Goals. In the security analysis, we demonstrate that the following security goals are satisfied in the proposed PSS scheme based on our assumptions.

Definition 2 (correctness). If there exist a portion $\epsilon > 2/3$ of honest shareholders, the correct secret can always be reconstructed. And any insider adversary who uses fake share in the share reconstruction phase can be identified.

Definition 3 (secrecy). If there exist a portion $\epsilon > 1/2$ of honest shareholders, the insider adversaries cannot learn any information of the secret before the secret is supposed to be reconstructed. Moreover, in the secret reconstruction phase, the traffic flows over the broadcast channel $\mathscr{C}$ reveal no information of the secret to the outsider adversary.

Note that the proposed PSS scheme aims to achieve information theoretical security. Hence, both of the above security goals do not rely on any computational assumption.

4. The Proposed PSS Scheme

In this section, we propose a (t, n) PSS scheme using asymmetric bivariate polynomials. There are two major differences between shares generated by a univariate polynomial and by a bivariate polynomial: (1) the shares generated by a univariate polynomial are integers in $\mathbb{Z}_p$, but shares generated by a bivariate polynomial are univariate polynomials over $\mathbb{Z}_p$; (2) the shares generated by a univariate polynomial can only be used to reconstruct the secret, but the shares generated by a

bivariate polynomial not only can be used to reconstruct the secret but also can be used to establish pairwise keys among shareholders.

4.1. Share Generation and Distribution Phase. At first, the dealer $\mathscr{D}$ selects a random asymmetric polynomial:

$$F(x, y) = a_{0,0} + a_{1,0}x + a_{0,1}y + \cdots + a_{t-1,h-1}x^{t-1}y^{h-1}, \quad (2)$$

where $F(x, y)$ is with degree at most $t - 1$ in x and with degree at most $h - 1$ in y (i.e., $h > t(t - 1)$; we will explain this condition in the security analysis), where $s = F(0, 0)$ is the secret, $a_{i,j} \in \mathbb{Z}_p$, and p is a large prime integer with $p > s$. The dealer $\mathscr{D}$ computes a pair of shares $s_i^1(y) = F(w_i, y)$ and $s_i^2(x) = F(x, w_i)$ for each shareholder U_i, where w_i is the public information associated with the corresponding shareholder U_i. The dealer sends the pair of shares $\{s_i^1(y), s_i^2(x)\}$ to each shareholder U_i through the secure channel.

4.2. Secret Reconstruction Phase. Without loss of generality, assume that u (i.e., $t \leq u \leq n$) shareholders $\{U_1, U_2, \ldots, U_u\}$ are participating in the secret reconstruction phase:

(1) Between every pair of shareholders, they compute two shared keys. For example, the shareholders U_i and U_j (i.e., we assume that $i < j$) can compute the shared keys as $k_{i,j} = s_i^1(w_j) = s_j^2(w_i) = F(w_i, w_j)$ and $k_{j,i} = s_i^2(w_j) = s_j^1(w_i) = F(w_j, w_i)$.

(2) Each shareholder U_i then uses her share $s_i^1(y)$ to compute a *Lagrange Component* δ_i as

$$\delta_i = s_i^1(0) \prod_{j=1, j \neq i}^{u} \frac{-w_j}{w_i - w_j} \pmod{p}. \quad (3)$$

(3) For each pair of shareholders, they use their shared keys to build a secure channel and then use this channel to exchange their Lagrange Components. For example, the shareholder U_i computes $c_{i,j} = E_{k_{i,j}}(\delta_i)$, where $E_{k_{i,j}}(\delta_i)$ denotes the one-time pad encryption of δ_i using the key $k_{i,j}$, and sends $c_{i,j}$ to the shareholder U_j through the authenticated broadcast channel $\mathscr{C}$. Similarly, U_j encrypts her share δ_j by one-time pad using the shared key $k_{j,i}$ and sends $c_{j,i}$ to U_i using the authenticated channel $\mathscr{C}$.

(4) After receiving the ciphertexts $c_{j,i}$ for $j \in \{1, 2, \ldots, u\} \setminus \{i\}$, the shareholder U_i can decrypt them individually as $D_{k_{j,i}}(c_{j,i}) = \delta_j$, where $D_{k_{j,i}}(c_{j,i})$ denotes the decryption of $c_{j,i}$ using the key $k_{j,i}$.

(5) Finally, each shareholder U_i computes the secret as $s = \sum_{j=1}^{u} \delta_j$.

5. Security and Complexity Analysis

In this section, we first prove the correctness and secrecy of the proposed scheme; that is, neither type of adversaries can achieve its objectives based on our assumptions. Then, we briefly analyze the complexity of the proposed scheme.

5.1. Security Analysis

Theorem 4. *The proposed scheme achieves the correctness property. That is, if there exist a portion $\epsilon > 2/3$ of honest shareholders, the correct secret can always be reconstructed. And any dishonest shareholder who uses fake share in the share reconstruction phase can be identified.*

Proof. To prove this theorem, we first consider the situation that there are no dishonest shareholders. Then we justify why less than a portion of $1/3$ dishonest shareholders cannot prevent the correct secret from being reconstructed. In step 2 of the secret reconstruction phase, each shareholder U_i uses her share $s_i^1(y)$ to compute the Lagrange Component of the secret s as

$$\delta_i = s_i^1(0) \prod_{j=1,j\neq i}^{u} \frac{-w_j}{w_i - w_j} = F(w_i, 0) \prod_{j=1,j\neq i}^{u} \frac{-w_j}{w_i - w_j}. \quad (4)$$

Since $F(x, 0)$ is a univariate polynomial with degree at most $t - 1$, the secret s can be obtained in step 5 through Lagrange Interpolation as

$$s = F(0, 0) = \sum_{i=1}^{u} F(w_i, 0) \prod_{j=1,j\neq i}^{u} \frac{-w_j}{w_i - w_j}. \quad (5)$$

Therefore, if all shareholders are honest, the correct secret can be reconstructed. However, if there exist some dishonest shareholders, they may use fake shares in the secret reconstruction phase. In the proposed PSS scheme, the secret can be reconstructed by any subset of t or more than t shareholders. Hence, we assume that there are at most $t - 1$ dishonest shareholders. Otherwise, the dishonest shareholders working together will have the ability to reconstruct the secret. In this case, any polynomial $F(x, 0)$ that passes n points agrees at most $t - 1$ points and it disagrees at least $n - t + 1$ points. In other words, these polynomials have a Hamming distance $n - t + 1$, and this distance can correct any number of errors that is less than $(n - t + 1)/2$ according to Coding Theory. Therefore, if $t - 1 < (n - t + 1)/2$, the correct secret can always be reconstructed. Note that $t - 1 < n/3$ is another form of this inequality. To speed up the decoding process, either the Euclidean decoder or the Berlekamp-Massey decoder can be used. Moreover, if the correct secret is determined, the invalid shares can be identified as well. This is because any subset that contains invalid shares will interpolate into an incorrect secret. □

Theorem 5. *The proposed scheme satisfies the secrecy property. That is, the outsider adversaries cannot obtain any information of the secret. Moreover, if there exist a portion $\epsilon > 1/2$ of honest shareholders and the condition $h > t(t - 1)$ holds, then t or more than t shares can recover the secret, but fewer than t shares cannot reveal any information of the secret.*

Proof. Although the shareholders exchange information through the authenticated broadcast channel $\mathscr{C}$ in the secret reconstruction phase, all messages are encrypted. Based on the assumption that the asymmetric polynomial is randomly selected over $\mathbb{Z}_p$ by the dealer $\mathscr{D}$, the messages and the shared keys are all randomly distributed within the same space $\mathbb{Z}_p$. Moreover, since the messages are exchanged only once, one-time pad can be used here to encrypt these messages. Therefore, even if the outsider adversary has unlimited computational power, she cannot obtain any information of the secret. Next, we prove that if $\epsilon > 1/2$ and $h > t(t - 1)$, the insider adversaries cannot learn the secret before it is reconstructed. Regarding the first inequality, it just simply states that there should be a majority of honest shareholders. Otherwise, the dishonest shareholders will have all the abilities that the honest ones have, that is, reconstruct the secret. Note that this requirement is widely used in most of the existing secret-sharing schemes. Regarding the second inequality, recall that the polynomial $F(x, y)$ is an asymmetric polynomial of degree $t - 1$ in x and degree $h - 1$ in y. It contains th different coefficient. In the proposed scheme, each share $\{s_i^1(y), s_i^2(x)\}$ contains two univariate polynomials with degree $h - 1$ in y and degree $t - 1$ in x, respectively. In other words, each shareholder can use her share to establish at most $t + h$ linearly independent equations in terms of the coefficients of the bivariate polynomial $F(x, y)$. When there are $t - 1$ colluded shareholders with their shares together, they can establish a total of $(t + h)(t - 1)$ linearly independent equations. If the number of coefficients of the bivariate polynomial $F(x, y)$ is larger than the number of equations available to the colluded shareholders, that is, $th > (t + h)(t - 1)$, the $t - 1$ dishonest shareholders cannot recover $F(x, y)$. Hence, they cannot learn any information of the secret. Therefore, these two inequalities together ensure that fewer than t shares cannot reveal any information of the secret. □

5.2. Complexity Analysis.

In this section, we analyze the complexity of our proposed scheme and compare it with the one in Shamir's secret-sharing scheme. Regarding the share generation and distribution phase, in our proposed PSS scheme, each share $\{s_i^1(y), s_i^2(x)\}$ consists of two univariate polynomials: one is $t - 1$ degree in x and the other is $h - 1$ degree in y. Therefore, $t + h$ coefficients in $\mathbb{Z}_p$ need to be transmitted from the dealer to each shareholder, and each shareholder needs to store these coefficients. The storage requirement for each shareholder is $(t + h)\log_2 p$ bits, where p is the modulus. In Shamir's secret-sharing scheme, each share is a single value in $\mathbb{Z}_p$. Therefore, only one value in $\mathbb{Z}_p$ needs to be transmitted from the dealer to each shareholder, and the storage requirement for each shareholder is $\log_2 p$ bits. Note that, when evaluating the polynomials, Horner's algorithm can be used to reduce the computational cost in both our proposed scheme and in Shamir's secret-sharing scheme.

Regarding the secret reconstruction phase, in step 1, each shareholder needs to compute pairwise shared keys with the other shareholders. Note that this step does not involve any interaction. Using Horner's algorithm, evaluating the polynomials of degree $h - 1$ and degree $t - 1$ requires h steps and t steps, respectively, where each step consists of one multiplication and one addition. In step 2, each shareholder needs to compute $\delta_i = s_i^1(0)\prod_{j=1,j\neq i}^{u}(-w_j/(w_i - w_j))$. Since $s_i^1(0)$ is the constant coefficient of the polynomial $s_i^1(y)$, there is no need to compute this value. Therefore, the computational cost of evaluating δ_i is identical to that in Shamir's secret-sharing scheme. Finally, there are $u - 1$ one-time pad encryptions in step 3 and $u - 1$ one-time pad decryptions in step 4.

Based on the above analysis, the computational complexities are similar in both schemes. But, compared with Shamir's secret-sharing scheme, more information needs to be transmitted and stored by each shareholder in our proposed scheme. The price is paid to achieve an additional property that the recovered secret is not revealed to nonshareholders. This property is desirable in many applications and our proposed scheme achieves it even if the adversaries have unlimited computational power. Although including a pairwise key establishment protocol [18, 28] with Shamir's secret-sharing scheme can protect the secret from nonshareholders as well, most pairwise key establishment protocols are computationally secure (not information theoretically secure) and the complexity of key establishment protocol will have a quadratic relationship with the number of shareholders participating in the secret reconstruction phase.

5.3. Some Future Works. In the last three decades, many fascinating works about secret-sharing have been proposed in the literature, and different types of secret-sharing schemes can provide different properties. For example, verifiable secret-sharing (VSS) scheme [15–17] not only allows the shareholders to verify the validity of their received shares in the share generation and distribution phase but also allows the verification of the revealed shares in the secret reconstruction phase. In proactive secret-sharing schemes [29–31], shareholders can refresh their shares periodically without the dealer being involved, so that the shares obtained by the adversaries will become obsolete after the shares are updated. Moreover, the threshold can be dynamically adjusted when some shareholders join in or leave. In multiple secret-sharing schemes [32–34], each shareholder can use her share to recover multiple secrets at different stages. In this paper, we have not considered these additional properties, and the existing secret-sharing schemes have not considered the issue of protecting the secret(s) from nonshareholders. Therefore, incorporating the ideas presented in this paper with these different types of secret-sharing schemes will be interesting, and we consider these further investigations as our future works.

6. Conclusion

A new type of secret-sharing, called protected secret-sharing (PSS), has been introduced in this paper. In a PSS scheme, the shareholders' shares not only can be used to recover the secret but also can be used to protect the shares against nonshareholders in the secret reconstruction phase. A (t, n) PSS scheme using a bivariate polynomial is proposed, and we provide security and complexity analysis of the proposed scheme. Some possible future works are also discussed in the paper. Note that our method is generic enough to be directly applied with threshold cryptosystems for the same purpose.

Authors' Contributions

The authors have equal contribution to this paper.

Acknowledgments

This work was partially supported by the National Natural Science Foundation of China (Grants nos. 61772224, 61601337, 61672398, and 61503289), the Key Natural Science Foundation of Hubei Province (Grant no. 2015CFA069), the Science and Technology Support Program of Hubei Province (Grants nos. 2015BAA120 and 2015BCE068), the Applied Fundamental Research of Wuhan (Grant no. 20160101010004), the Humanity and Social Science Youth Foundation of Ministry of Education of China (no. 15YJC870029), and the Research Planning Project of National Language Committee (no. YB135-40).

References

[1] A. Shamir, "How to share a secret," *Communications of the Association for Computing Machinery*, vol. 22, no. 11, pp. 612-613, 1979.

[2] R. Blakley, "Safeguarding cryptographic keys," *Proceedings of the National Computer Conference*, vol. 48, pp. 313–317, 1979.

[3] M. Mignotte, "How to share a secret," in *Proceedings of the Advances in Cryptology–EUROCRYPT '82*, T. Beth, Ed., Lecture Notes in Computer Science, pp. 371–375, 1982.

[4] C. Asmuth and J. Bloom, "A modular approach to key safeguarding," *Institute of Electrical and Electronics Engineers. Transactions on Information Theory*, vol. 29, no. 2, pp. 208–210, 1983.

[5] Y. Desmedt, "Society and group oriented cryptography: a new concept," in *Proceedings of the Advances in Cryptology–CRYPTO '87*, vol. 1987, pp. 120–127.

[6] Y. Desmedt and Y. Frankel, "Threshold cryptosystems," in *Proceedings of the Advances in CRYPTO '89*, vol. 435 of *Lecture Notes in Computer Science*, pp. 307–315, 1989.

[7] L. Harn, "Group-oriented (t, n) threshold digital signature scheme and digital multisignature," *IEE Proceedings: Computers and Digital Techniques*, vol. 141, no. 5, pp. 307–313, 1994.

[8] Y. Desmedt and Y. Frankel, "Shared generation of authenticators and signatures," in *Proceedings of the Advances in CRYPTO '91*, vol. 576 of *Lecture Notes in Computer Science*, pp. 457–469, 1991.

[9] A. De Santis, Y. Desmedt, Y. Frankel, and M. Yung, "How to share a function securely," in *Proceedings of the 26th Annual ACM Symposium on the Theory of Computing*, pp. 522–533, May 1994.

[10] R. Gennaro, S. a. Jarecki, H. Krawczyk, and T. Rabin, "Robust and efficient sharing of RSA functions," in *Proceedings of the Advances in CRYPTO '96*, vol. 1109 of *Lecture Notes in Comput. Sci.*, pp. 157–172, 1996.

[11] V. Shoup, "Practical threshold signature," in *Proceedings of the Advances in EUROCRYPT '00*, Lecture Notes in Computer Science, pp. 207–220, 2000.

[12] L. Ertaul and W. Lu, "Ecc based threshold cryptography for secure data forwarding and secure key exchange in manet,"

in *Proceedings of the International Conference on Research in Networking*, 2005.

[13] Y. Shang, X. Wang, Y. Li, and Y. Zhang, "A general threshold signature scheme based on elliptic curve," *Advanced Materials Research*, 2013.

[14] W. Gao, G. Wang, X. Wang, and Z. Yang, "One-round ID-based threshold signature scheme from bilinear pairings," *Informatica*, vol. 20, no. 4, pp. 461–476, 2009.

[15] M. Fitzi, J. Garay, S. Gollakota, C. P. Rangan, and K. Srinathan, "Round-optimal and efficient verifiable secret sharing," in *Proceedings of the 3rd Theory of Cryptography Conference, TCC '06*, Lecture Notes in Comput. Sci., pp. 329–342, Springer, 2006.

[16] R. Kumaresan, A. Patra, and C. P. Rangan, "The round complexity of verifiable secret sharing: The statistical case," *Lecture Notes in Computer Science (including subseries Lecture Notes in Artificial Intelligence and Lecture Notes in Bioinformatics)*, vol. 6477, pp. 431–447, 2010.

[17] A. Patra, A. Choudhary, T. Rabin, and C. Pandu Rangan, "The round complexity of verifiable secret sharing revisited," in *Proceedings of the Advances in Cryptology-CRYPTO '09*, Lecture Notes in Comput. Sci., pp. 487–504, Springer, Berlin, 2009.

[18] D. Liu, P. Ning, and L. I. Rongfang, "Establishing pairwise keys in distributed sensor networks," *ACM Transactions on Information and System Security*, vol. 8, no. 1, pp. 41–77, 2005.

[19] H. Liang and C. Wang, "An energy efficient dynamic key management scheme based on polynomial and cluster in wireless sensor netwoks," *Journal of Convergence Information Technology*, vol. 6, no. 5, pp. 321–328, 2011.

[20] S. Guo and V. Leung, "A compromise-resilient group rekeying scheme for hierarchical wireless sensor networks," in *Proceedings of the IEEE Wireless Communications and Networking Conference 2010, WCNC '10*, 2010.

[21] N. Saxena, G. Tsudik, and J. H. Yi, "Efficient node admission and certificateless secure communication in short-lived MANETs," *IEEE Transactions on Parallel and Distributed Systems*, vol. 20, no. 2, pp. 158–170, 2009.

[22] L. Harn and C.-F. Hsu, "Dynamic threshold secret reconstruction and its application to the threshold cryptography," *Information Processing Letters*, vol. 115, no. 11, pp. 851–857, 2015.

[23] B. Chor, S. Goldwasser, S. Micali, and B. Awerbuch, "Verifiable secret sharing and achieving simultaneity in the presence of faults," *Foundations of Computer Science*, pp. 383–395, 1985.

[24] R. Cramer, I. Damgård, S. Dziembowski, M. Hirt, and T. Rabin, "Efficient multiparty computations secure against an adaptive adversary," in *Proceedings of the Conference on the Theory and Applications of Cryptographic Techniques*, vol. 1999, pp. 311–326.

[25] R. Gennaro, Y. Ishai, E. Kushilevitz, and T. Rabin, "The round complexity of verifiable secret sharing and secure multicast," in *Proceedings of the Proceedings of the thirty-third annual ACM symposium on Theory of computing*, pp. 580–589, 2001.

[26] J. Katz, C.-Y. Koo, and R. Kumaresan, "Improving the round complexity of vss in point-to-point networks," in *International Colloquium on Automata, Languages, and Programming*, pp. 499–510, 2008.

[27] V. Nikov and S. Nikova, "On proactive secret sharing schemes," in *Proceedings of the International Workshop on Selected Areas in Cryptography*, Lecture Notes in Comput. Sci., pp. 308–325, Springer, Berlin, New York, NY, USA.

[28] R. Canetti and H. Krawczyk, "Analysis of key-exchange protocols and their use for building secure channels," in *Advances in cryptology—EUROCRYPT*, pp. 453–474, 2001.

[29] A. Herzberg, S. Jarecki, H. Krawczyk, and M. Yung, "Proactive secret sharing or: how to cope with perpetual leakage," *Lecture Notes in Computer Science (including subseries Lecture Notes in Artificial Intelligence and Lecture Notes in Bioinformatics)*, vol. 963, pp. 339–352, 1995.

[30] Y. Frankel, P. Gemmell, P. D. MacKenzie, and M. Yung, "Optimal-resilience proactive public-key cryptosystems," in *Proceedings of the 1997 38th IEEE Annual Symposium on Foundations of Computer Science*, pp. 384–393, October 1997.

[31] T. Rabin, "A simplified approach to threshold and proactive RSA," *Lecture Notes in Computer Science (including subseries Lecture Notes in Artificial Intelligence and Lecture Notes in Bioinformatics)*, vol. 1462, pp. 89–104, 1998.

[32] T.-Y. Wu and Y.-M. Tseng, "Publicly verifiable multi-secret sharing scheme from bilinear pairings," *IET Information Security*, vol. 7, no. 3, pp. 239–246, 2013.

[33] A. Endurthi, O. B. Chanu, A. N. Tentu, and V. C. Venkaiah, "Reusable multi-stage multi-secret sharing schemes based on CRT," *Journal of Communications Software and Systems*, vol. 11, no. 1, pp. 15–24, 2015.

[34] J. Herranz, A. Ruiz, and G. Sáez, "New results and applications for multi-secret sharing schemes," *Designs, Codes and Cryptography*, vol. 73, no. 3, pp. 841–864, 2014.

16

A Multidomain Survivable Virtual Network Mapping Algorithm

Xiancui Xiao,[1,2] **Xiangwei Zheng,**[1,2] **and Yuang Zhang**[1,2]

[1]*School of Information Science and Engineering, Shandong Normal University, Jinan 250014, China*
[2]*Shandong Provincial Key Laboratory for Distributed Computer Software Novel Technology, Jinan 250014, China*

Correspondence should be addressed to Xiangwei Zheng; xwzhengcn@163.com

Academic Editor: Lianyong Qi

Although the existing networks are more often deployed in the multidomain environment, most of existing researches focus on single-domain networks and there are no appropriate solutions for the multidomain virtual network mapping problem. In fact, most studies assume that the underlying network can operate without any interruption. However, physical networks cannot ensure the normal provision of network services for external reasons and traditional single-domain networks have difficulties to meet user needs, especially for the high security requirements of the network transmission. In order to solve the above problems, this paper proposes a survivable virtual network mapping algorithm (IntD-GRC-SVNE) that implements multidomain mapping in network virtualization. IntD-GRC-SVNE maps the virtual communication networks onto different domain networks and provides backup resources for virtual links which improve the survivability of the special networks. Simulation results show that IntD-GRC-SVNE can not only improve the survivability of multidomain communications network but also render the network load more balanced and greatly improve the network acceptance rate due to employment of GRC (global resource capacity).

1. Introduction

Network virtualization enables multiple virtual networks (VNs) to coexist on the same physical network dynamically, so that virtual network users can share the underlying physical network [1]. At the same time, network virtualization technology as a new technology means to provide a solution to cloud computing diverse services [2, 3]. In order to relieve the interdependence between network control and data plane [4, 5], network service operators are generally divided into two roles: the underlying infrastructure provider (InP) and the service provider (SP); their tasks are to deploy the underlying network resources and lease a number of underlying infrastructure providers to provide the underlying network resources to meet the custom scalability of virtual network services [6, 7].

This paper refers to the relevant algorithms in the literature [8–12] and combines the multidomain mapping problem with the network survivability. We classify process as two stages, the resource classification process and the network mapping process, and the resource classification process is further divided into two parts, the primary flow

and the backup flow resource, which can, respectively, form a complete underlying physical network topology. The characteristic of this paper is that we protect the security of node data by mapping the virtual nodes to different domains of the physical network. Simultaneously, in order to ensure the balance of network load, we choose a new measure, global resource capacity (GRC) [13], which can measure the potential mapping capability of nodes in the process of node mapping. IntD-GRC-SVNE is applied in a multidomain environment and when compared with the traditional algorithm of IntD-GREEDY-SVNE and random algorithm IntD-RANDOM-SVNE, the acceptance rate, network load balancing, and network revenue of IntD-GRC-SVNE all show better performance. In addition, the non-cross-allocation of the primary flow and backup flow resources in this paper can greatly improve the survivability of the network.

This paper is organized as follows: we review related work in Section 2. We introduce problem description in Section 3 and provide survivable virtual network mapping model in Section 4. The details of virtual network mapping algorithm are given in Section 5. Finally, we analyze experiments and provide discussion in Section 6.

2. Related Work

As the core of network virtualization technology, the goal of virtual network mapping is to provide node and link resources for dynamic virtual requests to meet their mapping service requirements. However, with the number of network users climbing, the user requirements for the stability of the network are getting higher and higher. In order to improve the survivability of the network, many researchers have done some researches and most of the current researches focused on both protection and backup [14].

Physical failure is generally divided into node failure and link failure. In order to deal with physical link failure, Rahman et al. [15] designed a SVNE method for passive allocation of backup resources, which is essentially a virtual link remapping method after a failure. However, because the node failure will inevitably lead to its adjacent link failure, it is necessary to rebuild the virtual nodes affected by the virtual node and the virtual nodes affected by the virtual link, so the recovery of node failure is relatively complex. Guo et al. [16] proposed a SVNE method for proactively allocating backup resources for virtual links in the initial mapping of VNs which can be timely recovery network failure. By this way, the economic losses caused by network failures can be minimized in the case of efficient use of resources.

In order to guarantee the survivability of VN under the influence of physical node failure, Yu et al. [17] designed method of reliable VN two-stage SVNE method; they firstly extended VN to a reliable network that backs up important virtual nodes by adding redundant nodes and corresponding redundant links to the original VN and secondly mapped the reliable VN to the physical network with the goal of maximizing shared backup link resources. Qiao et al. [18] used another two-stage SVNE method to further reduce the backup overhead, but, after a node failure, the method may need to migrate a large number of working virtual nodes in addition to migrating affected virtual nodes. Hu et al. [14] defined and solved the SVNE problem of the constraint position, emphasizing that the backup node used for remapping must satisfy the position constraint specified by Yeow et al. [19] who used the SVNE method of ORP (opportunistic redundancy pooling) to dynamically create and pool backup virtual nodes and made different VNs share backup virtual nodes for better fault tolerance and cost performance.

The number of researches in the literature on the protection of node data is still relatively small, especially in the event of a major natural disaster such as earthquakes and tsunamis which may lead to domain network failure and serious loss of node data in a moment [20–22]. In this situation, the existing node protection mechanism will lose its role. Therefore, implementing multidomain mapping can not only protect the independence of the various data sets but also avoid domain data loss caused by the failure. At this stage, there are a few studies; Papagianni et al. [9] used the advantages and related principles of cloud computing to achieve the distribution of files between multiple geographies and the process of document distribution for the cloud computing in this paper is actually the realization of a

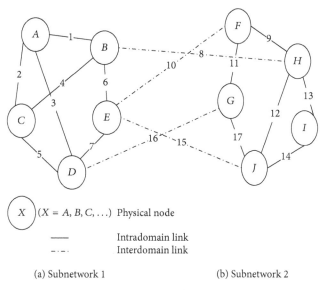

X $(X = A, B, C, \ldots)$ Physical node

————— Intradomain link
—·—·— Interdomain link

(a) Subnetwork 1   (b) Subnetwork 2

Figure 1: Physical network.

multiarea information exchange. Mijumbi et al. [8] also put forward using multidomain advantages to achieve resource allocation in the virtual network environment. Nonetheless, there are few existing literatures that really solve the problem of network mapping.

3. Problem Description

In this section, we first give a multidomain underlying physical network, virtual request network model, and their formal descriptions. Then we give a description of survivable virtual network mapping algorithm that supports multidomain mapping.

3.1. Physical Network. The underlying network topology is marked as a weighted undirected graph $G_s = (N_S, L_S, C_s^n, C_s^l)$, where N_s represents a collection of underlying network nodes, L_S represents a collection of underlying network links, C_s^n represents the computational power of the physical node, and C_S^l indicates the link bandwidth corresponding to the physical path. Figure 1 depicts an example of an underlying physical network which includes two subnetworks in different domains. Tables 1 and 2 show the geographical coordinates of the physical nodes in the two sub-networks, respectively represents the relative position between the physical network nodes and the available computing resources of the nodes CPU. Table 3 shows the available bandwidth resources of physical links.

As shown in Figure 1, circles filled with different English alphabets such as A, B, and C and so on represent different physical nodes. The physical node is a physical, active electronic device attached to the substrate network and can send, receive, or forward information via communication channel.

There are two types of physical links: the interdomain link which is used to complete the interdomain communication and the intradomain link in a single-domain network which

TABLE 1: Subnetwork 1 node information.

Physical node	Coordinate position (x, y)	Computing resources, CPU
A	(57, 54)	57
B	(36, 46)	39
C	(47, 60)	34
D	(40, 11)	24
E	(37, 33)	25

TABLE 2: Subnetwork 2 node information.

Physical node	Coordinate position (x, y)	Computing resources, CPU
F	(67, 74)	57
G	(76, 66)	39
H	(65, 60)	34
I	(70, 81)	24
J	(77, 63)	25

is used to complete intradomain communication. No matter what kinds of underlying links are there and how many virtual links can be mapped, the substrate connection is a physical communication channel between two substrates nodes.

3.2. Virtual Network.

The undirected graph of the virtual network request is similar to the undirected graph of the underlying network. The network topology map is marked as a weighted undirected graph $G_V = (N_V, L_V, R_V^n, R_V^l)$, where N_V represents a collection of virtual network nodes, L_V represents a collection of virtual network links, R_V^n represents the computing power requirements of the virtual node, and R_V^l indicates the bandwidth resource requirements of the virtual link. Figure 2 depicts an example of a virtual request with node constraints and link constraints. Table 4 shows the relative geographical coordinates of the virtual nodes, node computing resource, CPU, and maximum mapping distance which is defined as formula (1), and Table 5 shows the bandwidth resource requirement of the virtual links in a virtual request.

$$\text{Lim\_Dis}\left(\text{Lim\_Dis} = \sqrt{(x_1 - x_2)^2 + (y_1 - y_2)^2}\right). \quad (1)$$

As shown in Figure 2, hexagons filled with different English alphabets a, b, and c represent different virtual nodes. A virtual node is a software component that has a host or routing function, such as an operating system encapsulated in a virtual machine. Virtual nodes form a virtual network topology through the virtual link interconnection.

The lines identified as 1 and 2 are virtual links which are logical interconnections between virtual nodes. For a viutual network, the function of virtual link is to connect directly with the physical network and dynamically display the user's resource requirements.

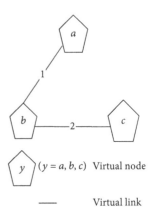

(y = a, b, c) Virtual node

——— Virtual link

FIGURE 2: Virtual request.

3.3. Global Resource Capacity.

In the node mapping phase, the corresponding mapping nodes need to be found on the underlying physical network for each virtual node. In general, all physical nodes with more resources than the resources required by the virtual node can be used as candidate nodes for virtual nodes. In this paper, we obtain the unit of measurement $GRC(N_i)$ which is used to measure the potential mapping ability of all the physical nodes through the global resource calculation method in the process of node selection. The calculation method is defined as follows:

$$\begin{aligned} \text{GRC}\,(N_i) \\ = (1 - d)\,C_r\,(N_i) \\ + d \sum_{v \in \text{Neb}(N_i)} \frac{\text{bw}\,(i, j)}{\sum_{k \in \text{Neb}(N_j)} \text{bw}\,(k, j)} \text{GRC}\,(N_j). \end{aligned} \quad (2)$$

In (2), d is set to a constant representation of the decreasing factor, $\text{bw}(i, j), (i, j) \in E$, represents link resources, and $\text{Neb}(N_i)$ represents a set of physical nodes adjacent to the node N_i. In addition, $C_r(N_i)$ represents the proportion of the node computing resources that occupy the entire network computing resource. The calculation formula is defined as follows:

$$C_r\,(N_i) = \frac{\text{CPU}\,(N_i)}{\sum_{N_v \in V} \text{CPU}\,(N_v)}, \quad \forall N_i \in V. \quad (3)$$

The calculation of GRC_S for all nodes using the vector format can be defined as follows:

$$\text{GRC} = (1 - d)\,C_R + dM_R\text{GRC}, \quad (4)$$

where $\text{GRC} = (\text{GRC}(N_1), \text{GRC}(N_2), \text{GRC}(N_3), \ldots, \text{GRC}(N_{|v|}))^T$ $C_R = (C_{r_1}, C_{r_2}, C_{r_3}, \ldots, C_{r|v|})^T$, and MR is a matrix of $|V| * |V|$ dimensions. Each dimension data corresponds to two adjacent contacts $m(u, v)$ value which is defined as follows:

$$m\,(u, v) = \begin{cases} \dfrac{\text{bw}\,(u, v)}{\sum_{x \in \text{Neb}(v)}, \text{bw}\,(x, v)} & (u, v) \in E \\ 0, & \text{other.} \end{cases} \quad (5)$$

TABLE 3: Link resource information.

Link serial number	Link available bandwidth resources (bw)	Interdomain communication link (Y: 1, N: 0)
1	74.827859	0
2	83.370701	0
3	77.140495	0
4	95.433926	0
5	66.452354	0
7	69.448338	0
8	56.235293	1
9	57.188120	0
10	77.287520	1
11	54.428015	0
12	96.737798	0
13	88.669225	0
14	81.164182	0
15	60.910143	1
16	51.048862	1
17	79.065118	0

TABLE 4: Virtual network node information.

Virtual node	Coordinate position (x, y)	Resources required, CPU	Distance limit (Lim_Dis)
a	(55, 50)	10	75
b	(37, 40)	35	60
c	(80, 96)	20	40

TABLE 5: Resource requirements of virtual links.

Link serial number	Link bandwidth resources required (bw)
1	74.827859
2	83.370701
3	77.140495

3.4. *Evaluation Indices.* The primary evaluation index of the network is defined as follows:

(1) Network Acceptance Rate

$$\frac{\lim_{T \to \infty} \sum_{t=0}^{T} \text{VNR}}{\sum_{t=0}^{T} \text{VNR}_S}. \tag{6}$$

In (6), $\sum_{t=0}^{T} \text{VNR}$ represents the number of virtual networks successfully mapped from $t = 0$ to T and $\sum_{t=0}^{T} \text{VNR}_S$ represents the total number of virtual network requests from $t = 0$ to T.

(2) Average Cost of the Network

$$\frac{\lim_{T \to \infty} \sum_{t=0}^{T} \text{Cost}(G_V, t)}{\sum_{t=0}^{T} \text{VNR}_S}. \tag{7}$$

In (7), $\sum_{t=0}^{T} \text{Cost}(G_V, t)$ represents the resources required to successfully map the virtual network from $t = 0$ to T.

(3) Node Pressure

$$\text{Node\_Load}(n^s) = \sum_{v \in E^v} \frac{\text{Map}_{n^s}(C_n^v)}{C_n^s}. \tag{8}$$

In (8), C_n^s indicates the node resources of the physical node n^s and $\text{Map}_{n^s}(C_n^v)$ represents the sum of the resources including all virtual nodes mapped on physical node n^s.

(4) Link Pressure

$$\text{Link\_Load}(l^s)$$

$$= \sum_{v \in E^v, p \in (p,v)} \frac{\text{Map}_{l^s}\left[C_{l_1}^v(p,v) + C_{l_2}^v(p,v)\right]}{C_l^s}. \tag{9}$$

Link pressure is divided into two parts, the primary flow link pressure and backup flow link pressure. As the former is used to provide link resources under the normal service of the network, the latter is used to provide backup link resources for network failure. In (9), C_l^s indicates a physical link l and $\text{Map}_{l^s}[C_{l_1}^v(p,v) + C_{l_2}^v(p,v)]$ represents the total resources consumption including primary and backup resources.

(5) Long-Term Network Revenue

$$\frac{\lim_{T \to \infty} \sum_{t=0}^{T} \text{Rev}(G_V, t)}{T}. \tag{10}$$

In (10), $\sum_{t=0}^{T} \text{Rev}(G_V, t)$ represents the total revenue obtained from the virtual network that is successfully mapped from $t = 0$ to T.

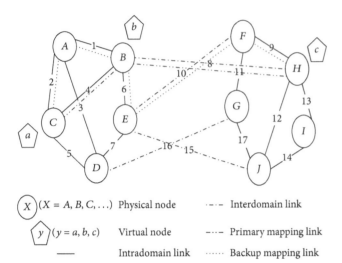

X ($X = A, B, C, \ldots$) Physical node $-\cdot-$ Interdomain link

y ($y = a, b, c$)   Virtual node $---$ Primary mapping link

——   Intradomain link $\cdots$ Backup mapping link

FIGURE 3: Network mapping.

4. Survivable VN Mapping Model for Multidomain Network

4.1. Mapping Problem Description. Virtual network mapping problems are generally defined as mapping: $M \in G_v(N_v, L_v) \rightarrow G_S(N_S, L_S)$ which usually include node mapping and link mapping. The number of physical network resources is deemed to be shown in Figure 1. When the virtual request arrives, in the node mapping phase, the candidate physical node satisfies two conditions: (1) the number of available computing resources is greater than the amount of CPU resources required by the virtual node and (2) the physical coordinates of the physical node meet the requirements of the virtual node.

As shown in Figure 3, the virtual nodes a and b are, respectively, mapped on the physical nodes B and C in subnetwork 1 according to the mapping requirements and the node selection method GRC. But the virtual node c cannot find the mapping node in subnetwork 1 under the limit of the maximum mapping distance. Based on previous studies, under the single-domain network provider environment, the virtual request in this paper will fail to map.

In order to minimize the geographical coordinates caused by the failed mapping and improve the acceptance rate of the network, the proposed IntD-GRC-SVNE in this paper supports multidomain network mapping, so we can find a feasible physical node in the network outside subnetwork 1. For example, as shown in Figure 3, the physical node H is found as the mapping node in subnetwork 2.

4.2. Data Security. As the nodes are mapped in different domain subnetworks, when a major accident happened in a subnetwork, such as earthquakes, floods, or other large natural disasters, mapping in different domain subnetworks can effectively avoid the loss of data and improve the security of the data.

As shown in Figure 3, for example, when a major natural disaster occurred at the location of the domain, subnetwork 2

will result in paralyzed service process and large loss of data. In accordance with the previous mapping, the virtual request mapped to subnetwork 2 will be interrupted. In this paper, the virtual request is mapped to different domain subnetworks; in the case of the paralyzed network, the mapping method of IntD-GRC-SVNE can not only ensure that some nodes and links work properly but also improve the node data security to a certain degree.

At the same time, in order to prevent the impact of link failure, IntD-GRC-SVNE sets the primary resources and backup resources and the proportion of the former is $\alpha(s)b(s)$ and the proportion of the latter is $\beta(s)b(s)$. These two types of resources cannot be crossed in order to ensure the effective use of resources; that is, $\alpha(s) + \beta(s) = 1$.

The network mapping process is shown in Figure 3, virtual link 1 is mapped to the primary flow path which is identified as $(a, b) \rightarrow (C, B)$, and the backup flow path is defined as $(a, b) \rightarrow (C, A, B)$. Virtual link 2 is mapped to the primary flow path which is identified as $(b, c) \rightarrow (B, H)$ and the backup flow path is defined as $(b, c) \rightarrow (B, E, F, H)$. Once the virtual request is accepted, the resources on the primary flow resource path are always used until the virtual request service ends, so the primary flow resource does not support resource sharing. The backup flow path is used to ensure that the network can quickly reroute and make the network reprovide normal service in the event of a failure.

4.3. Business Utility Model for Multidomain Mapping. Based on the description of the network mapping problem in Section 4.1, we give the function model of the problem in this section. During the virtual network mapping process, the cost of the network mainly includes two parts, the node cost and the link cost, and the latter includes intradomain link cost and interdomain link cost. The two costs are defined in different ways: the intradomain link cost is defined as (11) and interdomain link cost is defined as (12):

$$
\begin{aligned}
&\text{Inter\_Cost}\left(G^v\right)\\
&= \sum_{v \in E^v} \text{CPU}\left(n^v\right)\\
&\quad + \sum_{v \in E^v, p \in p(v)} \omega\left[b_1\left(p, v\right) + b_2\left(p, v\right)\right],
\end{aligned}
\tag{11}
$$

$$
\begin{aligned}
&\text{Dom\_Cost}\left(G^v\right)\\
&= \sum_{v \in E^v, p \in p(v)} Dom\_b_1\left(p, v\right) + Dom\_b_2\left(p, v\right).
\end{aligned}
\tag{12}
$$

In (11), n^v represents any virtual node in a virtual request and $\text{CPU}(n^v)$ represents the computing resource occupied by the virtual node n^v. In (11) and (12), $b_1(p, v)$ and $Dom\_b_1(p, v)$, respectively, represent the primary flow path within the intradomain and interdomain resource consumption, while $b_2(p, v)$ and $Dom\_b_1(p, v)$, respectively, represent the backup flow path within the intradomain and interdomain resource consumption. As ω represents the balance parameter between the node cost and the link cost, $\sum_{v \in E^v} \text{CPU}(n^v)$ represents the consumption of node resources. While $\sum_{v\in E^v, p\in p(v)} \omega[b_1(p,v) + b_2(p,v)]$ represents primary flow of interdomain resource consumption, $Dom\_b_1(p,v) + Dom\_b_2(p,v)$ represents backup flow of interdomain resource consumption. So the total cost is defined as follows:

$$TCO(G^v) = Inter\_Cost + \varphi Dom\_Cost. \tag{13}$$

The goal of the algorithm in this paper is to achieve greater revenue by improving the acceptance rate of the network as much as possible in the case of satisfying the requirement of users. The relevant constraints of this algorithm are as follows (see (14)~(19)).

Resource capacity limits of primary flows and backup flows of intradomain physical link and interdomain physical link are as follows:

$$\sum_{v\in E^v, p\in p(v)} \vartheta_s(p)\{b_1(p,v), Dom\_b_1(p,v)\} \leq \mathfrak{R}_\alpha(s),$$

$$\forall s \in E^s,$$

$$\sum_{v\in E^v, p\in p(v)} \vartheta_s(p)\{b_2(p,v), Dom\_b_2(p,v)\} \leq \mathfrak{R}_\beta(s), \tag{14}$$

$$\forall s \in E^s.$$

Resource capacity limits of primary flow and backup flow of virtual network link are as follows:

$$b(v) = \sum_{p\in p(v)} \{b_1(p,v), Dom_{b_1(p,v)}\}, \quad \forall v \in E^v, \tag{15}$$

$$b(v) \leq \sum_{p\in p(v)} \{b_2(p,v), Dom_{b_2(p,v)}\}, \quad \forall v \in E^v. \tag{16}$$

In (16), as the remaining resources of the primary flow are marked as $\mathfrak{R}_\alpha(s)$, the remaining resources of the backup flow are marked as $\mathfrak{R}_\beta(s)$ and $\vartheta_s(p)$ is a flag variable indicating whether the link is occupied; when the value is 1, $s \in p$; otherwise $s \notin p$.

The primary and backup flow resource cannot be crossed:

$$\vartheta_s(p)\vartheta_s(q)[\delta_1(p,v) + \delta_2(p,v)] \leq 1, \quad \forall s \in E^S$$

$$\{b_1(p,v), Dom\_b_1(p,v)\} \leq b(v)\delta_1(p,v),$$

$$\forall p \in p(v) \tag{17}$$

$$\{b_2(p,v), Dom\_b_1(p,v)\} \leq b(v)\delta_2(p,v),$$

$$\forall p \in p(v).$$

Range of variables is as follows:

$$\delta_1(p,v) \in \{0,1\}, \quad \forall v \in E^v, \forall p \in P(v), \tag{18}$$

$$\delta_2(p,v) \in \{0,1\}, \quad \forall v \in E^v, \forall p \in P(v). \tag{19}$$

In (18)~(19), δ_i is a flag used to represent whether the primary resource and backup resource are cross-occupied. The initial value of δ_i is set to 0; once the resources are occupied during the mapping process, δ_i will be set to 1.

5. Virtual Network Mapping Algorithm (IntD-GRC-SVNE)

5.1. Flow Chart of IntD-GRC-SVNE. The implementation of this algorithm is in accordance with the order of arrival of the events. At different time points, the algorithm will deal with different events which include two types of virtual network requests: the new virtual request waits for service and the virtual request leaves after service has been completed. The algorithm flow will not be completed until all the events have been processed.

In Figure 4, the core part of this algorithm is to find the mapping scheme in the multidomain environment and the key is to find the physical mapping nodes distributed in different domain subnetworks for virtual nodes on one link. Through the above mapping method, we can improve the node data security and avoid data loss due to domain failures and the process of finding a mapping scheme is illustrated in Figure 5.

5.2. Algorithmic Description of IntD-GRC-SVNE. The survivable virtual network mapping algorithm (GRC-SVNE) is described in Algorithm 1.

6. Experiments and Discussions

6.1. Experimental Settings. In this paper, the topology and location information of the network are randomly generated by the GT-ITM tools. The underlying network topology which consists of six domain subnetworks includes 100 nodes and 570 links. The node CPU resource and bandwidth resource in each domain subnetwork obey a uniform distribution of 50–100. The rest of the parameters involved in the paper are shown in Table 6. The numbers of nodes and intradomain links are shown in Table 7, while the number of interdomain links is shown in Table 8.

We assume that the number of virtual network requests arriving in 100 time-units obeys the *Poisson* process with an average of 5 and the lifetime of each virtual network is also exponentially distributed with an average lifetime of 500 time-units. For any virtual network request, the number of network nodes is uniformly distributed between 2 and 20, and any two virtual network nodes are connected with a probability of 0.8. The numbers of virtual network node resources and link bandwidth resource requirements are uniformly distributed between 0 and 50. The coordinates of the nodes x and y variables are uniformly distributed from 0 to 100, assuming that the location constraints D of all virtual network mapping requests are constants. Each simulation experiment runs about 10,000 time-units and contains 100 virtual network requests.

6.2. Results and Discussions. As IntD-GRC-SVNE supports multidomain virtual network mapping, in order to improve the network load balancing, the algorithm uses the existing metric GRC that measures the potential mapping capability of physical nodes to select the more reasonable nodes as the mapping nodes in node mapping phase. In addition, in order to demonstrate the performance of the algorithms

TABLE 6: Simulation parameters.

Node number of the substrate network	100
Link number of the substrate network	570
Initial available computing resources on substrate nodes	50–100 units
Initial available bandwidth resources on substrate links	50–100 units
Average lifetime of the VNRs	500 time-units
Bandwidth demand of a virtual link	0–50 units
Computing resource demand of a virtual node	0–50 units
Node number in a VNR	10–25
$\alpha(s)$	0.5
$\beta(s)$	0.5

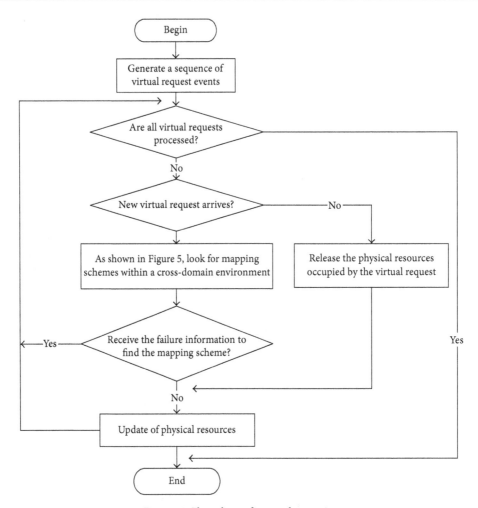

FIGURE 4: Flow chart of network mapping.

in multidomain networks, this paper applies the traditional random algorithm (named as IntD-RANDOM-SVNE in experimental results) and greedy algorithm (named as IntD-GREEDY-SVNE in experimental results) to multidomain network environment. The acceptance rate, average cost, and long-term revenue of the experimental comparison results between the three algorithms are shown in Figures 6–8.

As shown in Figure 6, IntD-GRAND-SVNE and IntD-GREEDY-SVNE are applied in the multidomain environment and then compared with the algorithm proposed

in this paper. Contrast simulation experiments show that IntD-GRC-SVNE reflects obvious advantages in the aspect of acceptance rate. IntD-RANDOM-SVNE, IntD-GREEDY-SVNE, and IntD-GRC-SVNE are all applied in the multidomain environment in this paper, and when compared with the traditional algorithm, IntD-GRC-SVNE proposed in this paper is more survivable. In addition, because IntD-GRC-SVNE uses a new node selection scheme (using a new metric GRC to measure the potential mapping capabilities of physical nodes), the process of selecting nodes is more

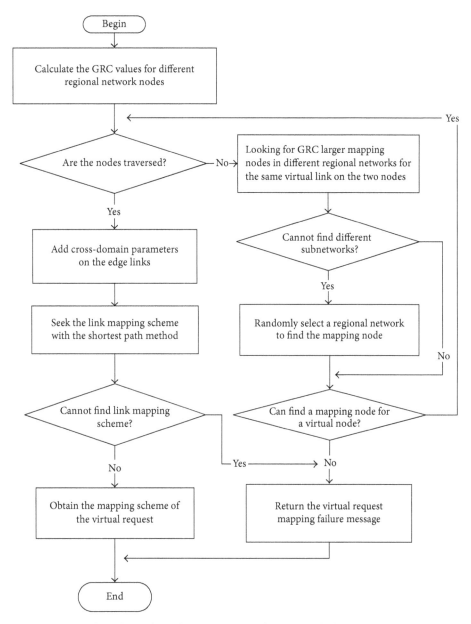

FIGURE 5: Flow chart of searching a mapping scheme in multidomain environment.

TABLE 7: Resource information for each domain subnetwork.

Domain network serial number	Number of nodes	Number of links
0	19	38
1	16	34
2	15	27
3	17	32
4	18	38
5	15	26

reasonable, which further makes the utilization of node resources more efficient and reduces node mapping failure rate. Therefore, the mapping success rate of IntD-GRC-SVNE is significantly higher than the other two traditional algorithms IntD-RANDOM-SVNE and IntD-GREEDY-SVNE.

In addition, the algorithms used in this paper preferentially look for mapping nodes in different network domains. So IntD-RANDOM-SVNE, IntD-GREEDY-SVNE, and IntD-GRC-SVNE have higher data security guarantees than those algorithms previously mapped in a single-domain network environment.

As shown in Figure 7, at the beginning of the runtime, the cost of IntD-GREEDY-SVNE is much lower than IntD-RANDOM-SVNE and the IntD-GRC-SVNE proposed in this paper. With the passage of service time, due to the unreasonable use of resources, the available resource in IntD-GREEDY-SVNE is not enough and further causes network costs to rise.

(1) Create a number of virtual network request events
(2) The physical link resources are divided into the primary and backup flow resources, and set the ratio as 1 : 1.
(3) **WHILE** (Virtual network events are not fully processed)
(4)   **IF** (The event type is a new virtual network request)
(5)   Calculate the GRC value of the physical node according to formula (1)
(6)   **FOR** (The number of virtual nodes)
(7)   **FOR** (The number of virtual links connected to the node)
(8)   The two nodes on the same virtual link are mapped in two different domain sub-networks.
(9)   **IF** (Cannot find a different sub-network)
(10)   Randomly select a domain network as a mapping network and put the candidate physical node number found in the candidate [i].
(11)   **ELSE**
(12)   Find the candidate physical node within the selected sub-network and place the serial number in the candidate [i].
(13)   **ENFIF**
(14)   **ENDFOR**
(15)   **IF** (!candidate [i])
(16)   Return Node mapping failed.
(17)   **ELSE**
(18)   Select the eligible physical node in the candidate [i] as the mapping node according to the value of GRC from large to small;
(19)   **ENDIF**
(20)   **ENDFOR**
(21)   Form a virtual request node mapping scheme;
(22)   **ENDFOR**
(23)   **FOR** (The number of virtual links)
(24)   Use the Dijkstra method to find the primary flow path and the backup flow path between *Node_From* and *Node_To*;
(25)   **IF** (!Primary flow path ‖ !Backup flow path)
(26)   **WHILE** (Candidate [i].size > 0)
(27)   Randomly re-select the physical node in Candidate [i] as the mapping node for the virtual node;
(28)   Delete the mapping node number in Candidate [i];
(29)   Use the *Dijkstra* method to find the primary flow path and the backup flow path for the new node scheme;
(30)   **IF** (Candidate [i].size ==−1)
(31)   Return Link mapping failed;
(32)   **ENDWHILE**
(33)   **ENIF**
(34)   **ENDFOR**
(35)   Form a new link mapping scheme;
(36) **ENIF**
(37) **ELSE** (The event type is the virtual network request to leave)
(38)   Update the virtual network request information;
(39)   Update physical network resources (including node resources, primary flow resources, and backup link flow resources);
(40) **ENDWHILE**

ALGORITHM 1

In general, the network cost consists of two parts: the node resource and the link resource. In the context of this experiment, the link resource includes the primary flow resource and the backup flow resource. In the case of its highest acceptance rate, the network cost of IntD-GRC-SVNE is still lower compared with the other two algorithms; this can fully show the rationality of the mapping scheme. As IntD-GRC-SVNE can not only realize the multidomain mapping to meet the data security requirements but also make network costs lower when compared to the traditional algorithms IntD-GREEDY-SVNE and IntD-RANDOM-SVNE in the

same multidomain network environment, the above experimental results and analysis demonstrate the practicality of IntD-GRC-SVNE proposed in this paper.

Figure 8 shows the degree of node load balancing. In order to show the network load gap between different algorithms, this paper uses the common variance solution method to get the pressure distribution characteristics of the node. As shown in Figure 8, IntD-GRC-SVNE is more balanced than the IntD-RANDOM-SVNE and IntD-GREEDY-SVNE nodes. Since IntD-GRC-SVNE not only supports the security of the multidomain mapping to protect the

TABLE 8: Interdomain link number information.

Domain subnetworks i	Domain subnetworks j	Number of communication links
0	1	24
0	2	34
0	3	22
0	4	21
0	5	9
1	2	23
1	3	29
1	4	8
1	5	18
2	3	28
2	4	42
2	5	28
3	4	22
3	5	37
4	5	30

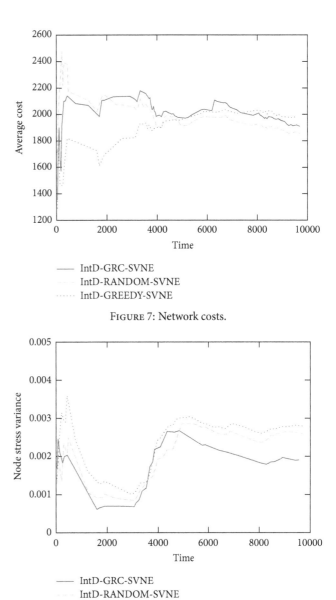

FIGURE 7: Network costs.

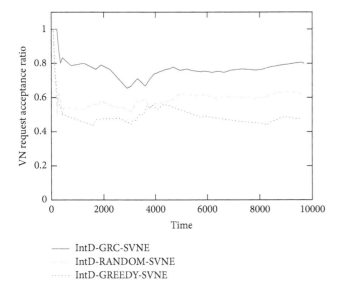

FIGURE 6: Acceptance rate.

FIGURE 8: Node pressure variance.

node data but also applies the existing measurement metric GRC to the survivability network environment to make the network load more balanced, in this paper, all the required resources need to be found in a multidomain environment. The different amounts of resources in subnetwork can easily lead to network load imbalance, as GRC which is used in the paper indicates that the node mapping capabilities in whole network; this can just solve network balance problem. IntD-GRC-SVNE proposed in this paper shows the improvement effect of load balancing compared to IntD-RANDOM-SVNE and IntD-GREEDY-SVNE.

Similar to the node pressure variance, Figure 9 shows the link pressure variance which is calculated by the traditional mathematical method. As shown in Figure 9, compared with IntD-RANDOM-SVNE and IntD-GREEDY-SVNE, the link

load of IntD-GRC-SVNE is obviously more balanced which can also explain why the algorithm cost is low. In IntD-GRC-SVNE, the use of link resources is relatively balanced, so there are sufficient resources to receive more virtual requests. In IntD-GRC-SVNE, the GRC metric is applied to select the appropriate mapping node in the node selection process as the GRC value is determined by two kinds of resources: resources of the node itself and the number of link resources directly connected and indirectly connected to the node. The node selection process will affect the subsequent link mapping process to a certain extent. So IntD-GRC-SVNE selects the physical node which has better potential mapping capability as the mapping node. At the same time, it chooses a physical node with better potential mapping capability as the mapping node will reduce the difficulty of finding mapping links. Through the mapping, most of the selected mapping links can be better connected with other physical nodes,

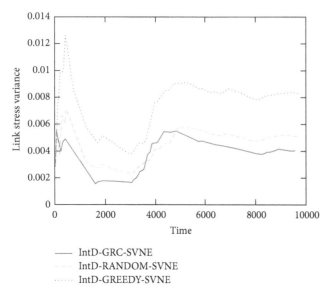

FIGURE 9: Link pressure variance.

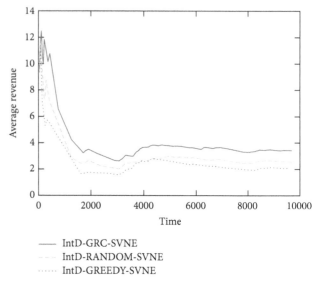

FIGURE 10: Average network revenue.

which not only improve the success rate of mapping but also improve the efficiency of the link and further make the link load more balanced.

There is also something that is worth emphasizing: because virtual requests are mapped across different domain networks, single-domain communication congestion is avoided. This also improves the load balancing of the network compared to the previous single-domain network mapping algorithm.

As shown in Figure 10, IntD-GRC-SVNE shows higher revenue when compared with the other two traditional algorithms, IntD-GREEDY-SVNE and IntD-RANDOM-SVNE. The average revenue from the network is derived from the associated costs of providing services for virtual requests. Therefore, to a certain extent, the amount of receiving virtual requests and the length of service time jointly determine the network provider revenue. As shown in Figure 6, IntD-GRC-SVNE has a higher receiving rate compared to the other algorithms and its corresponding network average revenue is also higher as shown in Figure 10.

In general, the mapping of virtual requests in different subnetworks can avoid the sudden termination of service due to domain disastrous paralysis of the network. Although the experimental results cannot directly reflect the algorithm to improve the security of the data as the three algorithms support multidomain network mapping to ensure the consistency of mapping conditions, in practical applications, there is no doubt that the virtual request mapping in multidomain network environment will improve data security.

7. Conclusion and Future Work

After summarizing the existing research on network survivability and node data security, this paper proposes a survivable virtual network mapping algorithm (IntD-GRC-SVNE) that supports multidomain network mapping. A new metric, GRC, is used to represent the potential mapping capability of the node in the node selection phase. In order to facilitate the comparison of the experimental results, this paper has applied the existing greedy algorithm and random algorithm to the multidomain network environment, which are called IntD-RANDOM-SVNE and IntD-GREEDY-SVNE, respectively, in experimental results. The simulation results show that IntD-GRC-SVNE proposed in this paper not only realizes the multidomain mapping but also improves the survivability of the network. When compared with the two traditional algorithms, the acceptance rate, the network load, and the network revenue of IntD-GRC-SVNE embody the obvious advantages.

Further work mainly focuses on the following two aspects: (1) studying IntD-GRC-SVNE's adaptability in different physical network environments and the impact of physical resources on algorithm performance and (2) studying the multidomain network problem and attempting to reduce the impact of network services failure.

Acknowledgments

The authors are grateful for the support of the National Natural Science Foundation of China (61373149 and 61672329).

References

[1] J. Carapinha and J. Jiménez, "Network virtualization," in *Proceedings of the the 1st ACM workshop*, p. 73, Barcelona, Spain, August 2009.

[2] N. Feamster, L. Gao, and J. Rexford, "How to lease the internet in your spare time," pp. 61–64.

[3] X.-W. Zheng, B. Hu, D.-J. Lu, Z.-H. Chen, and H. Liu, "Energy-efficient virtual network embedding in networks for cloud computing," *International Journal of Web and Grid Services*, vol. 13, no. 1, pp. 75–93, 2017.

[4] X. Cheng, Z. Zhang, S. Suet et al., "Review of Virtual Network Mapping Problem," *Journal of Communications*, vol. 32, no. 10, pp. 143–151, 2011.

[5] X. Cheng, S. Su, and Z. Zhang, "Virtual network embedding through topology-aware node ranking," *SIGCOMM Computer Communication Review*, vol. 41, no. 2, pp. 38–47, 2011.

[6] N. M. M. K. Chowdhury and R. Boutaba, "A survey of network virtualization," *Computer Networks*, vol. 54, no. 5, pp. 862–876, 2010.

[7] M. Chowdhury, M. R. Rahman, and R. Boutaba, "ViNEYard: virtual network embedding algorithms with coordinated node and link mapping," *IEEE/ACM Transactions on Networking*, vol. 20, no. 1, pp. 206–219, 2012.

[8] R. Mijumbi, J. Serrat, and J.-L. Gorricho, "Self-managed resources in network virtualisation environments," in *Proceedings of the 14th IFIP/IEEE International Symposium on Integrated Network Management, IM 2015*, pp. 1099–1106, can, May 2015.

[9] C. Papagianni, A. Leivadeas, and S. Papavassiliou, "A cloud-oriented content delivery network paradigm: modeling and assessment," *IEEE Transactions on Dependable and Secure Computing*, vol. 10, no. 5, pp. 287–300, 2013.

[10] X.-C. Xiao and X.-W. Zheng, "A proposal of survivable virtual network embedding algorithm," *Journal of High Speed Networks*, vol. 22, no. 3, pp. 241–251, 2016.

[11] G.-P. Gao, B. Hu, and J.-S. Zhang, "Design of a miniaturization printed circular-slot UWB antenna by the half-cutting method," *IEEE Antennas and Wireless Propagation Letters*, vol. 12, pp. 567–570, 2013.

[12] X. Yu, H. Wang, X. Zheng, and Y. Wang, "Effective algorithms for vertical mining probabilistic frequent patterns in uncertain mobile environments," *International Journal of Ad Hoc and Ubiquitous Computing*, vol. 23, no. 3-4, pp. 137–151, 2016.

[13] J. Xu, J. Tang, K. Kwiat, W. Zhang, and G. Xue, "Survivable virtual infrastructure mapping in virtualized data centers," in *Proceedings of the 2012 IEEE 5th International Conference on Cloud Computing (CLOUD '12)*, pp. 196–203, June 2012.

[14] Q. Hu, Y. Wang, and X. Cao, "Location-constrained survivable network virtualization," in *Proceedings of the 35th IEEE Sarnoff Symposium (SARNOFF '12)*, May 2012.

[15] M. R. Rahman, I. Aib, and R. Boutaba, "Survivable virtual network embedding," *Lecture Notes in Computer Science (including subseries Lecture Notes in Artificial Intelligence and Lecture Notes in Bioinformatics): Preface*, vol. 6091, pp. 40–52, 2010.

[16] T. Guo, N. Wang, K. Moessner, R. Tafazolli et al., "Shared backup network provision for virtual network embedding," in *Proceedings of the 2011 IEEE International Conference on Communications (ICC '11)*, pp. 1–5, June 2011.

[17] H. Yu, V. Anand, C. Qiao, G. Sun et al., "Cost efficient design of survivable virtual infrastructure to recover from facility node failures," in *Proceedings of the 2011 IEEE International Conference on Communications (ICC '11)*, pp. 1–6, June 2011.

[18] C. Qiao, B. Guo, S. Huang, J. Wang, T. Wang, and W. Gu, "A novel two-step approach to surviving facility failures," in *Proceedings of the 2011 Optical Fiber Communication Conference and Exposition and the National Fiber Optic Engineers Conference (OFC/NFOEC '11)*, pp. 1–3, March 2011.

[19] W.-L. Yeow, C. Westphal, and U. C. Kozat, "Designing and embedding reliable virtual infrastructures," *ACM SIGCOMM Computer Communication Review*, vol. 41, no. 2, pp. 57–64, 2011.

[20] W. Li, Y. Jiang, and J. Wen, "Risk Assessment of Industrial Space Network in Earthquake Disaster Scenarios-Taking Toyota Motor in Japan as an Example," *Acta Geographica Sinica*, vol. 71, no. 8, pp. 1384–1399, 2016.

[21] B. Cao, J. Li, and Q. Sun, "Power grid suffered earthquake damage response measures and optimization design , For electricity," vol. 33, no. 3, pp. 76–82, 2016.

[22] Z. Li and C. Jiang, "Study on Emergency Logistics Network Model for Facility Arming Considering Interruption Scenario," *Periodical Issues*, vol. 30, 2016.

Permissions

List of Contributors

Vishal Sharma, Kyungroul Lee, Soonhyun Kwon, Jiyoon Kim, Hyungjoon Park, Kangbin Yim and Sun Young Lee
Department of Information Security Engineering, Soonchunhyang University, Asan-si 31538, Republic of Korea

Rabia Riaz and Nazish Yaqub
Department of CS & IT, University of Azad Jammu and Kashmir, Muzaffarabad 13100, Pakistan

Tae-Sun Chung
Department of Software, Ajou University, San 5,Woncheon-dong, Yeongtong-gu, Suwon 443-749, Republic of Korea

Sanam Shahla Rizvi
Department of Computer Sciences, Preston University, 15 Shahrah-e-Faisal, Banglore Town, Karachi 75350, Pakistan

Li Kuang, Yin Wang, Pengju Ma, Long Yu, Chuanbin Li and Lan Huang
School of Software, Central South University, Changsha 410075, China

Mengyao Zhu
School of Communication and Information Engineering, Shanghai University, Shanghai 200444, China

Ru Zhang, Yanyu Huo, Jianyi Liu and Fangyu Weng
Information Secure Center, Beijing University of Posts and Telecommunications, 10West Tucheng Road, Haidian District, Beijing, China

Rameez Asif and William J. Buchanan
Centre for Distributed Computing, Networks, and Security, School of Computing, Edinburgh Napier University, Edinburgh EH10 5DT, UK
The Cyber Academy, Edinburgh Napier University, Edinburgh EH10 5DT, UK

Tomasz Andrysiak, Łukasz Saganowski and Piotr Kiedrowski
Institute of Telecommunications and Computer Science, Faculty of Telecommunications, Computer Science and Electrical Engineering, University of Technology and Life Sciences in Bydgoszcz (UTP), Ul. Kaliskiego 7, 85-789 Bydgoszcz, Poland

Junling Lu, Xiaoming Wang and Lichen Zhang
Key Laboratory for Modern Teaching Technology, Ministry of Education, Xi'an 710062, China School of Computer Science, Shaanxi Normal University, Xi'an 710119, China

Zhipeng Cai and Zhuojun Duan
Department of Computer Science, Georgia State University, Atlanta, GA 30303, USA

Iván García-Magariño and Raquel Lacuesta
Department of Computer Science and Engineering of Systems, Escuela Universitaria Politécnica de Teruel, University of Zaragoza, c/Atarazana 2, 44003 Teruel, Spain
Instituto de Investigación Sanitaria Aragón, University of Zaragoza, Zaragoza, Spain

Huanyu Meng
School of Computer and Information Technology, Beijing Jiaotong University, Beijing 100044, China

Zhen Liu, Shuang Ren and Feng Liu
School of Computer and Information Technology, Beijing Jiaotong University, Beijing 100044, China Engineering Research Center of Network Management Technology for High Speed Railway of MOE, Beijing 100044, China

Mikel Iturbe, Iñaki Garitano, Urko Zurutuza and Roberto Uribeetxeberria
Department of Electronics and Computing, Mondragon Unibertsitatea, Goiru 2, 20500 Arrasate Mondragón, Spain

Rong Ma and Xingkai Wang
Shanghai Jiao Tong University, Shanghai, China

Zhenfu Cao
East China Normal University, Shanghai, China

Mahalakshmi Gunasekaran
Department of Computer Science and Engineering, NPR College of Engineering and Technology, Tamil Nadu 624001, India

Subathra Periakaruppan
Department of Information Technology, Kamaraj College of Engineering & Technology, Tamil Nadu, India

Qinlong Huang, Licheng Wang and Yixian Yang
Information Security Center, State Key Laboratory of Networking and Switching Technology, Beijing University of Posts and Telecommunications, Beijing 100876, China
National Engineering Laboratory for Disaster Backup and Recovery, Beijing University of Posts and Telecommunications, Beijing 100876, China

Fu-Hau Hsu, Chih-Wen Ou and Ya-Ching Chang
Department of Computer Science and Information Engineering, National Central University, Taoyuan, Taiwan

Yan-Ling Hwang
School of Applied Foreign Languages, Chung Shan Medical University, Taichung, Taiwan

Po-Ching Lin
Department of Computer Science and Information Engineering, National Chung Cheng University, Chiayi, Taiwan

Lein Harn
Department of Computer Science Electrical Engineering, University of Missouri-Kansas City, Kansas City, MO 64110, USA

Ching-Fang Hsu
Computer School, Central China Normal University, Wuhan 430079, China

Zhe Xia and Junwei Zhou
Department of Computer Science, Wuhan University of Technology, Wuhan 430071, China
Hubei Key Laboratory of Transportation Internet of Things, Wuhan University of Technology, Wuhan, China

Xiancui Xiao, Xiangwei Zheng and Yuang Zhang
School of Information Science and Engineering, Shandong Normal University, Jinan 250014, China
Shandong Provincial Key Laboratory for Distributed Computer Software Novel Technology, Jinan 250014, China

Index

Printed in the USA
CPSIA information can be obtained
at www.ICGtesting.com
JSHW051441221024
72173JS00006B/1540

9 781682 856512